P9-DGL-840

THE
GOLDEN AGE
OF
BASEBALL

FOREWORD BY ERNIE BANKS

Paul Adomites

Robert Cassidy   Dan Schlossberg

Bruce Herman   Saul Wisnia

 Publications International, Ltd.

Paul Adomites is the author of *October's Game* and coauthor of *Babe Ruth. H* Baseball, and *Sluggers! History's Heaviest Hitters.* He was a contributing writer to Baseball, *Players of Cooperstown,* and the *Encyclopedia of Baseball Team Histories.* H director for the Society for American Baseball Research (SABR) and founded and edited *The SAP* *Books* along with its successor, *The Cooperstown Review.* He also writes for several magazine

Robert Cassidy, a former collegiate baseball player, has covered the major leagues for *Newsday,* *Sportscene,* and *Inside Baseball.* He authored the title *Muhammad Ali: The Greatest of All Time* and coauthored *Sluggers! History's Heaviest Hitters* and *Boxing Legends of All Time.*

Bruce Herman is a sportswriter and editor and has served as editorial consultant for the Topps Company since 1991. A contributing writer for the books *100 Years of Baseball* and *Michael Jordan Scrapbook,* Bruce also contributes to *Sports Illustrated* and many other major publications and has been internationally syndicated by Tribune Media. He writes regularly for Major League Baseball Publications and Athlon Sports.

Dan Schlossberg is the author or coauthor of 25 baseball books, including *The Baseball Catalog* and *The Baseball Almanac: Big, Bodacious Book of Baseball.* A former AP news reporter, Dan also writes about travel and is managing editor of the syndicated radio show BallTalk. He is a longtime member of the Society for American Baseball Research (SABR).

Saul Wisnia is a former sports and feature correspondent for *The Washington Post.* His work has appeared in a variety of publications, including *Sports Illustrated,* the *Boston Herald,* and *Boston Magazine.* He is the author of *Baseball's Prime-Time Stars* and *The Wit & Wisdom of Baseball* and has coauthored many books on baseball, among them *Sluggers! Baseball's Heaviest Hitters.*

Factual verification by **Marty Strasen,** sports producer for TBO.com of *The Tampa Tribune.*

Ernie Banks delighted Chicago's Wrigley Field fans with his long home runs, steady fielding, and cheerful disposition. In his illustrious career, "Mr. Cub" belted 512 homers, five times hitting over 40 in a single season. After smashing a record five grand slams in 1955, he belted 47 round-trippers in 1958, the most by a major-league shortstop in the 20th century. He also became the first National Leaguer to win the MVP Award in consecutive years (1958 and '59). Banks's love for the game is exemplified by his signature phrase, "Let's play two!"

Copyright © 2003 Publications International, Ltd. All rights reserved. This book may not be reproduced or quoted in whole or in part by any means whatsoever without written permission from:

Louis Weber, CEO
Publications International, Ltd.
7373 North Cicero Avenue
Lincolnwood, Illinois 60712

Permission is never granted for commercial purposes.

Manufactured in China.

8 7 6 5 4 3 2 1

ISBN: 0-7853-8368-9

Library of Congress Control Number: 2003101566

Contents

FOREWORD: BY ERNIE BANKS • 4

PROLOGUE: THE DAWNING OF AN ERA • 6

'20s: THE JUDGE, THE BABE,
AND A HIGH, INSIDE FASTBALL • 14

1930s: LONG BALLS AND LIGHTS • 46

1940s: WAR, PEACE, AND JACKIE • 88

1950s: NEW YORK AND NEW FRONTIERS • 128

1960s: FASTBALLS AND FLEET FEET • 188

1970s: DYNASTIES AND DOLLARS • 258

EPILOGUE: A STATE OF FLUX • 307

INDEX • 312

Foreword

BY ERNIE BANKS

When I was a boy, I didn't like baseball—had no use for it. My father bribed me to play catch with him—first for pennies, later for dimes and quarters. (I may have been the youngest pro ballplayer ever!) I learned fast.

I didn't follow baseball; I had no baseball heroes. I didn't read the box scores or race home to listen to the games on the radio. I wasn't interested in sports at all, even though I was a batboy for my father's semipro team, the Dallas Green Monarchs. What I really wanted to be was a spy. That, I thought, would be pretty neat. But no one ever asked me to be a spy.

I didn't play any kind of organized ball until high school. And because the school didn't have a baseball team, I played softball. I was pretty good, or so the coach told me.

It wasn't until Babe Ruth died (in 1948) that I felt baseball's enormity and its power. I was amazed and shocked at the outpouring of love and affection for a man most people had only read about. Few had seen him, and fewer still knew him. It changed how I looked at the game. The game suddenly became real. Important.

I began playing with a semipro league in Amarillo, Texas, in 1948. In 1950 Cool Papa Bell saw me play and recommended me to Buck O'Neil, the manager of the Kansas City Monarchs. Buck signed me with the Monarchs that very year. After two years in the military (1951–52), during which time I played baseball for the Army in Germany, I rejoined the Monarchs. That was when my life as a professional ballplayer officially began.

Like many black players at the time, I had no aspirations to go to the majors. I liked what I did. I loved getting paid for doing something I loved to do. For me, it was seeing the country, meeting people, and playing ball—a simple, good life. Everyone thought all of us in the Negro Leagues were just itching to play in the majors. It simply wasn't true. Even after Jackie broke through, many of us were just happy doing what we were doing. For me, I enjoyed getting on a bus, eating a few peanut butter, jelly, and sardine sandwiches, and going to the ballpark to play ball. Life was good. Who needed all the media attention of being the first, second, or third black man to do this or to do that? I was very happy, content.

I did get a taste of the "bigs" when Jackie Robinson asked me to join his barnstorming team in 1950. It was similar to Satchel Paige's All-Stars years earlier. We traveled around the country playing semipro teams. I never really thought it would amount to much. Then a scout saw me play in White Sox Park—and the rest is what you call history.

I did achieve a few firsts, despite my attempts to avoid attention: I was the first black to play for the Cubs; the first player to have his number retired by the Cubs; and, this is not known by many, the first black manager in Major League Baseball. It was 1972 in San Diego, and I was a coach for the Cubs. It was late in the game, and all the other coaches and the manager, Leo Durocher, had been kicked out—I can't remember exactly why. I was the only coach left on the bench. So, for a couple innings, I was a manager in the National League. As he was leaving the dugout, Leo Durocher said, "Don't play Pepitone . . . whatever else you do, don't play Joe Pepitone." I played him anyway.

The '50s were a great time for baseball and a great time for me. When I joined the Cubs in 1953, they were out of the pennant race; the dugout was a rather solemn place. My teammates didn't make a fuss about me being there—the first black to play for the Cubs. The press made the fuss. It was a bigger issue to them than it was to us. Fans always ask me how it felt to be the first black to play for the Cubs. I always say, "No big deal. The guys were nice; they treated me well. No big deal." People have a hard time believing that, but it's true.

I got reacquainted with Jackie Robinson during my second game, when the Dodgers came to town. His advice to me was, "Listen and you will learn." I thought about that long and hard, maybe too hard. I listened a lot; I didn't say much. Some thought I was deaf or stupid. I was just learning. That served me well throughout my career.

I loved the All-Star Games in the '50s. I played with Stan Musial, Frank Robinson, Hank Aaron, and Willie Mays. I played against guys like Whitey Ford, Nellie Fox, and Ted Williams. These were highly talented men, but, more important, they were committed. They played every game like it was their last. That impressed me, inspired me. I wanted to play the game the way they did.

In 1955 the All-Star Game was in Milwaukee's County Stadium; I started at shortstop. The game was tied in the bottom of the 12th; Stan Musial was set to lead off. He said, "I'm going to wrap this up so we can all go home." A few of the guys scoffed; others chided him a bit. He took the first pitch (a fastball) and sent it out of the park. That was Musial's fourth All-Star home run, breaking a tie with Ted Williams and Ralph Kiner. He said after the game, "If you can believe it, you can achieve it." I never forgot that. I went on to hit five grand slams that year, and in 1958 and 1959 I won back-to-back MVP titles. (Interestingly, the 1955 All-Star Game took place on the same day funeral services were being held for Arch Ward, the *Chicago Tribune* sports editor who had founded the All-Star Game in 1933. There are no coincidences in life.)

The biggest event for me in the '50s came in 1959 in Dodger Stadium. I remember I was driving to the ballpark, listening to the radio, feeling pretty good. I hit two home runs that evening, then went to the hospital where my wife delivered twins. "You hit one for each of them," she said. That was quite a day.

Cubs owner William Wrigley was a wonderful man and wonderful to me. Without his efforts I would not have been a Cub for my entire career. Management tried to trade me several times. Mr. Wrigley blocked every attempt. A lot of people don't remember, but it was Mr. Wrigley who brought baseball west. He owned the Angels (Pacific Coast League) and the territory rights to the West Coast. Walter O'Malley owned a team in Fort Worth. I'm not sure how or why, but they swapped franchises, and in 1958 the Dodgers came to Los Angeles.

It seemed that everything was faster in the '60s. I'm not sure if the stats bear that out, but it sure seemed that way. Maury Wills stealing 104 bases in 1962 stands out in

my mind, as does Lou Brock's 94 in 1965. Sandy Koufax's strikeout record was amazing.

I never played in a World Series. But to play at Wrigley Field you'd never know it. We had (and have) the greatest, most loyal fans in the world. It's a fan base of regular people, working class people—moms, dads, and kids who just love the game. I always thought that Wrigley Field was one of those "Wonders of the World." It's just a great place to play and watch baseball. People connected to the game and were passionate about it. We played day games, and there was no advertising on the fences. It was pure baseball. That's why I think the Cubs' fans are the way they are.

On July 2, 1967, I didn't play because of an injury. It was the day Ferguson Jenkins pitched us to a 4-1 win over Cincinnati, tying us for first place with St. Louis. A flag was hoisted in the outfield, signifying that we were in first place. I watched as 40,000 people rose to their feet and cheered. It was as if we had already won the pennant. Of course, we finished third that year, 14½ games out of first.

People always ask about "Let's play two." It happened on July 3, 1969. The temperature was over 100 degrees. The team was tired, and we hadn't even played yet. I looked around, scanning the solemn faces of my teammates. It was like a wake or something. And then, it just came out: "Let's play two!" A couple writers wrote it down, and it stuck. I was just trying to remind my teammates how fortunate they were to be playing that day, on that field, for the Cubs. I never considered myself a leader. It just came out.

Every step of my life has been important—the wins, the losses, the good times and bad. I truly have lived the Golden Age. And with *The Golden Age of Baseball*, you, too, can live the greatest moments of the game.

Ernie Banks

Prologue

THE DAWNING OF AN ERA

Long before it reached its Golden Age, baseball had already earned its rightful status as America's game. Colonists, in one of their more innocent attempts to break from England, were altering the British pastimes of cricket and rounders even before the Declaration of Independence. Soldiers took some of the many variants on the road during the Revolutionary War, and while at Valley Forge none other than George Washington said that he passed the day by playing catch with one of his aides. By the 1830s, games such as "one old cat" and "town ball" were being played throughout the fledgling nation.

Here is where fiction and fact meet up. According to the bulk of sports history books written between 1910 and 1960, baseball was not developed from these roots at all. In 1839, the legend went, a man named Abner Doubleday drew up the game's first rules from scratch in the tiny hamlet of Cooperstown, New York. Doubleday was actually nowhere near this town at the time, and while he did achieve true fame as a Civil War general, there is no proof he ever even saw a baseball game. The myth was popularized for no apparent reason during the early 20th century by Albert Goodwill Spalding, whose contributions to the game as an ace pitcher, team owner, and sporting-goods giant were otherwise noteworthy. In subsequent years the truth came out, but the Cooperstown locale of baseball's Hall of Fame is a constant reminder of this far-reaching fable.

Albert Spalding was baseball's first true power broker as well as the man who promoted the Cooperstown legend. He later cofounded the National League and won its first pennant as player/manager of the Chicago White Stockings.

"Base ball" began as an informal social game. As its popularity grew, contests such as this one between the New York Nine and the New York Knickerbockers planted the seeds of professionalization throughout the nation.

The facts are now well documented. On June 19, 1846, at the Elysian Fields in Hoboken, New Jersey, the first game of what can be considered true baseball—complete with a diamond and foul lines—was played between the New York Knickerbockers and the New York Base Ball Club. The lopsided 23-1 score did little to curb growing enthusiasm for the game, and rules continued to evolve. Twenty-five teams formed the National Association of Base Ball Players in 1857, and within a few years its ranks had grown to some 60 amateur clubs from Maine to California. Thousands of fans attended major contests, and box scores started appearing in newspapers. Although several key changes were still in the future—pitchers still threw underhanded, for instance, and fielders wore no gloves for protection—the seeds of the modern game had been planted.

Players came from big cities and small towns, with a strong Irish influence and many other immigrant groups represented: a true melting pot. "I see great things in baseball," young poet Walt Whitman wrote during this period. "It's our game—the American game. It will take our people out-of-doors, fill them with oxygen, give them a larger physical stoicism. Tend to relieve us from being a nervous, dyspeptic set. Repair these losses, and be a blessing to us." As both a blessing and a diversion, baseball was played by young men on both sides of the Mason-Dixon Line during the Civil War. Games even took place in prison camps, and Abraham Lincoln (who himself played) was known to watch the action on the "White Lot," a diamond erected on the grounds behind the White House.

Given its popularity, it was only a matter of time before baseball became a business. Done quietly at first, this movement went aboveground in 1869, when team president Aaron B. Champion announced that he would pay all members of his Cincinnati Red Stockings. Even with a 60-0 record touring the country that summer, this first "professional" club didn't make its stockholders rich. Still, the players enjoyed earning steady

Brothers George (left) and Harry (right) Wright were among the first to be paid to play. Though both starred on the diamond, Harry—sometimes called "the Father of Game"—became more noteworthy for his efforts to professionalize the sport and for his many innovations, which included batting practice and the hidden ball trick.

pay—led by shortstop George Wright's $1,400 annual salary. When the amateur National Association attempted to thwart the idea of pro teams following the 1870 season, a coup occurred that resulted in a new nine-team circuit bearing the same name as its predecessor.

Baseball's first true major league, the "new" National Association, attracted the country's top players. The bulk of them, including George Wright, his brother/manager Harry (who also played outfield), and pitcher Al Spalding, suited up in Boston for the relocated Red Stockings. This powerhouse club won four straight championships, but the player-run league suffered from problems. The only paid prerequisite for a team's admission to the circuit was a $10 entry fee, and there were no fixed schedules. Teams doing poorly in the standings or at the gate would simply fold in midseason, and franchise shifts to new cities were common. Players left to govern themselves were free to jump to different clubs for salary hikes whenever they liked, and game-fixing and drunkenness (sometimes on the field) emerged amidst the casual atmosphere.

After the Red Stockings had blown away the competition in 1875 with a 71-8 record in league play, the next critical point in the game's history occurred. Resolved to end Boston's reign, Chicago White Stockings President William A. Hulbert convinced ace Red Stockings hurler Spalding and three of his teammates to head west for more cash. Knowing the move would prompt an outcry from other National Association owners, Hulbert convinced some of his well-heeled friends with investments in other teams to jump ship and form yet another new circuit where owners would call the shots: the National League of Professional Base Ball Clubs.

Starting the 1876 season with teams in Boston, Chicago, Cincinnati, Hartford, Louisville, New York, Philadelphia, and St. Louis, the National League (or NL) enforced strict rules that curtailed many of the National Association's problems and led to the latter's swift demise. NL clubs agreed to play each of their rivals ten times per season or be expelled, and each ponied up $100 in annual operating expenses to govern disputes and pay umpires. Better team financing and a ban on gambling, liquor sales, and Sunday games further solidified the NL's status, and, even while enduring its own struggles to make money, the league remained afloat as other circuits came and went. The schedule eventually expanded to 154 games, where it would remain for most of six decades.

As played in the 1890s by stars including outfielders Ed Delahanty, Billy Hamilton, and "Wee" Willie Keeler, third baseman John McGraw, and pitcher Kid Nichols, baseball began to evolve more and more into the modern game. Pitchers were now throwing overhand, padded fielding gloves and catcher's masks were deemed acceptable defensive equipment, and four pitches constituted a walk (down from nine a decade before). A far more dreadful practice that arose during this time was the expulsion of black players from the major leagues. While a handful of African Americans had performed alongside whites in earlier years, a "gentleman's agreement" among owners kept the pro game segregated for the next half-century.

"Wee" Willie Keeler (batting) stood 5'4" and weighed barely 140 pounds, but his .384 batting average from 1892 through 1899 was the highest of the 19th century. Using his great speed and magical bat-handling, he played 15 years before encountering a sub-.300 season.

Although a few sluggers did emerge as the 20th century dawned, home runs were mostly in short supply. A strategic, one-run-at-a-time approach to play called "inside baseball" ruled. Bunts, hit-and-runs, steals, and squeeze plays were common offensive tactics, and homers were seen as an oddity unbecoming this rough-and-tumble style. Further hampered by heavier, scuffed-up balls that were seldom (if ever) replaced during a game, home run leaders rarely approached 20 in a season. Spiking an opposing player while sliding into a base and engaging in fistfights on the field were considered acceptable practices, but, while some rowdier fans enjoyed the ruckus, others were losing interest.

The quest for a "cleaner" alternative prompted Byron Bancroft "Ban" Johnson, a successful minor-league president, to establish the eight-team American League (or AL) in 1901. Like the NL before it, the newest major league stole many of its rival's top players with offers of higher salaries. Fighting and drinking among the ranks were discouraged, and in cities with two teams, such as Boston, the AL took a further step of charging fans just a quarter for admission—half the going NL rate. This combination firmly entrenched the "Junior Circuit" as a formidable foe to NL supremacy, and baseball's rock-solid foundation was finally established. For the next half-century, the same 16 teams would play in the same 11 cities as symbols of consistency in an ever-changing world.

Competition between the leagues prompted the arrangement of a 1903 grudge match pitting the AL-champion Boston Pilgrims (now the Red Sox) against the NL's Pittsburgh Pirates in a best-of-nine postseason playoff. Made up primarily of raided National League stars such as third baseman Jimmy Collins and pitcher Cy Young, the American League prevailed,

Cy Young pitched the AL's Boston Pilgrims to the first "World Series" championship in 1903. An unpretentious and ultimately beloved figure, his 511 career victories and 7,354⅔ innings pitched are among baseball's records that almost certainly will never be approached.

The best-of-nine 1903 "world's championship" was billed as a grudge match between the established National League—championed by the Pittsburgh Pirates—and the three-year-old "junior circuit," represented by the victorious Boston Pilgrims. A crowd of 16,242 witnessed the opener in Boston, and the spectacle soon became a rite of fall.

Once a game populated mostly by rowdies, farmhands, and the uneducated working class, baseball had become much more diverse by World War I. Players such as the college-educated Christy Mathewson—an upstanding, almost regal figure as well as a spectacular pitcher—brought a principled respectability to the game.

and the "World Series" was born. Within a few years, this annual October ritual became the premier event on the sports calendar. Crowds of thousands would congregate outside newspaper offices waiting for telegraphic word of scores from far-off Series games, and as radio emerged so did the practice of rushing home from school or work before the first pitch of the fall classic.

Mirroring the changing American landscape, big-league rosters became more diverse than ever between 1900 and 1920. Refined, college-educated players such as legendary New York Giants pitcher Christy Mathewson were now suiting up beside southern farmhands and midwestern coalminers' sons, with French, German, and Jewish immigrants from the country's teeming eastern cities thrown into the mix. All had their own rabid fans. During the teens, Red Sox ace pitcher Babe Ruth was the quintessential embodiment of the street-kid-turned-big-league-hero. The son of German-born parents who owned a bar along the tough Baltimore docks, he ran loose from an early age and spent his formative years in an industrial school for "bad boys" with a rough crowd before his quick leap to the majors.

The exploits of such pitchers as Mathewson, Ruth, and Walter Johnson of the Washington Senators and top hitters such as Pirates shortstop Honus Wagner and Detroit Tigers outfielder Ty Cobb were brought to an ever-widening audience through expanded sports coverage in newspapers, and the size of the crowds attending games soared. Smallish wooden stadiums constructed in the 19th century soon became inadequate and were replaced with concrete-and-steel ballparks that seated 25,000 or more. The regal Shibe Park in Philadelphia was the first new structure to go up, in 1909, and within seven years every big-league team had such a home. This rapid expansion left no doubt; other sports such as college football and boxing were popular, but baseball was king.

Babe Ruth is shown here as a Red Sox hurler in 1919, the last year in which he pitched more than two games. He also set a record with 29 home runs that season, and soon his exploits as baseball's original "slugger" gave the game its first real superstar.

It seemed nothing could stop the game's steamroller success, but in the period from 1914 to 1920 several strong attempts at derailment emerged. First came the start-up of the Federal League, a well-financed venture that in its brief existence (1914–15) managed to lure away several AL and NL stars and prompt bidding wars for many others that sent player salaries skyrocketing. The Federal League threat coincided with an economic depression that caused attendance to drop even as new ballparks were still sprouting up.

Honus Wagner was one of baseball's first stars of the 20th century. His career began in 1897, but from 1900 until he retired in '17, the Pirates shortstop had more hits (2,967), extra-base hits (865), and runs scored (1,521) than anyone in the game.

America's 1917 entry into World War I temporarily depleted rosters as players enlisted, and it prompted a shortening of the 1918 season. The war's end brought back many fans the next year, and these crowds were thrilled by the slugging exploits of Ruth, who, now taking a regular turn in the outfield when not pitching, hit a record 29 home runs in 1919.

What transpired next, however, would quickly overshadow that feat in the public's consciousness. Ever since the establishment of the National League in 1876 had shifted the balance of baseball's power from players to owners, those wielding control had done so with a strong arm. A reserve clause in each major-

Connie Mack's Athletics took up residency in Philadelphia's Shibe Park in 1909. The largest ballpark in the world at the time, it was a prototype of the "modern" facility, a concrete-and-steel structure with a capacity of more than 20,000, built to accommodate the coming groundswell of baseball's popularity.

league player contract bound (or reserved) that player to his club for a season following the contract's expiration—even if a new pact hadn't been agreed upon. A team could keep, trade, or sell a player as it saw fit, and there was little negotiation when it came to salaries. The brief taste of higher pay during the Federal League years only magnified the players' frustration. Repressed by the system, several players—Highlanders/Yankees first baseman Hal Chase being the most notable—had taken to clandestinely supplementing their income by teaming up with gamblers to bet on, and even intentionally lose, games.

In 1919, this not-so-secret practice was taken to a new low when eight members of the White Sox—whose owner, Charles Comiskey, was perhaps the most penurious of them all—accepted bribes from gamblers to throw the World Series to Cincinnati. The first sign something was amiss was when a heavily favored Chicago club featuring the likes of .351-hitting outfielder Joe Jackson, slick-fielding second baseman Eddie Collins, and 29-game-winner Eddie Cicotte dropped several games to the Reds on uncharacteristic errors and shoddy pitching. Sportswriters speculated in print about a possible fix even before Cincinnati wrapped up the Series, but nobody wanted to believe it was true.

Although talk quieted down somewhat by the start of the 1920 season, a grand jury convened in Cook County, Illinois, that fall to examine allegations of other instances of gambling in the game—and soon looked at the 1919 World Series as well. Eight Sox players were called to testify, and several, including Jackson and Cicotte, admitted knowledge of the fix. All eight were indicted for conspiracy to defraud the public and injure "the business of Charles Comiskey and the American League," and while the group was acquitted due to lack of evidence when Jackson and Cicotte's testimony "disappeared," the damage had already been done in the form of huge black headlines across the country. Baseball, America's game, was facing its darkest hour.

The sport, however, was about to turn a historical corner. The change would be much bigger, much more dramatic than what anyone could predict. As America entered the Roaring Twenties, baseball entered its Golden Age—a stretch of glory that would last for more than half a century.

Baseball's Golden Age was preceded by its blackest hour— the 1919 World Series–fixing scandal in which Shoeless Joe Jackson emerged as a shameful symbol. Though Jackson and the alleged co-conspirators were acquitted by a jury, they were convicted in the court of public opinion.

1920s

THE JUDGE, THE BABE, AND A HIGH, INSIDE FASTBALL

After the cynical greed of the Black Sox scandal, baseball needed not one, but two heroes. Fortunately, baseball was blessed with a pair of stalwarts who arrived just in time: two men who could not have been more unalike—high-living athletic genius Babe Ruth and high-principled Federal Judge Kenesaw Mountain Landis. One helped restore the nation's faith in the game's fun; one helped restore faith in the game's honor. However, a third, much more somber factor was what truly made baseball roar like the '20s themselves. When Cleveland's Ray Chapman died in 1920 after being hit by a pitch, a new rule was put into effect, shifting the power from the pitcher to the batter. Starting in 1921, batters would see only new, spotless white balls. Fence busting had arrived, and not just by Babe Ruth.

At 13, George Ruth was known to hit a baseball 400 feet—farther than almost any major-leaguer of the time. He hit his final major-league home run at age 40, a shot launched over the right-field grandstand at Forbes Field in Pittsburgh. It was estimated to have traveled 600 feet.

Baseball didn't just turn a historical corner in the 1920s. It was much bigger, more dramatic than that. The sport was booted upstairs to a whole new level, one that delighted fans as never before and matched the tone of the nation like never before or since. The Landis/Ruth/Chapman trio made the difference. Perhaps baseball would have eventually overcome the ugly venality of the Black Sox episode, but with Ruth, Landis, and Chapman the revolution began almost instantly. It was fast; it was furious; it was baseball in the 1920s.

THE BABE IS SOLD

He hit the ball farther than anyone ever had. By late 1919 everyone connected with the baseball world knew who he was. But it wasn't until he moved to New York City that he grabbed the game by the scruff of the neck and shook it silly.

Babe Ruth was a fine pitcher, probably the best lefty in the league, but after being moved to the outfield he shocked the baseball world by belting 29 home runs, two more than anyone else had ever hit (and *that* record was set during a fluke year in a fluke ballpark). Harry Frazee, Red Sox owner, knew he had a prize. Unfortunately, he had something else as well: a lot of debt. He hadn't yet hit his stride as a super impresario. So when the Yankees asked if Ruth was for sale, Frazee said the price was $125,000. The Yanks reacted with a loud chuckle. But they surely wondered how many long balls the kid would hit in their home park, the Polo Grounds, a much more homer-friendly

In 1927, with Yankees business manager Ed Barrow (standing) and owner Jake Ruppert looking on, Ruth inked a three-year contract for the groundbreaking sum of $210,000. Five years later, he took a pay cut after hitting "only" .373 with 46 homers.

American schoolkids in the Roaring Twenties, "graduating" from traditional, less athletic games such as hopscotch and marbles, embraced baseball in backyards and vacant lots. Many schools organized ball teams and even instituted "sports days."

space than the Sox's Fenway. The Yanks came back, and a deal was struck by the end of December: In exchange for Ruth, Frazee got $25,000 in cash, plus three promissory notes of $25,000 each and a $300,000 loan against the mortgage on Fenway Park. The deal was announced in January 1920.

The Yankees were the newest team in the 20-year-old American League. Named the Highlanders, soon thereafter changed to the Yankees, they were losers more often than winners. Until Ruth, that is. The Red Sox, on the other hand, had won three pennants in the previous five years. In the early part of the decade, however, star pitchers Herb Pennock, Carl Mays, Red Ruffing, and Waite Hoyt, as well as everyday stalwart Joe

BOUNTY IN BALTIMORE

Before the advent of the farm system, independent minor-league teams supported themselves by selling star players to major-league clubs. Nobody did it better than Jack Dunn of the International League's Baltimore Orioles. From 1919–25, his team won seven straight pennants while developing a roster of men who became impact players in the majors.

Dunn, who owned Oriole teams from 1910–28, enjoyed his greatest success long after selling Ruth to the Boston Red Sox. His 1921 team went 119-47, posting a .717 winning percentage fueled primarily by pitcher Jack Ogden's 32-8 season. The team had a 27-game winning streak, and Ogden won 18 in a row.

Fellow pitcher Jack Bentley had a 12-1 record that was overlooked because he also led the International League with a .412 batting average and 24 home runs. Maryland native Lefty Grove had a 25-10 record in his first full year with Baltimore, then followed with 18-8, 27-10, and 26-6 seasons before Dunn sold him to the Athletics for a record $100,600—topping by $600 the 1920 sale of Babe Ruth from the Red Sox to the Yankees.

Jack Dunn

Dunn's ability to judge talent allowed his club to keep winning even while he sold off many of his top players. In addition to Ogden, Bentley, and Grove, the list included Frank Baker, Max Bishop, Joe Boley, Ben Eagen, George Earnshaw, Fritz Maisel, and Bob Shawkey.

President Calvin Coolidge may have thrown out the first pitch at this 1925 Senators–Athletics game, but he often was bored by baseball. It was his wife, Grace, who was the true fan. She frequently restrained her husband from leaving games early.

Dugan, were sold to New York to help Frazee's cash position. It would be a long time before the Sox were winners again.

Babe and the Big Apple were made for each other. In addition to being an athlete of unparalleled talent, Ruth was the ultimate media star and party animal in a town that was becoming both the media capital of the world and a hopping party scene. The '20s began to soar. In 1920 Babe hit 54 homers, more than any other *team* in the American League and double the record he had broken the year before. Baseball fans had recognized years before that Babe Ruth was great, but in 1920 the kid from the Baltimore slums moved the boundaries. The fans in New York City were just the start; soon the whole country was captivated by the awesome skills of the Babe.

Baseball was waking up to the joys of noisier offenses. Some stalwarts made fun of this "ridiculous" home run "craze." The AL improved its runs scored total by 1,283 over the previous year (the Yanks themselves provided 260 of that total). Even in the National League, where the home run leader knocked 39 fewer balls out of the park than Ruth, 20 players batted over .300. The expected cry was heard: "The ball's been juiced!" But it wasn't.

Actually, the ball did have something to do with the louder batwork: "Trick" pitches had been banned in the 1919–20 off-season. Anything that smacked of uncleanliness—spitters, shineballs, emery balls, Vaseline balls—was heretofore illegal, although 17 pitchers were allowed to keep their favorite pitches until they retired. The fans loved the greater offensive output. Over nine million fans spun the turnstiles that season, shattering the old record, set in '09, of 7.25 million.

ENTER THE JUDGE

Ray Chapman was killed by a pitch in August 1920, and the Black Sox news broke about a month later. Baseball reacted to the first event by making sure new balls were in use for nearly every play. No longer would the same ball be used for a full nine innings, battered and softened, dirtied by saliva and chaw until it became nearly impossible to see—especially late in the game, in waning sunlight. Baseball reacted to the second by hiring Kenesaw Mountain Landis as its commissioner just three weeks after the indictments were handed down against the eight players and five others involved in the fix. At Landis's demand, he was given supreme power over the game.

Baseball's dictatorial but effectual commissioner from 1920 through '44, Kenesaw Mountain Landis—who was named for the site at which his father lost his leg in a Civil War battle—presided over the game's conscience in the wake of the Black Sox scandal.

"Ken" Landis had come to the attention of baseball's owners because he had a finely honed sense of public relations. Through a series of high-profile, though ultimately ineffective, decisions from the bench, the judge had crafted a reputation for himself as a man who backed down from no one when he felt he was right (which seemed to be all the time). In the mid-teens, Landis was chosen to rule on the lawsuit filed by the Federal League owners against Major League Baseball. Landis, acting with masterful judicial prudence, stalled. The Federal League, losing more money every day the case went on, was finally forced to settle out of court. MLB moguls were filled with delight at Landis's no-decision. So even though it probably wasn't true that Landis was simply handed the job, the appointment may have had less to do with Landis's legal abilities and more with his appearance.

For no one *looked* more like a judge (particularly one with "complete power") than Kenesaw Mountain Landis. Named

THE CHAPMAN TRAGEDY

The only on-field fatality in major-league history occurred in New York on August 16, 1920. During an afternoon game at the Polo Grounds, Yankee pitcher Carl Mays, a sidearming right-hander with a deceptive submarine delivery and a reputation for pitching inside, beaned Cleveland shortstop Ray Chapman in the head with a high fastball. The fleet shortstop, who had been crouched over the plate in his usual stance, died the following day after a midnight operation failed to save him.

"Chapman was one of the gamest players and one of the hardest men to pitch to in the league," Mays told *The New York Times*. "I always dreaded pitching to him because of his crouching position at the bat."

The pitcher first thought he had hit Chapman's bat. When the ball bounced back to him, he picked it up and threw it to first base. Only then did he realize that umpire Tommy Connolly was calling for a physician.

Players of the period did not wear helmets, though some American Leaguers started doing so in the wake of the Chapman incident. Helmets did not become mandatory, however, until 1971—more than a half-century after Ray Chapman's death. (In 1957, the National League dictated that all players wear protective headgear—often cap liners—and the AL followed suit a year later.) Even more amazing, it took *another* 23 years before single-earflap helmets became mandatory.

Chapman played in more than 1,000 games for the Indians, had a record 67 sacrifice hits in 1917, and led the Indians in stolen bases four times. He died just over a month before eight White Sox players were indicted and eventually expelled for allegedly fixing the 1919 World Series (the Black Sox Scandal). Rumors of the fix had previously prompted team owners to clean up the game. They banned the spitball and other freak deliveries and ordered that newer, whiter balls be used in games.

The result was the sudden end of the dead-ball era and an explosion of home run hitting, led by newly acquired Yankee slugger Babe Ruth.

Ray Chapman

after the mountain where his father was wounded in the Civil War (although his dad got the spelling wrong), Landis, despite being short and slight, posessed a craggy visage and scowl that virtually oozed moral rectitude. As Will Rogers said in the book *Judge Landis*, "Somebody said: Get that old boy who sits behind first base all the time. He's out there every day anyhow."

Landis rapidly established that he wasn't kidding about "supreme power." J. G. Taylor Spink, founding editor of *The Sporting News* (often referred to at the time as "Baseball's Bible"), said, "The club owners first came to him hat in hand, and in his long subsequent baseball career he never showed a great deal of respect for them. It almost seemed he felt a secret contempt." Landis immediately ticked off AL president Ban Johnson by ignoring the idea that he was supposed to serve as head of a three-person "Commission." The rule of the game was his and his alone.

The Black Sox trial began June 27, 1921. Because the written testimony from their grand jury appearances had somehow "disappeared," the gang was delivered a verdict of not guilty. They celebrated at an Italian restaurant in a long-lasting party; many of the jurors joined them. The next day, Landis

banned them all for life. His famous words: "Regardless of the verdict of juries, no player that throws a ball game, no player that entertains proposals or promises to throw a game, no player that sits in a conference with a bunch of crooked players and gamblers where the ways and means of throwing games are discussed, and does not promptly tell his club about it, will ever play professional baseball." Included in the eight were the obviously guilty, like pitcher Eddie Cicotte; at least one who seemed to have done nothing wrong, Buck Weaver; and at least one who was somewhere between the two, because of stupidity or guile or both, Joe Jackson.

Before long, Landis had tossed close to 20 men out of the game for gambling-connected offenses and had nearly come to fisticuffs with Giants coach Cozy Dolan over such an accusation. He heard testimony in cases involving such superstars as Ty Cobb, Tris Speaker, and Joe Wood. Kenesaw Mountain Landis restored the confidence of fans in the game by coming down hard on gambling and anything that even remotely smelled of it.

Eddie Cicotte (right) threw knuckleballs, spitballs, shineballs, and—apparently—the 1919 World Series. The diminutive, wise-cracking, and formerly popular ace of the White Sox, pictured here with teammates Jim Scott and Ed Walsh, said of the bribe, "I did it for the wife and kiddies."

Joe Jackson was no stranger to the courtroom. After the Black Sox scandal, in 1924 Shoeless Joe sued the White Sox for $16,700 in back salary and bonuses. A jury found in his favor, but the ruling was overturned by a judge who ordered the former player jailed for perjury.

For everything else they were, the Judge and the Babe were quintessential 20th-century celebrities, the earliest of their species so identified. Both knew how to milk the media for maximum benefit.

It could be said of Ruth that he just loved the camera and the attention, and as such was less a manipulator than a talented innocent. But just as everything about the Babe indicated he was here for maximum fun, the Judge's craggy visage implied that he would stand for no nonsense, no how.

Even though the game needed them both, a battle between the two seemed inevitable. It happened during the final days of the 1921 World Series, the first Series in which Ruth's Yankees appeared. In those days players looked to extend their season and their income by playing postseason games in less-than-major-league locales. They called it "barnstorming," from an old vaudeville term that implied the performers were so eager to strut their stuff they'd even play in a barn during a storm. Among the more common postseason games were "city championships," in which players from the two St. Louis, two Chicago, or two Philadelphia teams would play each other in exhibitions designed to fatten their wallets. The very first "World Series" in the 1880s were similar events, except they were multigame tournaments played across the country. One of the most common barnstorming tours was a

This group of White Sox players showed up in court to defend themselves against accusations that they had thrown the '19 World Series. Acquitted, but banned from baseball, they were dubbed the "Black Sox" not out of ignominy (as many might think), but rather due to their propensity to dirty their uniforms with their hardscrabble playing style.

continuation of that year's World Series: The two teams, or at least several members of each, would get together for a series of games—sometimes a few, sometimes dozens.

Landis hadn't been on the job a year yet. But he had made his presence felt, with suspensions and expulsions of "dirty" players and consolidation of his own power. The World Series was his special interest. What happened within the leagues was the purview of the league presidents, but the Series was Landis's own. He understood that having an exhibition "Series" after the actual Series was over diminished the value of the original. There were rules in place that forbade such behavior, but no one was enforcing them. Landis decided to set things straight by telling Babe Ruth himself that he was not allowed to go on a barnstorming tour.

The Judge had tried to reach Ruth to let him know he was laying down the law. Ruth, ever the big kid, didn't return the Judge's phone calls until after the final game of the Series, late in the afternoon on October 13. Ruth explained he had a contract to play in the barnstorming series, which he couldn't (or wouldn't) break, and he was about to catch a midnight train to Buffalo to start the tour. Landis snarled, "If you do, it will be the sorriest thing you ever do in baseball."

It was the biggest power play in baseball history. The game's superstar versus the game's center of power. Babe had to feel he held the cards; who could stand up to *him*? When asked about Landis's wrath, Ruth replied, "Ah, let the old guy go jump in the lake." Babe appealed to the Yankee owners; they backed the Judge. Although Babe was joined by big Bob Meusel and no-name pitcher Bill Piercy, several other Yankees bailed when

The American public, already in a foul mood from the beginnings of a postwar depression, racial disharmony, and other social ills, was nauseated when its grand old game brought upon itself a brand new shame.

THE CHANGING WORLD

[Copyright: 1920: By The Chicago Tribune.]

"THE BEAUTY ABOUT BASE BALL IS THAT IT'S ALWAYS BEEN KEPT STRAIGHT AND CLEAN"

POLITICS HIGH FINANCE

PUGILISM HORSE RACING

BASE BALL

Our national sport as it has been regarded.   *It now joins the "Black Eye club."*

they heard about Landis's edict. The trip itself turned out to be a disaster. The weather turned rotten, and some towns canceled the games, also fearful of the Judge. The tour was cut short.

To punish the miscreants, Landis first withheld their World Series shares. Then he let them dangle until December, at which time he made his pronouncement: They would be fined the amount of their Series shares and suspended until May 20, 1922. They couldn't play until the 40th game of the season. The Judge had laid down the law, and even Babe Ruth had to toe the line. Some advised Ruth to beg for leniency; he went quail hunting instead. The next year, Judge Landis further clarified his hold on the World Series: He abandoned the best-of-nine experimental format that had been in place since 1919, due to the owners' greed, in favor of a cleaner best-of-seven format, and he negotiated the first radio contract for the Series.

THE GREAT OFFENSIVE MOVEMENT

In 1920, with the arrival of Ruth in New York and the banning of nasty pitches, offenses began to take charge. Both leagues outperformed their previous year's totals of runs, homers, batting average, slugging, and on-base percentage. The old dead-ball style flashed one last glorious gasp in 1920: The World Series-bound Brooklyn Robins played the Boston Braves to a *26-inning, 1-1* tie, the longest big-league game ever. Total pitchers used by both clubs: two, Joe Oeschger of Boston and Leon Cadore of Brooklyn.

The fans responded by turning out. Attendance jumped to nine million. But the offenses weren't really exploding yet, just simmering. Several times previously the National League had scored more runs than it did that year.

So while offenses started to perk in 1920, it wasn't until 1921, when the dirty balls were thrown out of the game, and safer, whiter balls were required,

The Braves' Joe Oeschger (pictured) went arm-to-arm with the Dodgers' Leon Cadore for 37 innings in less than a month in 1920, allowing only two runs but coming away without even a win to show for it. After losing an 11-inning, 1-0 duel in April, he and Cadore met again and fired all 26 frames of a 1-1 tie in May.

Ty Cobb: A Great Hitter in Any Era

When Babe Ruth began launching home runs at a frenetic pace, he forever changed the game of baseball. Throughout the dead-ball era, however, the most important facet of hitting was bat control. With good bat control a hitter could make consistent contact and place the ball in all fields. There were few players who handled a bat as well as Ty Cobb, the era's most prolific hitter.

In the height of the dead-ball era, Cobb won nine straight batting titles and hit over .400 three times. He also knocked in over 100 runs seven times (five times in the dead-ball era). Cobb's unconventional batting stance afforded him more control over the path of the ball once contact was made. He batted left-handed, choking up from the knob and gripping the bat with his hands held slightly apart. He felt that keeping his hands apart allowed him to better manipulate the bat. It also gave him the option to quickly drop a bunt, or to feign bunting

at the last moment and slash the ball past charging infielders.

Cobb also rarely planted his feet in the batter's box. Instead, he shifted his position, stepping forward or back and inside or out depending on the pitch. Throughout his career, he resisted the temptation to swing with power and began to resent Ruth, who was rapidly

Ty Cobb

emerging as the game's best offensive player.

It wasn't that Cobb lacked power. He was capable of swatting the long ball, but he preferred to use his exquisite control to place the ball where he wanted it.

One of the most cerebral players of his time, Cobb was able to out-think opposing pitchers and fielders. He believed that the home run would ruin baseball, stripping the game of strategy and skill. It was one of the few times when Cobb's baseball instincts were wrong. The home run craze was growing with each season.

Leading up to Ruth's power surge in 1920, rules that favored pitchers were changed and the quality of the balls used in the major leagues was improved. Still, Cobb remained steadfast in his approach to hitting and continued to enjoy great success. He batted .401 in 1922 and .378 in 1925. Ultimately, Ty Cobb, with a .366 lifetime batting average, proved he could hit in any era.

that hitting headed for the stratosphere. And the next ten years delivered even more of the same.

The most glaring difference in the two eras was in the hands of the Babe: home runs. The National League hit 199 more of them in 1921 than in 1920. In 1929 the NL swatted nearly 300 more than in '21. The American League had hit more than 200 homers in a season only three times until 1920. From there through 1930, however, the AL topped 400 in every year but two, and they beat 500 four times. On an individual level, the change was even more startling. In the first two decades of the century, there were only 49 occasions when an NL player topped 10 homers in a season; only twice did anyone hit as many as 20. The AL was even less powerful; from 1901 through 1920, just 35 times did someone belt more than 10 homers. But over the next ten years, long balls became the name of the game. More than 180 NLers topped 10 in a season; 17 knocked 30 or more in one year; five hit more than 40, and Hack Wilson had one of the top batting seasons in NL history in 1930 when he belted 56 (and drove in 191). In the AL, the gang following Ruth was even larger: 21 players slugged more than 30; 40 was surpassed 10 times; and the Babe hit more than 50 four times, including the magical 60 once. And who knows what Oeschger and Cadore were thinking on August 25, 1922, when the Cubs toppled the Phils, 26-23, in a game that featured a total of 51 hits, including 12 doubles, off seven pitchers.

But unlike today's homer-happy times, where muscle-bound bombers in tiny ballparks slug tons of homers while batting around .260, the batsmen of the '20s were great hitters who took advantage of the cleaner balls to hit homers *and* hit for high averages. Ruth, of course, was the noteworthy example, with a lifetime average of .342 and 714 homers. Hack Wilson, Rogers Hornsby, and Harry Heilman also combined power and average in a way not seen before or since.

Early on, this phenomenon of slugging plus average was noted by the pundits of the day. In 1921, *Baseball Magazine* questioned: "In five short years the number of total bases have [sic] risen in the major leagues more than 30 percent. How are we to reconcile the fact that slugging has not resulted in a

Brooklyn's Leon Cadore, a curve-balling righty, allowed 5 walks and 15 hits in his 26-inning matchup with Boston's Joe Oeschger on May 1, 1920. In '31, he married Mae Ebbets, whose father Charles was the namesake for the Dodgers' Ebbets Field.

"Babe" Ruth, Mighty Batsman Who Has Broken Home - Run Record

falling off of batting? On the contrary, slugging . . . has been accompanied by soaring batting averages." Perhaps even more amazingly, strikeouts declined as power numbers soared.

Batting averages were juiced. From 1901 through 1921, no one in the National League had batted .400. In just the next nine years it was accomplished four times. Nap Lajoie, Ty Cobb, and Shoeless Joe Jackson each batted over .400 (Cobb twice) in the first dozen years of the AL's existence. From 1920 through 1923 it was accomplished four times. And in 1927 Harry Heilman hit .398.

The combination of power and average that is the "total bases" statistic demonstrates the amazing hitting phenomenon of this era most succinctly. Of the top 20 total-base seasons of all time, 12 occurred between 1921 and 1932. It truly was the Big Bang Era.

BABE'S COHORTS

What was the reason for this explosion? The "rabbit ball" myth has been largely put to rest (although research indicates the ball was hopped up in 1930 and again in 1932), but searching for

Babe Ruth claimed the secret to his stroke—here analyzed in sequence by the publication Mid-Week Pictorial—*was simply to swing his 54-ounce bat as hard as he could. "I hit big or I miss big," he admitted.*

Rogers Hornsby was such a single-minded hitter that he rarely read or attended movies because he believed it would weaken his eyes. Over the course of his 23-year career, he cracked 102 more home runs than any other second baseman in the game.

reasons still generates lively discussion among historians. An interesting analysis is offered by William Curran in *Big Sticks: The Batting Revolution of the Twenties*: "No one seems to have taken into account the increased physical size of the players." The likely explanation is three-sided (after all, baseball is a game of threes): one, the ball was easier to see and therefore hit; two, baseball at that time just plain had a crop of incredibly great hitters; and three, America wanted it.

With the exception of Ruth himself, none of those great hitters was better than Rogers Hornsby. Described by longtime St. Louis sportswriter Bob Broeg as "sturdy, dimpled, rosy-cheeked," "The Rajah" was almost the anti-Ruth. First off, he was nobody's pal and wasn't apt to be found playing catch with kids outside the ballpark. In fact, he was downright nasty. He stood deep in the batter's box, and even though he looked vulnerable to low and outside pitches, he often slugged them for extra-base hits. The period of 1920–25 was, in another delightful Broeg turn of phrase, Hornsby's "reign of terror" over National League pitchers. For the five years from 1921–25, Hornsby averaged nearly .400—no one else has *ever* done that.

His .424 average in '24 still ranks as the highest in the 20th century. He captured the batting title for six consecutive years, an NL record. Hornsby also captured the on-base and slugging titles each of those years and won two homer crowns. He led the NL in hits, doubles, and RBI four times each and in runs scored five times. In 1922 he bagged 450 total bases (only one other hitter has ever had more). With a .358 lifetime average, second only to Cobb, Hornsby is without a doubt the greatest right-handed batter in baseball history. But he

There was nothing odd about Harry Heilman except his habit of winning batting titles in every odd year from 1921 to '27. In two of those instances, the Tigers flychaser won narrow races only by his performances in final-day double-headers, each time refusing to sit out the nightcap to protect his lead.

was such an irascible, surly so-and-so that he was traded three years in a row. Hitting was his sole passion. He never smoked or drank, and he even refused to read books or newspapers or go to the movies: He thought those activities were bad for the eyes. As a manager he had some success several times, but inevitably his players would tire of his sour disposition.

Bill Terry was another player who wasn't likely to win any congeniality contests. To him, baseball was a business, and nothing but. "I'm giving this game the best years of my life," he said. "I'd make any other business pay for that. Why should baseball be any different?" Terry swatted quite a few businesslike line drives. In the dozen years he played regularly (all for the Giants) he failed to hit .300 only once. He finished his career with a lifetime .341 average and more than 1,000 RBI. Terry's best season was everybody's best season: In 1930 he batted .401. No NLer has done it since.

Harry Heilman had shown potential in his first few seasons as a big-league hitter. But when Ty Cobb took over the reins as Tiger manager, he became Heilman's tutor. The timing was perfect. It was 1921. Heilman learned enough from his personal batting coach to rap the ball at a .394 clip. With Bobby Veach, the entire Tiger outfield batted a collective .374 and drove in an amazing 368 runs, still an AL record. Then in 1922 they did it again. Cobb batted .401 and Heilman .356. From 1921 through 1927, Heilman hit greater than .390 four times and won four batting titles. Throughout the '20s,

Ty Cobb once called George Sisler "the nearest thing to a perfect ballplayer." His notoriety diminished, perhaps, by his quiet demeanor, "Gorgeous George" was a two-time batting champ, a swift runner, a brilliant first baseman, and (early in his career) a hard-throwing pitcher.

Heilman finished in the top five in RBI every year but two. Heilman's teammates nicknamed him "Slug," both for his ungraceful running style and his potent bat.

George Sisler was simply a supreme athlete. During his first season in the bigs he played first base *and* pitched, and he once out-dueled the great Walter Johnson in a 1-0 game. Fleet of foot, he often led the AL in stolen bases and may have been the most graceful first baseman ever. Branch Rickey, who signed Sisler, referred to his "perfection of reflexes." But in spite of all that, his greatest strength was as a hitter. Twice he batted .400: in 1920, when he set the major-league record with 257 hits, and in 1922, when he knocked the ball around at a simply preposterous .420 clip. However, a bad case of the flu in that off-season intensified an ongoing sinus problem, which in turn damaged his eyes. He was forced to sit out the entire 1923 season. When he came back, he used his smarts and athleticism to bat better than .300 six more times. But it is a sad story. Few people in baseball history operated at a level of batting efficiency like George Sisler before his illness.

THE DOMINANT TEAMS

It seems counterintuitive at first, but baseball history has proved it several times: When everyone is hitting, pitching becomes more important than ever. This is probably why, even though there were sluggers all over the landscape, the decade of the '20s was dominated by a mere handful of teams. In the American League, after the Indians' 1920 championship, the Yankees put together their first decade of greatness, capturing the AL flag every year but two until 1929.

The only other AL team to notch a pennant was the Senators of Washington, led by estimable hurler Walter Johnson, who was coming to the end of his career but was finally surrounded with enough talent to snag consecutive flags in 1924 and '25. Pitching made the difference in '24: While

Jim Bottomley (left, with cap tilted over his left eye, as was his trademark) and Chick Hafey (right) formed a potent Cardinals left-right punch. In 1931, their last of eight years as teammates, Hafey hit .3489 to Bill Terry's .3486 to Bottomley's .3482 in the closest NL batting race ever.

four other teams scored more runs than Washington, no team had a lower ERA. The Nats had Johnson's 23 victories, two other pitchers with 15 wins or more, and Firpo Marberry, the game's first great relief pitcher, who appeared in nearly one-third of their games. The team was fast and played sound defense. Goose Goslin led the league in RBI, and 27-year-old Bucky Harris, in his first year as player-manager, provided a galvanizing dose of leadership. They squeezed past the Yanks in '24 and easily outpaced the A's in '25. Johnson and new addition Stan Coveleski each won 20 games, and Firpo saved 15 again.

Over in the National League, four teams won pennants between 1921 and 1929: the Giants, Cards, Pirates, and Cubs. The decade began under the sway of the Giants and John McGraw, easily the dominant personage in the game until Ruth and Landis came along. In winning the pennant the first four years of the decade, the Giants just plain did everything right, and if a weakness appeared, McGraw knew how to correct it. In Major League Baseball records, two men are perched atop the list for most pennants won by a manager: Casey Stengel and John McGraw, with ten each. McGraw managed the Giants until 1932 but never finished first after '24.

The Pirates, who had been in second or third place every year, came into their own in 1925. The Bucs' lineup was stocked with bangers: Only one regular batted less than .300 (and he hit .298!), and the team scored 912 runs. But once again it was outstanding pitching that made the difference. In 1926 there was an upsurge of internal

A WINNER FOR WASHINGTON

Throughout a 21-year career spent entirely with the Washington Senators, Walter Johnson showed an uncanny knack for winning with bad ballclubs. Though he won 417 games, second only to Cy Young, he went to the World Series only twice. But his fearsome fastball, pinpoint control, and reputation as a gentleman who wasn't afraid to pitch inside earned him baseball immortality as a charter member of the Baseball Hall of Fame.

Walter Johnson

Variously called the "Big Train" (because the velocity of his heater matched the speed of a steam locomotive) and "Barney" (after early auto-racing legend Barney Oldfield), Johnson didn't drink, smoke, or swear. He didn't even play cards until late in his career. The 6'1", 200-pound right-hander was only 19 when he leaped from his Kansas farm overalls into a major-league uniform. His discovery was even more unlikely: A traveling liquor sales rep spotted Johnson pitching for a semipro team in Idaho and notified Washington manager Joe Cantillon.

That sales rep had a good eye: Johnson led the American League in victories six times, won a dozen strikeout crowns, and proved himself such an intense competitor that he won 38 times by the score of 1-0. He won 69 games in 1912–13 alone.

For Johnson, the pinnacle of his career occurred in 1924, when he was almost 37. After posting losing records in two of four previous seasons, he went 23-7 to pitch the Senators to their first flag. Though he lost his first two World Series starts against the Giants, he got an unexpected third chance in Game 7.

With the score tied 3-3, Johnson's appearance in the top of the ninth whipped the Washington crowd into a frenzy. The right-hander responded with four scoreless innings but waited in vain for his teammates to score. They finally did, thanks to a series of Giants misplays and a well-placed pebble, in the bottom of the 12th. Though Johnson went on to win two World Series games in 1925, he never won another ring.

Forced to retire three years after a broken leg and a severe bout with influenza, Johnson finished his illustrious career with a record 110 shutouts and a dozen 20-win seasons. He once pitched 56⅔ consecutive scoreless innings, a record that stood for 75 years. He won 16 straight games in 1912 but was even better in 1913, when his 36-7 record netted an .837 winning percentage.

Johnson's last winning season came in 1925, while he was still basking in the glow of his Game 7 heroics of the previous fall. For the Big Train, that glow never faded.

squabbling on the team, which they shook off to garner the league championship again in 1927, under new manager Donie Bush. The Waner brothers had joined the team. Paul's 131 RBI and .380 average led the league, and shortstop Glenn Wright and third sacker Pie Traynor were both superb fielders and 100-plus RBI guys, too. Carmen Hill, a new addition to the starting rotation,

The Giants' Frankie Frisch (left) and the Senators' Bucky Harris (right) were competing second basemen in the 1924 World Series. Both hit .333, but Harris's two home runs—including one in Game 7—helped Washington prevail.

won 22 games. Hill and Lee Meadows both wore glasses, a rarity for the time, making the '27 Bucs the first pennant winners with two "four-eyed" hurlers. But the season still was tainted: Young superstar Kiki Cuyler got tangled in a power struggle with manager Bush and lost. He didn't play an inning in the World Series. Soon after, he was shipped to the Cubs, where he became a big part of their winning ways.

The Cardinals had twice finished third in the early '20s, but they began to establish themselves as a powerful bunch (only the Yankees have won more World Series) by taking pennants in 1926 and '28. Under less-than-lovable manager Rogers Hornsby in '26, the Cards just outslugged everyone else, leading the league in runs, hits, homers, and slugging average. The next year, Hornsby was swapped to the Giants for star infielder Frankie Frisch. In 1928, "Sunny" Jim Bottomley led the league in three categories and rising star Chick Hafey had a breakout batting season. The Cards nosed out the Giants by two games.

THE YANKEES ARE BORN

The 1920s were most notable for the appearance of the New York Yankees as a force. They have become the most successful franchise in sports history, but until Babe Ruth showed up, the Yankees were third-class citizens in their own town, behind McGraw's Giants and the lovable Brooklyn Robins. In fact, they weren't even the Yankees until 1913; before that they were called the Highlanders, because they played in Hilltop Park.

Their new name came when McGraw let them share the rebuilt Polo Grounds as home field. But even as Yankees, they just weren't very good. From the team's founding (as the Baltimore Orioles) in 1901 until Ruth arrived, they never won a pennant. But the "two colonels," Jacob Ruppert and Tillinghast Huston, began to make some moves. They picked up promising hurler Bob Shawkey from Connie Mack's A's. In 1919 the perennially cranky Carl Mays (he of the pitch that killed Ray Chapman) whined his way off the Boston Red Sox, and the Yanks grabbed him. In 1920, Ruth was the second BoSox snapped up. The next season, former Sox manager Ed Barrow became the Yank GM, and Yankee money began to howl as he bought more and more Red Sox. Soon pitchers Waite Hoyt, "Bullet Joe" Bush, and "Sad Sam" Jones were dealt from the Sox to the Yanks. Catcher Wally Schang came along in the Hoyt deal; infielders Everett Scott (who held the record for consecutive games played until Lou Gehrig) and Joe Dugan also were plucked from Boston.

Ruth and his pals proved good enough to take AL flags in 1921, '22, and '23. The Giants disposed of them without much difficulty in the first two of those three World Series. But McGraw could see the tremendous gate attraction of Ruth. When the Yanks began to regularly outdraw McGraw's team, he revoked their park-sharing deal. The Yanks were forced to build their own place to play.

The Yankees' Earle Combs, one of the first great leadoff hitters, singles to open a 1928 tilt against Philadelphia. Years later, the club hired Combs to teach a young rookie named Joe DiMaggio how to play center field at the Stadium.

But it was not a "ballpark." It was no "field." It was, in classic monumental terms, a "stadium." It quickly earned another name, too: Appropriately, Fred Lieb dubbed it "The House that Ruth Built."

The Yanks finished second in 1924 and seventh in 1925. But that year a 21-year-old who had attended Columbia University moved into Wally Pipp's slot at first base. Lou Gehrig had become a Yankee, and true Yankee greatness was underway. The lineup of Gehrig, Tony Lazzeri, Mark Koenig, Ruth, Earle Combs, and Bob Meusel stayed together for three years, and the Yanks went to the World Series all three, making it a total of six Series appearances in the first eight years of the decade. Many have called the 1927 team the greatest of all time, even though its catching was barely average and the pitching more efficient than star-studded. The World Series of 1927 and '28 were both four-game sweeps. But what was intriguing was who held the broom. With Ruth, Gehrig, and Meusel, the Yanks were downright scary. The '27 team had the top three run-scorers in the American League as well as the top three in home runs and total bases; the top two in hits, RBI, triples, and walks; two of the top five in batting average; two of the top three in on-base average; and the top two in slugging. Even in a decade of unparalleled offensive power, the moniker "Murderer's Row" seemed apt. As historian A. D. Suehsdorf said, "If you didn't like the Yankees it was a tough time to be alive."

BASEBALL'S GENERAL

John McGraw was a gritty, hard-charging ballplayer for the Baltimore Orioles, baseball's preeminent team of the 1890s. He approached the game with passion and intensity and sometimes allowed his temper to dictate his play.

The traits that made him a successful player also served him well as a manager. He had an aggressive style, favoring the hit-and-run, double steals, and the art of intimidation. Whether it was his own players, opposing players, umpires, or his managerial counterparts, no one was spared McGraw's wrath. And while he may not always have been popular in the clubhouse, he always had his team's respect and loyalty. Winning, it seems, covered a multitude of sins.

Nicknamed "Little Napoleon," McGraw could be arrogant and combative, but he understood all facets of the game. He was a great strategist and was the first manager to call pitches from the dugout. He is also credited with being the first man to utilize relief pitching as it is known today.

John McGraw

McGraw managed his Baltimore team for three seasons and then, in 1902, took over as skipper of the New York Giants. He would remain the Giants' manager for 31 seasons. Over that span, his teams took 10 National League pennants and finished second 11 times. They won three world championships along the way. To this day he ranks second on the all-time career wins list with 2,763, behind only Connie Mack (3,731).

THE FALL CLASSICS

When great teams face off in short series, exciting things can happen. Not just great, hard-nosed, eyeball-to-eyeball baseball, but the extraordinary, wacky, even bizarre can happen, too. The

World Series of the '20s may have had more strange twists and turns than those of any other decade.

For example, the 1920 battle between the Brooklyn Robins and the Cleveland Indians had several doses of historic flavor. For one, it featured the first championship matchup between two teams each nicknamed to honor a specific person: The Brooklyn Robins got their moniker from their manager, Wilbert Robinson; the Indians were so called in memory of their moment-of-blazing-glory star, Louis Sockalexis, a Penobscot American Indian. It also featured (in one game) the first grand slam in World Series history (Cleveland's Elmer Smith), the first Series home run by a pitcher (Cleveland's Jim Bagby), and the only unassisted triple play in Series history (Cleveland's Bill Wambs-

Bob Meusel, Babe Ruth, and Earle Combs (left to right) were three key "inmates" of "Murderer's Row," the Yankees' lineup of sluggers. But 11 days after this photo was snapped in 1926, they were upset by St. Louis in the World Series.

Yankee Stadium, "The House that Ruth Built," opened in 1923 on a plot of land granted to a "yankee" named John Lion Gardiner before the Revolutionary War.

ganss). Oh, and by the way, it was the last time Brooklyn would be in a Series for 21 years, and the last time Cleveland would see Series action for 28 years.

The World Series of the next three years all featured the same two teams: the Giants versus the Yankees. The first two were played totally in the Polo Grounds, with teams changing uniforms from gray to white each day. McGraw's men dominated, winning the first contest five games to three. The final outs (in a 1-0 game) came on a stunning double play in which Giant second sacker Johnny Rawlings knocked down what looked like a sure single in short right field to rob the Yankee batter, and heads-up first baseman George Kelly made a super throw to nail an overly aggressive Yank baserunner at third.

The Giants swept the '22 Series four games out of five. (That's not a misprint.) Umpire George Hildebrand called the second game at about 4:45 in the afternoon "because of darkness" with the score tied. Landis was furious. "I don't pretend to be the smartest person in the United States, but at least I can tell day from night," he roared. To prove to fans that there was nothing untoward about the ump's decision, Landis seized the day's gate receipts (around $120,000) and gave them to charity.

Although fans at the Polo Grounds—the site of every game of the 1921 World Series—ultimately cheered their Giants to an eight-game win, they saw the Yankees' Carl Mays (here fielding Ross Youngs's bouncer) blank them in Game 1, 3-0.

WHAT'S IN A NAME?

When it came to doling out nicknames, old-time players could be rude and crude—yet often quite hilarious. They had no qualms about calling outfielder Nick Cullop "Old Tomato Face" or labeling fidgety Lou Skizas "The Nervous Greek." Because of his tiny stature and oversize ears, Walter Maranville was renamed "Rabbit." Even his wife called him that! Here are some of the great nicknames of the Golden Era:

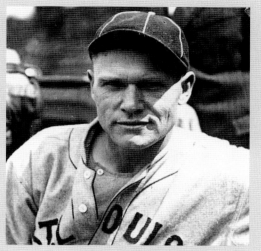

Baby Doll Jacobson

Luke "Old Aches and Pains" Appling
Hank "Bow Wow" Arft
Luis "Yo-Yo" Arroyo
Abraham Lincoln "Sweetbreads" Bailey
Boom-Boom Beck
Bill "Ding Dong" Bell
Joe "Bananas" Benes
Don "The Weasel" Bessent
Emil "Hill Billy" Bildilli
Bingo Binks
Ewell "The Whip" Blackwell
Paul "Motormouth" Blair
Bob "Butterball" Botz
Frank "Turkeyfoot" Brower
Downtown Ollie Brown
Pee Wee Butts
Sammy "Babe Ruth's Legs" Byrd
Ron "The Penguin" Cey
Dain "Ding-a-Ling" Clay
Fidgety Phil Collins
Jack "Sour Mash" Daniels
Yo-Yo Davalillo
Pickles Dillhoefer
Spittin' Bill Doak
Joe "Burrhead" Dobson
Shufflin' Phil Douglas
Leo "The Lip" Durocher
Fred "Moonlight Ace" Fussell
Phil "Scrap Iron" Garner
Burleigh "Stubblebeard" Grimes
Ron "Louisiana Lightning" Guidry
Mike "The Human Rain Delay" Hargrove
Ed "The Wild Elk of the Wasatch" Heusser
Handy Andy High
Johnny "Hippity" Hopp
Al "The Mad Hungarian" Hrabosky
Joe "Poodles" Hutcheson
Reggie "Mr. October" Jackson
Shoeless Joe Jackson
Baby Doll Jacobson

Al "Bear Tracks" Javery
Sheldon "Available" Jones
Willie "Puddin' Head" Jones
George "Highpockets" Kelly
Ellis "Old Folks" Kinder
Tobacco Chewin' Johnny Lanning
Tony "Poosh 'Em Up" Lazzeri
Sal "The Barber" Maglie
Willie "The Say Hey Kid" Mays
Sudden Sam McDowell
Cliff "Mountain Music" Melton
Benny "Earache" Meyer
Russ "The Mad Monk" Meyer
Hugh "Losing Pitcher" Mulcahy
Johnny "Grandma" Murphy
Julio "Whiplash" Navarro
Lou "The Mad Russian" Novikoff
Blue Moon Odom
Camilo "Little Potato" Pascual
Tom "Money Bags" Qualters
Babe "The Sultan of Swat" Ruth
George "Twinkletoes" Selkirk
"Bucketfoot" Al Simmons
Harry "Suitcase" Simpson
Lou "The Nervous Greek" Skizas
Mose "The Rabbi of Swat" Solomon
Dick "Dr. Strangeglove" Stuart
Jim "Abba Dabba" Tobin
Bill "Mumbles" Tremel
Dixie "The People's Cherce" Walker
Walt "No-Neck" Williams
Charlie "Swamp Baby" Wilson
Jimmy "The Toy Cannon" Wynn

John McGraw made sure Ruth was no factor in the Series, calling every pitch to the Babe from the bench and effectively limiting him to just a .118 average.

The Yankees finally paid back the Giants by winning the 1923 Series, four games to two. The teams alternated home and away for each game once again, but this time half the games were played in the old Polo Grounds and half across the river in brand-new Yankee Stadium. The Giants took Game 1 with a two-out, top-of-the-ninth, inside-the-park home run by Casey Stengel. Casey was only 33 years old, but he became forever known as "Ole Case" when a pad inside his shoe slipped during the sprint around the bases, making his gait look clumsy and old. At least one writer called it "the greatest baseball game ever played." Stengel also won Game 3 with an over-the-fence homer, the only score of the game, and he thumbed his nose at the Yankee crowd, which miffed Yankee manager Miller Huggins quite a bit. Landis said Stengel deserved to have some fun. The Yankees came back from a 4-1 deficit in the last game to

Thousands of ebullient Cardinals fans congregated to welcome their first-time World Series participants home after two games in New York. St. Louis would win the '26 Series in seven.

win it with five runs in the ninth inning. The New York press stated, "It is by common agreement the greatest game in World Series competitions until that time." Lesson for historians: New York hyperbole is nothing new.

The 1924 Series between the Giants and the Senators featured three terrific games and ended on a weird play coupled with sense of déjà vu. In Game 1, Giant ace Art Nehf lost a 2-1 lead in the bottom of the ninth, but the Giants won in 12, 4-3. In Game 2, the Giants scored twice in the top of the ninth to tie the contest but lost in the bottom of the ninth, 4-3. The teams alternated wins in Games 3 through 6. Game 7 was something out of the twilight zone. The Giants took a 3-1 lead into the eighth, but with two outs and the bases loaded, Senators player/manager Bucky Harris chopped a ground ball that hit a pebble, or something, and bounced over the head of third baseman Fred Lindstrom. Score tied. Walter Johnson, who had already pitched 20 innings in two starts and lost them both, came on in relief. The Giants put men on base in each of the next four innings, but Walter hung tough. In the last of the 12th, Muddy Ruel popped up behind home plate, but Giant catcher Hank Gowdy stepped in his face mask while trying to catch it ("It hung on his foot like a bear trap," Fred Lieb said) and couldn't make the play. Given new life, Ruel doubled. Earl McNeely knocked what looked to be a sure out toward third, but that ball *also* hit something (the same pebble?) and bounced over Lindstrom's head. Game over. The Senators had won their first Series.

The next year the Nats were in the Series again, but the Giants were not. Their string of four consecutive pennants was broken by the Pirates of Pittsburgh. Senator shortstop Roger Peckinpaugh had just been given the Most Valuable Player Award for the season. He proceeded to make eight errors, directly accounting for six Pirate runs, including a two-out bad throw in the bottom of the eighth of Game 7, which was followed by a Kiki Cuyler double that gave Pittsburgh a 9-7 win. The losing pitcher was Walter Johnson. The Pirates became the

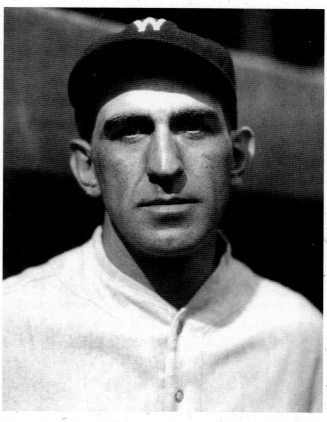

In 1914, Roger Peckinpaugh became—at just 23 years old—the youngest manager ever, skippering the final 20 games of the Yankees schedule. In 1925, he was voted AL MVP in his last season as a full-time shortstop, but he cost the Senators the World Series with his eight errors.

first team to win a seven-game Series after being down three games to one. And the people who give out awards stopped giving them out until *after* the World Series.

In 1926 the Cardinals made their first Series appearance, and the Yankees were back. The heavily favored New York gang led three games to two. Ruth belted three homers in Game 4. But ancient star Grover Cleveland Alexander, who had pitched a complete-game four-hitter for the Cards in Game 2, tossed another complete-game victory in Game 6, tying the Series. Though known for the resilience of his rubber arm, he hardly expected to pitch again the next day.

Legend has it the 39-year-old celebrated long and loud after his second victory of the Series. He was still recuperating in the bullpen in Game 7 with the Cards clinging to a 3-2 lead. The Yanks loaded the bases in the last of the seventh with two out when St. Louis starter Jesse "Pop" Haines developed a blister on his pitching hand. Card manager Rogers Hornsby called for grizzled veteran "Old Pete" Alexander. Alexander, allegedly asleep in the bullpen, was rushed into the fray. It is said that Hornsby met him as he reached the mound and stared in his eyes to see if he was still suffering from a hangover. The puritanical Hornsby wanted a sober Pete. A control artist who could warm up quickly, Alexander assured his manager he was fine.

Batting for New York was rookie star Tony Lazzeri, who had slugged 18 homers and knocked in 114 runs that season. The kid knocked one far but foul. Then Old Pete struck him

Grover Cleveland Alexander, who had seen everything since starting his pro career in 1909, said of Tony Lazzeri's foul liner in the '26 World Series, "A few more feet and he'd have been a hero and I'd have been a bum."

out. Alexander retired the next five men but walked Ruth with two outs in the bottom of the ninth. (It was the 11th time the Cards had put him on in the Series.) That brought up slugger Bob Meusel, representing the potential winning run. Before he could do any damage, however, Ruth tried to surprise St. Louis by stealing second. Catcher Bob O'Farrell fired to Hornsby, who tagged a sliding Ruth to end the Series and give St. Louis

its first world championship. And the Series came to a strange and bitter end for the Yanks.

The Yankees swept the Pirates in the 1927 Series and did the same to the Cards in 1928. The first Series featured a couple of close games and ended on a wild pitch by Buc hurler Johnny Miljus (his second of the inning). In the second Series the Cards decided not to walk Babe Ruth. They pitched to him, and they paid for their arrogance. Ruth batted .625 with three home runs and three doubles; his partner in power Lou Gehrig batted .545 and slugged at a 1.727 clip. Grover Cleveland Alexander pitched five innings and finished with a 19.80 ERA.

The 1929 Series featured the first appearance in 15 years of Connie Mack's Philadelphia Athletics in the Series. They were facing the Chicago Cubs, in their first World Series since 1918. Mack pulled off a bit of trickery in Game 1. Without making any announcement, he started veteran hurler Howard Ehmke, who had pitched in just 11 games during the regular season, instead of either of his superstars, George Earnshaw or Lefty Grove. The story goes that Howard told Mack, "I think I've got one more good game left in this old arm." The truth is,

Babe Ruth slugged three of his four 1926 World Series long balls in Game 4. After the Babe repeated his Series "home run hat trick" two years later, the feat was not accomplished again until Reggie Jackson did it in '77.

Mack didn't care about the age of Ehmke's arm; the manager knew that sidearmer Ehmke's deliveries would appear to be coming out of the shirts in the left-field bleachers as they headed toward the Cub batters. Ehmke won the game 3-1 and broke Ed Walsh's record for strikeouts in a World Series game, with 13. But the tide of the Series really turned in Game 4. After losing Game 2, the Cubs took Game 3 and were cruising toward a tie in the Series with an 8-0 lead in inning seven of Game 4. Then the Cubbies collapsed. Al Simmons led off the A's seventh with a homer. The next four A's singled. Hack Wilson misplayed a fly ball into a three-run homer, and before the second out was made, Jimmy Dykes's double had knocked in runs 9 and 10 for the A's. The A's comeback in Game 5 to win the Series, with three runs in the bottom of the ninth, seemed almost anticlimactic.

Connie Mack's once-proud Athletics returned to the World Series in 1929, their fans voracious for their first pennant in 15 years. These team employees sorted through mounds of ticket requests for the fall classic, won by Philadelphia over the Cubs in five games.

WHEN ALL IS SAID AND DONE, THERE IS REALLY ONLY ONE

The world was an exciting new place for Americans in the 1920s. With the terrible events of World War I behind them, Americans felt safe, fresh, and new. "The pursuit of happiness" promised in the Declaration of Independence became the "pursuit of pleasure." Americans spent money like never before on entertainment, from speakeasies and dance halls to "flickers" and theater. Professional sports were a huge part of the entertainment world. Every sport had its stars, but each had one personage who dominated his game so much that he reached another level, becoming bigger than the game, even bigger than life. Tennis had "Big Bill" Tilden, winner of seven U.S. Opens and three Wimbledons in the 1920s. Golf had Bobby Jones, the quiet gentleman with the machinelike perfect swing who won the Grand Slam (all four majors) in one year and then retired— at age 28. Boxing had Jack Dempsey, "The Manassa Mauler," who knocked out his opponents 49 times in his 78 fights (25 times in the first round—once in 14 and once in 18 seconds). Football had Red Grange, "The Galloping Ghost," who captivated the nation as a collegian and then singlehandedly put pro football on the map.

But of all the talents of this great sporting era, only one became an icon. He had a great nickname, too: "The Sultan of Swat." Babe Ruth was like Elvis Presley in that he created something new that no one else ever succeeded in doing better. And, like Elvis, Ruth had to learn how to mature while in the public eye, to control his outsize appetites for food, drink, women, and just plain rollicking.

The statistics Ruth compiled are so stunning, and so outrageously bigger than anything that had come before, that they are hard to believe. His record of 12 homer titles in 14 seasons leaves everyone else in the dust. It took Hank Aaron nearly 3,000 more at-bats to equal Babe's 714 homers. But consider the mark he left on baseball history apart from his batting prowess. With Babe in the lineup, his Yankees won seven pennants and four World Series. With the money that generated, the Yanks were able to construct a farm system second to none, and as a result won 25 pennants and 19 World Series in the next 54 years. Ruth cast a long shadow.

But even at that, one writer put it best when he said, "Trying to describe Babe Ruth with statistics would be like trying to keep up with him on a Saturday night." For Babe was as exces-

Otherwise unnoteworthy Indians Bill Wambsganss (left) and Elmer Smith (right) accounted for two World Series firsts in 1920: an unassisted triple play and a grand slam, respectively. Cleveland fans showered the League Park diamond with straw hats upon Wambsganss's feat.

sive in his personal life as in his batting swing. "Once my swing starts, I can't change it or pull up on it," he said. "It's all or nothing." Babe drove too fast, ate and drank more than he should (until second wife Claire got him in line), and womanized in ways that have become legend (again until Claire). He was the first athlete to endorse all kinds of products, and (after Christy Walsh took charge of his finances) he made an incredible amount of money. He also gave barrels of it away. A $50 bill as tip for a nickel cup of coffee wasn't uncommon. It is said that only the president had his name in print more often than the Babe, and that nobody in Ruth's lifetime was photographed more often.

Scientists at Columbia University performed a battery of physical tests on Ruth early in his Yankee career. On tests for strength, stamina, coordination, vision, and the like, the Babe tested off the charts. One scientist pontificated, "It's unlikely that more than one person in a million would score so highly on all these tests." The New York media loved it: "Babe One in a Million" their headlines shouted. Of course people weren't as

The New York Giants were relieved to see Babe Ruth hustling back into first base in the seventh inning of Game 2 of the 1923 World Series. He had hit home runs in both the fourth and fifth, setting up a 4-2 Yankees win and, ultimately, his team's first world title.

used to large numbers then as they are today. By that standard, there would have been 106 "Babe Ruths" alive in the United States at that time. The fact is, it is more likely that Babe's physical skills would rank him one in *30 or 40 million* people.

And of course there was that wink. Captured on film more than a few times, it was as broad as his smile and just as captivating (subtlety wasn't to be found in any Ruth gesture). Babe Ruth's wink let everybody know that we are all in on the same joke. With that look, he told you that life was sheer, exultant joy. It also told you he knew he wasn't fooling anybody; he didn't have to. He'd wink at folks in the stands, at girls on the street, even at the opposing third baseman when he circled the bases

after knocking the stuffing out of an unsuspecting baseball, again. "This is easy," the winking Babe was saying. "This is fun."

One photograph of Babe Ruth stands apart. The shot was taken in what seems to be a rural setting. In the middle of a sea of nearly 100 children, one face, above a bow tie and below a straw boater, stands out. Babe Ruth's grin spreads from ear to ear. All the bad times, the bellyaches, the tantrums, the strikeouts are forgotten. Because he was such a child himself, the kids loved him, and he returned their love completely. He was the all-time superstar, but he was also always the Babe.

By the end of the 1920s, Americans were spending nearly $5 billion a year on entertainment and recreation. The 1920s had seen the largest single-decade rise in American population ever. And baseball was reaping the benefits. Attendance for the decade was 93 million, nearly 3,000 more per game than in the 1910s. Baseball revenues were up 40 percent over the previous ten-year period. It was a truly Golden beginning to the game's Golden Age. But trouble wasn't far away.

The Babe was the most recognizable American of his era, a magnet for starstruck young fans and the first celebrity from whom an autograph was considered a treasure. "I won't be happy until we have every boy in America between the ages of six and sixteen wearing a glove and swinging a bat," he once said.

1930s

Long Balls and Lights

While the nation suffered through the Great Depression, the lords of the game gave the fans what they wanted—offense and more offense. But even though that tonic produced some mind-boggling stats, it couldn't cure an ailing economy, so attendance continued to slide. To promote attendance, new ideas were born, from night games to uniform numbers. And somehow baseball found new ways to grow, as broadcasting and barnstorming expanded the audience to a truly national one. Meanwhile, a quiet revolution took place in St. Louis, as Branch Rickey's redefinition of what makes a big-league team reaped benefits. A new owner in Boston promised to right the foundering Red Sox ship, and in New York, Lou Gehrig finally got out from under the Babe's shadow.

After playing in 2,130 straight games, Lou Gehrig finally asked just to watch the ninth contest of the 1939 season (pictured). "I honestly have to say that I've never been tired on the field," claimed "The Iron Horse."

BASEBALL GETS OFFENSIVE

There was never a worse season to be a big-league pitcher than 1930. In every way, it was the culmination of the new slugging that had started with Ruth's arrival in New York ten years earlier. Some have called 1930 "the year of the hitter," but "the year of *every* hitter" would probably be more appropriate. Briefly, here's what the stats say. First, the National League batted at a .303 clip. Remember: That's the *entire league.* No team in history had ever scored 1,000 runs in one season (that's 6½ runs per game), but in 1930 the Cardinals *and* Yankees did it, and four other teams scored more than 900. The Yankees, by the way, despite that offensive barrage, finished third, 16 games out of first. The team that relished the offense but also suffered from it the most was the Phillies. That season they batted .315 as a team and slugged .458. Their star, Chuck Klein, had one of the great batting years of all time: a .386 average, 40 homers, 170 RBI,

Chuck Klein (left) and Bill Terry (right) dominated the batting charts from 1929 to '35. During that time, Terry led all major-leaguers with a .357 average, and Klein was just behind at .345.

DOUBLE-NO-HIT

Inability to control his fearsome fastball kept Johnny Vander Meer out of the Hall of Fame. But when he was on, the 6'1", 190-pound left-hander was almost unhittable.

That was certainly true in June 1938, when he became the only man in baseball history to pitch consecutive no-hit games. Never mind that his victims were the Boston Braves and Brooklyn Dodgers, two second-division clubs, or that the second gem coincided with the first night game in Ebbets Field history, in which the lighting was very poor, making it difficult to see. A no-hitter is a no-hitter.

A New Jersey native who reached the majors with the Reds in 1937, Vander Meer was a four-time All-Star and three-time strikeout king. But he never won more than 18 games in a season, and he finished his 13-year career two games under .500 (119-121).

Variously known as "The Dutch Master" or "Double-No-Hit," Vander Meer was a hard-throwing southpaw whose best pitch was a sinker. But it didn't always sink: The

Johnny Vander Meer

pitcher led the National League in walks in both 1943 and 1948.

Even during his second no-hitter, on June 15, Vandy's tendency to walk batters almost proved to be a problem: Before 40,000 fans, most of them lured by the novelty of night baseball in Brooklyn, he walked the bases loaded in the ninth before getting Leo Durocher to end the game with a fly ball to center on a 1-2 pitch. Even though he had more walks (eight) than strikeouts (seven) that night, the lefty was able to post a 6-0 win, twice the margin of his June 11 daylight victory at home against Boston.

Vander Meer, 23 at the time, was not only the first pitcher to notch consecutive no-hitters but was also the first to pitch a pair in the same season. Only 11 previous pitchers had even tossed two in their careers.

158 runs scored, 250 hits, and 445 total bases (fourth best ever). They scored 944 runs, yet finished *40* games out of first. Why? Easy guess: Their team ERA was 6.71. Only one team in baseball had a team ERA less than 4.00, and three others joined the Phils with marks over 5.00. All in all, 45 big-leaguers sported batting averages higher than .313 (in 1968, "the year of the pitcher," only four did); nine were better than .360; five hit better than .380, and Bill Terry became the last NLer to reach the .400 mark.

Baseball owners have always had a love-hate relationship with offense. Plenty of run-scoring usually means higher attendance, which means more revenue. But higher batting averages also usually translate into demands from hitters for higher pay. The stock market crash after the 1929 World Series put the fear of God into baseball's magnates. To keep fans coming, they added a little juice to the ball and lowered the seams, making it harder to throw a pitch that would break. The fans loved it. Gate receipts from 1930 (more than 10 million fans in attendance!) were the highest ever, and it would be a long time before attendance went that high again.

But perhaps no one enjoyed that slugging ride more than Hack Wilson, dubbed by someone as the "hardest hitting hydrant of all time." At 5'6" Hack wasn't tall, but he was thick, at a rock-solid 190 pounds. His tree-trunk legs ended in a tiny pair of feet, only size six. Hack was power personified; some said his nickname came from his resemblance to a German wrestler, but it's just as much fun to believe it came from the way he approached his job at the plate. He was as tough as he was sturdy; no one wanted to scrap with Wilson. He proved he had slugging skills with four fine seasons as a Cub, topping .312 every year, knocking home at least 109 runs, and homering 21 times or better. But in 1930 he was positively unstoppable. Fifty-six homers, 190 RBI (since changed to 191), and 423 total bases (then fifth best of all time, now eighth). His Cubs finished just two games behind the Cards for the NL pennant. His 1930 manager, Joe McCarthy, knew how to get the most from his happy-go-lucky slugger. But late in the season, McCarthy was ousted in favor of tactless Rogers Hornsby, and under Rajah's constant harping and withering criticism, the big little man just seemed to give up. He never batted .300 or hit 25 homers again, and his career was essentially over after just three more seasons.

Hack Wilson, here in the spring of '31 following his monumental season, was virtually washed up at age 30. A short, stocky ballplayer, he died destitute at 48 but was named to the Hall of Fame on the basis of a five-year stretch in which he hit .321 and averaged 141 RBI.

MR. MACK'S ATHLETICS

It's no wonder the Philadelphia A's of 1929–31 don't get much respect as a great team. They were stuck in the middle of a couple of Yankee dynasties, and they were disassembled shortly thereafter. But great they surely were, winning three consecutive AL flags (by an average of 13 games over the second-place team) and two of three World Series. What makes them truly stand out is that they accomplished all that while Ruth and Gehrig were both in their prime.

Connie Mack, the angular, patrician owner/manager of the A's, had tasted success with his team earlier in the century, winning pennants in 1910, '11, '13, and '14. These were the teams of Eddie Collins, Stuffy McInnis, and Frank "Home Run" Baker, with legendary hurlers such as Jack Coombs, Eddie Plank, and "Chief" Bender. Either financial pressure from the Federal League to raise salaries or his own greed (both stories are told) led Mack to sell off his best players. The A's tumbled to the basement and pretty much stayed there for a dozen years.

With savvy and the occasional big check, Mack began to rebuild. Muscular youngster Jimmie Foxx wasn't expensive to sign. Al Simmons, born Szymanski, and also a born slugger, was picked up on the cheap because his "bucketfoot" batting style looked vulnerable. (It wasn't.) Pacific Coast League Portland didn't want to part with its brilliant young catcher, Mickey Cochrane. Mack's solution? Buy the team. Then Mack spent

Athletics owner Connie Mack is flanked by the on- and off-the-field leaders of his finest teams: catcher Mickey Cochrane (left) and pitcher Lefty Grove. For Philadelphia's three pennant-winners from 1929 through '31, Cochrane batted .345 and Grove racked up a record of 79-15.

the unheard-of sum of $100,600 to buy Lefty Grove from Jack Dunn's International League Baltimore Orioles. The collection Connie was amassing was young, talented, and growing up together. By 1925 they had sneaked into second place. In 1926 they were third, then two consecutive seconds preceded their three-year championship run.

What a run it was. The Athletics, called by one historian "the most complete team" of all time, won 104, 102, and 107 games those three years. Al Simmons batted .365, .381, and .390. His outfield partners, Bing Miller and Mule Haas, were reliable batters as well. Cochrane, whom some still consider the greatest catcher of all time, hit between .331 and .357. Simmons was in the top five in batting in the AL each of those years; Cochrane in four of them.

In 1932 Jimmie Foxx slugged 58 home runs, just two shy of Babe Ruth's then record. Interestingly, Foxx lost two would-be long balls to rainouts that season. The slugger earned the second of two MVP awards in '33, the same year he won the Triple Crown.

At first base was the still-growing Jimmie Foxx. He was only in his second full season, but he had power to spare. The man whom Lefty Gomez said "had muscles in his hair" belted 33, 37, and 30 homers those years. (The following year he hit 58, as close as anyone would come to Ruth's record for nearly 30 seasons.) His homers went long distances, and he hit them when they counted: Four times in his career he topped 155 RBI.

The difference between the mini-dynasty A's and the second-place Yanks was their pitching. George Earnshaw and Lefty Grove both won 20 games or more for the A's each of those seasons. Grove didn't even reach

Mickey Cochrane was the era's best defensive catcher and the highest-hitting (.320) retired backstop ever. "Black Mike"—so-named for his mood after defeats—homered in the final at-bat of his career. His playing days were curtailed in his next trip to the plate by a beanball that left him comatose for ten days.

the majors until he was 25, because Dunn wanted to keep him in Baltimore. By the time he got to the bigs he seemed angry about it. As Jack Kavanagh says in *The Ballplayers*, "he led the American League in strikeouts seven consecutive years, victories four times, . . . ERA nine times (no one else ever did more than five) and winning percentage five times. Grove also led in shredded uniforms, kicked buckets, ripped-apart lockers and alienated teammates." His 2.06 ERA in 1931 was more than two runs a game less than the league average. Grove was the Walter (or Randy) Johnson of his era, with a fastball that was unhittable and a canny sense of where to throw it.

But like many investors, the crash of the market hurt Connie Mack sorely. Fans stopped coming even though the A's were winning. Before long the A's of the early '30s were sold off, and Connie Mack had built, then taken apart, not one but *two* great teams.

RICKEY, THE FARM SYSTEM, THE CARDS

The Cardinals were nicknamed the "Gashouse Gang" in 1934, but they had been playing with that style—hardscrabble players in a hardscrabble era—for years already.

And the man behind this collection of talented characters? Branch Rickey. While Rickey may have had the deepest, savvi-

Prior to the 1934 season, the brash Dizzy Dean (right) predicted he and brother Paul (left), also known as Daffy, would win 40 games. Together, they piled up 49, then won two more apiece in the World Series.

est baseball mind ever, his style was pompous and arrogant, and he was breathtakingly cheap. While managing the Cardinals in the early '20s, Rickey saw clearly that his team would never generate enough revenue to be able to buy the big stars from the minor leagues. In order to improve, he needed to do something. So he created something new: the farm system. The Cards would *own* their minor-league teams—and all the players. This ran counter to the way the talent pipeline had come to work in baseball, and none other than Judge Landis didn't like the idea. In fact, Landis's first decision as commissioner had nothing to do with the Black Sox or Babe Ruth, but was instead a dressing-down of Rickey in 1921 for hiding ballplayers. Landis accused Rickey of having "secret agreements." It was all true, but despite Landis's frequent slaps on the wrist, Rickey rolled on.

A canny business executive, and legally trained, Rickey was often able to buy shares in a team, then gradually establish control without expending much more money. At its peak, the Rickey-created Cardinal system owned 33 teams, including every team in the Nebraska State League. (Today's typical big-league club has "working agreements" with five or six minor-league aggregations.) Rickey lost his job as field manager of the Cards in 1925, but he comfortably moved upstairs to the general manager's post, where he oversaw his amazing creation. He believed that speed and strong arms were the two skills to look for; the rest could be taught. So Rickey trained a team of scouts, instituted tryout camps on a huge scale, signed thousands of players, and developed a method of teaching that was consistent throughout the Cardinals organization. The next team to follow Rickey's example? The New York Yankees.

By 1938, Landis had enough on Rickey to slam him hard. The Judge issued an edict turning more than 70 Cardinal farmhands free. Other teams, including the Tigers, also felt Landis's anti–farm system ire. In *Judge Landis: Twenty-Five Years of Baseball*, J. G. Taylor Spink sarcastically titles the chapter on this action "The Great Emancipator."

But while the farm system was in place, the talent that percolated through it produced some exciting, high-caliber baseball for Cardinal fans. The Cards started winning in the '20s, taking NL flags in 1926 (the year Grover Cleveland Alexander fanned Tony Lazzeri to help win Game 7 of the World Series) and again in '28 (the year Ruth and Gehrig bombed them into submission in a Series sweep). By 1930 they were back again. Their batting attack that year was described as

With as many as 33 farm teams, the Cards under Branch Rickey (right) saw numerous stars rise through their ranks. Joe "Ducky" Medwick (left), a home-grown Cardinal, won the National League Triple Crown in 1937 (.374-31-154). Medwick also led the circuit in runs (111), hits (237), and doubles (56).

1930s
LONG BALLS AND LIGHTS

"balanced hitting of a kind unseen before or since" (William B. Mead, *Low and Outside*). Every Card regular, and four bench players, batted better than .300. Their catchers, usually weak links in the offense, batted .318 and .366. Stars Jim Bottomley, Frankie Frisch, Taylor Douthit, and Chick Hafey helped them score 1,004 times. However, the A's disposed of the Card batting machine in six games in that year's World Series.

The next year, things got rocking. Both the A's and Cards repeated as league champs. But the Cards had a secret weapon, and he was to become one of World Series history's most unlikely heroes. John Leonard Roosevelt "Pepper" Martin was fast. Very fast. Growing up on the plains of Oklahoma, he developed foot speed galore and a gutbucket attitude toward the game and life in general. If it wasn't fun, Pepper would make it so. Pepper's attitude toward life was always refreshing. He was wacky and fun-loving, and he kept things exciting for the Gashouse Gang and Cardinals fans.

A veteran of six minor-league seasons, Martin was ready for the bigs—so ready that once he appeared, the Cards

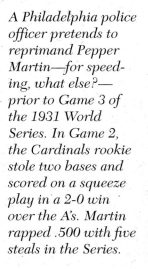

A Philadelphia police officer pretends to reprimand Pepper Martin—for speeding, what else?—prior to Game 3 of the 1931 World Series. In Game 2, the Cardinals rookie stole two bases and scored on a squeeze play in a 2-0 win over the A's. Martin rapped .500 with five steals in the Series.

swapped super outfielder Taylor Douthit early in the year. Pepper batted .300 and swiped 16 bases.

In the Series, Game 1 looked like it was shaping up to follow the pattern of the year before and the year before that. Lefty Grove wasn't perfect, but he was good enough to down the Cards 6-2. Pepper Martin had three hits and a stolen base in the game. Then Game 2

Player/manager Frankie Frisch (left) and St. Louis ace Dizzy Dean celebrate after Diz blanked the Tigers in Game 7 of the '34 World Series. The two, who were among the most quotable teammates in baseball history, both went on to become radio broadcasters.

arrived, and Pepper stole the show with a double, a single, and two swiped bases. The Cards took the Series lead in Game 3 when Martin swatted a double and scored twice off Grove. Interestingly, Game 3 was notable for another reason as well: When President Herbert Hoover made an appearance at the game, Prohibition-era fans reacted with a rudeness unheard of for the time. They began to boo, then chant, "We want beer! We want beer!"

The Cards lost Game 4 when they were able to muster only two hits, but both belonged to Martin. In Game 5 the Cards scored five times; Pepper drove in four of them. At this point in the Series, Martin was batting .667 (against Grove and Earnshaw!) and had a full dozen hits. And this was just Game 5! The A's kept Pepper from getting another base hit for the rest of the Series, but he wound up scoring once more and ended the final game with a gutsy snatch of a sinking liner.

The Cards stumbled badly in '32 and '33, but a new manager (the college-educated Frank Frisch), a new pitching duo (Dizzy and Daffy Dean), and a revitalized Pepper Martin (now at third base to make room for Joe Medwick) turned things around for them in 1934. Leo Durocher joined the team at shortstop. This was the "Gashouse Gang," even though that nickname didn't stick until the following year. But these were the brawlers, the hot-foot artistes, the men of wacky stunts and

dirty uniforms. The fact that they led the National League in runs, hits, and doubles made it even more fun. But they might not have made it to the Series at all if not for a verbal indiscretion on the part of Giants manager Bill Terry. On January 25 that year, in a standard preseason interview, a writer asked Terry for his analysis of the teams his world champs would be facing. "And what about Brooklyn?" the reporter prompted. "Brooklyn?" Terry said. "Are they still in the league?" The wounded Dodgers took the last two games of the season from the Giants, opening the door for the Cards to slip in.

CATS AND BIRDS

In 1934 the Cards faced the Detroit Tigers in the World Series. Like the A's, the Tigers had been an early-century mini-dynasty, taking consecutive flags in 1907, '08, and '09. Since then, however, their performance had been mosttly second-division. But Connie Mack's financial straits benefited the Tigers; they

Detroit's "G-Men"—Goose Goslin, Hank Greenberg, and Charlie Gehringer (left to right)—of the 1930s slugged the Tigers to a pair of pennants. All three remained in baseball after their playing days and ultimately were elected to the Hall of Fame.

obtained catcher Mickey Cochrane, still only 31 years old, and made him their playing manager. The Tigers were an intriguing mix of old and new. Manager Cochrane was joined by several other over-30 regulars. Longtime quality-hitter Goose Goslin took the field in right, and Charlie "The Mechanical Man" Gehringer, who earned his nickname because, as teammate Doc Cramer once said, "You wind him up on Opening Day, put him out there, and he hits .350," lined up at second. Gehringer became a regular in 1926; he didn't bat below .298 until 1941. Billy Rogell and Marv Owen handled the left side of the infield. Stars-to-be took their places at first base and in the outfield: Hank Greenberg, in his second full season, knocked 63 doubles, still the fourth-highest total in major-league history. Jo-Jo White, just 25 years old, had the best year of his career, batting .313.

That year's World Series featured one of the worst displays of fan behavior ever seen during a championship game. The Tigers and Cardinals were knotted at three games apiece when Game 7 began in Detroit, with submariner Eldon Auker pitching for the home team and Dizzy Dean on the mound for St. Louis.

Frank Frisch doubled in two runs in the third inning, and the Cards tacked on five more before the dust settled, taking a 7-0 lead. With two outs in the sixth, Joe Medwick whacked a ball off the bleachers in right-center. As he rounded the bases, he slid hard into Tigers third baseman Marv Owen. The two had words, but it seemed to end there—until Medwick headed out to left field, that is, with a team lead of 9-0. The Detroit

HAMMERIN' HANK

Long before Jackie Robinson broke baseball's color line in 1947, another talented young player survived a slew of threats and racial epithets en route to a Hall of Fame career.

A native New Yorker whose parents were Jewish immigrants from Romania, Hank Greenberg attracted attention from pro clubs as a schoolboy. After a semester at New York University, he signed with the Tigers in 1930, reaching the majors three years later.

Hank Greenberg

The prevailing anti-Semitism of the Depression era also infected the playing field. According to Aviva Kempner's documentary film *The Life and Times of Hank Greenberg*, opponents often riled Greenberg, who was still wearing his Tiger uniform when he marched into the Yankee clubhouse after a game to challenge the race-baiters. No one was willing to take him on.

The 6'4", 215-pound Greenberg found few challenges on the diamond either. After working hard to perfect his fielding at first base, he helped the Tigers take consecutive pennants in 1934–35, earning his first Most Valuable Player Award in the process. In 1937 Hank amassed 183 RBI, just one less than Lou Gehrig's AL single-season record.

His 1938 challenge of Babe Ruth's single-season home run mark again raised the ugly specter of anti-Semitism. With five games to go and just two homers shy of 60, Greenberg received a steady diet of intentional walks—partly because opposing pitchers didn't want a Jew to break Ruth's record.

Though he missed nearly five seasons to wartime military service, Greenberg won four home run crowns and two MVP awards while hitting .313 with 331 home runs. His .605 career slugging average remains fifth best of all time.

Tigers fans pelted Joe Medwick with food, bottles, and other projectiles in Game 7 of the 1934 World Series after the Cardinals left fielder slid hard into third baseman Marv Owen, setting off brief fisticuffs. "Ducky" was removed from the game for his own protection, but St. Louis won anyway.

fans, who no longer had any reason to enjoy their lunches, began to pelt Medwick with fruit, soda bottles, and all manner of garbage while booing him unmercifully. Landis called a conference and ordered Medwick out of the game for his own safety. The riot may have made the Detroit fans forget their woes for a while, but it didn't do them any good: The final score was 11-0.

THERE WERE GIANTS IN THOSE DAYS

After four consecutive pennants at the start of the '20s, the Giants didn't take another until 1933. But they were nearly always in the thick of the hunt. And even though John McGraw had been supplanted by Babe Ruth as "Mr. Baseball," he remained one of the canniest men in the game. Before he retired in 1932, handing the managerial reins to Bill Terry, McGraw made two moves that set the Giants up for future contention.

The first move was to make certain Mel Ott remain unspoiled. "Master Melvin" had a strange hitting style. The diminutive left-hander raised his right foot into the air as he began his swing, his hands holding the bat high in the air. He looked like he might fall over. But as he swung, the bat moved down into a perfect flat arc, often depositing the ball quite a distance away. McGraw signed the 17-year-old, then sat him down on the bench to teach him the game. McGraw knew that in the minors, out of his view, some eager manager would mess up that odd but highly efficient batting style. So McGraw kept Ott on the bench for two years, pointing out correct plays and mistakes, gradually building his confidence. No 19-year-old was ever more ready to step into a major-league starting lineup.

Ott became the dominant National Leaguer of his era: a great hitter with power (he led the NL in homers six times) and a superb right fielder. He averaged 12 assists a season and held the record for lifetime walks for 35 years. He was the first National Leaguer to hit 500 homers, and no batter ever enjoyed home cooking more: Of Ott's 511 career homers, 323 were hit in the Polo Grounds, the most ever by one batter in one park. Pirates manager Pie Traynor said of Ott, "No other player can beat you so many ways."

McGraw's other move involved lefty hurler Carl Hubbell, who was aging but still had plenty of promise. McGraw encouraged him to stick with the screwball, the pitch Hubbell had

A dead-pull hitter who aimed at the Polo Grounds right-field fence just 257 feet away, Mel Ott defied theories of hitting mechanics by lifting his leg and "stepping in the bucket." When killed by a drunken driver in 1958, he was still the NL's all-time home run hitter.

developed but which his former team had told him not to use. Hubbell, of course, became the dominant pitcher in the National League with that marvelous oddity. He put together five consecutive 20-win seasons and led the NL in wins once and ERA three times. In the 1934 All-Star Game he fanned Babe Ruth, Lou Gehrig, Jimmie Foxx, Al Simmons, and Joe Cronin in order, all with screwballs. In 1936 he won 16 straight decisions, and in 1937 he put together a string of 45⅓ consecutive scoreless innings. Knuckleballer "Fat" Freddie Fitzsimmons and curvemeister "Prince" Hal Schumacher delivered sterling mound work for the Giants on Hubbell's days off, and the team copped flags in 1933, '36, and '37. They captured the World Series in '33 but ran into the Yankee juggernaut the other two years.

HUBBELL FANS FIVE HALL OF FAMERS

Carl Hubbell enjoyed tremendous success over the course of his 16-year Hall of Fame career. The New York Giants' southpaw was known as the master of the screwball, but he is best remembered for his brilliant performance at the 1934 All-Star Game.

Hubbell, pitching before almost 50,000 spectators at the Polo Grounds, allowed the game's first two AL All-Stars to reach base. With Babe Ruth up next, the crowd began to percolate in anticipation of an offensive explosion. Even though Hubbell was pitching in his home park and could rightfully expect to have the fans behind *him*, few moments in baseball could rival the excitement of Ruth stepping to the plate. Fans couldn't help but cheer the Babe on.

Hubbell responded by striking out Ruth, who stood frozen as a screwball brushed over the outside corner of the plate. The next batter was Lou Gehrig, who worked the count full before swinging through the third strike. The crowd then quickly shifted behind Hubbell, cheering for another strikeout. He didn't let them down, fanning Jimmie Foxx to end the inning.

Carl Hubbell

In the top of the second, Al Simmons struck out swinging at several pitches outside the strike zone, a testament to Hubbell's delightfully devious screwball. Joe Cronin went down swinging as well, and that brought Bill Dickey to the plate. Dickey ran the count to 2-1 before lining a single to left. The streak was over, but Hubbell ended the inning by whiffing opposing pitcher Lefty Gomez.

Although the American League beat the National League 9-7, the game would forever be remembered as the day Hubbell struck out the mighty Ruth, Gehrig, Foxx, Simmons, and Cronin in succession.

THE YANKS ROLL ON

While other great teams emerged, the New York Yankees slugged it out throughout the '30s. Even though Mack's Philadelphia team kept the Yanks out of the World Series from 1929–31, the Babe and the talented young Lou Gehrig, the most amazing slugging duo in history, weren't exactly taking it easy. In those three seasons Ruth batted .345, .359, and .373 and averaged nearly 47 homers and 160 RBI; Gehrig hit .300, .379 (second in the AL), and .341 while swatting close to 42 dingers a year and averaging 161 RBI. The 184 he drove in in 1931 is still the all-time AL record. The 174 he sent home in 1930 is fifth best.

Of course, while Babe and Lou were setting batting records, the Yanks were getting outpitched by Lefty Grove and George Earnshaw and Mack's other hurlers. It wasn't until 1932 that the Yanks once again earned the top spot. New pitchers Lefty Gomez and Red Ruffing (obtained from the Red Sox—sound familiar?) helped solidify the rotation, and veteran

George Pipgras recovered some of his gas. The Yanks led the league in runs (as usual), but this year they also led in team ERA. Connie Mack's guys could manage no better than 13 games out of first.

For the third time in three World Series appearances (1927, '28, '32), the Yanks swept the opposition (this time the Cubs). The Chicagoans were settling in as one of the better teams of the era. They took the NL flag four times in ten years, every three years like clockwork: 1929, '32, '35, and '38. (In 1938, however, it took a remarkable comeback late in the season for them to pull within striking distance of the league-leading Pirates, and then, in late September, Gabby Hartnett effectively knocked the Pirates out of the race with what is now registered in baseball lore as his "Homer in the Gloamin'.")

The '32 Series between the Yanks and the Cubs was one of the nastiest Series of all time, at least in terms of invective hurled and billingsgate dished out. The two teams flat-out

In 1939 Yankees Bill Dickey, Joe DiMaggio, Charlie Keller, and George Selkirk (left to right) all hit over .300, and all but Keller were named to the All-Star Team. That year New York so sustained its talent monopoly that owners passed a rule prohibiting AL teams from trading with the prior year's pennant-winners.

didn't like each other. The Yankees were full of themselves, particularly since they were back where they felt they belonged—playing for the world championship. They also didn't cotton to the fact that their former teammate, Mark Koenig, who was now batting .353 as the Cubs' shortstop, had been voted only a one-half Series share in Chicago. You can bet the Babe called the Cubbies tightfisted more than once.

The Yankees had no trouble taking the first two games, played in New York. When they arrived in Chicago for Game 3, the fans were all over the Babe. His response was typical. Noting the great hitting backdrop in Wrigley Field during batting practice, Ruth exclaimed (as only he could), "I'd play for half my salary if I could hit in this dump all the time."

Ruth came to bat in the fifth inning with the score tied at 4 and the bases empty. The crowd was screaming; both benches were roaring at each other. What happened next lies somewhere between myth and legend. Some say that after two strikes Ruth pointed to center field, indicating that's where the next pitch was headed. (The Cub on the mound, Charlie Root, wasn't easily intimidated. He often said if Ruth had actually pointed, the next pitch would have ended up in his ear.) Some say Babe just kind of waved toward the outfield, or toward the Cubs bench, with his bat. Cubs third baseman Woody English (as close to the action as one could get) said in a 1991 interview that after noting each of the first two strikes with a raised index finger, Ruth was just pointing at Root ("Okay, go ahead").

Everyone agrees on what happened next. Babe smoked a line drive deep into the center-field stands, then circled the bases laughing. The next hitter, Gehrig, chuckled and shook Babe's hand as the big guy crossed home. Then Gehrig himself knocked one out of sight. The Yanks won that

HARTNETT HITS HOMER IN THE GLOAMIN'

As darkness descended upon the friendly confines of Wrigley Field on a late September afternoon, hope for the beloved Cubs was still flickering in the twilight.

The Cubbies and Pirates were separated in the standings by half a game, and on September 28, 1938, they went head-to-head at Wrigley. The score was tied 5-5 in the bottom of the ninth inning with two outs. Had Pittsburgh managed to procure the third out, it was likely that the umpires would have called the game due to darkness. (Night baseball had been introduced to the majors in 1935, but it was still considered a novelty at this time, and it would be another 50-plus years before lights were installed at Wrigley.)

As the last rays of sun sank and twilight wrapped itself around the park, Chicago's catcher/manager Gabby Hartnett launched a two-strike pitch into the left-field seats, securing a dramatic 6-5 win. The ecstatic crowd spilled onto the field and, along with the rest of the Cubs, joined Hartnett in a jubilant dash around the bases. The Cubs, who trailed the Pirates by as many as nine games in August, had finally climbed into first place as the sun was setting over Wrigleyville. Three

Gabby Hartnett

days later they clinched the National League pennant. Although they were swept in the World Series by the Yankees, Hartnett's heroics had provided the Cubs with their fourth NL crown in ten seasons, continuing their odd pattern of appearing in the World Series every third season.

day and the next to sweep the Series, and the Babe's World Series career came to an end—with 12 straight wins.

Two years later, Babe and the Yanks parted ways. It was sadly unpleasant. Babe had always ached to manage his beloved team (or any big-league team, for that matter). But he felt it was somehow his birthright; he didn't need to work for it. He rebuffed offers to manage a high minor-league Yankee club. (And the high minor-league Yankee farm teams of this era were pretty amazing.) He passed on a chance to head up the Tigers. The story goes that just about this time Yankee owner Jacob Ruppert uttered a pretty hurtful remark: "How can he manage a ball team when he can't even manage himself?"

The truth is, Babe's days of out-of-control carousing had pretty much ceased since his marriage to Claire Hodgson. He still loved his fun, but after the World Series each year Babe drank only beer until the big New Year's Eve party they always threw, and then nothing until spring training was over and the season was well underway. Babe's emerging belly and weak knees were more a result of age than of bad behavior.

Depending on whom you believe, this painting depicts Babe Ruth either "calling his shot" before hitting a home run at Wrigley Field on October 1, 1932, or—as most of the Cubs claimed—pointing toward Chicago's bench-jockeying dugout. Ruth's own accounts of the event were generally evasive or contradictory.

Three key members of the 1937 Yankees were in a celebratory mood after dismissing the Giants in five World Series games. Lefty Gomez (center) had two wins, while Tony Lazzeri (left) and Joe DiMaggio carried the offense by together batting .324, compared to rest of their teammates'.227.

The Yankees didn't want him, so the Boston Braves signed Ruth for the 1935 season. He believed it was a stepping-stone to management, when actually it was a sham devised to hype attendance for one of the game's worst teams. Babe grew tired of it quickly.

The end of Ruth's career took place in May 1935, in a somewhat muted blaze of glory. Playing the Pirates in Forbes Field (in a far-from-full park), Ruth homered his first two times up, singled the next, and then knocked a ball completely over the right-field grandstand. Pitcher Guy Bush said, "I never saw a ball hit so hard before or since." Ruth was the first batter in the ballpark's 26-year history to do it, and it would happen only 16 times more in the park's next

Yankees manager Joe McCarthy won seven world championships. Known for staying seated squarely in the middle of the dugout (which he called his "command post"), he claimed never to have challenged an umpire on anything but rules and never to have gone to the mound to remove a pitcher.

35 seasons. Within a few days, the Babe had hung it up as a player for good. For 13 years he waited for the phone to ring, hoping he'd be asked to return as a manager to the game he loved. A 1938 stint as a coach with the Dodgers was another waste of time.

THE GREAT GEHRIG

Back in 1925, Ruth had lost a good part of the season due to an intestinal problem; only one Yankee pitcher had an ERA below 3.00; and the New York behemoths finished in seventh place, 28½ games out of first. It was their lowest finish since 1917, and it would be their lowest for 40 more years. But there was a silver lining. Because the team was struggling, manager Miller Huggins saw no reason to limit the playing time of that new kid at first base, the big strong one, Lou Gehrig. Lou rose to the occasion.

Gehrig was not just a great player. He was intensely durable, playing in 2,130 consecutive games. (Late in his career, doctors x-rayed Gehrig's huge hands and located 17 fractures—broken bones that had healed themselves as Gehrig continued to play, and play brilliantly.) Cal Ripken, Jr., who broke Lou's record in 1995, was a very good player himself, but when it came to greatness Gehrig was in another universe.

Over the 11-year span from 1927 to '37, Lou Gehrig averaged 153 RBI per year for the Bronx Bombers—a prodigious level of sustained offensive excellence.

Of course he got much less attention because he played in the shadow of Babe Ruth. Who could compete with the all-time home run hitter and party animal? When asked about that fact, Lou replied with typical modesty, "It's a pretty big shadow."

Gehrig's numbers are positively breathtaking. He had a lifetime average of .340, 15th best of all time. Only 16 players have ever had a 400-total-base season. Three did it twice; Chuck Klein did it three times. Gehrig did it *five* times. Over a 13-season span he *averaged* 147 RBI a year. And he accomplished that while batting immediately behind two of history's greatest base-cleaners, Ruth and DiMaggio.

Gehrig won the Triple Crown in 1934, but even that performance could only drag the Yanks to within seven games of the Tigers. The next year the Babe was gone to Boston, and the Yanks finished second again.

But in 1936 a new kid showed up. The kid was quiet like Gehrig, but fleet of foot and longball-strong. Joe DiMaggio had about as exciting a rookie season as one could imagine: 206 hits, a .323 average, 29 homers, 125 RBI, and a league-leading 15 triples. He also struck out 39 times; for the rest of his career he never had a season in which he struck out more. Red Ruffing was also in fine form, and besides Gehrig and DiMag, four other Yanks batted over .300 (including a sensational .362 from catcher Bill Dickey—his highest average ever among ten

Gehrig admired Ruth tremendously, but he came to feel slighted playing in the Bambino's shadow. Allegedly, the two were once so at odds that they went six years without talking away from the field.

THE LUCKIEST MAN ON THE FACE OF THE EARTH

On July 4, 1939, the Yankees saluted Lou Gehrig in a sold-out tribute ceremony at Yankee Stadium. Here's what he *really* told the more than 60,000 fans in attendance. (The movies changed it for dramatic purposes.)

Lou Gehrig

Fans, for the past two weeks you have been reading about the bad break I got. Yet today I consider myself the luckiest man on the face of the earth. I have been in ballparks for 17 years and have never received anything but kindness and encouragement from you fans. Look at these grand men. Which of you wouldn't consider it the highlight of his career just to associate with them for even one day? Sure I'm lucky. Who wouldn't consider it an honor to have known Jacob Ruppert? Also, that builder of baseball's greatest empire, Ed Barrow? To have spent six years with that wonderful little fellow, Miller Huggins? Then to have spent the next nine years with that outstanding leader, that smart student of psychology, the best manager in baseball today, Joe McCarthy? Sure I'm lucky. When the New York Giants, a team you would give your right arm to beat, and vice versa, send you a gift—that's something. When everybody down to the groundskeepers and those boys in white coats remember you with trophies, that's something. When you have a wonderful mother-in-law who takes sides with you in squabbles with her own daughter—that's something. When you have a father and mother who work all their lives so you can have an education and build your body—it's a blessing. When you have a wife who has been a tower of strength and shown more courage than you dreamed existed—that's the finest I know. So I close in saying that I may have had a tough break, but I have an awful lot to live for.

As Gehrig fought back the tears, old pal Babe Ruth, to whom he hadn't spoken in years, walked up and applied a Ruthian hug. Gehrig didn't live two more years. It is said that his powerful swing and graceful fielding made him a star; his tragic death made him a legend. Only imagination can hint at how many records he might have shattered if his body hadn't let him down.

.300-plus seasons), and they finished 19½ games ahead of everyone else. A new era of Yankee greatness was unfolding.

In the '36 World Series, they went face to face with the Giants for the first time in 13 years. The Yanks had no great trouble with Bill Terry's men, taking the Series in six games. In typical Yankee style, two of the games were complete blowouts. The next year they took the flag by 13 games, and the Giants won only once in the Series. In 1938 the Red Sox "sneaked" to within 9½ games to no avail; the Yanks again headed to the Series, this time sweeping the Cubs. In 1939 the Yankees took the flag by 17 games and then swept the Cincinnati Reds in the World Series.

Over the course of this amazing run, the Yanks won the AL pennant by an average of nearly 15 games and racked up a 16-3 record in World Series play. Measuring dominance against the league, several researchers have claimed that this was truly the greatest Yankee team of all time, much better than the storied 1927 or 1932 teams. It's true that this team had much better pitching than either of those two: Red Ruffing and Lefty Gomez were a dynamite one-two punch, and it also had Bill Dickey behind the plate. And though it didn't have Ruth, it surely had Joe DiMaggio. During this era, Yankee farm teams were pretty much unbeatable, too.

But by early in the 1939 season, people were starting to notice a difference in Gehrig. Plays he used to make easily he could no longer accomplish. Balls he would have slugged into the next county were lazy fly-outs. He played only eight games before taking himself out of the lineup, ending his consecutive-game streak. Shortly thereafter, he was diagnosed with amyotrophic lateral sclerosis, a very rare degenerative disease (now forever known as "Lou Gehrig's Disease"). Though Lou Gehrig could no longer play baseball, he remained the Yankees' captain for the rest of the season. He died just two years later, at age 37.

NEWS IN BEANTOWN

While the Yankees were continuing to build powerhouse teams, the Boston Red Sox, long bled dry of good players by Frazee and his successors, were sold to Tom Yawkey. Yawkey's money came from his adoptive father's success. Tom took possession of his inheritance on his 30th birthday, February 21, 1933. Four days later, the Red Sox were his.

The Sox had finished last 9 times in the previous 11 seasons. Fortunately, Yawkey wasn't afraid to spend his dough. He began by purchasing the contracts of older, established players who would add instant credibility (if not instant championships) to his team. Before the 1936 season began, Yawkey had Jimmie Foxx, George Pipgras, Lefty Grove, Rube Walberg, and Joe Cronin on his roster. The team showed some improvement; the Sox were no longer cellar dwellers, but they didn't move out of the middle of the pack until 1938. That year a kid named Bobby Doerr became their second baseman; the next year "The Kid," Ted Williams, became their left fielder.

Boston owner Tom Yawkey, one of the few owners with disposable income during the Depression, acquired superstars Joe Cronin (right) in 1935 and Jimmie Foxx, "Old Double-X," (left) in 1936. Anticipating Foxx's monstrous blasts, Yawkey installed a screen atop Fenway Park's left-field wall to keep his homers in the stadium.

The Sox were about to taste glory again for the first time since Ruth had been sold to New York.

ECONOMIC TURMOIL

Although major-league baseball set an attendance record in 1930, the onset of the Great Depression over the next few years took its toll on every American family. Fans just couldn't afford tickets to see the big-leaguers, and ticket revenue was still the largest source of income for the game. After a profit of nearly $1.5 million in 1930, in 1932 the game *lost* $1.2 million. Three years later baseball was back in the black, but the glory days of the '20s were just memories. Even though they hadn't really juiced the ball in 1920 or '21, they certainly did in 1930, and they tried again later in the decade as well in an effort to produce more fans with more offense. Commissioner Landis and NL President John Heydler took voluntary pay cuts in 1932.

To save money, teams reduced their rosters from 25 to 23 players, and many teams saw the cost advantages of paying a star once to be both player and manager. That's why the '30s featured more people wearing both hats than any other time period. There were no player/managers in 1930. The next year there was just one. But by 1932 there were five. In 1934, the National League alone had five. For the rest of the decade, each league had three or four every year. In the World Series of 1933, '34, and '35, both teams were skippered by men who also took their turns at bat.

A SCHOLAR, A CATCHER, AND A SPY

Moe Berg lived a life shrouded in mystery and marked by contradictions. He played alongside Babe Ruth, Lefty Grove, Jimmie Foxx, and Ted Williams; he moved in the company of Nelson Rockefeller, Albert Einstein, and international diplomats; and yet he was often described as a loner. He was well liked by teammates but preferred to travel alone. He never married, and he made few close friends.

Intellectually, Berg was brilliant. He graduated magna cum laude from Princeton, studied at the Sorbonne in Paris, earned a law degree from Columbia, and spoke a dozen languages. However, he was content to wallow in mediocrity as a backup catcher for 15 major-league seasons.

Berg broke into the majors in 1923 as a shortstop with the Brooklyn Robins (later the Dodgers). He was converted to catcher and spent time with the White Sox, Senators, Indians, and Red Sox throughout his career. He was a solid defensive player but was hardly a threat at the plate. His final batting average was .243, and he slugged just six career home runs.

His feeble bat led sportswriters to note, "Moe Berg can speak 12 languages flawlessly and can hit in none."

Berg's intellect and elusive lifestyle were ideal for a post-baseball career as a spy. He first raised eyebrows in the intelligence community at the start of World War II when he shared home movies of Tokyo's shipyards, factories, and military sites that he secretly filmed while on a baseball tour of Japan.

Moe Berg

In 1943, he joined the Office of Strategic Services (OSS), which preceded the CIA as the United States' first national intelligence agency. His most important mission for the OSS was to gather information on Germany's progress in developing an atomic bomb. He worked undercover in Italy and Switzerland and reported information to the States throughout 1944.

Berg's unusual career turns were later immortalized in the Nicholas Dawidoff book *The Catcher Was a Spy*.

Attendance totaled just 81 million for the decade, 12 million less than the previous decade. Take away that record-breaking 1930 season, and the picture becomes that much bleaker. (However, by 1940, the ten million mark had been reached again.)

According to historian Bill James, the game changed little or not at all from 1929 to 1939. It was the least change of any decade ever. On the field, he was right. But off the field the whole sport was scurrying to find new ways to engage the fans.

Some of the things owners did to court fans sound like gimmicks, although they quickly became reliable aspects of ballgame tradition. Ladies' Day, on which a woman accompanying a full-paying man got in free, had first been tried back in the 1880s. The Depression brought it back, and it remained a staple until the rise of feminism. Another "innovation" was allowing fans to keep balls hit into the stands. Although today it's obvious that foul balls are meant to be souvenirs, up until the '30s failure to throw back a foul ball was reason for expulsion from the park.

There was no more avid presidential baseball fan than Franklin Delano Roosevelt, who threw out the first pitch of the 1937 season in Washington. Later that year, he would become the first chief executive to attend an MLB All-Star Game.

BASEBALL ON SUNDAY: FEAST OR FAMINE

Believe it or not, baseball games were once prohibited on Sundays. The National League not only banned Sunday ball when it was founded in 1876, but voted two years later to expel clubs that violated the rule. The league relented in 1892 after merging with the American Association, but many cities still mandated no games on the Christian Sabbath.

Teams tried to skirt local blue laws by sandwiching concerts around games, declaring contests "exhibitions" instead of games, or increasing the price of scorecards to match the price of tickets. Cities in the northeast held out the longest, with New York lifting its ban in 1919, Boston in 1929, and Philadelphia in 1934 (following a public referendum). Several cities, including St. Louis, allowed their teams to play on Sunday but did not broadcast the games.

Hall of Fame pitcher Christy Mathewson and longtime executive Branch Rickey were among a handful of religious baseball personalities who refused to play on Sunday. Others appreciated the opportunity, scheduling Sunday doubleheaders as a magnet to increase gate revenue. Offering two games for the price of one proved to be a great attraction. Although occasional twin bills were played as early as 1876 (the NL's first season), scheduled doubleheaders were rare until the '30s. Cardinal owner Sam Breadon, bucking the opinion of fellow executives, initiated the practice in St. Louis after attendance of the club's Houston farm team skyrocketed for Sunday twin bills.

Teams started putting numbers on the players' uniforms to encourage scorecard sales. Public address systems announced the starting lineups and lineup changes. And by the end of the decade every club was allowed to play baseball on Sunday. So-called "blue laws" had kept entertainment off the Sabbath until that time. This was also the first decade when "community involvement" became significant to big-league clubs. Teams organized speakers' bureaus and even made instructional films to be shown for free in the community. To make all of this happen, major-league teams began hiring professional "press agents" (public relations experts) to see that their product got all the free press it deserved.

THE YEAR THE STARS CAME OUT

Another innovation of the 1930s was the All-Star Game, an idea conceived by Chicago sportswriter Arch Ward to serve as part of the Chicago World's Fair. Judge Landis wasn't keen on the idea until Ward suggested all proceeds be used to augment the pension fund for needy ex-players. With purse strings so tight, the penurious Landis saw the wisdom of that. The first game was held July 6, 1933, in Chicago's Comiskey Park.

Via a newspaper poll, fans from all over the country selected the players to represent the two leagues. The top vote-getter was the A's Al Simmons, followed by Chuck Klein of the Phils. (Philadelphia fans were doing a lot of voting.) Babe Ruth

finished sixth overall. But the Babe didn't let that bother him. In the third inning, with the score tied at two and Charlie Gehringer on base, Ruth lined a homer to right that opened up the game for good. Baseball's first All-Star Game had been decided by its greatest player.

The double bonus of added publicity for the game during the dog days of midsummer and added revenue for the players' pension fund proved irresistible. The All-Star Game became an annual part of the baseball season. (Years later they even tried two a year.)

Legends Carl Hubbell (left) and Lefty Grove (right) toiled as closers in the inaugural All-Star Game in 1933. NL starter Wild Bill Hallahan, who said he was thrilled to be on the same field as Babe Ruth, surrendered a two-run homer to the Bambino, the key blow in the AL's 4-2 win.

HONORING GREATNESS

After more than 20 years of sniping among baseball insiders about what kind of awards to give players, in 1931 the Baseball Writers Association of America (BBWAA) stepped up and created the Most Valuable Player Award. Frankie Frisch won the MVP for the National League, Lefty Grove for the American. This award was later combined with similar awards presented by *The Sporting News*.

Five years later, in 1936, baseball came up with its ultimate reward—the Hall of Fame. The story goes back a few years. The Depression-weary baseball establishment—desperate for a gimmick that might start the turnstiles spinning again—began making elaborate plans for the game's 100th birthday. Those plans, announced in March 1936, would link the centennial with a national baseball museum and Hall of Fame in Cooperstown, New York. Why Cooperstown? Based on legend, word of mouth, and the 1907 report of the Mills Commission, it had been determined that Cooperstown was the birthplace of baseball, as devised by Abner Doubleday in 1839. This "creation myth" has since been debunked from so many angles it seems positively ridiculous now, but it was accepted as truth back then. The 1934 discovery of an old, homemade baseball in a nearby farmhouse attic gave the idea momentum. Local resident Stephen C. Clark, heir to the Singer Sewing Machine fortune, purchased "the Doubleday ball" and conceived the idea of putting it on display, along with other baseball artifacts. With baseball establishment already thinking about ways to mark the game's centennial anniversary in 1939, National League President Ford Frick welcomed the idea and went one step further, suggesting that a Hall of Fame gallery be part of the baseball museum. He enlisted the support of American League President Will Harridge and baseball Commissioner Kenesaw Mountain Landis. Stephen Clark put up about half of the original construction cost to convert the village gym into the National Baseball Hall of Fame and Museum. Filling the hall was left to baseball.

Two elections were held in 1936 to determine who should be enshrined: one by the 226 members of the BBWAA; the other by a special 78-member veterans committee. Interestingly, no criteria were ever spelled out for what made someone a Hall of Famer. Stats? Character? Winning? A combination? It

Ten of the 11 living Hall of Fame inductees in 1939: (back row, from left) Honus Wagner, Grover Cleveland Alexander, Tris Speaker, Nap Lajoie, George Sisler, Walter Johnson; (front row, from left) Eddie Collins, Babe Ruth, Connie Mack, Cy Young.

just seemed obvious; anyone could tell who was a Hall of Famer and who wasn't.

In balloting announced February 2, 1936, the writers chose five men. Ty Cobb drew 222 of 226 votes, Babe Ruth and Honus Wagner polled 215 each, Christy Mathewson 205, and Walter Johnson 189. No one else received the required 75 percent. In the next three years, 21 more men were chosen in additional elections, from Nap Lajoie and Grover Cleveland Alexander to Wee Willie Keeler and George Sisler.

By the time the building was dedicated more than three years later, on June 12, 1939, 20 more players had been selected. All 11 living Hall of Famers attended that initial induction ceremony, with Landis, Frick, Harridge, and National Association President William Bramham officiating. As part of the centennial ceremonies, U.S. Postmaster General James Farley attended the unveiling of a baseball stamp at the Cooperstown post office.

THE REAL FATHER OF BASEBALL?

While the precise origins of baseball are probably forever impossible to determine, the likelihood is that it evolved gradually from several different games. What can be unequivically stated, however, is that Alexander Joy Cartwright—Alick, to his friends—had a large hand in the game as we now know it.

Cartwright, a New York bank teller and talented draftsman whose rules were introduced seven years after Doubleday's "invention" of baseball, was the first to suggest teams of nine players, regular batting orders, equidistant bases, and three outs per inning. The first game under Cartwright's rules was played at the Elysian Fields in Hoboken, New Jersey, on June 19, 1846.

Abner Doubleday's credibility as the inventor of baseball wasn't helped by the dozens of diaries he wrote after retiring from the U.S. Army in 1873. Neither the diaries nor the Doubleday obituary that appeared in *The New York Times* 20 years later mention baseball, and most researchers today believe Doubleday was a West Point plebe who did not go to Cooperstown in 1839. In fact, the Hall of Fame plaque of Alexander Cartwright credits him as "the Father of Modern Base Ball," while Abner Doubleday, the man responsible for the placement of the Hall of Fame in Cooperstown, has himself never been enshrined.

Alexander Joy Cartwright

UNDER THE LIGHTS

Two of the largest changes in the roots of how baseball is enjoyed (and paid for) took place in the 1930s. The first was night baseball. According to David Pietrusza in *Total Baseball*, the first experiment of artificially lighting a ball field to play at night happened in 1880. At least four other tries were made before the Federal League considered it in 1915 as a way to counter the excessive economic power of the National and American Leagues. Over the years the technical problems encountered were gradually sorted through and solved.

But "the great breakthrough," according to Pietrusza, happened in April 1930. On that evening, both the Independence, Kansas, minor-league team and the Kansas City Monarchs of the Negro Leagues played a night game. (The Monarchs' innovation was quite snazzy: The lights were portable and were carried on a truck behind the team bus so the team could play under the lights anywhere.) About two weeks later the Des Moines Demons hosted a night game. By the end of the 1930 season, there were lights in most minor leagues. By 1934, 15 of the 19 minor leagues had at least one lit park.

Crosley Field, home of the Cincinnati Reds, was the site of the first regular-season major-league game ever to be played under the lights. On May 24, 1935, President Franklin Roosevelt illuminated 614 GE Novalux floodlights at the park by pushing a button 500 miles away in Washington, D.C.

The first major-league night game was an exhibition in 1931 between the White Sox and the Giants in Houston. In 1935, forward-thinker Larry MacPhail of the Reds put lights up in his home park, Crosley Field. Three years later, when he got a job with the Dodgers, he did the same. By the end of 1939, four more big-league teams could play games at night. By the 1941 season, four more. Then the need for raw materials to fight World War II limited the expansion of lit parks—but not for long. By the 1960s, the roles had reversed, and day games had become a relative rarity. Night baseball, a radical innovation dredged up to help the game in the 1930s, became the standard mode of major-league ball. By 1971, major-league baseball saw fit to play a World Series at night. By 1985, no World Series game saw the light of day.

AIRWAVES

The next innovation (and the one that made all the difference) was the arrival of radio, the first electronic medium. It had begun early in the previous decade. In 1921, radio was simply a novelty. Harold Arlin, an engineer for Westinghouse Electric in East Pittsburgh, Pennsylvania, took a microphone and some transmitting equipment to Forbes Field on August 5, 1921, and "broadcast" the Pirates game. The next day he announced the U.S. Open tennis tournament, and two months later he called the plays for the first football game ever aired. That fall the first broadcast of a World Series game was heard by a handful of high-tech aficionados on the East Coast. But things change fast: By the next year, the Series was heard live by 5 million people, and the re-creation of the game was heard on *three continents*.

In the 1930s Ronald Reagan broadcast major-league games without ever leaving WHO's studio in Des Moines, Iowa. As a play-by-play recap came over the ticker, Reagan described the action as if he were watching it live. When the ticker went dead during one game in 1934, Reagan made up his own play-by-play.

However, baseball owners seemed to live in constant dread that if they "[gave] the games away," no one would ever pay to see one again. History kept proving them wrong, but as of 1922 most of them were worried about this new gadget's effects on their revenues. Sure, some radio stations offered to pay for the broadcasting rights, but it didn't seem sufficient to

It was heady stuff for a rookie to shake the hand of despotic commissioner Judge Landis as the 1932 World Series opened. But Cubs outfielder William Jennings Bryan "Billy" Herman was a polished personality whom Casey Stengel once called "one of the two or three smartest players" to play in the NL.

make up for the fans who might choose to listen to the game on the radio rather than come to the ballparks.

Others, however, saw the light and realized how greatly radio could expand their audience. Radio had an immediacy no newspaper writeup ever could have. A great game heard by a lot of folks on Monday might encourage more ticket sales for Tuesday. In 1925, Cubs owner Phil Wrigley invited all the Chicago radio stations to carry all the Cubs games, free of charge. Soon thereafter, Sam Breadon of St. Louis began to build a regional following for his team in the same way. (In truth, few other teams in baseball are stronger regional attractions than the Cubs and Cards, even today.)

The first great radio networks, NBC and CBS, were formed in 1926 and '27. People had been buying radios for a while, but by 1929 Americans spent nearly a *billion dollars* to put crystal sets in their homes—a leap of nearly 1,600 percent in seven years. Broadcast revenue, less than one percent of baseball's income a few years earlier, was more than seven percent by the end of the '20s. Beginning in 1933, *The Sporting News* ran a regular feature on baseball broadcasting, "On the Air," and every year ran a survey asking fans to name their favorite broadcaster. They also asked the important question: Does listening to games keep you from attending them in person?

Travel expenses and the technical difficulties of broadcasting far from the studio and transmitter meant that most teams only did live broadcasts of their home games. Away games were "re-created," in real time, from ticker tape reports, using recorded crowd noises, blocks of wood to simulate bat-ball contact, and other creative special effects.

No group was more terrified by the potential of losing money to radio than the owners of the three New York teams. In 1932 they banned *all* radio, even re-creations by visiting teams' broadcasters. In the meantime, the energetic and brilliant Larry MacPhail, working with radio manufacturing magnate Powel Crosley,

Babe Ruth is escorted out of the ballpark following what turned out to be his last game as a Yankee in 1934. He desperately wanted to become the team's manager, but, instead, he wound up playing briefly for the Braves in '35 when he was not re-signed by the Yanks.

took over the Cincinnati Reds in '33. MacPhail made sure Crosley sold plenty of radios. He hired Red Barber, a soft-spoken Southerner with an easy use of engaging colloquialisms, as his announcer. After MacPhail's cantankerous ways led to his firing by Crosley in 1938, he took a job with Brooklyn. MacPhail, who had instituted night baseball and team airplane flights, brought Barber with him and broke the New York radio ban. Baseball was changed forever. (The next year, a new medium was used to broadcast baseball for the first time: Television.)

THE BABE IN YOUR BACKYARD

The tight economic straits of the 1930s (salaries were cut, rosters sliced) encouraged major-leaguers to capitalize on the longstanding practice of barnstorming. And this, too, had an impact on the game as appreciated by its fans.

Off-season touring by major-leaguers, either as part of their regular teams or as individual stars backed by lesser players, had been going on since as far back as 1867. In 1888 Albert Spalding (looking to expand the market for his sporting goods company) took two squads of big-leaguers on a 14-nation "world" tour. They even played a game under the shadow of the Sphinx.

The most prolific barnstormers, of course, were the Negro Leaguers. With shorter league schedules and smaller crowds to play for, they would hop on a bus and go anywhere to play any-one for a cut of the gate. Their skills and showy presentation captivated old fans and created new ones around the country, as well as in Canada, Latin America, and Japan. And it was lucra-tive, too. Some say that by the late '30s, sensational star Satchel Paige was making $40,000 a year as a barnstormer, which was about what Bob Feller was making for the Indians. On occa-sion, even though Landis was opposed to the idea, games show-casing both Negro Leaguers and big-leaguers were played. Unfortunately there weren't nearly enough of those contests to settle the debate of how good the Negro Leaguers really were—they merely fueled the fire.

The 1930s, while tough on the economic end, were big years in opening up baseball to a national audience. The twin factors of broadcasting, whereby a fan thousands of miles away from a major-league game could hear it, and barnstorming, whereby real big-leaguers and Negro Leaguers could play at the field down the street, helped expand baseball's audience in very direct ways.

In 1934 Satchel Paige (left) and the Kansas City Mon-archs played six games against a team of barnstorming major-league stars headed by Dizzy Dean (right). Satchel and his teammates took four of the contests from the big-leaguers at Chicago's Wrigley Field.

THE NEGRO LEAGUES

They played in small towns and major cities. They ran the bases of the sandlots as well as those of sold-out stadiums. The players of the Negro Leagues may have been shunned by Major League Baseball, but they embraced the sport and played it with a passion that was palpable to their fans.

The diamond, any diamond, was their sanctuary.

The halcyon days of the Negro Leagues ranged from 1935 to 1948. But from the moment Fleetwood Walker played his last major-league game in 1884 until the day Jackie Robinson broke baseball's color barrier in 1947, black ballplayers played the game with spirit, flair, and intensity. They turned 63 years of exile into a lifetime of glory.

That glory, though, came at a price. Life in the Negro Leagues was a hardscrabble existence, particularly on the barnstorming circuit. Most teams traveled by bus, sometimes driving all night to make a scheduled game. There are stories of a typical day beginning with a game at 9:30 A.M., followed by a doubleheader at noon, and then a drive to a neighboring city for a night game.

"We'd just eat and ride and play," said Kansas City Monarchs pitcher Chet Brewer in *A Complete History of the Negro Leagues*. "That was the size of it. It wasn't easy street."

The players were denied accommodations at many hotels and restaurants, which still catered exclusively to white customers. They would stay at black boarding houses or in the homes of people within the African-American community. In the worst scenario, they'd pitch a tent in the outfield and sleep there until the game the next day. Sometimes they would literally fish for their dinner in nearby lakes and rivers.

But to many of the men who donned Negro League uniforms, the opportunity to play professional baseball was worth enduring such conditions.

The Newark Eagles cheer their teammates from their spot in the dugout.

"It was thrilling to me," said James Moore, who played first base for the Atlanta Black Crackers, Baltimore Elite Giants, and Newark Eagles over 11 seasons. "We'd have dates booked ahead of time and we'd travel from city to city playing baseball. We knew in a lot of cities we couldn't stay in the hotels. So we'd usually find boarding houses. Being raised in the South, it didn't effect me that much. Segregation was a part of my life. I wasn't trying to disobey any laws. I was playing baseball and I just loved it."

In the league's heyday, the average player made between $200 and $300 per month. It wasn't great money, but they earned more in baseball than they would have working anywhere else. While official league games were played primarily on the weekends, teams would schedule exhibition games against local teams throughout the week to bring in more money.

"Many teams carried several young pitchers, they called them 'sock-a-mayocks,'" said James A. Riley, an author and one of the foremost historians on the Negro Leagues. "These were guys who'd pitch against local white teams or semipro teams. It was their way of saving the starting pitchers while giving young pitchers a chance to develop and learn. When teams barnstormed during the week, it was referred to as 'scuffling' because they were fighting just to turn a small profit. When they played in major-league parks, they called it 'getting even day' because they knew they'd make more money from that one game than they did all week."

The season's highs and lows created an incredible duality in the lives of players, who would soak up the prestige of playing in big-league parks a day removed from "scuffling" against amateurs. The games against American Legion teams, local police departments, or semipro clubs didn't count toward Negro League statistics. That's why some career statistics of the players include the phrase "Against all levels of competition." Motivated by the extra money and the opportunity to stay sharp between league contests, players usually accepted all forms of competition.

"I have no regrets," said Wilmer Fields, who played for the Homestead Grays from 1939 to '50. "I was doing what I wanted to do. I always wanted to play baseball in the Negro Leagues. I didn't play for the money, I played for the love of the game."

Many statistics of the Negro Leagues cannot be verified for a number of reasons. Some teams couldn't employ scorekeepers, and the itinerant nature of many clubs made it difficult to track statistics. While the African-American media covered the league, the game's rise in popularity grew out of eyewitness accounts passed on by fans from town to town.

The lack of documentation lends itself to a perception that Negro League baseball was composed of barnstorming bush-leaguers who played their way across baseball diamonds large and small. While there may be a level of truth in that, it is vastly misleading. When Negro League teams played each other, the competition was fierce and the play was major-league quality.

When Major League Baseball began to falter in the Great Depression, the Negro Leagues flourished— so much so that at times the

Satchel Paige

Homestead Grays sold more tickets at Griffith Stadium than the Washington Senators. Ultimately, it would take an event the magnitude of World War II for the country to begin to grasp the absurdity of segregation in baseball. At that time, people began to slowly realize that men of color were expected to die on the battlefield for America, just like the white soldiers, but were not allowed to share a ballfield with white players.

Integration

In 1938, a poll was conducted among National League players. Seventy-five percent of them said they would have no objection to blacks suiting up in the majors.

"The white players gave them credit," said Riley. "I interviewed a lot of them and they'd say, 'Yeah, they could play in the major leagues.' For the most part, I think the players would have integrated sooner if it were up to them. I don't think it was the players as much as the owners. Once the owners saw Jackie Robinson putting people in the stands and helping his team to reach the World Series, they saw that integration wasn't hurting business."

Jackie Robinson played just one season in the Negro Leagues, 1945, for the Kansas City Monarchs. The next year he was signed by the

Pittsburgh Crawfords Oscar Charleston, Rap Dixon, Josh Gibson, Judy Johnson, Jud Wilson (left to right)

Brooklyn Dodgers and played Triple-A baseball in Montreal. Then, on April 15, 1947, he took his place at first base for the Dodgers at Ebbets Field, marking the first modern-day appearance by an African American in the major leagues.

It was a historic moment, but one that must have been rooted in ambivalence. Robinson afforded all black ballplayers the dream of entering the major leagues. But at the same time, progress signaled the demise of the Negro Leagues.

"Integration just killed us," said Fields. "It just stopped us dead. We would draw 15,000 or 20,000 to a game. Then we were drawing 4,000, maybe 5,000."

A year after Robinson debuted with the Dodgers, the Negro Leagues began to dissipate. In 1948, the Black Yankees went out of business and the Grays pulled out of the National League in favor of barnstorming. When the Newark Eagles relocated to Texas later in '48, the Negro National League disbanded.

The success of Robinson, who was named major-league Rookie of Year, provided the impetus for more Negro Leaguers to enter white baseball. Larry Doby, Don Newcombe, and Roy Campanella soon followed him into the big leagues.

By 1957 the Negro American League had also folded, leaving just the Kansas City Monarchs and Indianapolis Clowns to "scuffle" along the barnstorming route. The Monarchs' final season came in 1965.

Moore was succinct in his assessment of baseball's integration. "It helped some and hurt others," he said flatly.

The opportunity to play major-league ball had finally become a reality, but for those not picked up by pro franchises, the only options were to barnstorm or to play in Latin American countries. The glory of the Negro Leagues was gone, but not its legacy.

"As a young player, when I found out I could never play in the major leagues, my ambition was to play in the Negro Leagues," said Moore. "Just to be in the league was a great thrill. I was fortunate to go as high as I could when I could. I helped pave the way for some of the other players."

The Negro Leagues were a celebration of black independence and culture. The fact that black baseball existed for as long as it did serves as a testimony to the perseverance of its athletes, but also as a reminder that they were excluded from pursuing the American dream. In the end, what is left to ponder is whether the Negro Leagues were a tragedy or a treasure.

Ultimately, they were both.

Josh Gibson

Legends: Gibson and Paige

Seventeen residents of the Baseball Hall of Fame spent all or most of their careers in the Negro Leagues: Cool Papa Bell, Oscar Charleston, Ray Dandridge, Leon Day, Martin Dihigo, Rube Foster, Willie Foster, Josh Gibson, Judy Johnson, Buck Leonard, John Henry "Pop" Lloyd, Satchel Paige, Bullet Rogan, Hilton Smith, Turkey Stearnes, Willie Wells, and Smokey Joe Williams.

Other stars—such as Willie Mays, Hank Aaron, Jackie Robinson, Roy Campanella, Elston Howard, Ernie Banks, Larry Doby, and Monte Irvin—got their start playing in the Negro Leagues.

The two greatest players associated with Negro League baseball are Gibson, the power-hitting catcher, and Paige, the charismatic pitcher. Gibson's life would be tragically cut short while Paige would go on to appear in a major-league game at the age of 59.

Gibson broke into the Negro National League in 1930, catching for the Homestead Grays at the age of 18. He has been credited with more than 800 home runs over the

course of his career and was hailed for hitting tape-measure bombs.

"Let me put it to you this way," said Wilmer Fields, who played with Gibson on the Grays. "He's the best hitting catcher I've ever seen."

It has been said that he hit three balls out of the cavernous Griffith Stadium, a 512-foot home run in Monessen, Pennsylvania, and a 580-foot homer at Yankee Stadium. In 60 recorded at-bats against major-league pitchers, he batted .426.

Over the course of his career with the Grays and the Pittsburgh Crawfords, Gibson developed into a strong-armed defensive catcher. James Moore played against Gibson many times and was a teammate of Roy Campanella on the Baltimore Elite Giants before Campy began a Hall of Fame career with the Brooklyn Dodgers.

"Campanella was one of the greatest I've ever seen. He had an arm that was outstanding," said Moore. "But I'd have to put Josh ahead of him because of his power. And Josh could throw the ball just like Campy."

Historian James Riley observed, "In my opinion Gibson's the best catcher ever, black or white. I'd take him over Bill Dickey and Mickey Cochrane, the best major-league catchers of his time. I'd even take him over modern guys like Johnny Bench. Roy Campanella, who is in the Hall of Fame, was nowhere near as good as Gibson. Gibson hit for tremendous power. I think he would have challenged Babe Ruth's single-season home run record."

Sadly, he never got the chance. In 1942, Gibson developed a brain tumor that put him in a coma.

When he awoke, doctors wanted to operate but he refused. Despite recurring headaches, he continued to play, assaulting Negro League pitching for several more seasons. He died of a brain hemorrhage in 1947, just three months before Jackie Robinson broke baseball's color barrier. He was 35 years old.

The undisputed hero of Negro League baseball was Paige, the tall, lean, right-handed pitcher whose explosive fastball intimidated batters and enthralled fans. Paige was also a born entertainer, and his presence in a game made it a can't-miss social happening. As his legend grew, Paige became black baseball's most sought-after star.

"He's one of the best pitchers of all time," said Riley. "He compares favorably with Dizzy Dean or Bob Feller. He threw a fastball most of his career, he didn't need much else."

Paige was a power pitcher who effectively varied his release point. He would deliver his fastball over the top, sidearm, or three-quarters, and each angle provided the ball with different movement. Later in his career he adopted an efficient curveball, but his reputation was forged on the heat of his fastball.

With Paige on the mound, fans got plenty to watch. He would call his outfielders off the field and often held running conversations with opponents. At times he promised to strike out the first nine batters he faced or whiff the first three on nine pitches. There was also his famous "Hesitation Pitch." He'd push off the rubber, hesitate at the top of his windup, and then finish his delivery, putting the batter completely off-stride.

While the average Negro League player made just enough money to survive, Paige often made more than his white contemporaries in the majors. At the height of his career, he earned $40,000 per season by commanding a healthy percentage of the gate.

Always in demand, Paige rarely stayed with the same team for very long, which illustrates to some degree the lack of structure in the Negro Leagues. (Imagine Babe Ruth deciding to switch from the Yankees to the Tigers midseason because Detroit offered him more money!)

Nonetheless, Paige wore the uniforms of no less than eight Negro League teams, and in the off-season he would barnstorm the countryside or travel to places such as the Dominican Republic, Cuba, or Puerto Rico. He welcomed the travel—and the appearance

fees—pointing out that fans could only see major-leaguers in big cities, but they could see him pitch in small towns all over.

While legend has it he tossed 55 no-hitters and won 2,000 games, the best measure of his talents comes from his six-year major-league career. When you consider that Paige debuted for the Cleveland Indians in 1948, nearing the age of 42, his ability comes into much sharper focus. In his first season, he went 6-1 and pitched two shutouts. He also posted a 2.48 ERA. In five big-league seasons, working mostly as a reliever, Paige compiled an ERA of 3.29, nearly 25 percent lower than the league average.

Most of Paige's notoriety was built while barnstorming against white stars. In 1934, he and Dizzy Dean toured the country, with each fronting a team of All-Stars. He also toured with major-league star Bob Feller in '46, and the games played to sold-out stadiums throughout the country.

Exhibition Games and All-Stars

Throughout the prime years of Negro League baseball there were many exhibitions between white and black All-Stars. These contests made for great press but rarely pitted equally matched teams. The white teams generally had one or two stars, while the rest of the roster was assembled from the mediocrity of the major leagues.

"When I first began to play I thought we were inferior to the white ballplayer," said Moore. "That was the general idea that society had. I hadn't played competitively

The Newark Eagles square off against the New York Black Yankees in 1936.

against white players. At first I was skeptical. They had better fields, better training facilities. I played against a lot of major-league ballplayers. We beat them some and they beat us some. I realized they were human and we were human. It really made me feel good to be hitting the ball against guys who were in the major leagues."

Baseball history is replete with documentation of Gibson homering off Dean and Stan Musial taking Paige out of the park. Indeed, the games provided many legitimate moments. But players from both sides understood that top priority was to never jeopardize the windfalls these games produced. So at times entertainment value, professional courtesy, and avoiding injury obstructed true competitiveness.

"The games meant more to the black players because it was their chance to prove they were as good as the major-leaguers," said Riley. "The white players were looking for the payday. The biggest names in the Negro Leagues didn't mean anything to white fans, but if you had a Lefty Grove pitching or a Jimmie

James "Cool Papa" Bell

Foxx playing against a Negro League team, that drew quite a crowd. The black players understood that these major-leagues stars were lending their names to the game. They all shared the same pie."

In 1933, following baseball's first All-Star Game, the Negro Leagues adopted their own All-Star Game. It was called the East-West Game and was hosted every year at Comiskey Park, home of the Chicago White Sox. The game regularly drew between 30,000 and 40,000 fans. In 1941, when Paige returned after a five-year hiatus, more than 50,000 witnessed the game, which was more people than Comiskey had seats.

In 1938, '42, '43, '46, and '47 the East-West Game drew more fans than that year's major-league All-Star Game. The largest black sporting event in the country at the time, it drew African-American celebrities such as Joe Louis, Cab Calloway, and Louis Armstrong. The greatest East-West Game ever played occurred in 1935 when the West assembled the most prolific lineup in Negro League history. It included Gibson, Bell, Oscar Charleston, Jimmie Crutchfield, Stearnes, Mule Suttles, and Willie Wells. But the East team was a cast of veterans that included a pair of Cuban-born players: Luis Tiant, Sr., and Martin Dihigo, who started the game in center field and finished it on the pitching mound.

The West trailed 4-0 going into the ninth but rallied to force extra innings. The East immediately responded with four runs in the 10th, only to see the West tie the score again in the bottom of the inning. Suttles finally ended the

Buck Leonard

glorious game with a dramatic two-out, three-run homer off Dihigo in the bottom of the 11th.

Great Games, Great Teams

Twice in its history the Negro League put forth a pair of viable leagues that competed in a World Series at the close of the season. The first time (1924–27) pitted the winner of Rube Foster's Negro National League against the winner from the Eastern Colored League. The Kansas City Monarchs won the inaugural series, defeating the Hilldale Giants over ten games.

The second time was 1942–48, when the second incarnation of the Negro National League played against the Negro American League. One of the primary differences between Major League Baseball's World Series and the Negro League World Series was that Negro League teams didn't play a home-and-away series. Instead, the teams that reached the Series would each host a game, and then the other contests would be played in cities with large African-American communities.

One of the most famous postseason moments occurred in the '42

World Series, featuring the Kansas City Monarchs and the Homestead Grays. Paige was hurling for Kansas City, and Gibson, his former batterymate, was with the Grays. The Monarchs were leading 2-0 in the seventh inning of Game 2. With a man on and two out, Paige intentionally walked Howard Easterling and Buck Leonard just to face Gibson with the bases loaded. It was the ultimate showdown, and Paige emerged victorious, striking out Gibson on three pitches.

The dominant teams of the Negro Leagues included the Kansas City Monarchs, Homestead Grays, Birmingham Black Barons, and Pittsburgh Crawfords. The Monarchs were the longest-running franchise and ultimately sent the most players to the major leagues. They were a charter member of the Negro National League in 1920, won over a dozen pennants in 37 league seasons, and existed for 42 years. Among the greats who wore the Monarch uniform were Paige, Cool Papa Bell, Turkey Stearnes, Buck O'Neil, Jackie Robinson, and Ernie Banks.

The Grays won 12 National League pennants, including nine straight from 1937 through 1945. They were led by the likes of Hall of Famers Bell, Gibson, Judy Johnson, Buck Leonard, and Martin Dihigo. In 1943, '44, and '47, the Grays defeated their American League rival, the Black Barons, for the Negro World Championship.

"We were very proud of what we accomplished," said Fields, who went 16-1 and won a pair of postseason games in 1948, the Grays' final championship season. "The Homestead Grays won 11 pennants. Everyone respected the Grays. White teams, black teams, major-leaguers. They're still talking about the Grays."

Perhaps the biggest rivalry was between the Grays and Crawfords. Both teams competed in Pittsburgh (though the Grays also played in Washington, D.C.), and their games were often played at Forbes Field. The rivalry turned bitter when Crawfords owner Gus Greenlee signed Gibson away from the Grays. As the stature of the Crawfords grew, Greenlee built his team a 7,500-seat stadium—Greenlee Field. Opening Day was April 30, 1932, with Paige pitching to Gibson. The game was a sell-out, and ultimately 120,000 fans came to Greenlee Field during the 1932 season.

Many Negro League games were played in minor-league parks and other smaller venues. But as far back as 1910, major-league stadiums were rented to Negro League teams. As black baseball grew in popularity in the late '30s and into the '40s, some teams began to book their league games inside major-league parks.

"I pitched in Yankee Stadium, Griffith Stadium, and Forbes Field," said Fields. "The thing about pitching in a major-league park was that in those games you knew you were facing the opposing team's best pitcher. You had to be on your game to win. We drew great crowds to those parks."

Still, only a handful of teams played in big-league parks on a regular basis. The New York Black Yankees played home games at Yankee Stadium, the Cuban Giants played at the Polo Grounds, and the Homestead Grays split their home games between Forbes Field in Pittsburgh and Griffith Stadium in Washington, D.C.

It was a simple business decision for the white owners of the stadiums: When their major-league clubs were out of town, they would rent the otherwise empty ballpark to Negro League teams. The black teams often drew great crowds to those hallowed fields, but in keeping

Negro League fans take a break from their Depression-era troubles to enjoy a game.

with the Jim Crow policies of the day, the locker rooms were strictly off-limits.

"When I first played at Yankee Stadium it was the thrill of my life," said Moore. "I had read all about it growing up. I was elated to play in the House that Ruth Built. We had to change at the hotel and come to the game in our uniforms. We couldn't use the facilities, the bath or the showers. But I was used to segregation. I never thought I'd get to play in a place like Yankee Stadium because of the color of my skin."

1940s
WAR, PEACE, AND JACKIE

It was almost as if baseball could sense what was coming. While the Second World War crept ever closer to American soil, baseball provided fans with one of the most amazing seasons in the history of the game. In 1941 fans were treated to a knuckle-gnawing NL pennant race, a stunning World Series, and, in the middle of it all, record-shattering performances by its two greatest stars. Baseball, like every other American institution, was dramatically altered by World War II: cheap balls, northern spring training, and inferior play—although sensational pennant races were the rule rather than the exception. And when the war ended, a new America was born. Fans flocked to baseball in record numbers, and racial segregation finally ended on the ballfield as a noble young man (and several brave older ones) had the guts to make a difference.

In this World Series game in 1947, Jackie Robinson upended both Phil Rizzuto and any myths that baseball could or should persist in its whites-only prejudices. The season began with some teammates drafting a letter threatening not to play with a Negro and ended with Robinson being voted the first Rookie of the Year.

The Most Competitive Decade

By 1940 the war in Europe was raging. The mood in the United States was strongly isolationist; few Americans wanted any part of that war "over there." But before the next decade turned, the world, the game, and the entire nation experienced huge upheavals.

On the field, it was the most competitive decade of all time. Six pennants were decided by fewer than two games, which often meant final-Sunday decisive contests, and ten ended with the winner less than three games out in front. The Cardinals and Dodgers, both ultimately the product of the same man—Branch Rickey—wrestled each other in five bruising battles for the pennant that decade; only once was the margin of victory more than 2½ games. From 1939 to 1949, *eight* different teams (of 16 total) made World Series appearances.

In 1940 the Tigers snuck past the Indians—who were publicly scolded as "crybabies" for their complaints about their manager—then fell to the Reds in a seven-game World Series. The Reds victory was undercut with sorrow, however: In August, Redlegs backup catcher Willard Hershberger had committed suicide while playing on the road in Boston. Suicides are rare for baseball players (for all athletes, actually), and the story of Willard Hershberger is one of the strangest and saddest ever.

A Tragic Ending

On August 2, 1940, Reds catcher Willard Hershberger caught the second game of a doubleheader and had a bad day at the plate. He was hitless in five trips, leaving men on base every time. It wasn't that Hershberger was a poor player, and it wasn't that he was on a bad team. On the contrary, he was batting .309 and his team was in first by six games. But the pressure and the heat (it was one of the hottest summers on record) were too much for the troubled young man. Late in the game his manager, Bill McKechnie, was upset when Hershberger failed to make a play on a slow roller near the catcher's box; Hershberger remained stock-still while the pitcher completed the play. Confused, McKechnie asked the catcher if anything was wrong. Plenty, Hershberger answered. They talked after the game; Hershberger sobbed for two hours and told McKechnie that his father had taken his own life and so would he. He was found the next morning in the Boston hotel after the rest of the club had gone to the ballpark, his throat slashed with his roommate's razor.

The next day's game was dedicated to his memory, and the Reds players surely had him in their thoughts for the rest of the season as they continued their championship drive.

Willard Hershberger

The Yankees started the season poorly and never recovered; some said they were all afraid they had been "infected" by the disease that struck Lou Gehrig. Stan Hack of the Cubs took the NL batting title with the lowest winning average to that point. But 1941 was the season everybody still talks about: If it wasn't the best of all time, it was certainly one of the most breathtaking.

THE SUMMER OF '41

It was as if some foreboding over the tremulous state of the world pushed baseball in 1941 to sizzle at a previously impossible level. Writer Dan Daniel described "the tone and temper of 1941: its commitment to endurance as the most timely heroic virtue." It was as if Americans knew the war was coming their way, and that when it came, they'd be in it full tilt and for the long haul. So it made sense that the three remarkable stories of the 1941 season all featured stamina and endurance as their centerpieces.

Ted Williams (left) and Joe DiMaggio (right) were baseball's shining stars throughout the '40s. In '49, there were reports the heavy hitters would be traded for each other, but the Yankees declined when the Red Sox also wanted Yogi Berra included.

Two involved the game's greatest young stars (who would become two of the greatest players ever), and the other was a pennant race full of good old-time grit and guts. As icing on the cake, the All-Star Game was decided by a two-out, three-run homer in the bottom of the ninth (by one of the young superstars), and the World Series turned on a freak play and led to the introduction of one of the game's most poignant catchphrases, "Wait 'til next year."

The season's three main stories nested within each other. Joe DiMaggio took center stage first: His record-smashing 56-game consecutive hit streak lasted two months and was the first "stat event" to capture the imagination of the American populace. It was the precursor of Aaron and Rose chasing Ruth and Cobb, of McGwire and Sosa challenging each other and the ghost of Roger Maris, of Nolan Ryan breaking Sandy Koufax's single-season strikeout total—all statistically driven mini-dramas that engaged America's attention. Back in '41, people next took notice of Ted Williams's reach for a .400 batting average. Then, the Cardinal/Dodger scrum got hotter and hotter as the season wore on, with both Ted's feat and the NL pennant race reaching their climaxes on the final day.

BASEBALL ON THE RADIO

They say that during summer in the 1940s, a baseball fan could walk along Flatbush Avenue in Brooklyn and never miss an inning of a Dodgers game. The radio broadcasts could be heard through the open windows of apartment buildings and local merchants. Such was the power—and magic—of baseball on the radio.

The first radio broadcast of a major-league baseball game occurred on August 5, 1921, when Harold Arlin called a Pirates game for station KDKA. By 1938, the Dodgers, Yankees, Giants, Cubs, and White Sox had allowed their home games to be broadcast on a regular basis. More teams followed suit, and by the end of 1939 it was estimated that radio income represented 7.3 percent of the average team's income. The new revenue stream alleviated the concerns of owners who feared radio broadcasts would reduce attendance figures.

In contrast to the homogenized voices of today, each broadcaster of the time had his own authentic style. Red Barber, Mel Allen, Jack Buck, Vin Scully, and Ernie Harwell were some of the great announcers as the golden ages of radio and baseball meshed. Allen punctuated great plays by exclaiming, "How about that!" Buck was known for his simple, accessible, "less is more" approach to broadcasting. And when a batter took a called strike, Harwell proclaimed, "He stood there like the house by the side of the road and watched it go by." Their voices filled homes throughout each summer as they became the daily companions of the true baseball fan. Even today, many fans still recall their greatest baseball memories in the way in which the radio broadcasters described them.

Walter "Red" Barber

JOLTIN' JOE AND 56 STRAIGHT

Joe DiMaggio was a superb player who performed at a level of excellence that few ever attain. But more important was the way he did it. He created a mystique for himself with his understated grace and elegance. He managed to be quiet and commanding at the same time, both dignified and fiery—although his intensity seldom flamed visibly. His batting, running, and fielding styles seemed destined for radio, where Mel Allen described them with eloquence. His personality was more tangled; Roger Kahn called him a "neurotically private public man," but he *did* wed Marilyn Monroe. The greatest player on the greatest team marries America's most famous sex symbol: It was the stuff of storybooks.

As the 1941 season began, the world thought highly of DiMaggio's skills, but it would be safe to say he had not yet been awarded a spot in the Yankee pantheon. DiMaggio was frequently a holdout; he was constantly trying to wrangle a better salary from Yankee management, and that didn't sit well with Yankee fans. He was often booed when he began the season, which was sometimes several days after the rest of his team took the field due to holdouts or small but bothersome injuries.

Until Jason and Jeremy Giambi combined to hit 61 in 2002, the DiMaggios held the record for sibling home runs in a season. In 1937, Joe (center) and Dom (right) paired for 59, a total the DiMaggios matched in '41 with the help of 21 from eldest brother Vince (left).

DiMaggio, here signing autographs for young fans, was enormously popular everywhere he played. At Yankee Stadium he was treated with such deference that his teammates routinely allowed him to trot out of the dugout ahead of them so fans could first applaud him individually.

This single on July 16, 1941, gave Joe DiMaggio 23 hits in his last 40 at-bats, but it would be the final safety of his 56-game hitting streak. Eight years earlier, in his first full professional season, he hit in 61 straight games for San Francisco of the Pacific Coast League.

DiMaggio, who had once hit in 61 consecutive games in the minors, began the season hot as a pistol. He had at least one hit in each of the last 19 games of spring training and then did the same for the first eight games of the regular season: in effect, a 27-game batting streak (only two behind the Yankee record of 29).

But the Yanks couldn't get it in gear, and Joe rapidly cooled as well. By May 14 the team had a mediocre 14-13 record, and DiMaggio was batting a puny .194. Two weeks later Lou Gehrig succumbed to ALS, and the early passing of their longtime champion seemed to motivate the Bronxmen. They started rolling over the rest of the league, winning 41 of their next 47 games. DiMaggio had a hit in all of them but one. By late June the Yanks had far outpaced the Red Sox.

DiMaggio's batting streak lasted from May 15 until July 17. It wasn't mentioned by the press until May 29, but by the time Joe had hit in his 39th consecutive game, practically the entire country had taken notice. George Sisler held the old league record of 41. When DiMaggio broke it, a rare event occurred: All his teammates rushed from the dugout to congratulate him. This, of course, was long before home plate celebrations and curtain calls.

However, there was another hurdle to climb. A baseball researcher determined that the *all-time* record for consecutive games hit safely was 44, set by "Wee" Willie Keeler in 1897, before there *was* an American League. But Joe blew past that one, too. It was almost as if he was relishing the challenge and rising to the occasion: He batted .363 during the first 31 games of the streak (that's more than 40 points less than Williams hit for the *entire season*); but .461 for the last 25. The streak came to an end in Cleveland's League Park, against pitchers Al Smith and Jim Bagby, and it took two spectacular bits of defense by Indian third baseman Ken Keltner to do it. DiMaggio shrugged it off, and the next day he began another hitting streak, this one continuing for 17 games. If Keltner had failed to make either one of those plays, Joe DiMaggio may have hit in 74 straight games. The accomplishment has entered baseball lexicon as

From childhood poverty to his status as baseball's first $100,000 player, "Joltin' Joe" came to strike a larger-than-life pose. DiMaggio was named to the All-Star Team in all 13 of his big-league seasons. The Yankees retired his famed #5 in 1952.

"The Streak." Even though streaks are the essence of baseball history, only Joe's has earned this honorific.

As all-time-great columnist Red Smith once said, "Sometimes a fellow gets a little tired of writing about DiMaggio; a fellow thinks 'There must be another ballplayer worth mentioning.' But there isn't really, not worth mentioning in the same breath as Joe DiMaggio."

But the Yanks were so far out in front that there was no longer a reason to push. By August 2 they had a dozen-game lead, and DiMaggio's batting hit a rock. His average dropped 25 points in 17 days, and he finished the season at .357.

TEDDY BALLGAME AND .406

Ted Williams's season-long chase for a .400 batting average received much less press than Joe's streak. The .400 plateau had been reached just 11 years previously, and one didn't have to be very old to remember a fistful of other times before that. Now, of course, we can appreciate the immense mountains both

DiMaggio and Williams climbed that season.

In 1941 Ted Williams was only 22 years old. He was a skinny kid from California who didn't yet look anything like John Wayne. About the only person on the planet who would guarantee that Williams was going to be a great ballplayer was Ted himself. He was never shy about his ambition: "When I walk down the street, I want people to say, 'There goes the greatest hitter who ever lived.'"

Even though he began the season with a hobbling ankle injury, Williams's incredible season had an early charge. The day before DiMaggio began his batting streak, Ted started one of his own, and it lasted 23 games—the longest of his career. And while DiMaggio was getting a hit or two each night, Ted was absolutely brutalizing AL pitchers. During *his* streak, he knocked the ball at a .488 clip. In a Memorial Day double-header he had six hits, raising his average to a dizzying .429 (100 points better than Joe D.). He rose as high as .436 but was slumping briefly on June 24, a day when he had an especially appreciative audience: In the stands were the two greatest hitters ever (before Ted Williams, that is), Babe Ruth and Ty Cobb. By the All-Star Game, Ted's average was down to .405.

Arky Vaughan, hard-batting shortstop of the Pittsburgh Pirates, took charge of that year's midseason classic, belting a pair of two-run homers. At that time, in a way that anticipated the late 1990s, baseball had an exceptional number of sweet-swinging shortstops: Vaughan, Luke Appling, Lou Boudreau, Joe Cronin, Pee Wee Reese, Phil Rizzuto, and Cecil Travis. Interestingly, Travis, the least-remembered of that group, would in fact finish the season with more hits than either Williams or DiMaggio.

A 22-year-old Ted Williams was batting .402 when he posed for this picture in July 1941. He finished the season at a remarkable .406. Only six players since have come within 30 points of that last .400 season.

The National League's 5-3 lead looked comfortable as the last of the ninth began. But sparks began. The AL loaded the sacks with one out; DiMaggio came up and slapped a grounder but hustled to beat a relay throw to first that would have nailed a game-ending double play. One run scored. The next batter, "Teddy Ballgame," got his pitch and creamed it to deep right. Game over. American League 7, National League 5. The film of the event shows Williams as gleeful as he would ever be on a ballfield, clapping his hands in joy, almost bouncing up and down as he circled the bases.

He was often quoted later in his life as saying it was the most memorable moment of his career.

As the season wore on, Williams cooled off some and got injured. The last day of the season his Red Sox were playing a doubleheader against Connie Mack's A's in Shibe Park. Entering the games, Ted was hitting .39955, technically a .400 season. He could have sat out that final Sunday and claimed the .400 crown. But winning a batting title while sitting on the bench was not Ted's style. He demanded to play. In fact, he took special batting practice. As Williams came to the plate for the first time that final day, he received a message relayed from Connie Mack through catcher Frankie Hayes: "Mr. Mack told us if we let up on you he'll run us out of baseball. I wish you all the luck in the world but we're not giving you anything." Ted accepted the input, and he came through in true heroic style. Not only did he have six hits in eight at-bats that day, but his

For the two decades encompassing 1941–60, Ted Williams (left) and Stan Musial (right) were statistically dominant. Williams led the period in batting average (.346) and home runs (467), with Musial second in each. Stan was tops in hits (3,294) and RBI (1,741), followed by Ted.

Shirtless sluggers Ted Williams (left) and Jimmie Foxx (right) were Red Sox teammates from 1939 to '42. Williams once said he never saw a player hit a ball harder than "The Beast," a brawny farm boy whose .609 career slugging percentage is the highest ever by a right-handed batter.

final hit was a monstrous shot that hit a loudspeaker and tore a hole right through it. *Four-oh-six*—a number that rests regally in the stat pantheon in the hearts of all baseball fans.

Yet even though Williams's .406 average was accompanied by league leadership in runs, homers, walks, slugging average, and on-base percentage (his .551 would rate as the highest for more than 60 years), and even though he was just five RBI behind DiMaggio (or he would have won the Triple Crown), the American League Most Valuable Player Award that year went to Joe, not Ted. Simply stated, "The Streak" had captivated the baseball world.

During that season, each man created a position in baseball history that perfectly defined his ballplaying style. The

STAN THE MAN

Like Babe Ruth and George Sisler before him, Stan Musial parlayed his baseball debut as a left-handed pitcher into a career as a Hall of Fame slugger. Signed at 17 by the St. Louis Cardinals, Musial struggled with control in the minors before posting an 18-4 record for the 1940 Daytona Beach team. The manager liked Musial's bat, often playing him in the outfield when he wasn't pitching.

After Musial ruined his pitching shoulder while attempting a diving catch late in 1940, his manager convinced him to become a full-time outfielder. The conversion worked: Late in 1941, the 6-foot, 175-pound native of Donora, Pennsylvania, reached the majors to stay.

Over the next 22 seasons (a club record), Musial won seven batting titles and three MVP awards. He hit 475 career home runs, including five in one day in a doubleheader on May 2, 1954 (a feat duplicated by San Diego's Nate Colbert almost 20 years later).

A contact hitter, Musial owned a corkscrew stance that suggested a kid peeking around the corner to

see if the cops were coming. He appeared in the World Series four times and the All-Star Game 24 times, a record shared by Willie Mays and Hank Aaron. His best single season was 1948, when he hit .376 with 39 home runs, 135 runs scored, and 131 runs batted in. All were career bests for Musial, who finished one home run short of a Triple Crown but led the league in runs, hits, doubles, triples, batting, slugging, and RBI.

Nicknamed "Stan the Man" by Brooklyn fans because his bat was so potent at Ebbets Field, Musial led the league in hits six times, doubles eight times, and triples five times but never won a home run crown or hit 40 in a season. When asked how he pitched to Musial, Brooklyn's Preacher Roe said, "I throw him four wide ones and then try to pick him off first base."

The first Player of the Decade chosen by *The Sporting News,* Musial eventually retired after setting a laundry list of records, including NL records for most hits with 3,630 (since broken), games (3,026), at-bats (10,972), runs (1,949), and

Stan Musial

doubles (725). The first man to play at least 1,000 games at two positions (outfield and first base), he is one of three men (with Hank Greenberg and Robin Yount) to win MVP awards at different positions.

Stan Musial was elected to the Baseball Hall of Fame in 1969.

DiMaggio streak is a mark of consistent performance raised to the next level; it is the stuff of champions. The Williams .400 is a sign of dedication and commitment. Like the extra batting practice Williams took on the final day of the season, it indicates a star who is never satisfied; it is the stuff of perfection.

DiMaggio's and Williams's careers took intertwining turns after that. Both spent time in World War II military service. Both had to reshape their careers after they returned. Both faced aggravation from the press and guff from the fans; but they dealt with it in totally different ways. DiMaggio grew even more aloof, typically staring off into space; Williams grew more aggressively angry. He would snarl and spit. More than once rumors were heard that the Yanks and Red Sox were about to make the deal of the century: Williams for DiMaggio, straight up. Left-handed batter Williams would love that short right-field porch in Yankee Stadium, just as righty DiMaggio would wreak havoc with the "Green Monster" in Fenway Park's left field. But "The Trade" was to remain only a rumor.

Ted and Joe, along with Stan Musial, were the best batters of their generation. But there is one dramatic difference that will forever separate them. During his 13-season career, Joe DiMaggio's Yankees played in ten World Series and won nine of them. Ted Williams played in just one Series in his career, and his team lost it.

A TOP-NOTCH PENNANT SCRAP

While Ted and Joe were rattling the fences of American League parks in 1941, the National League was witnessing a crisp pennant race, the likes of which hadn't happened in baseball in quite a while. The St. Louis Cardinals, the flowering of Branch Rickey's farm system concept, were led by slugger Johnny Mize, smooth-as-silk shortstop Marty Marion, and a character who would have fit in perfectly with the Gashouse Gang of the previous decade, hard-charging outfielder Enos "Country" Slaughter. (In September, a pretty talented kid named Stan Musial joined them.)

Across the country, when Larry MacPhail moved from Cincinnati to Brooklyn, he made changes in a hurry. To please the fans, he installed lights so they could see games at night. He also blew apart the New York radio ban by airing the games.

In the 1940s, Johnny "The Big Cat" Mize endorsed Louisville Slugger bats, typically 35-ounce, 36-inch lumber he swung in a remarkable fusion of power and contact. Mize hit 359 career home runs yet struck out more than 50 times in a season only once.

And he brought in manager Leo Durocher, which proved that he *really* wanted to do what would please the fans; that is, bring home a winner.

The Brooklyn team had been the least successful (and interesting) of the New York teams since it last took a pennant, all the way back in 1920. MacPhail began making deals to acquire the kind of ballplayers Leo wanted. (Although he was full of himself—and full of vinegar—Leo was no dummy when it came to winning baseball.) Under Leo and Larry, the usually hapless "Bums" slid into third place in 1939 and second in 1940. The team signed the simply brilliant Pete Reiser before the 1940 season; he had been one of 73 Cardinal farmhands "set free" in one of Commissioner Landis's noisier punishments of Rickey. In June 1940, MacPhail obtained slugger Joe Medwick and pitcher Curt Davis from the Cards. Even though Medwick suffered a terrible beaning soon thereafter, he remained a potent hitter. Postseason deals brought flamethrower Kirby Higbe and stalwart defensive catcher Mickey Owen. The final hole: second base. Durocher wanted Cubs star (and one of the most intelligent players in the game) Billy Herman for the job, so MacPhail pulled off some fancy footwork to land Herman, who promptly rapped six hits in his first seven at-bats as a Dodger. Not a single Dodger regular was homegrown. It didn't matter.

Pete Reiser, seen here stealing home in 1942, might have been an immortal had it not been for numerous injuries—often incurred due to his breakneck style of play. One of the first true "five-tool" players, he led the NL in average (.343), doubles (39), and triples (17) at age 22 in 1941.

The Cards and Dodgers matched up in a wire-to-wire race. All season long they took turns at the top spot. And even when a string of incapacitating injuries assailed the Cards, they never fell more than a few games back. On September 10, the Dodgers started that day's doubleheader with their fattest lead in months: three whole games. But they lost both games, the Cards won both of theirs, and once again the lead was only one. They battled, they charged, they eked out close ones and ran home in romps, but neither team could pull ahead. In the last five weeks of the season the lead changed hands eight times. The outcome wasn't decided until there were only two games to go. Unable to overcome their raft of injuries, the Cards finally sank behind the boys from Brooklyn.

In the first game of that year's World Series, Durocher tried to pull off a Connie Mack. Instead of starting either of his 22-game winners, Whit Wyatt or Higbe, Durocher tried a surprise, sending 38-year-old Curt Davis to the mound against the Yankees. It didn't work. Davis allowed three runs in just over five innings, and the Dodgers lost 3-2. Each of the teams won one of the next two, and things were looking good for the Dodgers to tie the Series in Game 4.

THE ONE THAT GOT AWAY

In their long and tortured rivalry with the New York Yankees, there may not have been a more painful moment for the Brooklyn Dodgers and their fans than Mickey Owen's passed ball in Game 4 of the 1941 World Series.

Brooklyn reliever Hugh Casey was one strike away from victory. A win would have evened up the Series at two games each. With two out, the bases empty, and the Dodgers leading 4-3, Casey delivered a low, biting curveball to Tommy Henrich, who swung and missed. The ball glanced off Owen's glove and squirted away toward Brooklyn's dugout. Henrich raced to first, and the Yankees were still alive. Instead of erupting in celebration, the fans that filled Ebbets Field were dumbstruck. A quiet gloom settled over the stadium, and the fans could only watch in despair as Joe DiMaggio followed with a single and Charlie Keller put the Bronx Bombers ahead with a two-run double. After a walk to Bill Dickey, Joe Gordon put the final nail in the coffin with another two-run double. The Yankees now led the series 3-1.

"It was all my fault," said Owen, in a report filed the next day in *The New York Times*. "It wasn't a strike. It was a great breaking curve that I should have had. But I guess the ball hit the side of my glove."

The Yankees clinched the world championship the next afternoon. As they celebrated in the Bronx, the Dodgers' lament of "Wait 'til next year" was born.

Mickey Owen chases the ball that escaped him in Game 4 of the '41 Series.

They were leading 4-3 in the top of the ninth. Two men were out, and Dodger ace reliever Hugh Casey was on the mound. Tommy Henrich worked the count full, then swung at a big bending curveball. The umpire raised his hand to signal the third out. But the ball had zipped past catcher Mickey Owen. (As author John Leonard described it, "The condemned

Brooklyn Dodgers fans, here at Yankee Stadium in 1941, introduced the term "Bronx cheer" into the American lexicon by razzing the despised Yankees at every opportunity.

jumped out of the chair and electrocuted the warden.") With new life, the Yanks kicked it into gear and scored four runs. The Series was over the next day.

WAR

Even before the vicious attack on Pearl Harbor, Americans saw the need to prepare for the possibility of war. In September 1940, Congress passed a law establishing the Selective Service—the military draft. All males from 21 to 36 years of age were required to register. Naturally, team owners began to fret and wail, afraid of losing their stars (and the paying customers who followed them) to the service. What happened was much different. If precise statistics had held true, each team would have lost about one player to the draft. In fact, only five players total were drafted: Hank Greenberg, one-time threat to Babe Ruth's record of 60 homers; Hugh Mulcahy, whose misfortune of being stuck on poor teams left him saddled with one of the most unpleasant nicknames of all time—"Losing Pitcher"; and three others. The reason major-league teams were left largely intact is that volunteers, particularly from rural areas still suffering the Depression's blight, were making up the difference. To them the military service was an opportunity—a chance for three square meals a day, clean clothes, and a paycheck, most of which were still scarce where they hailed from. It's not as though Major League Baseball sat idly by, however: At the MLB annual meeting early in 1941, owners pledged $25,000 worth of baseball equipment for the men in the military.

However, with the bombing of Pearl Harbor on December 7, 1941, everything changed. In fact, Hank Greenberg had just been released from the service two days before. He turned around and immediately reenlisted.

Among the millions of questions on Americans' minds was the question of baseball. In 1918, a "work or fight" order let everyone know that baseball would receive no special privileges. This time Judge Landis wrote to President Roosevelt to ask. Roosevelt's response, which has come to be known as the "Green Light Letter," said this:

> *January 15, 1942*
> *My dear Judge—*
> *. . . I honestly feel that it would be best for the country to keep baseball going. There will be fewer people unemployed and everybody will work longer hours and harder than ever before.*
>
> *And that means they ought to have a chance for recreation and for taking their minds off their work even more than before.*

Ted Williams was sworn in as a naval aviation cadet in 1942 after hiding his intentions to enlist even from his teammates. During his fighter aircraft training, the natural athlete set records for gunnery, reflexes, coordination, and visual reaction time.

*. . . I hope that night games can be extended
because it gives an opportunity to the day shift to see
a game occasionally.*

*. . . [I]ndividual players who are active military
or naval age should go, without question, into the
services. Even if the actual quality of the teams is
lowered by the greater use of older players, this will
not dampen the popularity of the sport.*

*. . . Here is another way of looking at it—if 300
teams use 5,000 or 6,000 players, these players are a
definite recreational asset of at least 20,000,000 of
their fellow citizens—and that in my judgment is
thoroughly worthwhile.*

*Hank Greenberg
(here in Washington,
D.C., in 1942)
became the second
major-leaguer to join
the military for
World War II. Origi-
nally declared 4-F
and ineligible for the
draft because of flat
feet, he asked to be
reexamined. He not
only was inducted,
he voluntarily re-
enlisted after the
bombing of Pearl
Harbor.*

Some major-league owners had hoped Roosevelt would
give a blanket exemption to all players—as "recreational
assets." But even though they didn't get that, baseball had to be
thrilled at Roosevelt's response. Interestingly, Landis had just
slammed the door on a proposal from one owner to double the
number of night games allowed. (Until the war, each team was
allowed only seven.) But the wish of the President that night
ball be expanded meant that the owners would sooner turn a
profit on their expensive lighting systems.

Baseball and World War II were inexorably entwined. More than 1,000 big-leaguers served in the military during the war. Soldiers on some fronts (including these men, who heard the 1942 World Series from the jungles of Panama) were able to cheer their teams from distant reaches of the globe.

BASEBALL AT WAR

While the nation slowly mobilized during the summer of 1942, there still weren't many players called to active duty. The Phillies lost nine players to the service; the Senators eight; most other clubs lost four or five; Cincinnati only one. While the majority of the players drafted were hardly irreplaceable, the handful of stars gone to war included Hank Greenberg, Bob Feller, Cecil Travis, and Billy Cox. Many players received "necessary man" deferments (necessary to their business) until the season ended.

Baseball witnessed few surprises that first year of the war. The Yanks and Cardinals won their respective leagues, with St. Louis sneaking past the Dodgers by just two games. Stan Musial had a fine debut season with the Cards, and Mort Cooper and Johnny Beazley were the team's ace hurlers. Ted Williams won the Triple Crown (his first), but for the second year in row was denied the Most Valuable Player Award. (Joe Gordon, Yank second baseman, won it.) The Yankees won the first game of the World Series; the Cards took the next four. The same two teams repeated as champs in 1943, but this time it was the Cards' turn to get knocked off in five.

There was a dramatic change in the baseball hierarchy during this time. Larry MacPhail resigned from the Dodgers to

As the 1944 season dawned, more than 300 major-leaguers were wearing military, instead of baseball, uniforms. Joe DiMaggio, here with Brigadier General William J. Flood, enlisted in '42 and attained the rank of sergeant. He spent much of his stint playing baseball on Army teams stateside and abroad.

accept a commission in the Army. His replacement as Dodger GM was none other than the genius, Branch Rickey. People didn't know it at the time, but the first piece was now in place for the act that, four years later, would change baseball (and the nation) forever.

It's true that some of the big-leaguers who were drafted or had enlisted received easy duty in the military, spending a good bit of their time playing ball on camp teams. But these were young men of exceptional physical skills, and many of them served on the front lines with distinction. Ted Williams became an ace fighter pilot. Hank Greenberg and Bob Feller fought in the Pacific. Warren Spahn received a battlefield commission during the Battle of the Bulge, plus a Bronze Star and a Purple Heart. Former big-leaguers Harry O'Neill and Elmer Gedeon gave the ultimate sacrifice.

While the country—and the world—was enmeshed in the terror and horror of the war, an unexpected benefit arose for baseball and its fans. Just as the Civil War had introduced the game to Southerners in our own country, just as during the Depression barnstorming Negro Leaguers and big-leaguers showed people everywhere how great the game could be, now the sight of Americans—pros and others—playing baseball intrigued people wherever they went. In Europe and in Asia, the magic of the game was spreading. Baseball was on its way to becoming the "international pastime."

THE HOME FRONT

During the war, if you were a soldier or sailor in uniform, you could get into any ballpark in the country for free. But what kind of ball would you be watching? By 1943 the typical big-league team had seen 60 to 80 percent of its roster head off to military service. To conserve valuable resources, the games were played with inferior balls. "Balata," the term for the ball's construction, was defined by one author as "bastard rubber." These balls were very dead. In addition, fans were encouraged to toss back foul balls hit into the stands so they could be donated to the boys overseas. The already dead balls got deader. Not surprisingly, the long-ball adventures of the '20s and '30s disappeared.

What happened to the game was predictable. Basestealing and strategic plays such as the hit-and-run, which had fallen into disfavor during the big bang years, came back. The AL league leader in swipes in 1941 stole just 33 bases, the NL leader just 18. Two years later it took 61 steals to lead the AL. The fastest man in the game at the time was George Case, outfielder for the Senators. He led the American League in swipes six out of eight years, and his 349 lifetime steals are the most for any player who played between 1930 and 1960. George also knew how to turn a buck with his speed; he'd race anyone for money. He claimed that the only man who ever beat him in a race was legendary Olympic sprinter Jesse Owens.

As President Roosevelt predicted, the quality of play *did* go down. One writer titled his book on wartime baseball *Teenagers, Gray-*

With an impoverished talent pool producing little offense during the war years, a premium was placed on speed. Snuffy Stirnweiss (left) was a weak hitter apart from his 1944 and '45 seasons, when he batted .314 and stole 88 bases. George Case (right), probably the era's fastest man, retired with 349 swipes.

The pitching appearance in one 1945 game by wooden-legged Bert Shepard was quintessential war era machination: part gimmick, part valor. His limb lost when he was shot down in aerial combat and taken prisoner, Shepard was signed by Washington upon his return. After 5⅓ innings of one-run ball, he pitched again only briefly in the minors.

beards and 4-Fs. Before the war was over, major-league fans got to see such sights as a one-armed outfielder (Pete Gray) and a one-legged pitcher (Bert Shepard). At just 15 years old, Joe Nuxhall became the youngest man ever to play in a major-league game. And there were plenty of mediocre players who got their big chance during this time. Forty-year-olds and youngsters alike received big-league playing time. Hod Lisenbee ended his big-league career as a 46-year-old. There was a definite sense that the players on the field were simply caretakers keeping the game afloat until the "real" players returned from the trenches.

Historian Bill James has determined that around 40 percent of major-leaguers in the late war years were actually of major-league quality. He ran a study that showed that of the 64 regulars in the National League in 1945, only 22 played more than 100 games in 1946, and only 11 did it in 1949, much lower numbers than one would see under normal conditions. Of the top five hitters in the American League in 1945, only Snuffy Stirnweiss ever played another full season in the bigs.

Despite all that, it's possible to conclude (as some historians have) that the level of play wasn't really that bad, after all. Balata balls notwithstanding, none of the big-leaguers who

WOMEN GO TO BAT

As World War II depleted the minor leagues and wreaked havoc on baseball attendance everywhere, Cubs owner Philip K. Wrigley formed a committee of major-league executives to salvage America's waning interest in the sport. The solution they came up with was the All-American Girls Professional Baseball League.

It originally emerged as a softball league in 1943, but the committee quickly decided to combine elements of both softball and baseball in their new league. And while the idea was to play games at major-league parks when the big-leaguers were out of town, the four-team league ultimately took root in Racine and Kenosha, Wisconsin; Rockford, Illinois; and South Bend, Indiana.

The teams consisted of 15 players, a manager, a business manager, and a female chaperone. The four managers were male: Three of them were former major-league players, and the fourth was a one-time member of the NHL's Chicago Blackhawks.

Many of the players were drawn from the top softball teams in the United States and Canada, including the league's first star, catcher Mary "Bonnie" Baker of the South Bend Blue Sox. While the players signed to the league had to possess athletic ability, they were also required to comply with a dress code and a strict set of moral standards imposed by the league. Femininity was stressed. After practice, the women were often schooled in etiquette, dress, and personal hygiene. Each player was given a beauty kit and was instructed to use it daily.

The first game was played on May 30, 1943. The league was well received in '43, with 176,612 fans attending games. Fans and the media alike were impressed with the women's skill on the ballfield. Teams played 108 regular-season games, with the top two clubs competing in a playoff series to determine a champion.

Patriotism was widely promoted throughout the league. During the singing of "The Star-Spangled Banner" at the start of each game, the two teams formed a "V" for victory by lining up from home plate up the first- and third-base lines. The teams also played charity games to support the Red Cross and visited wounded players at veterans' hospitals to help boost morale.

In the host cities, junior AAGPBL teams were formed and provided girls 14 or older with an opportunity to play baseball. The league expanded with two additional teams in the 1944 season, and several games were played at major-league parks. However, during 1944, with the war drawing to a conclusion and major-league baseball looking healthy, Wrigley began to lose interest in the league and sold it to advertising executive Arthur Meyerhoff.

The league continued to thrive after the war ended in 1945, and it reached its high-water mark by drawing 910,000 fans for the 1948 season. Slowly, however, attendance began to slip, and the league survived only until 1954. Throughout the league's history, 600 female athletes were given the opportunity to play professional baseball—a chance they never would have gotten if it weren't for the war.

The women receive advice from their manager.

stayed with their team because of deferments set any records against the "inferior" competition they were seeing every day.

Wartime travel restrictions kept the teams from enjoying their springs in Florida. Preseason training took place north of the Ohio River and east of the Mississippi. The first nighttime All-Star Game was played in 1943, stirred by a little controversy. When Yankee manager Joe McCarthy was criticized for choosing so many of his own players to appear in the game, he refused to play them at all; he sat them on the bench. And in 1945 the All-Star Game was canceled.

In Brooklyn, the team, badly hurt by the loss of its best players, was sinking—as low as seventh place in 1944. But Branch Rickey, architect of the hugely success-ful farm system in St. Louis, seemed to grasp something other people did not. Briefly stated, Rickey knew that at some point the war would end. And, reminiscent of the "success from vol-ume" strategy of his

The big-league career of St. Louis's one-armed Pete Gray lasted only 77 games, over which he batted .218, in 1945. The year before, however, he swatted .333, hit five home runs, and led the Southern Associ-ation in stolen bases (63) and fielding percentage by an outfielder (.983).

Cardinal farm clubs, Rickey wanted to have as many players under contract as he could. He went on a spree of signing young players, giving out just minuscule "bonuses," and many a young soldier went off to war with a Dodger contract in his pocket. Who can say what incentive and hope the lure of a major-league uniform offered those men? At the same time, Clark Griffith, owner of the Washington team, began to send his scouts into Latin America to sign young men who weren't eligible for the U.S. military draft. It's a safe bet Rickey took notice. (Twenty years later there were more than 70 Latin-born players in the bigs.)

With so many of the better players off to war, talent was a little more evenly divided. As a result, one of the game's great miracles took place in 1944. The St. Louis Browns, who had been second-division dwellers for about 20 years (one year they

were 64½ games back!), actually won the AL pennant. Among the host of surprises the '44 Browns put together was Sigmund Jakucki (Ja-COOK-ee), a pitcher with few friends who had voluntarily retired from baseball eight years before with a big-league record of 0-3. He rewarded the Browns with a 13-9 record and a huge win over the Yanks on the final day of the season. The team began the season by winning their first nine games, then held off the Detroit Tigers, who were led by the vastly underappreciated Hal Newhouser, winner of 170 games during the decade and consecutive Most Valuable Player awards. As the batting leader of the "All 4-F Infield," George McQuinn became the only St. Louis Brown ever to hit a home run in a World Series, but in a pitching-dominated battle the Cards won the Series four games to two. It was the last World Series in which all the games were played at one stadium.

The mid-'40s was a great time to be a pitcher and have a medical exemption from the military. Hal Newhouser, despite having a heart defect, was the dominant moundsman of the era, winning back-to-back AL MVP awards in 1944 and '45 and finishing second the next year.

St. Louis Browns righty Sigmund Jakucki is probably unfamiliar to fans who have not heard David Frishberg's novelty tune, "Van Lingle Mungo." The lyrics consist solely of ballplayers' names. "Sig" didn't win a game until he was 34 years old, then collected 25 in two seasons and . . . just like that . . . he was gone.

By 1945 the quality of the game was at its lowest ebb. One-armed Pete Gray was a Browns regular. The Pirates had two 40-year-olds on their bench. The Senators' starting rotation was made up of four knuckle-ballers, one of them 41 years old. Judge Landis had died the previous November. But there was light on the horizon. In addition to the United States's successful campaigns in Europe and the South Pacific, baseball welcomed back an old hero. Hank Greenberg returned to the Tiger lineup on July 1 (his first big-league game in almost five years) and swatted a homer. Hank drove home 60 runs in the 78 games he played over the rest of the season.

By the last day of the season, the war was over, and the nation was in a dizzy mood. Greenberg's Tigers

Hank Greenberg was so tenacious about perfecting his swing that he would usually get to the park early to work on it, enlisting ushers or vendors if no one else was available to throw to him. Hammerin' Hank's grand slam on the final day of the 1945 season clinched the pennant for Detroit.

were scrapping for the flag. They were trying to outdo the Senators, who had hit only one home run in their home park all year (and it was an inside-the-park job!). Unlike the '41 race, neither team seemed to want to win; they both dropped crucial contests in the final two weeks of the season. On the last day, "Bingo" Binks, Senator outfielder, forgot to take his sunglasses out to his position; the ball he misplayed cost his team a victory that might have meant the pennant. Down to St. Louis by a run in the last of the ninth, Detroit loaded the bases and Hank knocked the cover off one. Grand slam! Tigers win! But when someone asked Chicago sportswriter Warren Brown his prediction for the upcoming Cubs–Tigers World Series, he replied simply, "I don't think either club has a chance."

The Series went seven games anyway, with Cub hurler Claude Passeau firing a one-hitter in Game 3. But Cub manager Charlie Grimm relied too much on Hank Borowy, the midseason acquisition from the Yankees who went 11-2 with Chicago. Hank pitched a complete game in Game 1 and was then used in relief for five innings in Game 5 and four in Game 6. He was weary. The first three Tigers in Game 7 cracked base hits off him; Borowy was gone, and so was the Series for the Cubs. They wouldn't make it back again in the 20th century.

FANS OR FANATICS?

During the late 1880s, German-born Chris Von der Ahe, owner of the St. Louis Browns in the American Association, openly admired a spectator who never missed a game. That fellow "is a regular *fan*-a-tic," he said, emphasizing the first syllable. Sportswriter Sam Crane overheard him and shortened "fanatic" to "fan."

Though rabid fans have always been part of the game, a few gained celebrity status in the '40s. One, a St. Louis rooter named Mary Ott, roamed the Sportsman's Park bleachers with a piercing laugh and booming voice described by one writer as "a neigh known to cause stampedes in Kansas City stockyards." That's particularly impressive when you consider Mary lived in St. Louis! The "Horse Lady of St. Louis" first came to national attention when revered umpire Bill Klem threatened to throw her out of a game in 1926.

Hilda Chester carried not one cowbell but two, ringing them in celebration or in mourning. She was such a trademark in Brooklyn that she became known as "The Bell of Ebbets Field." (One of the bells is now in Cooperstown.) Also called "Howling Hilda" before a heart attack forced her to keep quiet, Chester once sent a note to Dodger manager Leo Durocher, advising him to lift pitcher Whitlow Wyatt. Upon receiving the note from outfielder Pete Reiser, Durocher thought it had come from general manager Larry MacPhail. He removed Wyatt, then was livid when he discovered the true source of the note.

While Chester was ringing the bells one day from her customary spot in the center field stands, a five-piece band provided a stream of music from behind the Dodger bench. Broadcaster Red Barber dubbed it "the Dodger Sym-Phony," a name so well received that the drummer had it emblazoned on his instrument. The Sym-Phony specialized in music mocking the actions of opposing players, even playing "How Dry I Am" when one visited the water fountain.

Dodgers fans cheer for their team.

The fans were plentiful, and they were creative and passionate in their worship. Jack Pierce, another Brooklyn fan, idolized infielder Cookie Lavagetto and was convinced the Dodger infielder was the greatest player ever. To honor his idol, Pierce showed up at Ebbets Field every day, bought ten seats, and—using containers of gas he brought along—blew up dozens of balloons with "Cookie" on them and released them throughout the game. He even did it in 1942, when Lavagetto was in the military.

Compared to Cincinnati supporter Harry Thobe, however, Pierce practically blended into the crowd. Thobe showed up at the ballpark game after game, always dressed in the same attire: a white suit with red stripes, one red shoe, and one white shoe while carrying a red-and-white parasol. The retired bricklayer loved to dance jigs on the Crosley Field dugout.

Unlike other famous fans, Boston's Lollie Hopkins would never consider hollering. She shared her opinions with the Fenway faithful on a megaphone. And in polite New England style, she was perfectly willing to cheer for good play on the part of either team.

Another prominent fan was Pete Adelis, who rooted for the Athletics. Believed to weigh more than 600 pounds, Adelis had a voice to match. He was even barred from the raucous Ebbets Field, though the Yankees hired him as a heckler against the Indians when Cleveland came to New York for a critical series in the '40s. Connie Mack's Philadelphia Athletics had their own marathon man: Hyman Pearlstone made at least one road trip with the club for 44 straight seasons. George Doerzbach saw 55 consecutive Cleveland openers, and Atlantic City publicist Jimmie McCullough attended every World Series game for more than half a century, beginning in 1926. An AP dispatch described him as "the Babe Ruth of baseball fans."

Master promoter Bill Veeck, who considered each fan important, ran endless promotions to increase attendance. In 1948, as his Cleveland Indians were setting attendance records, Veeck even honored one letter-writing fan by sponsoring "Joe Early Night." The security guard and Indians fan received a car, refrigerator, washing machine, stereo, luggage, and more, becoming an instant local celebrity.

THE BOYS COME HOME

By the start of the 1946 season, 500 major-league players had returned to the game from military duty. Clubs had to expand their rosters to 30 men to fit everybody. America was being forced to redefine itself, both as a world power and (thanks to the GI Bill) as a newly vigorous economy. Luckily, Americans decided that baseball would be a big part of the entertainment once again.

Larry MacPhail, new Yankee partner, understood. Instead of holding drills and practices, his Yankees turned spring training into an extended barnstorming tour. By the time the season started, the Yanks had played 50 games in front of nearly a quarter-million fans.

And that was just the start! Fans came out like never before. The 1945 season had actually not been bad, all things considered. More than ten-and-a-half million fans came to big-league games, about on par with league-wide attendance at the peak of the slugfest era and pre-Depression. But 1946 was off the charts. Eighteen-and-a-half million fans paid their way to see the major-leaguers—an astonishing 71-percent jump, much more than any other increase before or since. Three-quarters of all teams set attendance records. Bill James, in the *Historical Baseball Abstract*, offered three reasons why: "[For one] the

Baseball was again the nation's "grand old game" by the end of the decade. These kids at the Alexander Graham Bell School in Chicago shared the dream of many others throughout the land—of one day becoming a big-league ballplayer.

Wealthy, eccentric Mexican League owner Jorge Pasquel (holding child) began raiding the majors for talent in 1946. Among players who accepted his generous salaries were Max Lanier, Vern Stephens, Sal Maglie, and Mickey Owen. (Pasquel is holding Owen's son.)

acceptance of night baseball...[Another,] the end of the War marked the end of a 15-year nightmare for America. [Third,] a nation suddenly more urban and more mobile was anxious to get out and move around...." In New York, the always-alert MacPhail was listening. He was a promoter with a fine sense of pleasing the fans, doing everything from installing lights in Yankee Stadium and building a women's lounge to putting on fashion shows.

But with the giddy exhilaration of the era, terms were being redefined and old traditions challenged. In one of the most potentially dire events ever to threaten the game, Mexican businessman Jorge Pasquel signed 23 major-leaguers to jump to the Mexican League, offering them big bucks and lots of perks. The owners were casually dismissive of the upstart's raids. However, when they got word of offers to Hank Greenberg and Bob Feller that exceeded $350,000, they demanded retaliation. New commissioner "Happy" Chandler leapt into action, coming down hard on the deserters. He banned them for five years, but offered a grace period during which they could return without punishment. Most did, and with the exception of a drawn-out court fight by jumper Danny Gardella, the threat was stillborn.

Perhaps because they had learned the value of group effort during their military duty, perhaps because the labor movement was growing in power throughout the nation, some players tried

to form a union, The American Baseball Guild. Attorney Robert Murphy headed the group, which accused the owners of failing to meet their obligations to the players relative to the GI Bill. An actual strike vote was taken in Pittsburgh before a game that year. The strike was voted down, and the Guild was disbanded soon thereafter. But this insurgence opened the owners' eyes, at least a bit. They agreed to changes in the basic players' contract and set a new minimum wage. It was the first significant step in the betterment of players' rights through labor organization.

A HERO IN WAR AND PEACE

Bob Feller was probably harmed more than any other great pitcher by World War II. While serving in the Navy, he lost nearly four full seasons—just as he was entering his prime. Had Feller's career been allowed to proceed without interruption, he might now be considered the greatest pitcher in history.

Feller was signed by Cleveland in 1935 for a dollar and an autograph while still a high school student in Van Meter, Iowa. Because he was just 16 years old, the signing was illegal according to the rules of the time and would have cost the Indians the rights to Feller had Commissioner Landis not feared a gargantuan bidding war among the other teams if Feller was made a free agent. For even as a teenager, he was renowned for the blazing fastball that would soon gain him the nickname "Rapid Robert."

Bob Feller

No one could have taught Feller what he possessed when he debuted with Cleveland in a July 1936 exhibition game against the Cardinals. Though only 17, Feller was already so swift that he fanned eight Redbirds in the three innings he hurled, causing home plate umpire Bob Ormsby to label him the fastest pitcher Ormsby had ever seen, Walter Johnson included.

When he returned from WWII, the right-hander picked up where he had left off. He helped the Cleveland Indians to a first-place tie in their division in 1946 and to a world championship two years later. During the '46 campaign, Feller won 26 games, one short of his single-season high, and fanned a then-record 348, topping Rube Waddell's mark—or so he thought. Waddell's record was 349 Ks, set in 1904, and Feller was not informed of that until after the season was over. An arm injury curtailed Bob's fastball, but he continued to be one of the game's top hurlers until 1955.

Feller fashioned two more 20-win seasons en route to a career record of 266-162. He threw three no-hitters and a dozen one-hitters, giving him a record 15 low-hit games before Nolan Ryan topped him. He led American League pitchers in complete games three times and shutouts four times. Feller was also the first to fan as many as 17 men in a game.

Years after his career ended, Rapid Robert admitted his record would have been better if he hadn't had problems with his control: He walked a modern-record 208 in 1938 and led his league in walks three other seasons.

But the real fun in 1946 took place on the field. For the first time in years, Yankee superiority wasn't automatic. Both Cleveland and the Red Sox were flexing new muscles. The Indians blossomed under the leadership of player/manager Lou Boudreau and the strong, strong arm of Bob Feller. In Boston, Bobby Doerr and Johnny Pesky provided an offensive-minded keystone combination, while Ted Williams seemingly didn't miss a beat upon his return from the military.

In the National League, the Cardinals were winding up one of the greatest runs of any team in history. After finishing second in 1941, they took the NL flag the next three seasons. They stumbled to second in 1945, then won the flag again in 1946. They ran out the decade with three more second-place finishes. But then the gas was gone; they didn't reach second again until 1957 or win the pennant again until 1964.

Hank Greenberg once again provided the power for the Tigers. He hit 44 homers, but his batting average dipped to .277. That made him the first 40-homer slugger *not* to bat .300. The Tigers figured he was washed up, but after the season the Pirates made him an offer he couldn't refuse: a ton of money, the left-field fence in Pittsburgh shortened just for him ("Greenberg Gardens"), and the opportunity to pass some of his wisdom to a rising talent, Ralph Kiner. It worked in a big way, as Kiner led or tied for NL league leadership in homers the first seven seasons of his career—an all-time record.

But to take the '46 pennant required a new bit of history. For the first time ever, a pennant race ended in a dead heat. The Dodgers and Cards both won 96 games and lost 58. The Cards took the first two playoff games, 4-2 and 8-4, to advance to the World Series.

It would be the only World Series ever to include Ted Williams. Unfortunately, Ted wasn't at his best. While the Cards and Dodgers were having their playoff battle, the Red Sox took on a team of "All-Stars" to stay sharp and generate some cash. A Mickey Haefner pitch whacked Ted on the elbow, and he wasn't himself for the Series. He finished with a meager .200 average and only one RBI. It is said that Ted was so embarrassed by his performance that he donated his entire World Series share (about $2,000) to the team's equipment manager.

Great defense kept the Cards in the Series, which extended to Game 7. The game was an instant classic. Sox center fielder Dom DiMaggio swatted a two-out double in the top of the eighth to tie the game at three, but in the process he hurt his ankle and was replaced by Leon Culberson. Culberson was nowhere near Dom's defensive equal, a fact Enos Slaughter knew full well. With two out in the bottom of the eighth, Slaughter was on first for the Cards. He took off when Harry Walker smacked a ball to left center. Slaughter, always a hustler, kicked into another gear to score the run that would win the Series, now enshrined in history as "Slaughter's Mad Dash." Did Culberson bobble the ball? Did Pesky hold it? It didn't matter. Enos provided a giddy ending to a glorious season.

Beginning in 1946, Ralph Kiner authored the unmatched feat of leading his league in home runs for seven straight years. Back problems abridged his career, but he was elected to the Hall of Fame in his final year of eligibility by just one vote over the minimum.

The Cardinals' Enos Slaughter was playing with a broken elbow when he made his "mad dash"—a sprint from first base to home on Harry Walker's hit that decided the 1946 World Series. Upon being traded to the Yankees in '54, Slaughter sat in front of his locker and wept.

JACKIE BREAKS THROUGH

As joyful as the return of the ballplayers was, as exciting as the resurgence of fan attendance, something far more important was also happening. In 1945 Jackie Robinson, former multi-sport star athlete at UCLA and second lieutenant in the U.S. Army, was signed to a minor-league contract by the Brooklyn Dodgers. With this act, Robinson became the first player of African-American heritage to step through the wall of segregation that had prevented blacks and whites from playing together at the highest levels since the 1880s. The signing of Robinson was part of Branch Rickey's plan to integrate the majors.

Robinson was a staggering amalgam of character, dignity, intelligence, pride, forbearance, and talent that made him an exquisite selection as "the chosen one" to break baseball's color barrier.

There are many reasons given why Rickey wanted to break this new ground. A grand storyteller, Rickey often spun a heart-rending tale of a black athlete he had played ball with in college. Racial discrimination had reduced his teammate to tears, as he desperately tried to rub the black off his skin so he could fit in. Rickey had not forgotten.

Blacks fought valiantly for America during the war, earning respect and greater acceptance, but the truth was that segregation and bigotry remained, and separate was *not* equal.

A savvy front-office man, Rickey also foresaw that signing Robinson would lead the way into a whole new source of championship-winning talent. And, bottom line, the payoff at the ticket window could be substantial, too, as Robinson attracted a whole new pool of fans to the ballpark.

Robinson was a highly talented athlete, to be sure, but there were other Negro Leaguers with more sheer skill. Rickey was looking for something beyond pure physical skills. He was looking for a man of patience and strong internal character, of courage and strength. He was looking for a man who would be able to undergo abuse and insults with dignity as he represented an entire people. Only Jackie possessed the traits Rickey knew were imperative for the man to break the "color" barrier. For one thing, Robinson was 28 years old—a grown man, not a nervous kid. As Robinson defined his role, in its most basic terms, "[My mission] was to show people that we could play together."

Another thing that attracted Rickey to Robinson was that he knew Jackie was not unfamiliar with standing up for himself; he had once taken on no less an adversary than the U.S. Army. He had been court-martialed for violating Jim Crow regulations but was acquitted and given an honorable discharge.

It was also no secret that Robinson didn't like playing in the Negro Leagues. He was used to integrated competition, the kind he had faced in college (although the Army had refused to let him play with whites). Before Rickey would sign Robinson, the old preacher made Jackie promise he would not exercise his right to fight back when challenged, threatened, or even injured by the white players. Robinson had to promise to turn the other cheek. A. D. Suehsdorf perceived something even deeper. "What Branch Rickey, bless his devious old soul, could see from the outset was that Robinson burned brightest under pressure, rose highest to a challenge."

And he had to rise to that challenge frequently. Even during his one year with the Montreal Royals, the Dodgers' Triple-A

Visionary Dodgers general manager Branch Rickey fabricated a non-white league as a front for his efforts to scout African Americans and integrate the majors. When Jackie Robinson showed up for an interview with Rickey, he had no idea he would be offered a contract to play for Brooklyn's farm club.

farm team, pitchers and other opposing players did everything they could to drive the black man from "their" game—and keep him out forever. Beanballs, spikings, threats...they were all part of the arsenal. Robinson responded to the pressure by batting .349 to lead the league, although by the time the season ended he admitted he was a nervous wreck.

With Rickey's plan in motion, Jackie took the next step. When Rickey sent his team to Cuba for 1947 spring training, far from the racist U.S. South, he sent Robinson with them, even though Robinson was still officially on the Montreal roster. A group of Dodgers got together a petition saying they didn't want Robinson on their team. When manager Leo Durocher heard of it, he called a team meeting in the middle of the night

After he paced the International League with a .349 average in 1946, there was little doubt Jackie Robinson was ready for the majors... whether or not they were ready for him. Here, he signs auto- graphs for Dodger fans five days prior to his historic big- league debut.

and told the rebels flat out where they could put their petition. And he added, "This man is going to make us all a lot of money." Rickey arrived the next day and backed Durocher up, and the revolt was over practically before it started.

Some of the worst attempts to rile Robinson came from Philly manager Ben Chapman. Chapman said he thought he was just doing what ballplayers always did: try to rile the opposition. But his language and attitude pushed way past even baseball's liberal boundaries on that issue. At one point, after several minutes of high-powered and highly obscene verbal abuse directed by Chapman at Robinson and his teammate Pee Wee Reese (a southern boy himself), Pee Wee walked over and put his arm around Robinson's shoulders. The gesture spoke louder than any words could have.

Chandler and National League President Ford Frick told Chapman to get into line, or else. He did. An attempted strike in late August by St. Louis players ended when Frick called each of the "strikers" into his office and laid down the law. He told them that even if half the league decided to strike, the league would remain integrated. He affirmed that every citizen of the United States of America has the same right to play baseball as the next.

Jackie Robinson was hit by 72 pitches— some as "retribution" for the color of his skin. The pitcher who plunked him here in 1947 was Pittsburgh's Hank Behrman, Robinson's teammate only weeks before. Behrman was dealt by the Dodgers for Al Gionfriddo, who made his famous World Series catch that fall.

AMERICAN LEAGUE PIONEER

Nearly three months after Jackie Robinson broke baseball's color barrier, Larry Doby became the first African American to play in the American League. Doby debuted as a pinch hitter for the Cleveland Indians on July 5, 1947. On that historic day, Doby was personally escorted to Chicago's Comiskey Park by Indians owner Bill Veeck.

Before his career with the Indians began, Doby was a standout second baseman for the Newark Eagles of the Negro National League. He was part of a legendary double-play tandem that also included future major-leaguer Monte Irvin.

Playing under immense cultural and social pressures, Doby did not fare well in his first season in Cleveland. The following season he was converted to center field and was personally coached by Hall of Fame center fielder Tris Speaker. That year, Doby batted .301 and helped the Indians to a World Series victory.

Doby was also an integral member of Cleveland's 1954 pennant-winning team, which won a record 111 games. In 13 big-league seasons, he was a seven-time All-Star who hit over 25 homers five times and drove in 100-plus runs five times. In 1962, he made history again when he and Don New-

Larry Doby

combe suited up for the Chunichi Dragons to become the first former major-leaguers to play in Japan. Doby was inducted into the Hall of Fame in 1998.

On the field, Robinson delighted fans everywhere with his aggressive style of baserunning, challenging pitchers and upsetting catchers with bluffs and steals. This kind of baseball, though quite familiar to Negro League fans, was something new to folks who were used to the Ruth/Williams school of "walk or hit the ball a mile." Robinson batted .297, and the Dodgers, even without Durocher, won the NL pennant. Baseball invented a new award that year: Rookie of the Year. Robinson was the first winner. Fifty years later the award was named after him, and at the same time every team in baseball retired his uniform number—the only time that has ever happened. Jackie was the first, but he was only the beginning. Within ten years of his debut, African Americans and Latin Americans had won seven MVP awards, eight Rookie of the Year awards, one Cy Young Award, and three league batting titles.

In retrospect, it's almost impossible to appreciate the symbolic value, as well as the practical sense, of making Jackie Robinson the first African-American big-leaguer in nearly 70 years. The U.S. military was not integrated for several more years. Blacks still faced uphill battles to real equality in many ways. But in this instance, Branch Rickey (and his three partners—they had to agree to hire Robinson, too) put a new face on America. Baseball was a leader in showing the world that Americans were willing to act on what they said they believed, that they were ready to do what they had been fighting for.

THE GAME ROLLS ON

The 1947 Yankees, who would face Jackie's Dodgers in the World Series, led the AL in runs scored and ERA that year, which is a pretty surefire way to win a pennant. The Red Sox mounted an assault early in the season, but in a four-game series in May at Yankee Stadium, the Yanks didn't just sweep; they annihilated, outscoring the Sox 40-5. Roger Kahn, in *The Era*, said, "After this incredible May series . . . , the Red Sox couldn't win an important game for a generation."

The 1947 World Series set several precedents. It was the first Series to generate two million dollars for the game, including $175,000 for radio rights and $65,000 for television rights. It

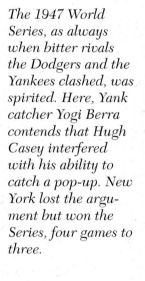

The 1947 World Series, as always when bitter rivals the Dodgers and the Yankees clashed, was spirited. Here, Yank catcher Yogi Berra contends that Hugh Casey interfered with his ability to catch a pop-up. New York lost the argument but won the Series, four games to three.

was the first Series ever televised. It was also the first Series to use six umpires.

The Yankees were up two games to one when Game 4 began, with Yankee Bill Bevens and Dodger Harry Taylor the starting pitchers. The Yanks were leading 2-1 going into the last of the ninth. Bevens had walked nine but amazingly hadn't yet allowed a hit. He was just one out away from the first World Series no-hitter when pinch runner Al Gionfriddo stole second. Yank manager Bucky Harris then violated a rule that had been in "the book" since Al Spalding was in diapers: *Never put the winning run on base.* But Harris ordered Pete Reiser walked, and then—spectacularly—pinch hitter Cookie Lavagetto swatted a double to right! Both runs scored, and, on that one swing, Bill Bevens lost his no-hitter and the game. In Game 6, Gionfriddo once again played a vital role, making a spectacular over-the-shoulder catch to rob Joe DiMaggio of a game-tying homer. Despite that October heroism, neither Gionfriddo nor

Al Gionfriddo never played another game after the 1947 World Series, but his catch in Game 6 emblazoned him into baseball history. Though he deprived Joe DiMaggio of a game-tying, three-run homer as the ball was about to clear Yankee Stadium's left-field fence, his Dodgers lost the Series the next day.

GETTING BETTER WITH AGE

To many, the signing of Satchel Paige at the age of 42 seemed like just another publicity stunt by Cleveland Indians owner Bill Veeck. Maybe it was, but it certainly paid dividends for the franchise.

Paige, a right-handed fireballer, had long been the Negro Leagues' best pitcher. The flamboyant star drew large crowds, and Veeck wanted to cash in on Paige's popularity. But Paige could help on the mound as well. The oldest rookie in major-league history was acquired midway through the 1948 campaign. He quickly made an impact on a Cleveland team that already featured such outstanding pitchers as Bob Feller and Bob Lemon. Paige appeared in 21 games and started 7. He went 6-1 with a 2.48 ERA while working as a spot starter or out of the bullpen.

Satchel Paige

The Indians went down to the wire in the American League pennant race in '48, finishing the season tied with the Boston Red Sox. The Indians won the one-game playoff to advance to the World Series and then beat the Boston Braves in six games to capture the fall classic. Paige made one appearance in the World Series, retiring the only two batters he faced.

While the strength in Paige's arm was not what it once was, he was still effective enough to pitch four more seasons in the majors. He remained in Cleveland one more year and then moved to the St. Louis Browns when Veeck took over the team. Used mostly as a reliever with the Browns, Paige had his best season in 1952. Although he was 46 years old, he went 12-10 with 10 saves and a 3.07 ERA and struck out 91 batters in 138 innings pitched. In 1953 he appeared in 57 games and notched 11 saves, fourth best in the AL. He also appeared in the '53 All-Star Game at the age of 47.

In 1965, in what was clearly a publicity stunt, Paige was signed by Kansas City Athletics owner Charlie Finley and became the oldest man to pitch in the majors. At age 59, Paige held the Red Sox to one hit and no runs in three innings of work. The appearance also helped Paige qualify for a pension from Major League Baseball. Paige was the first player elected to the Hall of Fame primarily for his play in the Negro Leagues.

Lavagetto ever played another major-league inning. But Bevens's blunder was only a stumble for the Yankees; they squeezed out a 2-1 win in Game 5 even though Joe DiMaggio uncharacteristically left seven men on base. And although they got bombed in Game 6, the men from the Bronx capitalized on 7⅔ innings of scoreless relief work from Ralph Branca and Joe Page in Game 7 to win it all.

In 1948, the pennant race ended in a tie for just the second time in history, but it was the second time in three years that this had happened. This time the tie occurred in the American League, where the Indians faced the Red Sox in a one-game playoff to see who would advance. Indian shortstop/manager

Lou Boudreau, called by many the smartest man in baseball, tapped rookie lefty Gene Bearden to start. Then Lou took charge, hitting two solo homers and scoring a third run himself.

The Indians headed to the World Series after drawing a then-record 2.6 million fans for the season. Part of the reason for the draw was quality baseball; part was savvy marketing. Promotional genius Bill Veeck kept the fans in stitches with gimmicks and goofiness. Satchel Paige, longtime Negro League superhero (and somewhere between 40 and 50 years old), contributed six wins to the Cleveland effort.

Over in the National League, the Boston Braves captured the flag. Somewhere along the line, someone described the Braves pitching staff as "Spahn and Sain and two days of rain." This is another example of a good soundbite elbowing reality into a ditch. Yes, there was a stretch in September when Warren Spahn and Johnny Sain, because of rainouts, started most of the team's games. But the truth is that a quick glance at the stats shows that while Johnny Sain did have a spectacular 24-15 year,

SPAHN AND SAIN AND PRAY FOR RAIN

When the 1948 Boston Braves found themselves in hot pursuit of the team's first pennant since 1914, manager Billy Southworth decided to ride the horses of his pitching rotation as far as they could go. He started Warren Spahn and Johnny Sain a combined 16 times in 26 games after September 3, helping the Braves to a first-place finish, 6½

games ahead of the closest team, the St. Louis Cardinals.

Sain, a 30-year-old right-hander, led the league in wins (24), starts (39), complete games (28), and innings pitched (314.2) while topping the rotation with a 2.60 ERA. He even made three relief appearances. The 27-year-old Spahn finished strong to end with a 15-12 record and 3.71 ERA, far from the 21-win form he flashed in 1947. But the left-hander, recuperating from a slow start that season, was at his best when it counted.

Both pitchers turned in winning performances when it mattered most, which was down the stretch. On Labor

Day, Spahn threw a 14-inning five-hitter to beat his longtime nemesis, the Brooklyn Dodgers, 2-1 in the opener of a doubleheader. Sain won the second game, 4-0. After two scheduled days off, the Braves' next game was rained out. That set the stage for Spahn and Sain, who again won back-to-back games. After a scheduled off-day, Boston's two other starters, Bill Voiselle and Vern Bickford, split a doubleheader. Then it was Spahn and Sain again, with the pair beating Chicago on September 14 and 15. After another off-day, Spahn and Sain topped Pittsburgh twice.

The stellar performance of Spahn and Sain fueled the Braves' drive to the pennant. When the aces weren't playing, the games seemed to get rained out. That situation, captured by a local columnist, soon turned into "Spahn and Sain and pray for rain."

Warren Spahn (left) and Johnny Sain (right)

Retained as player/manager in 1948 only because fans voted 10-to-1 to do so in a poll, Lou Boudreau (waving) guided the Indians to the world title. His performance as the AL's finest defensive shortstop, as well as his .355 average and 106 RBI, earned him the MVP Award.

Warren Spahn won only two more games than Bill Voiselle, and Vern Bickford added 11 wins himself. The Boston pitching staff as a whole led the league in both ERA and complete games. This was a balanced pitching staff backed by solid defense. To top off the 1948 season, Leo Durocher became manager of the Dodger-despised Giants. In other words, it was just another typical year in the 1940s.

In 1949 a black pitcher faced a black batter for the first time in modern major-league history. Ted Williams missed being the only person ever to win three Triple Crowns when he lost the batting title to George Kell by the amazingly thin margin of .00016. That year, Williams's teammate Vern Stephens matched the Splinter with 159 RBI. The Yankees hired a new manager—Casey Stengel, a man previously known mostly as for his clownish acts. Of course he won the pennant his first year there.

In 1945, '46, and '47, there were six different teams in the World Series, and all three Series went to seven games. The next year, two different teams made it to the fall classic. During the decade there were 11 different teams in the World Series, and the other five teams each made it into the first division (top four in the standings) at least once.

With Ted and Joe, then wartime, with teenagers and forty-somethings, Mollie Milosevich and Bingo Binks, then peace and Jackie Robinson breaking the color barrier, and the most competitive play in baseball history, the '40s were unlike any decade the sport has ever seen.

Ted Williams scores one of his career-high 150 runs in 1949, a year in which he also set personal bests in home runs (43), RBI (159), hits (194), and walks (162). His fine performance earned him his second and last MVP Award.

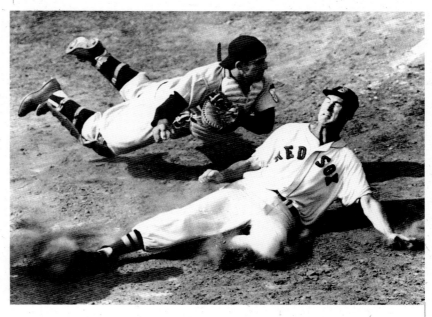

1950s

NEW YORK AND NEW FRONTIERS

New York reestablished itself as the capital of baseball in the 1950s. However, faced with dwindling attendance, five major-league owners picked up and moved their teams to where the fans were. The result was a shuddering upheaval in the game. Meanwhile, play on the field was dominated by slow, strong men who either hit the ball a mile or struck out; a stolen base was a "surprise play." Yet the era is lovingly remembered by millions of baby-boomer fans who first discovered baseball when it starred Willie and Mickey; showcased the Yankees, the Dodgers, and the Giants; and featured the joy of Ernie Banks, the lovable double-talk of Casey Stengel, and a new generation of superstars. The United States was in love with itself in the '50s, and baseball received quite a bit of that affection.

Brooklyn summoned reliever Russ Meyer to face Mickey Mantle with the bases loaded in Game 5 of the 1953 World Series, and the Mick launched his first pitch into Ebbets Field's upper deck for just the fourth grand slam in fall classic history.

THE NEXT YANKEE DYNASTY

The Yankees of Miller Huggins and Babe Ruth won three pennants in a row; their successors, skippered by Joe McCarthy and led by Gehrig and DiMaggio, won four in a row and took the world championship in each of those years as well. But the Yankees of 1949–53 raised the bar to another level: They won *five* straight pennants and never lost a World Series during that time. After missing out in '54, they won the flag again in '55, '56, '57, and '58. Then, after one more stumble, they won it *again* in 1960.

In fact, if you wanted to tell the abridged story of the decade it would be about the Yankees: how they won, and why they didn't the two times they lost. Because when the Yanks didn't win in the '50s, it was very large news.

But the money wasn't on the Yankees on October 12, 1948. That was the day they announced they had hired a new manager, the lovable, laughable 58-year-old Casey Stengel. Casey's first appearance before the New York press was clumsy and embarrassing. Dave Egan of the *Boston Record* even did a Casey impersonation in his evaluation of the hiring. "Well, sirs and ladies, the Yankees have now been mathematically eliminated from the 1949 pennant race. They eliminated themselves when they engaged Perfesser Casey Stengel to mismanage them for the next two years and you may be sure the perfesser

In 1949, the Yankees celebrated what would be their first of five straight World Series crowns. Casey Stengel (center, with ball) was their rookie manager, and Phil Rizzuto (left) their leadoff hitter.

Casey Stengel, who hid his deep intelligence behind a fanciful persona, revived the strategy of platooning and refined it into an art form.

will oblige to the best of his unique ability." Casey's garbled style of communication was well-known, as was his record as a big-league manager: almost nine years at the helm of the Dodgers and Braves, 581 wins, 742 losses, finishing as high as fifth place only twice in all that time. Conventional wisdom labeled him a clown, not a manager. Sure, he had plenty of baseball under his belt: His big-league career dated back to 1912. And Casey had learned plenty from John McGraw during the three seasons he served on pennant-winners under the old master. He was fun to have around, but to *manage* the *Yankees*? After all, wasn't he the guy who once tipped his cap to the fans only to have a bird fly out from under it?

Casey's instant success—winning the pennant and World Series in 1949—was a surprise to many, but most fans and historians don't realize what he had to overcome to accomplish it. For one thing, the team chasing his Yanks, the Boston Red Sox, was a formidable opponent that year. The Sox were rattling fences all around the league; Detroit's George Kell barely nipped Ted Williams in the batting average race to keep Ted from another Triple Crown. Five other Sox starters batted over .290, and both Williams and Vern Stephens knocked in 159 runs. On the Yank side, Joe DiMaggio missed nearly the entire first half of the season due to a heel injury. Yankee publicist Red Patterson counted up 71 disabling Yank injuries that year.

"Rookie" skipper Stengel was forced to be creative; he wound up using seven different players at first base. The season came down to the final two games, with the Sox holding a one-game lead. On Saturday, the Yankees stormed back from a 4-0 deficit after three innings to win 5-4. When the teams faced each other for the final game of the season, they were dead even. But Casey outmanaged legend Joe McCarthy, the BoSox exhibited some bad defense, pitcher Vic Raschi dominated, and New York headed to the World Series again.

While the sarcastic sportswriters had seen Stengel only as a manager of poor major-league teams, Yankee management had paid attention to something else: Casey's success in the minors with Pacific Coast League Oakland. There the "perfesser" had put together a second-, a fourth-, and a first-place finish in three years, learning how to get the most from less-than-star-quality players. It turned out the "clown" was much more than that. By 1960, when the Yankees fired him, he had become recognized as one of the most brilliant managerial minds of all time. A magazine article in the late '50s pointed out that Casey was "probably the only manager who wins more than two games a year with strategy." When the Yankee juggernaut under Stengel was at its most potent, some tried to claim Casey was a "push-button manager," one who didn't have to do anything for his team to be successful. The fact is, Casey did more to his team than almost any manager.

Like his mentor McGraw, Casey had no qualms about replacing a regular. In 12 seasons he had three different "regular" first basemen, four second basemen, four shortstops, and six third basemen. But one of Casey's most heralded moves was

Ed Lopat was the junk-balling southpaw Stengel sandwiched between hard-throwing right-handers Allie Reynolds and Vic Raschi during the Yanks' five-year spree of world titles from 1949 to '53. He is shown here in 1951, the year he won a pair of World Series games.

the reintroduction of platooning: playing left-handed batters against right-handed pitchers, and vice versa. Today it seems obvious: Number-crunchers have proved that platooning gives a statistical advantage. In Casey's time, however, the concept was based less on numbers than on common sense. Standing at the plate is more comfortable when someone is throwing the ball from the opposite side as you than when he's throwing from the same side. Platooning was widely used in the teens and even into the '20s, but it had been another casualty of Ruth and the Big Bang. Casey's logic for platooning at several positions was unassailable: You're not going to have superstars at eight positions, so you have to get the most from every player you have. Put each player in situations where he is most likely to succeed.

Stengel's handling of pitchers was analogous to platooning. He never had a set rotation. Instead, he chose the pitcher he felt had the best chance of winning that day. So he kept Whitey Ford off the Fenway mound, where right-handed bombers and the short porch in left field could be trouble. He used Allie Reynolds as both a starter and a reliever, to get maximum value from "The Chief's" rubber arm. Stengel realized that players past their prime could still play valuable roles in part-time, "swingman" positions.

Once Casey's ability to manage became clear, the press warmed to his amazing loquacity. His nonstop rambles were hilarious, even when he testified before the House Committee

STENGELESE AND YOGI-ISMS

The lexicon of baseball is filled with catchy phrases. A lazy fly ball is known as a "can of a corn." A double play is often described as a "twin killing," and runners on base are also known as "ducks on the pond." But for decades Casey Stengel and Yogi Berra spoke their own brand of baseball language. They were masters of the malaprop and the mixed metaphor. When Casey went on a rant, it was known as Stengelese. When Berra offered advice, it was a Yogi-ism.

Stengel managed his share of miserable teams, including the 1934–36 Dodgers, 1938–43 Braves, and 1962–65 Mets. But his legacy also includes the 1949–60 New York Yankees, whom he managed to ten pennants. During this time he became known as the "Old Perfessor." Warren Spahn pitched for Stengel with both the Braves and the Mets, prompting him to note that he played for Casey "both before and after he was a genius."

Stengel, a world-class raconteur, was known for sprinkling his stories with wisecracks. He called rookies "green peas," a good fielder was a "plumber," and a tough ballplayer was someone who could "squeeze your earbrows off." Among his notable quotes were, "Good pitching will always stop good hitting and vice versa," "I don't know if he throws a spitball, but he sure spits on the ball," and finally, "Being with a woman all night never hurt no professional baseball player. It's staying up all night looking for a woman that does him in."

Casey Stengel (left) and Yogi Berra (right)

Berra, a Hall of Fame catcher for the Yankees, was hardly a wisecracker. He was sincere and thoughtful, but sometimes translation was necessary after the words left his mouth. When he wanted to explain that playing successful baseball required equal amounts of physical talent and intelligence, he said, "Ninety percent of the game is half mental." When asked what size cap he wore, Berra answered, "I don't know, I'm not in shape yet." And perhaps his most famous baseball saying was, "It ain't over 'til it's over," citing the never-say-die attitude of his 1973 pennant-winning New York Mets.

Not all of his quips were related to baseball. Among his classics are, "When you come to the fork in the road, take it," and "I'm ugly. So what? I never saw anybody hit with his face."

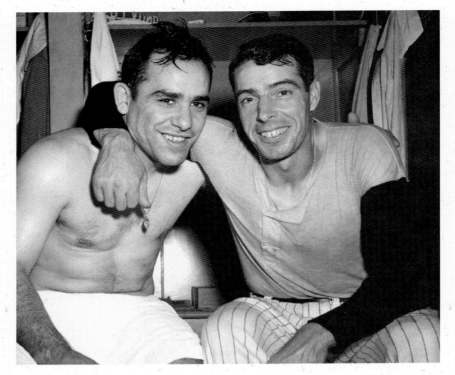

Yogi Berra (left) and Joe DiMaggio (right) were the only two players on either side to hit home runs in the 1950 World Series. The Yankees made short work of the Phils, dismissing them in four games. Of the seven Series sweeps to that time, the Yanks had six.

Hank Bauer is smooched by Phil Rizzuto (left) and Yogi Berra after making a terrific catch to end the 1951 World Series. Right fielder Bauer's shoestring stab of a low liner squelched a Giants rally and preserved a 4-3 Yankee victory in Game 6.

investigating baseball in 1957. After a sensational run of "Stengelese" that left many of the members of Congress in stitches, it was Mickey Mantle's turn to testify. "Well," he drawled, "my views are about the same as Casey's." But, as historian Mark Gallagher points out, "Make no mistake about this fact: Casey spoke Stengelese only when he wanted to and usually only to the press. His players understood Casey perfectly." Sure, some of his players grumbled about not getting enough playing time, and Joe DiMaggio and Case had run-ins late in Joe's career, but it was hard to argue with success. Even the men who didn't get to play every day still found themselves cashing a World Series check nearly every year. Casey managed the Yankees for 12 seasons; during that time they won ten American League pennants and seven world championships. The Yankees had dominated baseball before (and they would again) but never like they did the dozen seasons under Casey's reign.

One of Casey's first jobs in 1949 was to transform the talented young Yogi Berra into a catcher. Several teams had expressed an interest in signing the youngster from "Dago Hill" in St. Louis, but only the Yankees would give him what he wanted: the same signing bonus ($500) the Cardinals had given his pal Joe Gara-

giola. Berra's offensive capabilities were obvious, but behind the plate he was, frankly, an embarrassment. All-time great Bill Dickey was given the assignment of improving Yogi's defense. With hours and hours of hard work, Dickey and Berra turned things around. Yogi became the regular catcher for the 1949–60 Yank glory teams and was a frequent league leader in defensive categories. Despite his squat body, Yogi was a catlike athlete.

Stengel once said, "He springs on a bunt like it's another dollar." And Yogi knew how to handle pitchers: Some he coddled, some he cursed. He caught both of Allie Reynolds's no-hitters during the 1951 season.

Berra's most famous day of catching came in the 1956 World Series. The Yankee starting pitcher for Game 5 was Don Larsen, who was far from being a star. Just two years before, he had compiled a 21-loss season; he had never won more than 11 in one year. But that day Larsen was perfect. He threw just 97 pitches. Only once did he reach a count of three balls on a batter. Not a single Dodger reached base as Larsen threw the only perfect game ever in postseason play. When ump Babe Pinelli loudly signaled "Strike three!" at the final out, the dumpy Yogi rushed to leap into lanky Larsen's arms. It was a classic moment.

Don Larsen and catcher Yogi Berra embrace at the conclusion of the Yankee right-hander's perfect World Series game. To this day, people debate about whether the final called strike three to Brooklyn's Dale Mitchell was in the zone.

While Yogi was learning to be a first-rate backstop, he seemed to have been born a sensational batsman. He never got points for his knowledge of the strike zone, but if he figured he could hit it, he probably could, which made him even more dangerous. Despite his swings at balls nowhere near the zone, he was tough to strike out. And he was a great clutch hitter.

Casey Stengel bids farewell to Yankee Stadium for the 1957 season after his club dropped the World Series to the Braves. He returned to the Series the next year, in another seven-game thriller, to win a rematch with the boys from Milwaukee.

Longtime manager Paul Richards said Yogi was "the toughest man in the league in the last three innings." Berra set the career home run record for catchers, which wasn't broken until Carlton Fisk came along. And he was voted the league's Most Valuable Player three times.

With his knowledge of the game and his intuitive understanding of people, Berra served unofficially as Casey's assistant manager. Yogi himself managed in the bigs after his playing career was over and won pennants with both the Yankees and the Mets. But of course it was Yogi's mind-boggling, Zen-like quotes that added another dimension to his fame. "Nobody goes there anymore; it's too crowded." "It gets late early out there" (referring to the tough sun field in Yankee Stadium). Or, in appreciation of those who had sponsored "Yogi Berra Night," "I want to thank all the people who made this evening necessary." But in referring to the veracity of some of his "quotes," Yogi had the inimitable last word: "I really didn't say all the things I said."

PLAYERS OFF TO KOREAN WAR

In 1950 North Korean Communist forces invaded South Korea. The United Nations asked its members to assist South Korea, and President Harry S. Truman responded by sending American troops into the battle.

Baseball players once again responded to the call of duty. None figured more prominently than future Hall of Famer Ted Williams of the Boston Red Sox. Having already served in World War II, Williams again put his career on hold to fight in Korea.

As a Marine pilot, Williams flew 39 combat missions over Korea and missed the 1952 and '53 seasons. His plane was once hit by anti-aircraft fire, damaging the landing gear and forcing Williams to crash-land. Despite the

Ted Williams

incident, Williams continued to fly over the skies of Korea. He was the wingman for future U.S. Senator and astronaut John Glenn.

"There was no one more dedicated to his country and more proud to serve his country than Ted Williams," said Glenn.

Among the other major-league stars who served during the Korean War were Whitey Ford, Willie Mays, Jerry Coleman, Whitey Herzog, and Don Newcombe.

FIFTY AND FIFTY-ONE

Over in the National League, things weren't so predictable. The Phillies startled everyone by winning the NL flag in 1950. It was their first league title since 1915, when Grover Cleveland Alexander was their ace; it would be their last until 1980, when Steve Carlton was. The '50 Phils were called the "Whiz Kids" because they were young, hustling, and full of surprises. Their two star pitchers had been signed to large bonuses when they were still very young: Robin Roberts, who was just 21 when he signed, went 20-11; and Curt Simmons, who inked a contract the day he graduated from high school, finished 17-8. The top arm in the bullpen was Jim Konstanty, who began the season as a 33-year-old with 16 big-league victories on his baseball card. That season he added 16 more, all in relief; added 22 saves (retroactively); and won the league MVP crown.

They landed the flag on the last day of the season when Richie Ashburn threw out a Dodger at home plate in the last of the ninth (had he been safe, the game would have been over and the Dodgers champs). In the tenth, Dick Sisler, whose only previous claim to fame was that he was George Sisler's son, creamed a three-run homer, and the kids from Philly hung on to win. In the Series they were no match for the Yankees, who had no trouble sweeping them.

A 23-year-old Richie Ashburn penned chapter one of his Philly legend on the final day of the 1950 season. His perfect strike from center to nail a Brooklyn runner at home in the bottom of the ninth preserved a tie and set up a win to secure the NL pennant for the Phils.

Ebbets Field fans were jazzed for the National League's final game of the 1950 season, a winner-take-all match between the Dodgers and Phillies. A three-run, tenth-inning homer by Philadelphia's Dick Sisler sent the Dodger faithful home distraught, however.

Even though the "Whiz Kids" never recaptured pennant glory, Roberts built a long career marked by dependability and consistency. He had six straight 20-win seasons, beginning in 1950. For the decade, he never started fewer than 32 games a year or pitched less than 249 innings. Sad to say, for most years his team was mediocre at best. Roberts's forte was his marvelous control, but like all good things, it had its downside. Roberts routinely led the NL in homers allowed: Because batters knew he would always be around the plate, they dug in, and when they connected, the ball went far. He finished his career just 14 wins shy of 300.

The Phillies, who didn't clinch the NL pennant until extra innings on the final game of the season, had nothing left in the take for the World Series. Here, Yogi Berra completes a double play by nailing Granny Hamner at the plate in Game 4.

THE WHIZ KIDS

The 1950 Philadelphia Phillies were young. Very young.

At one point in the season, the starting lineup had an average age of 26, and their best seven pitchers averaged just over 27 years old. The club had finished in third place in 1949, 16 games behind Brooklyn, but had gained a valuable year of experience.

That experience paid off in 1950. The energetic, combative, and youthful Phillies team sprinted to a 7½-game lead in the National League by September 20. They played so hard that they were dubbed "Whiz Kids," a nickname once applied to a young University of Illinois basketball team.

Del Ennis, Willie "Puddin' Head" Jones, and Andy Seminick hit at least two dozen homers apiece, Richie Ashburn led the league with 14 triples, and a young

Robin Roberts won 20 games. But the surprise star of the team was Jim Konstanty, a 33-year-old right-handed relief pitcher who hardly qualified as a Whiz Kid.

En route to Most Valuable Player honors, the first ever given to a reliever, he led the league with 74

Jim Konstanty (left) and Andy Seminick (right)

appearances, at the time a major-league record, and finished with a 16-7 mark, saved 22 games, and racked up a 2.66 ERA.

With the Phils looking toward their first World Series since 1915, the veteran Dodgers caught fire, winning 13 of 16 down the stretch. The inexperienced Phils went 3-8 during that time and watched their lead shrink to one game. All the Dodgers needed to force a best-of-three playoff was a victory over the Whiz Kids on October 1.

The Phils hung tough. After fending off a serious Dodger threat in the bottom of the ninth, the Whiz Kids took the game and the flag when Dick Sisler hit a three-run homer in the tenth off Don Newcombe. Though they didn't win a game in the World Series against the Yankees, the Whiz Kids had made their mark.

The next year has gone down in song and story: The Giants, managed by erstwhile Dodger legend Leo Durocher, pulled off an insanely spectacular comeback to end the season tied with the Dodgers for first, and then an equally breathtaking comeback in the last half-inning of the final playoff game to cop the NL pennant.

The Dodgers of 1951 were a mature team: Seven of their regulars were 29 or older, including catcher Roy Campanella (winning his first of three MVP awards). Midseason outfield acquisition Andy Pafko was 30, and Jackie Robinson, third baseman Billy Cox, and Pee Wee Reese were all over 30. They had been through the white heat of a pennant race before, and they had tasted championships. But their pitching staff was comparatively young (with the exception of old-timer Preacher Roe, who went 22-3): Hurlers Don Newcombe, Carl Erskine, and Ralph Branca were in their mid-20s.

The Giants had finished five games back the year before, but for most of the previous decade, fourth place was the best they could muster. In terms of team structure, they were the opposite of the Dodgers. Among the regulars, only Eddie

Baseball had been integrated only a few years when Monte Irvin, Willie Mays, and Hank Thompson (left to right) helped anchor the great Giants teams of the '50s. Thompson and Irvin, respectively, were the franchise's first and second African Americans.

Stanky and Monte Irvin (who had spent a good part of his career in the Negro Leagues) were past 30 years old. Most of the other regulars were young; their center fielder was only 20, but he was Willie Mays. The Giant pitching staff, however, was full of grizzled veterans: Larry Jansen, Jim Hearn (who had the best ERA in the NL the year before), Dave Koslo, and Sheldon Jones were all 30 or close to it.

The most grizzled of all, at least in terms of looks, was Sal Maglie, who had a truly strange career. He was scary and grim in his facial appearance, always in need of a shave, looking positively like a movie villain. Maglie didn't make his major-league debut until he was 28, then jumped to the Mexican League and was blacklisted from the majors for nearly five years. When he returned in 1950, he posted the best winning percentage in the league. And in 1951, at age 34, he was the ace of the Giants' pitching staff, notching 23 wins and the second-best ERA in the league. Perhaps no major-leaguer ever had a more appropriate nickname: They called Sal "The Barber" for his willingness to pitch high and tight; in other words, to give the batter a "close shave."

The Giants began the season miserably, losing 12 of their first 14. The Dodgers, under manager Chuck Dressen, were rolling along. Even as late as August 11 there seemed to be no chance of a pennant race. Both teams split doubleheaders that day, and for a couple of hours between the Dodgers' loss in their first game and the Giants victory in their second, the gap between the two teams was 13½ games. The Giants were lucky to be in second place; the rest of the league was even further back.

But at that point something clicked for the Giants. They caught fire. They couldn't find a way to lose. After that first-game loss on August 11 they won 16 straight games. In their final 47 games they were the victors 39 times. What happened? Durocher said that he got lucky with a series of moves that worked and the team picked up on it, developing an almost mystical faith in every strategic decision he made. They believed; they responded; his hunches worked. Another opinion came to light a decade later: A former Giant said that during their 1951 hot streak they had been stealing the catcher's signs from the Polo Grounds' center-field stands. With an elaborate electrical wiring setup, the sign stealer rang a bell in the Giants bullpen, clearly audible to everyone there. Bullpen catcher Sal Yvars sat on the end of the bench with a ball. If the pitch was going to be a fastball he tossed the ball in the air. If not, he held onto it. The batter could easily see what Yvars did. Pitcher Al Corwin, who was recently interviewed for an HBO special on the team, called the sign-swiping technique "a cumbersome and not terribly reliable system."

It's hard to know whether to believe this stunning new accusation or not, although Durocher's description of his play-ers' almost mystical faith takes on a whole new light in this circumstance. Interviewed for the article that established the claim, both Bobby Thomson and Willie Mays said there was some sign stealing going on, but neither of them wanted to be tipped off. Strangely enough, the numbers don't back up the charge of cheating—the Giants' batting averages in the Polo Grounds, even during their streak, weren't significantly higher than their road aver-ages. In fact, some players actually batted lower when they were supposedly getting the signs. So even though we know the Giants pulled off the greatest comeback in history, we will probably never know for sure whether it was on the square or not—another one of the game's delicious histori-cal ambiguities.

It wasn't that the Dodgers fell apart; the Giants just won more often. In fact, it took a terrific defensive play in the 12th inning of the last game of the regular season followed by a 14th-inning homer—both by Jackie Robinson—for the Dodgers to squeeze out the tie.

The best-of-three playoff began in Brooklyn. Both Monte Irvin and Bobby Thomson swatted homers off Ralph Branca, and the Giants won 3-1. The next day, in New York, youngster Clem Labine

Ralph Branca was named an All-Star three times before his 24th birthday, yet his unfortu-nate legacy is his gopher ball to Bobby Thom-son that cost the Dodgers the '51 pennant.

*Though Bobby
Thomson's historic
home run to win the
1951 NL pennant
easily cleared the
left-field fence, the
self-proclaimed
"accidental hero" was
initially concerned
that the ball was
sinking too fast and
wouldn't make it.*

fashioned a six-hit shutout. Four Dodgers homered as the
Brooklynites won 10-0.

Game 3, Don Newcombe versus Sal Maglie, was tied at
one run each until the top of the eighth. Two poor plays by
Giant third baseman Thomson helped the Dodgers tack on
three runs. Newcombe was still looking strong in the bottom of
the ninth when the Giants' Alvin Dark bounced a single to the
right side of the Dodger infield. Manager Chuck Dressen inex-
plicably told first baseman Gil Hodges to hold the runner on,
even though Dark's run would mean nothing in a 4-1 game. The
bad decision came back to bite the Dodgers where it hurt when
Don Mueller singled through the spot where Hodges should
have been playing. Two Giants were now on. Ralph Branca and
Carl Erskine were both warming up in the Dodger bullpen
(Branca for the fourth time during the game—and he had
pitched eight innings just two days previously). Newk got
Monte Irvin to pop out. But Whitey Lockman doubled to left,
scoring Dark and advancing Mueller to third, where Mueller
twisted his ankle sliding and had to be carried from the field.
Clint Hartung replaced him on third base.

The Dodgers now led 4-2 with Giants on second and third
and one out. Dressen called the bullpen. "Who looks better?"

Bobby Thomson was mobbed at home after his "Shot Heard 'Round the World" sent the Giants to the 1951 World Series. Thomson was not just a one-hit wonder: Between '49 and '53, only six NL players hit more homers or drove in more runs than he did.

Bullpen coach Clyde Sukeforth answered that Branca looked better. "Okay, I want him," Dressen decided.

Bobby Thomson, who had homered off Branca just two days before, got ahold of the hurler's second pitch and ripped it into the left-field stands. Left fielder Andy Pafko thought he had a chance, but all he could do was look up and watch in dismay. On the radio, announcer Russ Hodges shouted "The Giants win the pennant! The Giants win the pennant!" over and over again, and the whole city went crazy. Those who weren't stunned simple were simply delirious. Film of the game shows Giant Eddie Stanky, rather than joining the crowd of players who surrounded home plate pummeling their hero Thomson, rushing past instead and charging out to the third base coaching box in order to leap in uncontainable joy on Leo Durocher's back. It was a great game to top off a sensational pennant race—the perfect fans' game, full of wonderful opportunities to second-guess managerial decisions. A lot of fans did just that—and are *still* doing it, in some Brooklyn enclaves. (Dodger club president Walter O'Malley did a little practical second-guessing himself; he had Sukeforth fired.) Three million Americans saw the homer on their TV sets at home. By some estimates, that many more watched it at the next most likely place—their local tavern.

Did Thomson know what Branca was going to throw? He denied it, but Branca later said that not only was Thomson's swing right on the money, he positively "attacked" the ball. According to Branca, Thomson definitely knew what was coming.

THREE CENTER FIELDERS

In Game 2 of the 1951 World Series, 19-year-old Mickey Mantle was playing right field for the Yankees, and legendary Joe DiMaggio was stationed in his own personal domain—center field. In a historic moment, arguably the three greatest players ever at their position connected for one instant—and with dramatic results. A fly ball was looped between Joe and Mickey by 20-year-old Willie Mays of the Giants. Mantle figured DiMaggio would take it. But Joe said nothing, so Mantle made a desperate last-second lunge for the ball. In doing so he stepped into a hole where a drainage cover hadn't been properly reinstalled, tearing up his knee. Truthfully, it probably was never right again. DiMaggio retired after that Series, and the job of Yankee center fielder became Mickey's.

Now in place was the triumvirate of New York flycatchers that would be hailed in song, a threesome of exceptional athletes and men that came to stand for what writer Roger Kahn called *The Era 1947–1957: When the Yankees, the Dodgers, and the Giants Ruled the World.* Willie, Mickey, and the Duke. Mays, Mantle, and Snider. Snider had two more full big-league seasons under his belt than the rookies Mays and Mantle, but in 1951 they were all still young, their glory seasons yet to come.

Two things made Willie Mays special: One was his absolutely unequaled collection of skills. He was a great hitter, a wonderful fielder with a super arm, a sensational slugger, and a baserunner of blazing speed and daring. Sure, for each of those talents there was someone who did it better. But no one else combined *all* of those abilities to such a degree. The other, equally magical side of his playing style was his childlike enthusiasm and love of the game, surpassing even other big-time fun lovers as Pepper Martin and Rabbit Maranville. Willie wasn't beating you to show you up; he was clobbering you because it was so much *fun.* He flew out from under his cap as he ran. He chased down fly balls with not only pure speed but also genuine exuberance. His trademark greeting, "Say hey!," somehow communicated his delightful attitude, the complete opposite of DiMaggio's quiet intensity or Ted Williams's relentless perfectionism.

Mantle points to a dent in the ball he hit 565 feet—the longest validated blast of his career—on April 17, 1953, in Washington. A computer program once calculated that, had it not struck Yankee Stadium's third deck facade, a ball Mick crushed in 1963 would have traveled more than 600 feet!

Early in the 1951 season, Willie was hitting the ball at a .477 clip for the Triple-A Minneapolis team when Durocher called him to join his Giants. After a poor start, Willie lost faith in his ability. Durocher found him weeping in the clubhouse and set the matter straight. "You're my center fielder as long as I'm the manager because you're the best center fielder I've ever seen." Willie broke out of his slump the very next day with a home run off no less than the great Warren Spahn. And Willie's incredible Hall of Fame career was off and running. Adding Willie to the lineup made it possible for Leo to move Bobby Thomson to a more comfortable position at third base, and before long Willie and the Giants were tearing up the league.

New York's center field guard changed in 1951: As Joe DiMaggio announced his retirement, the Yankees introduced rookie Mickey Mantle (left) and, across town, the Giants said "hey" to Willie Mays (right). Both Mantle and Mays would spend time in the minors, but Willie was NL Rookie of the Year.

Mays, shown here during a special day honoring him at the Polo Grounds in 1954, quickly became a fan favorite. He signed autographs tirelessly before and after games and sometimes would return to his Harlem home to play stickball with children.

Willie Mays wasn't just great, he was durable: His string of 13 consecutive 150-game seasons is an all-time record. Every year it seemed Willie's name was at the top of one statistical category or another: triples or homers (four times); batting or slugging average; runs, hits, or walks. (Not to mention his defensive prowess.) He was chosen as league MVP twice. As the best of the best, it made sense that every year Willie made the All-Star Game his own personal showcase. It was a treat that fans of the era anticipated and savored. Every year he seemed to be in the middle of every important play in the midseason classic—cracking a key double, stealing a vital base, making a critical circus catch.

By the time he retired he had hit more home runs than anyone besides Babe Ruth (660). And

Willie had lost two seasons to military service, too. Many baseball experts have called him the greatest player ever. Actress and baseball devotee Tallulah Bankhead once said, "There have been only two authentic geniuses in the world, Willie Mays and Willie Shakespeare." Who could argue with that?

Mickey Mantle was one of the most powerful players ever to play the game, and he was also one of the fastest. He invented the "tape-measure" home run, as Yankee publicists perfected the art of running out to where a long Mantle homer landed and whipping out the measuring device. Of one of his longest, a 565-foot monster smash in Washington in 1953, teammate Bob Kuzava offered, "You could have cut it up into 15 singles." Another homer, they say, would have traveled 602 feet if the Yankee Stadium facade hadn't gotten in the way.

Unfortunately Mickey missed many games with injuries and played in pain much of the rest of the time. As a teenager he had suffered a leg injury so severe that amputation seemed the likely outcome; only megadoses of the miracle drug penicillin saved his leg. During his 1961 chase of Babe Ruth's home run record he received a questionable hip injection from a doctor who wasn't exactly mainstream, the side effects of which cost him any chance at the crown. Mickey probably had more physical problems than any other of the all-time superstars. But in spite of that he still performed at a level of play that positively looms over mere mortals.

The New York Yankees all but ruled baseball from 1920–1964, and Mickey was the last representative of the line of superheroes who anchored the team: Ruth, Gehrig, DiMaggio...and the Mick. Before his rookie season, manager Casey Stengel, usually wisely circumspect when stating a player's skills, was unequivocal about the kid's prospects. He cited Mantle's exceptional power and speed and said that he should "lead the league in everything."

Mickey Mantle could not quite bring this one back in a 1951 game. Just days later in the World Series, Mickey caught his spikes in a drainpipe covering as he chased a Willie Mays fly ball. Mantle tore up his knee in the accident, turning a potentially monumental career into a merely great one.

Snider's bat over-shadowed his grace-ful center field play. In 1958, however, he hurt his arm trying to throw a ball out of the Los Angeles Coliseum—a stunt for which he was docked a day's pay.

In 1956 Mickey had the season of his career. With 52 home runs, 130 RBI, and a .353 batting average, he easily won the Triple Crown. Of course he won the Most Valuable Player Award (one of three he was voted), too. He retired with more than 500 home runs and 1,500 RBI.

With his all-American good looks and country-boy demeanor, Mickey was a superstar when it came to having fun, too. He had no problem enjoying all the pleasures New York City offered. As he said later in his life, "If I had known I was going to live this long I'd have taken better care of myself." The remark was made only half in jest: Both Mickey's grandfather and father had died of Hodgkin's disease in middle age. Late in his life Mickey came forward and publicly admitted his alcoholism. The noble fashion in which he faced his problem was easily the equal of all the heroism he had showed on the ballfield.

Although nowadays most people wouldn't mention Brooklyn's Duke Snider in the same breath as Willie and Mickey, Duke was a heck of a ballplayer himself, and a worthy member of the storied center field trio. Not many people realize that Duke, not Willie or Mickey, led the majors in homers (326) and RBI (1,031) for the decade of the '50s. Duke's batting stroke was perfectly tailored for the small dimensions of his home ballpark. ("When they tore down Ebbets Field," he said, "they tore down a piece of me.") From 1953 through '57, he hit at least 40 homers every season. In addition to fitting into his ballpark well, Duke fit in well with his team: As the sole lefty on a righty-dominated lineup, Duke hardly ever had to face the left-handed pitching that gave him trouble.

Snider possessed a different attitude than the freewheeling Mays or the fun-loving Mantle. In 1956 he and Roger Kahn collaborated on a magazine article titled, "I Play Baseball for Money, Not Fun." Regardless of his professional motivation, Snider was a smooth, graceful outfielder in the DiMaggio mold, but his arm was in a higher league. He once led his minor league with 25 assists. Stan Musial said Snider had the best throwing arm of any center fielder he had ever seen, and Stan's choice of his all-time NL outfield ranked Duke with Willie and Hank Aaron.

From a notoriety standpoint, Duke Snider played "third wheel" to fellow center field superstars Willie Mays and Mickey Mantle in New York. Even though Duke was the leading home run hitter for the decade of the '50s, his mother often felt compelled to write postcards to sportswriters complaining about Edwin's publicity deficit.

Classic Ballparks

So many things change in baseball. Players move on, teams vacate cities, and uniforms evolve with the styles of the day. But for much of baseball's Golden Age, the ballpark was a constant. To the fan, a local stadium was like a family heirloom, where generations of grandparents, parents, and children could gather in the warm sun and witness the history of the national pastime unfold before them.

Baseball's first great building boom occurred from 1909 to 1915, when some of the game's greatest parks were erected. Shibe Park, Forbes Field, League Park, Comiskey Park, Griffith Stadium, Crosley Field, Fenway Park, Tiger Stadium, Ebbets Field, Wrigley Field, and Braves Field all opened during that seven-season period.

The common trait of these new parks was that they were all built from concrete and steel. Shibe Park, home of the Philadelphia A's, was the first stadium built solely with those materials. It was ornate, built in French Renaissance style, and looked more like a bank or library than a sporting venue. The crown jewel was the domed roof—or cupola—that sat atop Connie Mack's third-floor office. It was also expensive, costing owners Mack and Ben Shibe more than $300,000 to complete. That was an exorbitant amount of money—especially compared to the roughly $10,000 spent on the wooden stadiums of that time.

While Shibe Park was built to fit inside an existing city neighborhood, many of the new fields were constructed in vacant lots, old garbage dumps, or abandoned farmland. As the urban population continued to expand, city neighborhoods rose around these hallowed ballparks. Eventually, the stadiums literally became diamonds in the rough, tucked away in a maze of urban development.

The great parks were, and still are, defined by their unique characteristics. Wrigley Field in Chicago has its ivy-covered walls. Fenway Park in Boston is home of the Green Monster. Yankee Stadium in

Forbes Field

the Bronx was rimmed with a white facade, and Ebbets Field in Brooklyn had a clothing advertisement along the right-field scoreboard that promised, "Hit Sign, Win Suit."

At Griffith Stadium, a beer advertisement adorned the right-field wall and a huge billboard shaped like a bottle jutted into the sky, 56 feet from the playing field. The outfield at Crosley Field rose as it met the wall, with the steepest incline in left and center. The right-field roof at Forbes Field was 86 feet high.

Many of the parks had been built in the dead-ball era, and the dimensions befitted a game that relied on pitching and contact hitting. Of the parks built from 1909 to 1915, the deepest center field was 515 feet (Shibe Park), while the shortest was 420 (Comiskey). By comparison, the deepest center field of any current ballpark is 435, at Minute Maid Park in Houston.

The foul lines were what generally provided each ballpark with its own unique shape and feel. The dimensions of the Polo Grounds, from left field to right field, measured 277, 433, and 258 feet. The left-field line at Ebbets Field was 419 feet away from home plate while the right-field line was a mere 301. The right-field wall, however, rose 38 feet from the ground.

Baseball's so-called "Jewel Boxes" were Ebbets, Fenway, and Wrigley. They were identified as such because they were considered small, quaint parks. The seating capacity at each of those three parks was less than 35,000, and they were designed with very little foul ground, which put the fans extremely close to the field.

"Ebbets Field was a special place, and playing in Brooklyn was special because of the fans," said Ralph Branca. "The fans were very close to the field. The grandstand was built high, not deep. I don't think it went more than 70 feet from the back of home plate to the top of the grandstand."

The Jewel Boxes quickly gave way to much larger stadiums. In 1915, Braves Field was built in Boston with a seating capacity of 40,000, which was expanded to 46,000 shortly thereafter. Yankee Stadium opened in 1923 with seats for

Wrigley Field

58,000, and Lakefront Park in Cleveland opened in 1931 with enough seating to accommodate 78,000.

Until the Dodgers and Giants left for the West Coast in 1958, New York City was home to three of baseball's classic parks—Yankee Stadium, the Polo Grounds, and Ebbets Field. Each park was unique in its structure, and throughout the 1950s, each had a Hall of Fame center fielder patrolling the outfield. Willie Mays ran down long drives in the cavernous Polo Grounds, Duke Snider perfected the nuances and oddities of Ebbets Field, and Mickey Mantle stood among the monuments at Yankee Stadium.

Perhaps it was the legendary players who roamed its grounds or the dominance of the franchise, but no other park in baseball history is as prestigious as Yankee Stadium. The Yankees originally shared the Polo Grounds with the New York Giants, the perennial National League powerhouse. But when the Yanks acquired Babe Ruth and began to outdraw the Giants at the gate, they were quickly asked to find a new home. The team settled across the Harlem River in the Bronx, which was merely a long

Ruth home run away from the Polo Grounds. On Opening Day, April 18, 1923, John Philip Sousa's band played, New York Governor Al Smith threw out the first pitch, and Ruth hit the first home run in the park that would forever be known as "The House that Ruth Built."

"When you look at Yankee Stadium there is just so much tradition," said Hall of Famer Whitey Ford, who pitched 16 seasons for the Yankees. "When I was nine years old I went to my first Yankee game and sat in the center-field bleachers. I never would have imagined I would be pitching on the mound. As a young player I remember the fun of playing at Ebbets Field and the Polo Grounds. They are gone but I wish they still had three teams in New York."

One of baseball's most ominous and recognizable architectural features is the Green Monster in left field at Fenway Park. To hitters, particularly those who are right-handed, it is an inviting target. To pitchers it is the source of many nightmares. The wall is 37 feet high and is capped by a 23-foot screen that protects the people and merchants of Lansdowne Street. It stretches 240 feet across left field, and at its base is one of baseball's last remaining hand-operated scoreboards. At the foul pole, the

wall is just 309 feet away from home, an inviting target indeed.

If Fenway's Green Monster makes hitters salivate, the canyonesque dimensions at Comiskey Park in Chicago surely made them sweat. When it first opened, the distance from home plate to the left and right field foul poles measured 362 feet. Center field was 420 feet away. The outfield wall was ten feet high. Further inciting the wrath of hitters was the distance between home plate and the grandstand, originally measured at 98 feet (later reduced to 85, then 60). All that room gave catchers plenty of space to chase down foul pops. The old Comiskey Park was always considered a pitcher's park. The reason? Chicago hurler Ed Walsh helped architects design the stadium.

Sadly, stadiums have also succumbed to the forces of change. Like many of its contemporaries, Comiskey has gone the way of the wrecking ball. Of the classic parks, only Fenway, Wrigley, and Yankee Stadium, remodeled in 1976, remain standing.

The memories, though, live on forever.

Ebbets Field

THE BOYS OF SUMMER

The Yankee team of the early '50s rightly goes down as one of the greatest ever. But the National League also featured a mighty tough aggregation—one that barely missed Yankee-like dominance. The Brooklyn Dodgers tied for the NL flag in 1946 (but lost the playoff), and then won it in 1947, '49, '52, and '53. Even more amazing, the 1946, '50, and '51 seasons each came down to the final game: If they had won those games, their record would have been an amazing seven pennants in eight years, including five in a row.

Managed by "Kindly Old Burt" Shotton through 1950 and by Chuck Dressen thereafter, this super team was perfectly suited to its cozy ballpark. In addition to featuring a crop of sluggers who could knock the ball over the fence, the pitching staff was canny and knew the value of keeping the ball down to neutralize opponents' power.

As far as sustained excellence, this was perhaps the greatest National League team of all time. There were All-Stars practically everywhere, and there were four future Hall of Famers in the starting eight. Roy Campanella had been a successful Negro League catcher, a stocky right-handed slugger who was tough as nails. "You didn't get hurt playing in the Negro Leagues," he once said. "You played no matter what . . . because if you didn't, you didn't get paid." With the glove, with the bat, and as a team leader who brooked no nonsense, Campy was among the best of all time. On a team this talent-laden, Campy's three MVP awards shine especially brightly.

In an era when there was no shortage of shortstop talent (Lou Boudreau, Marty Marion, Phil Rizzuto, Vern Stephens), Pee Wee Reese may have been the best of them all. Always among the league leaders in defensive categories, he also was a smart hitter who might lay down a surprise bunt to kick off a rally or knock one over the wall to

The support of Pee Wee Reese (throwing)—a team leader and a Southerner— was critical to Jackie Robinson's acceptance by Dodgers teammates. The team's offensive ignition, Reese ranked among the NL's top 10 in stolen bases 10 times, walks 11 times, and runs scored on 8 occasions.

Andy Pafko, Don Newcombe, and Jackie Robinson (left to right) enjoy a key late-season win in 1951. Pafko belted 30 home runs that year, while Newcombe went 20-9.

turn the tide. Pee Wee was a born leader; by the age of 19 he had already earned his nickname, "The Little Colonel."

Some historians say that this Dodger nine was simply the best defensive team of all time, and third baseman Billy Cox was a big part of that.

Casey Stengel once told Brooks Robinson that Brooks could field as well as Billy, but his arm wasn't in Cox's league. In right field the Dodgers had another man with a rifle arm, Carl Furillo, who was also a student of the many tricky hops and caroms of the Ebbets Field right-field fence. Furillo was a youngster with a minor-league contract in Reading, Pennsylvania, when Dodger scouts decided they wanted him. But the Reading people swung a tough deal. To land Carl, the Dodgers had to buy the whole team, bus and all. It cost them $5,000, but Furillo was worth it. In addition to his hard-nosed play and cannon throwing arm, he won the hitting title once and finished his career with a batting average just shy of .300.

On top of that, the Dodger pitching staff was the envy of the league. Carl Erskine, Clem Labine, and Johnny Podres joined longtime pros such as Preacher Roe (who joined the Dodgers in 1948 and suddenly discovered he could toss a mean spitter). Don Newcombe, despite his poor record in postseason play, was as dominating a righty as the NL had during this period. Joe Black and Billy Loes delivered quality innings as well.

Beyond their talent, their solid management, and their baseball smarts, the Dodgers were unique in baseball history. Their cramped ballpark, built in 1913, was a central space in the bustling urban life of Brooklyn. Perhaps because of that, the players developed a relationship with their fans that was absolutely ideal, a sympathetic connection unmatched in the history of the game. Brooklyn loved its Dodgers. The team wasn't made up of heroes on pedestals; the players were guys

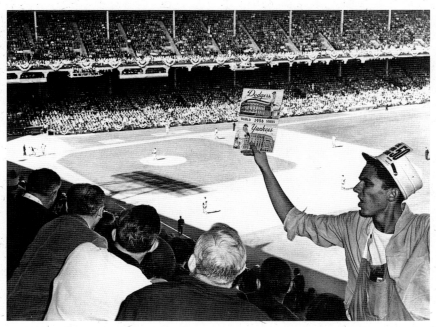

*The Yankees and Dodgers met in four of the
six World Series from 1951 to '56. This program (purchased for pennies at the time)
skyrocketed in value as a collector's item and
was worth about $300 half a century later.*

who lived down the street and who got their hair cut by the
same barber as your dad. It was more than familiarity; it was
kinship. This special connection inspired esteemed writers to
write wonderfully about the team and the people it played for.
No other baseball team (and perhaps no team in any sport) has
been the subject of anywhere near the
number of terrific books as the Brooklyn
boys. The concept of what it meant to be a
fan of "dem Bums" even extended beyond
the borough. As John Leonard put it, "It
was as if there were an underdeveloped
nation of social outlaws, the upwardly
mobile lower-middle class, and only one
baseball team with which to identify."

The team from Brooklyn had rested
comfortably in the lower reaches of the
National League from 1920 (when they
last won a pennant) until 1939, when Leo
Durocher was brought in to manage and,
together with Larry MacPhail, began to
build a great Dodger team. They visited the World Series to
play the Yankees in 1941, '47, and '49. Weird luck cost them a
few big games in those Series.

After the 1951 Thomson homer ended their season, manager Dressen tightened up his pitching staff for 1952, giving
more starts to fewer, but more dependable, pitchers. They took
the flag by 4½ games. They were buttoned up and ready to do
battle with those uptown guys, the Yankees, again.

Game 1 was vintage Dodgers. With the score tied at one in
the fourth, Carl Furillo snagged a line drive and made a terrific
throw to hold Phil Rizzuto at third. In the fifth, Andy Pafko
made a great throw followed by a great catch on back-to-back
plays. The Dodgers won 4-2 on two solo homers and a two-run
shot by Snider.

A five-run explosion in the sixth inning gave the Yankees a
7-1 win in Game 2. The Dodgers were up 3-2 in the top of the
ninth in Game 3 when a double steal by Reese and Robinson
led to two insurance runs and a 5-3 win. Allie Reynolds shut
them out in Game 4, and the Series was all tied up.

Game 5 was another Yank-Dodger matchup filled with
superlative play. A two-run homer by the Duke staked the
Dodgers to a 4-0 lead heading into the last of the fifth. But
Johnny Mize returned the favor, belting a three-run homer to
put the Yankees up 5-4. Then Carl Erskine tightened his belt

and retired the next 19 Yankees in a row. The Dodgers tied it in the seventh and won it in the 11th. It took a circus catch by Furillo to keep Mize's 11th-inning smash from landing in the seats, a play that sealed the Dodger victory.

The Yankees tied the Series at three games each with a 3-2 win in Game 6, although Duke Snider's two homers in that game tied him with Ruth and Gehrig for most ever in a World Series (four). Game 7 was another nail-biter. The Yanks tacked up single runs in the fourth, fifth, sixth, and seventh. The Dodgers scored single tallies in the fourth and fifth themselves, and in the last of the seventh, it looked like the Brooklyn boys were going to do some damage. They had two men on with Duke and Jackie due up. But Stengel reached into his bullpen and yanked out Bob Kuzava, the big, strong lefty they called "Sarge" for his no-nonsense style. It was one of those Stengel moves that, while it seemed questionable at the time, worked out the way Casey planned. Duke popped out to third. The runners were off and going when Jackie looped a lazy fly toward the right side of the infield. Sarge didn't move. Nei-

Lefty Bob Kuzava (hatless, in center) had a decade-long but undistinguished career—with one exception. In his only appearance in the 1952 World Series, he retired the last eight Dodgers to save the Yankees' 4-2 victory in Game 7.

ther did first baseman Joe Collins, who seemed to have lost the ball in the sun. Second baseman Billy Martin had to make a charging, lunging, knee-high grab to keep several runs from scoring. The Series was all but over, with nary a peep from either offense for the last two innings. The Yanks had done it to the Dodgers again, in another wildly sensational Series.

The 1953 Dodgers were probably the strongest of any of their clubs of this era. They batted .285 as a team (the highest team average to that point) and scored nearly 200 more runs than any other NL bunch. They were easily the top fielding team in the league. Once again Dressen made sure only four pitchers got more than 20 starts. But it took just six games for the Yankees to win the world championship, even though the last game was won in the bottom of the ninth on a single by Billy Martin. Martin batted .500 for the Series, and his even dozen hits were just one short of the record.

Roy Campanella's low center of gravity (at 5'8", 200 pounds) made him an uninviting target for runners trying to score. Here, in the 1953 World Series, the Yankees' Billy Martin bounces off him—tagged for the final out of Game 4.

"Next year" finally happened for the Dodgers in 1955. They had a new manager. Chuck Dressen, buoyed by his success, had asked for a multiyear contract after the '53 Series. Team management refused; they bounced Dressen and hired Walter Alston, who managed the team for the next 23 years with one-year contracts.

In this Series, the home team won every game but the last one. There was some bad blood between the two teams; they were getting familiar with each other. Robinson stole home in the first game (at age 36), but when Billy Martin tried to do the same, Roy Campanella didn't just tag the brash young Yank at the plate; he crunched him. After the game Campanella said matter-of-factly, "I

Jackie Robinson stole home 19 times in his career, the most memorable of which was his slither under Yogi Berra's tag in the opener of the 1955 World Series. Robinson was 36 years old at the time.

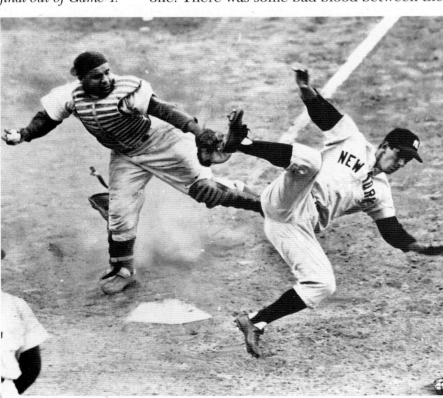

tagged him too low; I should have put it right in his mouth." In Game 7, with Brooklyn leading 2-0 and two men on base, Yogi Berra sliced a liner deep to left. Just-in defensive replacement Sandy Amoros tracked down the drive and turned it into a rally-killing double play with a super throw back to the infield. Johnny Podres, who had turned in a fine performance in Game 3, allowed just three singles in the final three innings. Finally, after seven tries (and five against the Yanks), the Dodgers were world champs. *The New York Times* headline read: "Bombers, conceding better team won, show no sadness in dressing room." The Yankees weren't "sad," but they weren't intimidated either. As usual, they returned to the Series in 1956. Even though they lost the first two games, they took the Series anyway when Don Larsen threw his masterpiece perfect game in Game 5 and 23-year-old Johnny Kucks tossed a three-hit shutout in Game 7.

Don Larsen saw the writing on the wall with two innings to go in his unprecedented and unequaled World Series perfect game against the Dodgers in 1956.

Years of being nothing but tailgaters in the Yankees' rearview mirror ended for the Dodgers in the '55 Series. This Game 7 catch by Sandy Amoros, followed by a throw to double-up a runner, preserved a lead and gave Brooklyn its first world title.

INDIANS' WARPATH REROUTED

As the 1954 season dawned, there was no reason to believe the Yankees wouldn't win another AL flag (and probably bounce the Dodgers in the World Series again). But that season was one of the two in that decade when the Yanks didn't taste AL championship champagne. It wasn't that Casey's boys weren't good. They won 103 games (no AL club had done that since 1946). They scored 805 runs to lead the league, and they had the best batting average and slugging percentage, too.

Amazingly, the Cleveland Indians were even better. Cleveland won 111 games (the second-highest win total ever in a 154-game season). Their pitching staff was one of the all-time juggernauts. Three Cleveland starters were nearly perfect. Early Wynn, he of the unshaven scowl, led the league in games started; Mike Garcia led in ERA; Bob Lemon led in complete games; and Wynn and Lemon tied for the league lead in wins. It was the pitching equivalent of Gehrig-DiMaggio-Keller. All three ranked in the top four in games started, innings pitched, and ERA, and Wynn finished third in complete games. Lemon and Wynn won 23 games each; Garcia won 19. But they weren't the only Tribe hurlers to rack up some amazing numbers. Even 35-year-old Bob Feller still had enough stuff to go 13-3 with an ERA just over 3.00. Hal Newhouser, who won back-to-back MVP awards in the '40s, also won seven games, and newcomers Don Mossi and Ray Narleski showed flashes of excellence throughout the season.

Over in the National League, Willie Mays, who had been in military service since early in 1952, came back and established himself as one of the great ones. Willie's 13 triples led the league, as did his .345 batting average and .667 slugging percentage, and he was third in homers with 41. The Giant pitching staff was on top with a 3.09 ERA, and Johnny Antonelli won 21 games.

The Series looked like it would be a challenging, drawn-out clash between two exciting and surprising clubs. Willie Mays turned that inside out in no time. Game 1 was knotted at two runs each as the Tribe batted in the top of the eighth. The men from Cleveland put runners on first and second with nobody out and big, strong Vic Wertz at the plate. Wertz creamed a Bob Lemon pitch to deep right center. Writers

The '54 Indians staff, who pitched their team to an AL-record 111 victories (since broken), has been called the best ever. Front row, left to right: Mike Garcia, Hal Newhouser, manager Al Lopez, Don Mossi, Bob Feller. Back row, left to right: Early Wynn, Bob Lemon, Bob Hooper, Art Houtteman, Dave Hoskins, Ray Narleski.

To prepare for his part as Grover Cleveland Alexander in the 1952 film The Winning Team, future president Ronald Reagan worked with Indians ace Bob Lemon. The role wasn't such a "stretch" for Reagan, who played ball at Eureka College in Illinois.

agreed that Willie Mays caught the ball with a sensational over-the-shoulder grab.

But this is the most famous example (Ruth's "called shot" is second) of how legend can slop over into exaggeration and the merely great becomes absurd. Some books say Mays caught the ball 460 feet from home plate. Others stretch the mileage to 505 feet (that would have put Mays halfway up the Knickerbocker beer sign in the center-field stands). While it's true that dead center field in the Polo Grounds was around 485 feet, Willie wasn't there; he was in front of the right-field bleachers, which are much more like 430 feet away, and he caught the ball before he reached the warning track. So it's reasonable to say the ball traveled more like 410 feet, or about where Bill Virdon later robbed Yogi Berra in the 1960 World Series. (No less a baseball luminary than Leo Durocher called the catch "routine—for Mays.") But the New York press immediately dubbed it "The Catch."

The truth is, what happened next was more incredible and much more important. After flagging the ball down, Willie unleashed a true miracle (which should be called "The Throw"), a spectacular heave back to the infield that kept the Indians from scoring. In an instant the gas seemed to disappear from the Tribe's balloon. In the last of the ninth Giant pinch hitter Dusty Rhodes whacked a three-run homer that landed barely 260 feet from home plate. Rhodes homered again in the second game and delivered a two-run, pinch-hit single in the third game. The surprising Giants had swept the potent Indians.

In what has become known forevermore as simply "The Catch," Willie Mays ran down this Vic Wertz drive late in Game 1 of the 1954 World Series. The most a-Mays-ing part of the play was "The Throw"—his feat of wheeling and firing the ball back in to prevent the go-ahead run from scoring.

Bobby Avila, here caught in a pickle during the World Series, was the 1954 American League batting champ. The Indians second sacker was formerly a pro soccer player in Mexico. Following his baseball days, he was elected mayor of Vera Cruz, Mexico.

THE ADVENT OF TELEVISION

Few fans owned television sets when Red Barber hosted the first televised game (from Brooklyn's Ebbets Field) on August 26, 1939. Within a dozen years, however, baseball had taken full advantage of the TV boom. Suddenly able to see the faces behind the voices, fans gave broadcasters celebrity status, making Mel Allen, Vin Scully, Harry Caray, and Barber as famous as Willie, Mickey, and the Duke.

On radio, broadcasters had used literary license to exaggerate on behalf of their employers—usually the teams they covered. Routine fly balls became hard drives to the fences; easy infield outs became spectacular plays. But television brought reality. A listener might be fooled, but a viewer could not.

According to the late Marty Glickman, one of those who made a smooth transition to television, "Announcers had to learn not to talk. With radio, you had to create the entire scene and situation because the listener couldn't see a thing. You had to be a story-teller, a word-painter. But brevity is the key to television reporting. Commentary should be succinct and should occur during lapses in the action. Don't tell the fans what they see but what they can't see, what they might expect, and what to look for."

Television personalized the game not only because fans could now see what was going on but also because announcers, with less to say about action on the field, began to reveal personal insights about the players. At the same time, advances in technology allowed TV viewers to see games from angles even ballpark fans couldn't see.

At first, television was trying. Announcers making the transition from radio to TV didn't know whether to talk more or less and realized their mistakes would become painfully obvious to fans who could now see as well as hear.

In 1948, when Chicago's WGN put the game onto the small screen, Jack Brickhouse kept one eye on the field and the other on the monitor. He also mistakenly placed his trust in the hands of an inexperienced camera operator.

"During one game," he said, "the batter hit a tremendous fly. I described the flight of the ball and the fielder chasing it and was sure I saw him catch the ball as it came down inside the park. But the camera followed it over the wall, over housetops, and on—until the cameraman realized he was not following the baseball at all but had picked up a bird in flight!"

Long before Brickhouse became a Chicago institution, Mel Allen had established himself as the Voice of the Yankees. His tenure ran from 1940 to '65, with three years out for wartime Army duty. Discovered as a

Mel Allen

PA announcer at college football games, the one-time Birmingham lawyer not only made a smooth transition from radio to television but convinced GM George Weiss to lure Red Barber from Brooklyn to the Yankee broadcast booth. Phil Rizzuto, the team's star shortstop, joined them after he retired in '56.

Hiring a former player was no surprise; Cleveland's Jack Graney had started the trend in 1932, when management decided popular ex-players on the air would attract listeners. Most of them openly rooted for their teams, irritating baseball purists.

"I am a Yankee rooter first and a broadcaster second," Rizzuto admitted late in his career. "I don't call myself a journalist because I just can't do a game straight. All announcers have favorites. My whole life has been the Yankees: 40 years as a broadcaster, 16 as a player, plus four in the farm system. What else could you expect?"

Reporting rather than rooting became a hallmark for several announcers who later received the Ford C. Frick Award, earning a niche in the broadcasters' wing of the Baseball Hall of Fame.

"The guys I emulated growing up were Vin Scully, Mel Allen, and Red Barber," said sportscaster Steve Albert. "All three had so much credibility without being homers or shills. They were basic, down-to-earth broadcasters who exuded professionalism."

Scully, who began with the Brooklyn Dodgers in 1950 and stayed with the team when it moved to California, is still the voice of the Los Angeles Dodgers. His voice is like a sunny day—relaxed, warm, and comforting. Scully's call of the final inning of Sandy Koufax's 1965 perfect game, noted for its poetic descriptions, is a baseball classic.

Said Steve Albert of Scully. "I only wish I could hear him more. If anybody wants to grow up to be an announcer, the way to do it is to study his style." One measure of how highly Scully is respected is the fact that the Dodger Stadium pressbox is named after him, even though he's still working.

Detroit's Ernie Harwell received the same honor in 2002 when he ended his 55-year career in the broadcast booth. Branch Rickey brought the soft-spoken Southerner to Brooklyn in 1948, actually trading a minor-league player for him after hearing him call an Atlanta Crackers game. Harwell was announcing the 1951 Dodger–Giant playoff game on television when Bobby Thomson hit his "shot heard 'round the world." He later worked for the Giants and Orioles before joining the Tigers in 1960.

Announcers have always had trademarks. Mel Allen popularized the home run call, "Going, going, gone." Russ Hodges said "Bye-bye, baby" when someone connected, while Vin Scully simply said "Forget it." Both Phil Rizzuto and Harry Caray often accented their accounts with exclamations of "Holy cow!"

Before television made such calls impossible, Pittsburgh's Rosey Rowswell reported Ralph Kiner home runs by yelling, "Open the window, Aunt Minnie, here it comes!" and then smashing a lightbulb, suggesting "Aunt Minnie" had failed to get her apartment window open in time.

Phil Rizzuto (left) and Russ Hodges

Bob Prince, who joined Rowswell as an assistant in 1948, soon won recognition for his slow, nasal twang, coupled with his knowledge of and passion for the game. He called the Pirates "Bucs" or "Buccos" and openly rooted for "a bloop and a blast" when the team trailed by a run.

Prince was capable of commanding an audience even when his team was likely to lose. Equally colorful off-mike, he won bets by diving from his third-floor window into the pool of the Hotel Chase in St. Louis, keeping quiet for a solid hour on an airplane trip, and parading in Bermuda shorts from the center-field clubhouse of the Polo Grounds to home plate, where Giants manager Leo Durocher kissed him on both cheeks.

Because broadcasters lasted longer than players and often received less money, teams were delighted to help them achieve celebrity status. Publicity stunts, such as broadcasting games from the stands, helped. Harry Caray, who thrived in his common-man image, was announcing from the Wrigley Field bleachers one day when he provided a graphic

description of Curt Flood's "spectacular catch" at the base of the center-field wall. In actuality, Caray could not even see the play as it occured because it was out of his line of vision.

Day in and day out Carey leaned out of the broadcast booth to lead the singing of "Take Me Out to the Ballgame" during the seventh-inning stretch. He was with the Cubs in '91 when he, his son Skip (announcing for the Braves), and his grandson Chip became the first three-generation family to announce the same game. The Carays, perhaps more than anyone else in baseball, proved the power of TV as an entertainment medium. Their commentary spanned the gamut from humorous to sarcastic and kept fans laughing even when team performance warranted the opposite reaction.

Some humor was inadvertent. Earl Gillespie of the Milwaukee Braves once said, "Al Deck is in the on-dark circle." And Phil Rizzuto, early in his career, said, "Here's the pitch. Yogi Berra swings and hits a high foul behind the plate. It's coming down . . . and Yogi Berra makes the catch."

Television broadcasters brought the game to an entirely new audience, teaching both casual fans and baseball neophytes the wonders of the game, bringing it directly into their homes and their hearts.

In fact, fans never again would have to leave their living rooms to see their favorite stars. To many, a ballgame on television with a soda and a snack was the perfect way to spend an afternoon.

LARGER THAN LIFE

Most people in postwar America had money to spend and a car to take them anywhere they wanted to go. There were more leisure activities available than ever before. Whereas in the past baseball had been primarily directed toward men, with the occasional "Ladies' Day" tossed in, 1950s baseball began to emphasize the *family* nature of a day or night out at the ballpark. The catchword of the era—"Togetherness"—became baseball's, too. Effort was made to improve the food and clean up the park (especially the restrooms). "Giveaways"—toys or trinkets given out to fans to make them think they were getting something for free—first came into existence. Attendance increased from 1946's amazing 18.5 million to as high as 20.8 million just two years later.

Actor Paul Newman once did a bit for I've Got a Secret, one of the most popular panel TV shows of the '50s, in which he posed as an Ebbets Field vendor. This little guy—name of Charley Potter—was the real thing, hawking trinkets in 1950.

In addition to encouraging families to enjoy a visit to the ballpark, Major League Baseball also made it easy for them to enjoy it at home. By 1950 every home game in New York City was televised. In just two years (from 1950 to '52), the percentage of U.S. homes with a television increased from 25 percent to 80 percent.

However, the American population was shifting. More Americans, with their new cars and new jobs, were headed out of the cities and into the suburbs. Or, they were extending the road trip even more, leaving the agrarian South and the industrial northeast for exciting places such as Florida or California, places that glistened with all the promise only America can conjure. The movement was reflected in ballgame attendance. By 1951 attendance had dipped to 16 million, and it continued to drop for the next five years. At first, ballclubs hardly felt the pinch; dollars for television rights easily made up the difference. But change was on the horizon.

According to Bill James in the *Historical Baseball Abstract*, "In the early part of the '50s, every team approached the game with the same essential offensive philosophy: get people on base and hit home runs." The base-on-balls and the homer became two of the most common plays in the game. The 1950 Red Sox were the proudest adherents of this philosophy. They became the last team for decades to score more than 1,000 runs in one season. They were also the last team ever to bat as high as .302. They finished third.

During this decade, the "stolen" base never seemed so truly illegal, so absolutely an act of pilferage. Just 15 steals led the American League in 1950—the fewest ever.

In 1946 Hank Greenberg had become the first man to hit 40 homers without batting .300. Before long, that became the rule. The rarity became the homer guy who *could* hit for average. Proof of this is that only once in the decade did a batter amass 400 total bases in one season (Hank Aaron in 1959). The muscular bombers with the puny batting averages were usually slow-footed left fielders or even slower first basemen who were frequently indifferent to defense. By 1959, there was such a complete rift between the two skills of slugging and batting for average that Harmon Killebrew tied for the AL home run lead but failed to bat even .250.

Harmon Killebrew was the son of a professional wrestler and the grandson of a man said to be the strongest soldier in the Union Army during the Civil War. "Killer," a big-leaguer at 18, muscled up for 573 home runs over 22 seasons.

After the 1959 season, famous wheeler-dealer general manager Frank Lane of Cleveland pulled off a stunning trade. He swapped the league's 1959 home run champ, Rocky Colavito, to the Detroit Tigers for the league batting average titleholder, Harvey Kuenn. Cleveland fans (particularly the bobby-soxers who took to the

An estimated 200,000 San Franciscans welcomed the arrival of the Giants from New York on April 14, 1958. The next day, sluggers Willie Mays (left) and Hank Sauer (right) helped their club beat the Dodgers, 8-0, in the first game ever played on the West Coast.

"dreamy" good looks of Colavito) were outraged by the trade. Lane's response: "What's the big deal? We just got a steak for a hamburger."

But it was more than Rocky and Harmon. There seemed to be dozens of sluggers who couldn't hit anything but homers. Big strong guys like Gil Hodges, Bobby Thomson, Hank Sauer, Ralph Kiner, Luke Easter, Joe Adcock, Gus Bell, Walt Dropo, Vic Wertz, "the original" Frank Thomas, and Wally Post. In 1956 a brash kid named Dick Stuart hit 66 home runs in the minors. In the majors his total lack of interest in defense earned him one of the game's great nicknames: "Dr. Strangeglove."

THE MAN

At the same time these "partial" players were flourishing, there was a player appearing in the box scores every day who was a *total* star. He did everything well, even though his team didn't make much news during the '50s. His name was Stan Musial. Beginning in 1941, and for the better part of 20 seasons, he did it all. He was fast. He played superb defense in left field before being moved to first base later in his career. He hit doubles and triples as well as homers. He was sturdy—from 1946 through 1955 he missed only 17 games. In 1948 Stan hit .376 and cracked 39 homers (one more dinger and he would have claimed the Triple Crown), 131 RBI, and 46 doubles and 18 triples among his 230 hits. His 429 bases were the highest accumulated since 1930, and no one topped that number for the rest of the century.

Musial is the only person to rank in the top 20 lifetime in singles, doubles, triples, and homers (though his rank has since slipped to number 22 in homers). When he retired he held the NL record for hits, games

Four-time NL wins leader Robin Roberts once pitched 28 consecutive complete games. In 1950, he clinched the pennant for Philadelphia's "Whiz Kids" with a ten-inning gem in the season finale—in his third start in just five days.

played, and runs scored. There are two reasons why Stan Musial's name doesn't leap to everyone's mind as one of the greatest players ever: One, without the bravado of Ted Williams or the elegance of Joe DiMaggio, Stan frankly just didn't call attention to himself; and two, Stan the Man played in St. Louis, a much smaller media market than New York or Boston.

On June 3, 1955, Elvis "The King" Presley played a free show in Lubbock, Texas, but one had to buy a ticket to Ebbets Field that day to see Stan "The Man" Musial "rock" his 300th home run. Weeks later, he hit another to beat the AL, 6-5, in the 12th inning of the All-Star Game.

BIG BOBS

Along with the big sluggers, every team in the '50s seemed to have a big pitching ace: a strong right-handed hurler who threw more than 250 innings every year and both won and lost in double figures. With big guys swinging for the fences, the issue of pitching in the '50s was consistency. Pitching was defined as something you counted on. Reliability was the keyword. And it seemed like almost every other pitcher was named Bob. There was Bob Feller, of course, and Robin Roberts. Other "Big Bobs" include Friend, Rush, Buhl, Lemon, and Turley. Others who pitched in this "Bob" style included Don Newcombe, Early

Wynn, Frank Lary, and Virgil Trucks. Trucks had an absolutely impossible year for the Tigers in 1952. He pitched two no-hitters, becoming one of just a handful of big-leaguers to toss a pair of "no-nos" in one season. But those two victories were 40 percent of Virgil's season total. He finished the year 5-19.

With big, strong hurlers flinging pitches at big, slow batters, baseball decided it was time to try to increase the game's safety factor (and protect their investment). Not surprisingly, Branch Rickey was at the forefront of the innovation. The first team required to wear batting helmets was the 1952 Pittsburgh Pirates, where Rickey had gone after being squeezed out of Brooklyn in a management power play. Oddly, the '52 Bucs may have been the team *least* in need of protection of all time. They lost a breathtaking 112 games (out of just 154). Joe Garagiola, then Pirate backup catcher, was fond of killing time by doing pretend radio interviews with other guys in the bullpen. He asked one teammate, "Do you think these helmets would be better if they had chlorophyll in them?" (Chlorophyll was then the hot new ingredient in many consumer products.) "No," was the response, "I think they'd be better if they had some ballplayers in them." All kidding aside, by 1955 every National League player was required to wear a helmet when batting. The AL passed a matching rule in 1956. Rules requiring players to keep the helmets on when they reached base weren't implemented for a while.

At the end of the 1954 season, only two active pitchers had six 20-win seasons on their résumés, and both pitched for the Indians. The "Bobs"—Lemon (left) and Feller—had contrasting weapons. Lemon's was a sinker, and Feller fired a nasty fastball once crudely timed at 107.9 mph.

CAREERS CUT SHORT

With Willie Mays, Mickey Mantle, and Hank Aaron among its talented stars, baseball enjoyed a bountiful harvest of new players during the '50s. But fortune failed to smile on all.

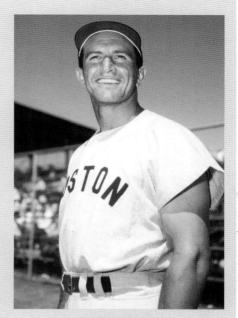

Harry Agganis

Injuries have always been part of the game. Though Ray Chapman was the only on-field fatality, the long list of career-stopping injuries includes Hall of Famers as well as workaday players. Lou Gehrig retired at 36 after being diagnosed with amyotropic lateral sclerosis, which took his life in 1941; Mickey Cochrane suffered a triple skull fracture when hit by a pitch in 1937; and arthritis forced Sandy Koufax to retire at age 31.

Roy Campanella, three-time league MVP and All-Star catcher of the Brooklyn Dodgers, was permanently paralyzed in January 1958 when his car skidded off an icy street, slammed into a telephone pole, and flipped over. Confined to a wheelchair, Campy eventually went to work for Los Angeles Dodgers management.

Less than one year earlier, star Cleveland left-hander Herb Score (named 1955's AL Rookie of the Year after he fanned a rookie-record 245 batters) had appeared to be en route to a Hall of Fame career. But on May 7, 1957, he was struck in the eye by a line drive hit by Yankee infielder Gil McDougald. Score was never the same again. He pitched only two more full seasons, 1959 and '60, before retiring at age 29.

The story of Harry Agganis may be the saddest of all. A New England high school star, Agganis became an All-America quarterback at Boston University. The "Golden Greek" signed with the Red Sox, then drove in 57 runs as a Sox rookie in 1954. Agganis opened '55 with a .313 average through 25 games before leaving the team for good. Agganis succumbed to leukemia, dying that June when he was just 26 years old.

Another rule change in the 1950s seems positively quaint today. Until 1954, players routinely just tossed their gloves on the field when they went in to take their turns at bat. The tradition probably began way, way back in history. But at this time, someone high up in the baseball establishment must have decided there could be a problem—someone could trip over a glove on the field, or a ball could bounce off one, so a new rule was instituted. Players had to carry their gloves all the way back to the dugout every inning. While the logic seems clear, the most amazing part of all this is that no baseball historian has ever been able to find one single incident of a glove on the field interfering with the game being played *in any way*.

THE BRAVES REAPPEAR AND STUN THE YANKEES

The Boston Braves, whose 1948 World Series appearance couldn't make up for decades of futility, moved to Milwaukee in 1953, becoming the first big-league team to pack up and go elsewhere since the Baltimore Orioles became the New York Highlanders (later the Yankees) in 1903. The move sparked something in the team; a crop of talented youngsters emerged, and with Milwaukee fans coming out in droves and shouting their heads off, the Braves began to build a terrific team.

Bill Bruton was a speedy center fielder who seemed to chase everything down on defense and also used his fleet feet to make himself an offensive force, swiping bases and knocking triples. At shortstop, Johnny Logan was a super fielder with some pop in his bat. There were two bright lights at first: slick-fielding Frank Torre and big bomber Joe Adcock, whose 18 total bases in one game in 1951 set a record that lasted half a century. (Two games after setting the record, he was beaned and had to be carried from the field.) Del Crandall was widely accepted as the league's best backstop.

At third was Eddie Mathews—a man Ty Cobb claimed had one of the four sweetest swings he had ever seen. Eddie had three straight seasons of more than 40 homers and 100 RBI, and his defense was smooth, too.

Henry Aaron was beginning to show the power and speed that would put him among the game's immortals. Aaron was that most curious of characters: a baseball natural, with physical talent beyond belief, who spent long hours at work to make himself better. While Ted Williams studied hitting, Aaron studied pitchers, so he was terrific at anticipating what he would see on each offering from each hurler. His batting style was unorthodox: He hit almost totally off his front foot. (This is very hard to do well, which is why most batting coaches suggest their students do otherwise.) But with his incredibly strong wrists, Aaron could afford to wait— and wait—to swing. With his keen eye, he made absolutely sure of the pitch's velocity and location, then quickly made needed adjustments and swatted the ball. Far. Aaron's unhurried style was not unlike Joe DiMaggio's, but while Joe D. was

The sky was the limit for 20-year-old rookie Eddie Mathews in 1952. Braves manager Tommy Holmes already had concluded that Mathews could "hit a ball farther than any man who ever played baseball."

Hank Aaron, here safe at home in a 1956 game, scored 100 or more runs every season from '55 to '67. That 13-year streak still stands as the record along with Lou Gehrig's from '26 to '38.

In 1951, the Yankees traded Lew Burdette to the Braves for Johnny Sain (pictured). Six years later, Burdette came back to haunt the New Yorkers with a World Series tour de force: three complete-game victories over the Yanks—two of them (including Game 7) shutouts.

praised for his "elegance," one would occasionally read of Aaron's "laziness." Though Americans had grown up a lot since the arrival of Jackie Robinson, the race card was still there.

Aaron was cool and steady. He wasn't likely to make circus catches like Mays or unleash jaw-dropping throws like Roberto Clemente, and he didn't challenge pitchers to throw at him and then settle the issue with fists like Frank Robinson. But he out-homered all of them (and Babe Ruth, too) and ranks among the top three batsmen of all time in homers, RBI, extra-base hits, total bases, runs, and hits.

On the mound the Braves had no less than Warren Spahn and Lew Burdette as their two aces, along with such second-liners as the ever-reliable Bob Buhl. Spahn's 363 lifetime wins are still the most ever by a left-hander. His career ERA was 3.09, and he hurled 63 shutouts. Perhaps even more amazing, in today's era of "get-one-guy" relief specialists, setup men, and closers, is that Spahn threw 382 complete games in his career, an impossible total to even consider, much less appreciate, nowadays, when a mere handful of complete games is enough to lead the league. Twelve times Spahnie had more than 20 complete games in a season. Throwing from the classic full looping lefty windup (nothing abbreviated or rushed for Spahn), he understood his job perfectly. He described a pitcher's role simply as upsetting the hitter's timing. Someone

once said, "If an alien from outer space landed on the ballfield where Warren Spahn was pitching, he may not have any idea what Spahn was doing, but he could tell in an instant that Spahn was the best in the world at doing it."

Spahn's cohort on the hill, Lew Burdette, had been a Yankee farmhand, but the New Yorkers dealt him away in 1951 for Johnny Sain and threw in $50,000. Burdette's secret weapon was his spitball, or non-spitball. Often accused of dampening up the sphere, he was never caught doing it and always denied it. Maybe he did wet up an occasional offering or two, maybe he didn't, but just the thought of it in the hitters' minds in effect gave Burdette an extra pitch. For nine years he was one of the top righties in the league. He retired with one of the best control records (walks/nine innings) of all time (not, incidentally, what you'd expect from a spitballer).

In 1956, the Braves were in first place much of the year. Their five-game losing streak in early September started their decline, and by the end of the month the Dodgers were on top to stay, even though the final margin was just one game.

Early in 1957, the Braves acquired Red Schoendienst to be their second baseman, and they were on their way. Future Hall of Famer Schoendienst was terrifically reliable, both offensively and defensively. His 200 hits for the season led all NLers. Even a season-ending injury to center fielder Bruton in July couldn't hold the Braves back. They promoted a minor-leaguer named Bob Hazle (with the wonderful nickname "Hurricane") to fill Bruton's slot. In his first game in the starting lineup the rookie cracked a double and a single, and the Braves took off on a ten-game winning streak. During that streak Hazle hit .545. By the time the season ended

AN INSPIRATIONAL COMEBACK

Jimmy Piersall was a highly touted young ballplayer in the Boston Red Sox organization and was ready to make an impact on the major-league level when his career came to an abrupt halt. Depression and anxiety overcame the center fielder and drove him from the baseball diamond to a mental hospital. He missed most of the 1952 season after suffering a mental breakdown.

Helped by electroshock therapy, Piersall overcame his illness to have a fine major-league career. He returned to baseball in 1953 and went 6-for-6 in his first game back. In 1956, he batted .293 and led the AL with 40 doubles. He was elected to the All-Star Team in 1954 and '56 and earned Gold Glove honors in 1958 and '61. Over 17 big-league seasons, Piersall batted .272.

Opposing fans often taunted him, but Piersall adopted the philosophy that playing baseball should be fun. Armed with a carefree attitude, Piersall offset the pressures of baseball by pulling more than a few zany pranks. He once hid behind the center-field monuments at Yankee Stadium during a game, and he circled the bases backward after belting his 100th career home run. "That way I can see where I've been," he said. "I always know where I'm going."

Piersall's comeback inspired a book, which was made into the 1957 film *Fear Strikes Out*, starring Anthony Perkins as Piersall.

Jimmy Piersall

In 1957, Milwaukee's Red Shoendienst, Lew Burdette, and Hank Aaron (left to right) helped wrest the World Series trophy away from New York City for the first time since '48.

he had batted .403. Alas, lightning, even in a Hurricane, doesn't strike twice: '58 would be Hazle's last year in the majors, but he had forever earned himself a spot among baseball's one-year wonders. Twenty-three-year-old Aaron had a breakout season and was named league MVP as he and Mathews combined for 76 homers and 226 RBI. The Braves finished eight games ahead of St. Louis. The fans in Milwaukee were beside themselves with joy. They hadn't had a major-league team in town since the 1880s; this was only their fifth year with the Braves, and they were in the World Series.

The Yankees were where everyone expected them to be: 13-5 favorites to take the World Series. The Yankees, typically, were full of themselves. They had been in the Series every year but one in the past eight and had racked up six world championships in that time.

Whitey Ford bested Spahn in Game 1, but Burdette tossed a seven-hitter in Game 2 to even the Series. Someone in the Yankee organization (the culprit has been variously iden- tified as Mickey Mantle, Casey

Mickey Mantle, here forced at third as the Yanks were shut out in Game 7 of the World Series, won his second of three American League MVP awards in 1957. During the Series, however, he suffered a shoulder injury that hampered him the rest of his career.

Stengel, and some front office flack) saw the wild Milwaukee celebration after the Game 2 victory and proclaimed it "bush" (comparing it to an unprofessional, amateur celebration). That was a mistake. When the Yankee team arrived in Milwaukee for Game 3 of the Series, they were greeted with thousands of signs saying "Welcome to Bushville."

Bob Buhl and five other Brave pitchers got tagged with a 12-3 defeat in the third game. A tenth-inning homer by Mathews won Game 4. Burdette was called on again for Game 5, which he won by pitching a shutout. The game's only run was scored via consecutive singles by Mathews, Aaron, and Adcock. In Game 6, Frank Torre, Hank Aaron, Hank Bauer, and Yogi Berra all homered, but Yogi's was the only non-solo job, and the Yanks took the game 3-2.

The Braves gave the ball back to Burdette for Game 7. He wasn't intimidated. All "Nitro Lew" did was shut out the Yankees again, by the score of 5-0, in his third complete game of the Series. The Braves had a moment of unease in the ninth when the Yankees loaded the bases, but Mathews was able to snag a Bill "Moose" Skowron smash down the third-base line

The Braves, habitual also-rans, stunned the Yankees in a seven-game World Series in 1957, igniting celebrations both on and off the field. In Milwaukee, Wisconsin Avenue was crammed with revelers who, said the local newspaper, rose up for "the craziest, wildest night Milwaukee has ever known."

Thanks to Bill Skowron, the 1958 Yankees became the first team in almost 35 years to recover from a three games-to-one deficit to win the World Series. "Moose" delivered the key blows against the Braves: the winning RBI in Game 6 and a three-run homer in the eighth inning of the finale.

and step on the base to end the game. Burdette's feat of three Series victories was just the second of its kind in 37 years, but Lew hadn't only notched three victories, he had hurled two shutouts, and he had done it against the nearly invincible New York Yankees.

The Braves commandeered the NL flag again in 1958 and once again ran up against the Yanks in the Series. The Braves were leading three games to one at the start of Game 5, but the Yanks rocked Burdette, and Turley pitched a shutout. Game 6 was a tight one. The men from New York scored two in the top of the tenth to break a 2-2 tie. In the last of the inning, a walk and two singles brought one run in for Milwaukee, but they left men stranded on first and third. Game 7 was also tied at two runs apiece going into the eighth, but the Yankees unleashed a little "Five O'clock Lightning," including a three-run homer by Moose Skowron, and the Series was effectively over.

THE HUSTLER AND THE MIDGET

Several baseball historians have pointed out that baseball was in deep trouble by the mid-'50s, but the moguls who ran the game seemed blind to the facts. Attendance was down nearly everywhere, for several reasons. Frankly, the slow, slugging style of play wasn't very attractive. The dominance of the Yankees, and the two other New York teams as well, made it a great time to grow up a baseball fan in New York City, but fans elsewhere weren't so enthralled. And when there are dynasties, there are also schlubs, perennial losers. Besides New York, baseball had four multiteam cities: Chicago, St. Louis, Philadelphia, and Boston. Most of the time at least one of those teams was pretty

miserable. The '52
Boston Braves
couldn't reach
300,000 in atten-
dance—and they
had won the pen-
nant just five sea-
sons before. In
Philadelphia, the A's
drew just 304,000
fans—fewer than
4,000 per game—in
1954. But the worst
were the St. Louis
Browns, who drew
fewer than 250,000

*Shortly after acquir-
ing controlling
interest in the St.
Louis Browns, Bill
Veeck introduced
himself by personally
distributing free
beverages during
"Drink on the House
Night" in July 1951.*

people in 1950. The impact of television on big-league ballgame attendance can't be overstated; why pay to see rotten teams when you can watch much better teams from the comfort of your home—for free? Proof of TV's power is that by the end of the decade the minor leagues had seriously shrunk, and the Negro Leagues were completely gone.

One man seemed to have the magic touch when it came to boosting home attendance, and doing it fast. That man was Bill Veeck, and his blatant hucksterism was a skill that few other owners wanted any part of. Veeck had grown up in a ballpark, as he himself put it. His father had changed jobs from sports-writer to Chicago Cubs executive and finally team president. Young Bill started his first job at age 11, serving as soda pop vendor and office gopher for the Cubs. Bill moved up in the Cubs organization (he even claimed to be the person who planted the ivy on the outfield walls of Wrigley Field), but when he realized he had reached the ceiling there he joined up with some friends to buy the Milwaukee club in the American Asso-ciation in 1941. Veeck was just 27, but he was already exploding with ideas. The first thing he did was make the ballpark a nicer place to be: new paint job, comfy seats, cleaner restrooms. Then he gave the fans reasons to show up.

The Veeck promotional style was unique. He never announced his promotions ahead of time, so folks would show up with no idea what to expect. What they got were giveaways such as live lobsters, buckets of nails, or hosiery. They got fire-works, live bands, and ballet. Anything could happen, and the fans loved it. Another benefit of attending a game run by Bill

Veeck was that fans got a chance to talk to the prez. He spent his time during the games out in the stands, chatting with the fans, joining them for a beer, talking baseball, having a grand time. What most people don't realize was that at the same time, Veeck was doing market research (in a most cost-efficient way!). He asked the fans what they wanted—and he listened to their answers. When one shift worker (this was wartime) asked for morning games, Veeck scheduled 8:30 A.M. starts for some games, and he himself was out at the park serving bowls of cereal to the fans when they arrived.

In 1943 there was talk that Veeck wanted to purchase the down-and-out Phillies. The story may be apocryphal, but it does sound like Veeck: It is said he planned to load up the Phils with Negro League stars, but when word of this "plan" reached the commissioner's ears, Landis put a speedy kibosh on the deal.

Veeck had his greatest success as lead member of a ten-person syndicate (which included comedian Bob Hope) that bought the Cleveland Indians in 1946. Veeck pulled out his promotional skills, moved the Indians into huge Municipal Stadium on a full-time basis, and attendance doubled the next year to 1.5 million. Then they blew the roof off the place. Veeck integrated the American League, signing slugging outfielder Larry Doby and ageless pitcher Satchel Paige. The Lou Boudreau-led Indians tied the Red Sox for the pennant in '48,

Gimmick-meister Bill Veeck twice brought ageless Satchel Paige out of retirement. In 1948 (here), the 42-year-old former Negro Leagues star shockingly went 6-1 for the Indians. In '52, Paige won 12 games and saved 10 for Veeck's St. Louis Browns.

then won the playoff and the World Series. Indians fans came out in record numbers: 2,620,627—the most ever for any team in either league. The record stood for nearly 30 years.

Veeck was unlike any other owner. While the other big-league moguls still wore steamed shirts and stickpins, Veeck never—ever—wore a tie. He much preferred the company of the bleacher fans to that of millionaires and movie stars. He was creative, fun-loving, and had a good time. Naturally, the other "Lords of Baseball" found him quite threatening. He called his autobiography *The Hustler's Handbook*, which severely rankled the other "sportsmen" who owned teams.

A costly divorce settlement forced Veeck to sell his share in the Indians a few years later, but baseball was still in his blood. He was able to scrape up enough money to purchase the St. Louis Browns in 1951.

But even Veeck couldn't turn the tide for the American League club in St. Louis. He doubled their attendance in one year, but that was only to half a million. It wasn't like Bill wasn't trying. In addition to his regular slew of wacky promotions, he tried an idea that caused tremors in the league president's office. By August 19, 1951, the Browns were about 50 games out of first. Their opponent, the Tigers, were about a dozen games out. But a good-size crowd had gathered for the game that day because Veeck had let the word out that something special was going to happen. The fans were to help celebrate the 50th anniversary of the American League; everyone

In a publicity stunt hatched by Browns owner Bill Veeck, 43-inch, 65-pound Eddie Gaedel emerged out of a cake wearing uniform number ⅛ and was sent up to pinch-hit against the Tigers on August 19, 1951. Batting out of a crouch, he was walked on four straight high pitches.

received a slice of birthday cake as they entered the gate. Between games of the doubleheader, a fake birthday cake was rolled out onto the field, and out of it jumped a little person (called a "midget" in those days) wearing a Browns uniform with the number ⅛ on his back. The fans were moderately amused. But in the last of the first inning of the second game, a pinch hitter was announced for Browns leadoff batter Frank Saucier. It was the little fellow from the cake: Eddie Gaedel, who stood all of 43 inches high and weighed in at 65 pounds. The opposing manager charged out of the dugout to protest, but the Browns showed him Gaedel's contract, certified by the

league office. The fans were in hysterics. Then Gaedel took his batting stance; the little guy actually was in a crouch! The Tiger catcher had to get on his knees to give his pitcher a target, and Gaedel walked on four pitches. The fans' joy notwithstanding, the Browns lost anyway. (The next day, AL President Will Harridge banned the use of little people from the game.)

In a 1951 game, Browns owner Bill Veeck staged "Fans Managers' Night," in which he passed out signs at Sportsman's Park so patrons could cast their votes for strategic decisions. Manager Zack Taylor, seated in a box behind the plate, was assigned to count the votes.

At a game the following week, every Browns fan entering the ballpark received a packet of cards with a specific play on each card: Bunt, Walk, Hit and Run, Steal, Warm up a Reliever, and so on. Manager Zack Taylor was told to consult with the fans before he made any move. Should we bunt? Taylor looked around and counted the votes, then sent the sign that followed the fans' advice. The fans actually managed the team to a victory. The next day Taylor regained control of his team; they lost five of the next six.

When Veeck realized that even he couldn't make the second team in St. Louis profitable, he looked at Los Angeles, Florida, Baltimore, and Milwaukee during 1952 and '53. But AL owners wouldn't give Veeck approval to move his team. At the same time, the National League gave Lou Perini the okay to move the Braves from Boston to Milwaukee. In 1952 Boston attendance

Veeck, flanked by a sample sign that would petition crowd opinions of managerial moves in an upcoming Browns game against the Athletics, sorts through letters he solicited from fans vying for free passes. (Thanks to the heroics of Sherm Lollar and Hank Arft— both "voted" into the lineup—St. Louis won the game, 5-3.)

was down to about 20 percent of what it had been in the Braves' pennant-winning year of 1948. Their first year in Milwaukee, 1953, it was up 649 percent. In fact, they passed their previous year's attendance figure in just 13 games in the new city. Milwaukee County Stadium was the first park to be constructed using public funds (except for Cleveland's Municipal Stadium, which was built in hopes of attracting the Olympics). Veeck had pointed the way to new success for old teams, but the AL ignored him.

In 1954, Veeck had it in mind to move to Baltimore. The league gave grudging approval, with one condition—Veeck had to sell his share of the Browns. Despite his success, despite his ability to see the next great direction for the game, what it boiled down to was that the "lords" wanted Bill to hand back his baseballs and go home. After his sale of the Browns, Veeck lay low for several years. In 1959, however, he bought the White Sox and continued his outrageous promotions for 21 fun-filled years.

Before the 1955 season the Philadelphia Athletics became the third big-league team in three years to shift cities—after no team had moved in 50 seasons. But the real tremor in the major leagues was about to come from New York, where the teams were all winners, not doormats. Walter O'Malley and Horace Stoneham had been watching closely, and they saw what happened when teams moved.

Bill Veeck (left), a vendor and office clerk at Chicago's Wrigley Field at age 11, later concocted the idea of planting ivy along its walls. Here in 1955, he confers with Cubs owner P. K. Wrigley, comparing a photo of Wrigley Field in Chicago to a proposed enlargement should baseball head west.

LOVABLE LOSERS

While the worst teams in the American League were packing up and shifting home bases, the two predominant cellar dwellers in the NL—the Chicago Cubs and the Pittsburgh Pirates—were staying put. These teams didn't just live in the cellar; they held the long-term lease. For the bulk of the decade they shared the last two places in the league. The Cubs landed in seventh or eighth six times in the '50s; the Pirates sat there eight times. These were two very bad teams. (The Pirates of 1952, in fact, lay claim to being the worst non-expansion team of the century; their 42-112 mark landed them 54½ games out of first place, which is another way of saying they were mathematically eliminated around August 1.) But there was a critical difference. While the Cubs had Ernie Banks, the Pirates had Branch Rickey. Chicago took Ernie to its heart. Banks was the centerpiece of the '50s Cubs, a team that seemed capable of hitting home runs at almost any time but was lacking in other basic skills—getting on base, pitching, and fielding. The Cubs were the NL's geriatric ward, with 35-year-old players getting regular jobs. The highlight of their 1955 season was when "Sad Sam" Jones became the first African-American pitcher to throw a no-hitter. Oh, and the team he beat? Who else— the Pirates.

It's hard to believe, but the 1950s-era Pirates were even worse than the Cubs. But a closer look indicates that what was going on in the Steel City was much different

MR. CUB

Ernie Banks ranks with Kirby Puckett as one of the most delightful human beings ever to play the game. Even when his team was floundering around the basement, Ernie's attitude was upbeat and joyful. "What a beautiful day for baseball! Let's play two!" became his catchphrase.

Though he never appeared in the World Series, Ernie Banks was such a formidable force that he twice won Most Valuable Player awards while his team finished fifth (in an eight-team league). In fact, he was the first man in National League history to win the honor in consecutive seasons. When someone groused about the choice, opposing manager Jimmy Dykes offered this opinion: "Without Ernie Banks, the Cubs would finish in Albuquerque." It didn't hurt that Banks hit 47 home runs during his first MVP season and knocked in 143 runs during the second.

Ernie Banks

A star in football and basketball at his Dallas high school, Banks began his baseball career with a black barnstorming team that paid him $15 a game. He was playing for the Kansas City Monarchs, a Negro League team, when the Cubs decided to make him their first African-American player. He hit his first homer late in the '53 season and succeeded Roy Smalley, Sr., as the team's regular shortstop the following spring. Banks had strong legs but not overpowering upper-body muscles. Similar to Hank Aaron, his power came from his wrists. "His wrists go up to his armpits," one teammate said. Banks became the first shortstop who was a true power hitter.

Like many hitters, Ernie enjoyed the "friendly confines" of Wrigley Field and its all-daytime baseball. Ernie gave a hint of things to come with a record five grand slams in a season (1955). He had five 40-homer campaigns, won two home run crowns, and finished his career with 512 long balls (290 at Wrigley), which at the time ranked ninth on the all-time list. He hit more home runs than any other major-leaguer from 1955 to '60 and held the single-season mark for home runs by a shortstop until Alex Rodriguez broke it in 2001, 43 years later.

Mr. Cub led NL shortstops in fielding twice prior to moving to first base in 1962 after leg injuries interfered with his range at short. He won a fielding title at the new position and led National League first basemen in assists five times. Banks was elected to the Baseball Hall of Fame in 1977.

from what was happening in Chitown. When Branch Rickey, the man with the great baseball mind, became their general manager in November 1950, they had a super slugger in left field—Ralph Kiner—and not much else. The team was loaded

When forkballing Elroy Face retired with 193 saves in 1969, only Hoyt Wilhelm had more. Often credited as the inspiration for the modern notion of a "closer," Face still holds the best single-season record: 18-1 for the '59 Pirates.

with never-weres, old-timers, and retreads (some of them ex-Cubs). Rickey began to shake things up, and although some of his ideas struck the press and populace of Pittsburgh as a little strange, "The Mahatma" wasn't about to be dissuaded. Rickey announced his "Five Year Plan" in 1952: He signed 435 prospects; the team lost 112 games.

But look at who Rickey was signing: Bob Friend wasn't yet 22, but he was a starter on the '51 team. Rickey chose Roy

Face, a short pitcher with a big heart, from the Dodger draft list in 1953, then the next year (despite the Dodgers' nearly secret-agent efforts to prevent it) did the same to grab Roberto Clemente, a man who would become one of the game's all-time greats. Rickey also dealt away Ralph Kiner—to the Cubs. Pirate fans were outraged, but Kiner's back problems ended his career two years later. By 1958 the team that had been called the "Rickey Dinks" managed to finish second. In 1960 they won the World Series.

It was not uncommon for ballplayers of the '50s and '60s to take off-season employment—some of which paid more than their "summer jobs." Selling cars was one of several modes of employment pursued by the great Ernie Banks.

GO WEST, YOUNG MEN

Of all the stats of the 1950s, from the Yankees' team and individual efforts to the Dodgers' miraculous near-pennant domination, one stands out: In 1947, the three New York teams combined for a total attendance of 5.6 million. In 1957, that number was 3.2 million—down about 40 percent, and the bulk of that drop was on the National League side.

There were several reasons for the slide. Television played a large part. But aging ballparks (Ebbets Field had been built in 1913; the Polo Grounds in 1911) and the deterioration of the inner-city neighborhoods where they were located meant they were less desirable places to go. Had the neighborhoods been the same as before, and if the ballparks had stayed "green cathedrals," the impact of television probably wouldn't have been so devastating.

Walter O'Malley made himself a reputation during the Depression as a lawyer handling bankruptcy cases. The Brooklyn Trust Company, the bank that held the mortgage on Ebbets Field (as well as some other substantial loans) hired O'Malley in 1941 to investigate why the Dodgers weren't making their mortgage payments when their attendance seemed about where it should be. The reasons were simple enough: Club president Larry MacPhail was a spendthrift. He spent money in droves, and no one bothered to reign him in.

A 67-year era of New York baseball ended at the Polo Grounds with a Giants loss to the Pirates on September 29, 1957. Some fans made one last, futile plea for the ballclub not to continue with its move to San Francisco.

It didn't take a financial expert to figure out that they needed a better system. But O'Malley, called "The Great Manipulator" by baseball writer Roger Kahn, saw a grander opportunity. Of course he could fix things... but only if he were made director of the team. The bank lent him $250,000 to buy 25 percent of the Dodgers, and naturally he cleaned up the money mess in no time. Even more important, he was on his way to becoming a baseball mogul.

Branch Rickey, another of the Dodgers' 25-percent partners, had attracted powerful enemies throughout his baseball career, from Judge Landis to Leo Durocher. He and O'Malley seldom saw eye-to-eye. While no one could dispute Rickey's baseball acumen, O'Malley knew boardrooms and balance sheets. So in order to exert power over Rickey, O'Malley recruited the other partners to his side, giving him a three-to-one voting advantage. However, Rickey still got all the press. The fact is, when Rickey signed Jackie Robinson, O'Malley and his other partners had to approve the act. But Rickey got all the credit—baseball's great emancipator. An O'Malley assistant claims that Rickey's reputation for integrating baseball was the first step in driving O'Malley out of Brooklyn and on to Los Angeles. O'Malley couldn't stand the blustery old man.

O'Malley engineered a way to get Rickey tossed out of the Dodger organization in 1950, but The Mahatma got the last laugh. Through the terms of the agreement, Rickey had to sell his shares back to O'Malley at market value.

MAULERS OF THE MINORS

In 1956, two years before the Dodgers arrived from Brooklyn, Los Angeles already featured a star slugger. That season, the Los Angeles Angels of the Pacific Coast League featured an overweight first baseman named Steve Bilko. In '56, Bilko hit .360 with 55 homers, 164 RBI, 163 runs scored, and 215 hits. A year later, he smashed 56 homers, four short of Tony Lazzeri's long-held Pacific Coast League record. Bilko won his third straight PCL MVP Award and was named Minor League Player of the Year by *The Sporting News* in '57. A bust in the bigs, Bilko was nonetheless such a hero in the minors that a young Neil Simon used his name in creating television's Sergeant Bilko character, portrayed by Phil Silvers.

Minor-leaguer Joe Bauman didn't merit a TV show, but he did carve a niche in minor-league history. Capitalizing on the high altitude and long schedule at Roswell, New Mexico, of the Class C Longhorn League in 1954, he hit .400 with 72

Joe Bauman

home runs, 224 RBI, and a .916 slugging percentage. A four-homer game on September 1 helped him produce baseball's first 70-homer season.

Dick Stuart came close to that mark in 1956: He collected 66 homers and 158 RBI while playing for Lincoln, Nebraska, of the Western League. One of his homers was measured at 610 feet. Though Ken Guettler of Shreveport (Texas League) and Frosty Kennedy of Plainview (Southwestern) joined Stuart at the 60-homer level in 1956, only Joe Hauser and Bob Crues (with 69 each) and Bauman rank ahead of Stuart on the minor-league home run list. Hauser (the only man to do it twice), Moose Clabaugh, and Lazzeri were the only other players to produce 60-homer seasons in the minors. Guettler won more home run crowns (eight) than anyone else in the minors.

Minor-league pitchers also had their share of glory in the '50s. Two of the best were Ron Necciai of Bristol (Appalachian League), who fanned 27 batters in a 1952 game, and teammate Bill Bell, who pitched three no-hitters, two of them in succession, that same season.

At spring training in 1957, Pee Wee Reese (left) and Don Zimmer commiserate with fans who make their opinions clear on the Dodgers' intention to move the team from Brooklyn to Los Angeles.

O'Malley figured Rickey's stock was worth about half a million dollars, but Rickey produced a written offer for over $1 million. O'Malley went to his grave certain that the offer was bogus, but he paid up anyway. At least he was getting rid of Rickey.

In 1955, the year the Dodgers won their first World Series, O'Malley took in somewhere around $2 million in profit. (Baseball was far from his only business; he owned several other companies, along with parts of the Brooklyn Borough Gas Company and the Long Island Railroad.) But he also noticed the Yankees had drawn 1.5 million people to Brooklyn's 1 million. Worse yet, the team that had just moved to Milwaukee had drawn 2 million.

By 1956, O'Malley was busily hatching a plan to move the Dodgers. But he was canny enough to be working on several different angles. On one hand, he was trying to get Brooklyn to give him land on which to build a new ballpark. He also hired an architectural firm to design a new Brooklyn Park. On the other hand, he started talking to the county of Los Angeles about moving his Dodgers out west. He began to pile up money. He sold Ebbets Field for about three million dollars and then persuaded the new owner to give him a short lease (so he could move quickly when he had to). He sold other ballparks he owned in Fort Worth and Montreal. He swapped the Fort Worth minor-league team to the Cubs ownership for the

Local pols—plus about 200 members of the media and two bands—greeted Walter O'Malley in Los Angeles in 1957, as the Dodgers owner arrived to begin organizing his team's move from Brooklyn. While touring the city in a sheriff's department helicopter, he spotted Chavez Ravine, future home of Dodger Stadium.

181

minor-league Los Angeles Angels so he could establish geo-
graphic rights on the West Coast.

He kept asking New York to provide him with a new site;
Robert Moses, the immensely powerful commissioner of parks
(also responsible for highways, bridges, and other urban proj-
ects), said no. He had his team play seven games in Jersey City,
New Jersey, during the 1956 season, a veiled threat. The fact is,
Walter O'Malley's Dodgers were making money, but he wanted
more. And New York City wouldn't play ball. Meanwhile, other
teams were being courted by Los Angeles at the same time: Both
the Indians and the Senators heard presentations on going west.

The situation with the New York Giants was much worse.
Even though the capacity of the Polo Grounds was much
greater than Ebbets Field, the Giants had passed the million
mark only once since 1951, in their pennant-winning season of
1954. The park was falling down; the neighborhood wasn't
good. Giants owner Horace Stoneham obtained Jackie Robinson's contract from O'Malley in December 1956 in exchange for
Dick Littlefield and $30,000, and then offered Jackie $60,000 in
salary in a desperate move to boost attendance. But Jackie
retired rather than join the hated Giants. Stoneham wailed, "I
can't stay where I am. If I don't move my team, I go bank-

*Following the
Giants' final game in
New York, manager
Bill Rigney assists in
the packaging of a
square of sod to be
shipped to San
Francisco for place-
ment into the
outfield of Seals
Stadium, the team's
new home for 1958.*

rupt. . . . All my relatives would starve." With a long and healthy relationship in place between the Giants and the city of Minneapolis, Stoneham made plans to move his team there. The league secretly approved the moves of Stoneham to Minnesota and O'Malley to California on May 29, 1957. Not long thereafter Stoneham received a call. "Hey," O'Malley said, "why not move to California with me?" and he brokered the deal that landed the Giants in San Francisco, which was perfect for the National League. One trip to the West Coast meant two teams to play, which would keep down traveling expenses. Stoneham announced his move in August. O'Malley waited until October 8, when New Yorkers were engrossed in the Yankees–Braves World Series.

The Dodgers were no longer the boys of Brooklyn. At the time, it was almost unbelievable. In retrospect, the O'Malley move only seems shocking because the team was (apparently) so deeply rooted in the borough. Ballclubs moving had ceased to be news. To Brooklynites, however, this really was *their* team—not just a local business, but an ongoing public trust. The Dodgers had been there before O'Malley; there was no reason to believe they wouldn't be there long after. The sad truth is that it was a matter of an immovable object—Parks Commissioner Robert Moses—and an irresistible force— Walter O'Malley. O'Malley had every right to make as much money as he could with his ballclub, and to take it wherever he wanted. The success he would find on the West Coast was beyond all imagining. However, to this day, people from the borough of Brooklyn curse his name.

At Ebbets Field in 1953, Carl Erskine struck out 14 Yankees in a World Series game—a record at the time. Seven years later, he "pitched" the demolition ball that razed the Dodgers' home of 45 seasons. (In '64, the very same ball was used to atomize the Polo Grounds.)

The upheaval of teams changing cities in the 1950s was simply a matter of adjusting to the changing demographics of the postwar era. In short, baseball had woken up to the fact that not many cities could still support a pair of big-league teams. Baseball was going where the people were.

THE NEW FRONTIER

When the Los Angeles Dodgers and the San Francisco Giants began the 1958 season, the new ballparks they had demanded as part of their New York "exit strategy" weren't ready for them. So they were forced to play in less than desirable venues. The Giants were stuck in Seals Stadium, a cramped little bandbox that held only 23,000 bodies—fewer than the Polo Grounds did. But they still drew twice as many fans as they had the season before. The Dodgers had to play in the Municipal Coliseum, a football stadium. It seated more than 90,000. They squeezed in the baseball field in rather unsuitable fashion. The right-field foul pole was very close to home, but the fence immediately swung out to extreme depth in right center. In left field the fence was just 250 feet away, so they constructed a high screen. It was jokingly said the stadium could easily fit 93,000 paying fans in the yard but only two outfielders. The Dodgers finished in seventh place but drew more fans than they ever had before, and over one million more than they had in 1957.

In 1959, a new team arose to end the Yankee domination. The Chicago White Sox (now

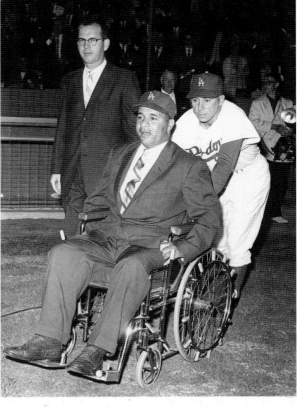

Luis Aparicio set a standard of athleticism for shortstops with his acrobatic defense and baseline-burning speed. "Little Louie" won nine Gold Gloves and the same number of consecutive stolen-base titles.

A record crowd of 93,103 turned out for a Dodgers–Yankees exhibition game in 1959 at which a paralyzed Roy Campanella (wheeled by Pee Wee Reese) was feted. In the fifth inning, the lights were turned off and candles lit in a moment Campy called the greatest thrill of his life.

owned by Bill Veeck) took the American League flag, finishing five games ahead of Cleveland. The Yanks finished 15 games out. The ChiSox played a different style of ball than fans had seen for most of the '50s. Only one of their players hit as many as 20 home runs that year. Their RBI leader drove in just 84. As a team they batted just .250, and five teams in the league outscored them.

Their offense was remarkably simple in concept: Leadoff batter Luis Aparicio would get on, steal second, be bunted or grounded over to third by number-two hitter Nellie Fox (the league's Most Valuable Player), and come home however he could. Their pitching staff was led by a crop of old-timers including Early Wynn, the rugged old coot who never feared knocking a batter on his butt. (When asked if he'd knock his own grandmother down, Early answered, "Granny was a helluva hitter.") The staff also included smooth and canny left-hander Billy Pierce and seasoned veterans Dick Donovan in the rotation and Turk Lown in the bullpen. Their fourth starter was youngster Bob Shaw. Wynn won 22 games that year, Shaw won 18.

THE GO-GO SOX

With a string of four consecutive American League pennants, the New York Yankees were heavy favorites heading into the 1959 baseball season. They had finished ten games ahead of the Chicago White Sox in '58 and were confident of keeping a comfortable margin of victory.

The Sox had other ideas, however. Guided by Al Lopez, the last non-Yankee manager to win an AL flag (with the '54 Indians), Chicago took advantage of early-season Yankee struggles that included a fall to last place on May 20.

A combination of speed, defense, and a potent bullpen enabled the ChiSox to jump to first place on July 28 and stay there, thanks in part to a four-game sweep of Cleveland on August 28–30. The Indians finished first in batting, slugging, and home runs but ended up in second place, five games out, as the White Sox won their first flag in 40 years.

The Go-Go Sox, whose Comiskey Park fans yelled "Go! Go!" when one of their speedsters reached base, led the league in triples, stolen bases, ERA, and saves. Only two players, catcher Sherm Lollar and left fielder Al Smith, reached double digits in homers as the team

Nellie Fox

perfected the art of manufacturing runs. Shortstop Luis Aparicio stole a league-high 56 bases, DP partner Nellie Fox hit a team-best .306 en route to a surprise MVP Award, and center fielder Jim Landis coupled 20 steals with stalwart defense, making the team especially strong up the middle.

Early Wynn, who had starred for Lopez in Cleveland, won 22 games at age 39 and teamed with Bob Shaw, an 18-game winner, in a formidable 1-2 punch. They got strong support from veteran relievers Turk Lown and Gerry Staley, who combined for 17 wins and 29 saves.

The miracle didn't extend into October, however. Though late-summer waiver pickup Ted Kluszewski hit .391 with three homers and ten RBI in the World Series, the Sox fell to Los Angeles in six games.

Over in the National League, the uniform still read "Dodgers," but the cap featured an interlocking *L* and *A*, no longer the slightly gothic *B*. Gil Hodges, Duke Snider, and Jim Gilliam were still around, but their teammates were Don Zimmer, Don Demeter, and John Roseboro, not Jackie Robinson and Roy Campanella. Their left fielder, Wally Moon, had perfected an inside-out swing that let him pop balls over the left-field fence at the Coliseum, which were promptly dubbed "Moon shots."

The Braves tied the men from L.A. for the pennant (the third National League playoff ever—all of which had included the Dodgers). The first playoff game featured solid pitching by Dodgers Danny McDevitt and Larry Sherry and a John Roseboro homer for a 3-2 win. The second game went 12 innings and featured a delicious Dodger comeback. With Lew Burdette on the mound and the Braves up 5-2 in the last of the ninth, the Dodgers slapped together five singles (the last one a pinch-hit job by old man Carl Furillo) to tie the score, then took the victory against Bob Rush.

HEARTBREAK FOR HADDIX

Even though Harvey Haddix won 136 games for five major-league teams from 1952 to '65, he's remembered most for one he lost.

On May 26, 1959, a night when fog and mist made conditions at Milwaukee County Stadium more suitable for ducks than for baseball, Pittsburgh's slim left-hander took the mound against Lew Burdette, star right-hander of the powerful Milwaukee Braves.

Inning after inning, the defending champions sent hard hitters Hank Aaron, Eddie Mathews, and Joe Adcock to the plate. Haddix had little trouble handling them, or any of the Braves, on that dank evening. Through 12 innings, he was perfect: 36 batters up, 36 batters down, a feat unmatched in major-league history before or since. Burdette, on the other hand, scattered 12 hits but, like Haddix, he also had not allowed any runs.

In the bottom of the 13th, Felix Mantilla finally broke the spell, reaching first with no outs on an error by Pirate third baseman Don Hoak. Mathews sacrificed, moving Mantilla to second, and Aaron drew an intentional walk, setting up a potential double play. After all those innings of futility, however, Adcock came through: He got ahold of a pitch and knocked it over the fence. Aaron ran to second, then headed directly for the Milwaukee dugout. Maybe he thought the ball had hit the wall. Adcock, well into his home run trot, didn't notice and passed the spot Aaron had vacated.

Harvey Haddix

Although Mantilla scored, Adcock's hit was ruled a double. It took several days before the league ruled that the final score was 1-0. And Haddix, who had pitched 12 perfect innings, ended up with a loss.

The World Series trophy found a West Coast home for the first time in 1959, when the Dodgers defeated the White Sox. Larry Sherry, here greeting catcher John Roseboro after the final out, earned Series MVP accolades for his two wins and two saves.

The 1959 World Series opened in Chicago. In Game 1 the Sox were nearly unrecognizable. First baseman Ted Kluszewski slugged a pair of homers, and the Chicagoans took a completely baffling 11-0 win. But it was about all the Sox had left. They had a 2-1 lead in the seventh inning of Game 2, but Chuck Essegian slugged a pinch-hit homer, Charley Neal hit one himself two batters later, and Larry Sherry sealed the win for Los Angeles.

Games 3, 4, and 5, in L.A., set records for World Series attendance: 92,394, 92,650, and 92,706 filled the seats, respectively. Sherry continued his fine relief work, and except for a 1-0 loss to the Sox's pitching trio of Shaw, Pierce, and Donovan in Game 5, the Dodgers were having all the fun. Essegian hit his second pinch-hit long ball in Game 6, and the Dodgers closed it out 9-3. Larry Sherry had two wins and two saves, the first pitcher ever to figure in all his team's decisions in a World Series.

In the 1950s, baseball was torn up by its roots as owners sought greener pastures away from decaying old cities. For 50 years there had been three teams in New York, two in Philadelphia, two in Boston, and two in St. Louis; now those towns had just one each. Before long, the guard itself would change; the old-time dominators would take a step back, replaced by a new crop of players with African-American and Latino backgrounds. The nature of the game itself would change too, as big bombers took a backseat to speedy runners.

Los Angeles's Wally Moon slides in under White Sox catcher Sherm Lollar's tag in 1959, and the Dodgers give their new West Coast constituency its first taste of World Series conquest.

1960s
FASTBALLS AND FLEET FEET

The 1960s closed the door on the career of baseball great Ted Williams, but before long there were dozens of new faces as new teams were invented in response to a challenge from a longtime baseball gadfly, Branch Rickey. With a little help from baseball's executives, the offense/defense pendulum swung all the way to the hurlers' side, and pitchers began to dominate as they had in the days of Christy Mathewson and Walter Johnson. Players were forced to expand their list of tools, and basestealing as a thrilling art form was resurrected by Luis Aparicio and Maury Wills. Although it had to happen someday, it was still stunning when the seemingly invincible Yankees fell apart, ending their reign of excellence. During the '60s, nearly every World Series was a nail-biter or house-rocker, making it the best decade for fall classics ever.

Sandy Koufax would not open the '65 World Series because it fell on the Jewish holiday of Yom Kippur, but he gladly closed it—with a three-hit shutout of the Twins in Game 7. In 57 Series innings throughout his career, Koufax compiled an astonishing 0.95 ERA.

TWO HOMERS END AN ERA

The long ball drew down the curtain in the last games of Ted Williams as a player and Casey Stengel as Yankee manager. On September 28, 1960, when Ted played his last game, there were about 13,000 people in the Fenway Park stands. Ted had refused offers from other teams to honor him in his final swing around the league, so it wasn't surprising he didn't want much adulation in his final game in Boston, either. Williams, who was named "Player of the Decade" for the 1950s by *The Sporting News*, was never one to covet the spotlight. In a brief ceremony before the game, announcer Curt Gowdy gave a rundown of the highlights of Williams's sensational career. He finished by saying, "I don't think we'll ever see another one like him." Ted accepted an award from the Boston Chamber of Commerce, and the mayor of Boston declared the day "Ted Williams Day". and presented Ted with a check for the Jimmy Fund (a charity for children with cancer)—the charity Williams had supported with cash and hard work for so long.

Ted stepped to the mike and made a typically terse set of remarks, just three sentences. First he got in one last shot at the Boston sportswriters, who had caused him so much grief over the years, then closed with: "If I were starting over again and someone asked me where is the one place I would like to play, I would want it to be in Boston, with the greatest owner in baseball [Tom Yawkey] and the greatest fans in America. Thank you."

In the bottom of the eighth inning, with one out, Ted Williams capped off his prolific career with a long home run off Oriole pitcher Jack

Ted Williams said goodbye to the Fenway faithful on September 28, 1960, prior to his final game. Though "Teddy Ballgame" was choked with emotion, his address to the crowd of barely 13,000 was brief and straightforward.

Ted Williams's home run in his final at-bat, in Boston in 1960, was one of the most dramatic moments in baseball history. He refused a curtain call, then trotted out to his position the next inning, where he was immediately replaced—thus ending his career.

Fisher. As always, he didn't acknowledge the fans' rabid cheers, just circled the bases with his head down and gave a perfunctory handshake to next batter Jim Pagliaroni. The ecstatic fans roared for a curtain call, but Ted wasn't interested. Glenn Stout described it perfectly in *Ted Williams: A Portrait in Words and Pictures*: "Ted stayed in the dugout, sitting by himself saying nothing, a secret grin on his lips. The first-base umpire motioned for Ted to acknowledge the cheers. Williams stayed put. There was no reason to move. . . . He had spoken to the crowd already, in the best way he knew. There was nothing more to add."

Williams's career was beyond great; it was the stuff of legend. He not only hit .406 in 1941, the highest average of any player since, but he also hit .388 in 1957 at age 40 (when he wasn't beating out many infield grounders for singles), the highest average any player would reach until 1977. Ted won six batting titles in his career, twice took the Triple Crown (and once missed it by the thinnest of hairs), and won four home run titles and two MVP awards. In the midst of all that he found time to be a war hero, flying fighter planes in World War II and Korea. So no one was surprised when one of the greatest players ever ended his career in a way that inspired the great American writer John Updike to pen one of the most memorable sports essays of all time, about Ted's final day and final dramatic homer, "Hub Fans Bid Kid Adieu."

The home run that closed the door on the career of Casey Stengel as manager of the Yankees was dramatic as well. This one was hit by the Pirates, however, not the Yanks, and it ended Casey's last World Series on a bitter note. No one has yet found the words to adequately capture the 1960 World Series: Topsy-turvy, weird, and wacky all fall short. The men from New York dominated the statistics in record-breaking fashion and still came up losers. The Yankees were, as usual, full of themselves, and probably more deservingly so than any team in history. After slipping to third place in '59, they returned to the top of the AL, where they figured they belonged, and won the title by a comfortable eight games. It marked the tenth time in the past 12 seasons that they had taken the AL flag.

The 1960 season would mark the last of Casey Stengel's 12 years as Yankees manager. Despite winning ten AL pennants and seven world championships, the Old Perfessor—shown here on the day after his 70th birthday—was fired for being too old.

They were facing the Pirates of Pittsburgh, the polar opposite of a Yankee dynasty. The Pirates were making their first World Series appearance in 33 years. The last time this franchise had seen a fall classic, the Yanks of Ruth and Gehrig had skunked them in four straight games. The Pirates had spent the bulk of the 1950s gazing up from the cellar.

But this team was the fruition of Branch Rickey's minor-league development plan and some savvy trades by post–Rickey GM Joe L. Brown. The Bucs were a scrappy team that played great defense, had solid pitching, and never gave up. Every member of the team contributed in one way or another. And they weren't intimidated by the Yankee mystique. In fact, the

Pirates took Game 1 at home, aided by a Bill Mazeroski homer and a great double play to end the game.

Game 2 was different. The Yanks unveiled their power and clobbered the Pirates 16-3. They did it again in Game 3, winning 10-0. But the Buccos took Games 4 and 5 in tight matches that ended 3-2 and 5-2. Down three games to two, the Yankees, with their backs against the wall, responded with a definitive 12-0 win to even the Series and bring on Game 7.

There have been dozens of truly terrific games in World Series history, where leads changed hands several times, weird plays baffled players and spectators alike, and the unlikeliest of heroes were crowned. But this has not often happened in Game 7. (In fact, the greatest World Series games tend to happen in Game 6, when one team has everything to lose but the other doesn't.) For a cold shower of unexpected thrills, Game 7 of the 1960 World Series remains unmatched.

Down 4-0 in just the second inning, the Yankees battled back to take a 5-4 lead, then extended it to 7-4 going into the last of the eighth. It was time for the Pirates to demonstrate their vaunted comeback ability. Pinch hitter Gino Cimoli

New York's Whitey Ford spun a pair of shutouts in the 1960 World Series. He still holds fall classic records for most consecutive scoreless innings (33), victories (10), and strikeouts (94).

A ball hit by Bill Virdon took one of the worst hops in Yankees history in Game 7 of the 1960 World Series. A sure double-play grounder leapt up to hit shortstop Tony Kubek in the throat, setting up a five-run eighth inning that put the Pirates in position to win in the ninth.

The Pirates scored less than half as many runs as the Yankees in the 1960 World Series but won their first world title in 35 years. Bill Mazeroski's decisive ninth-inning homer brought the players and Pittsburgh fans to thier feet in celebration.

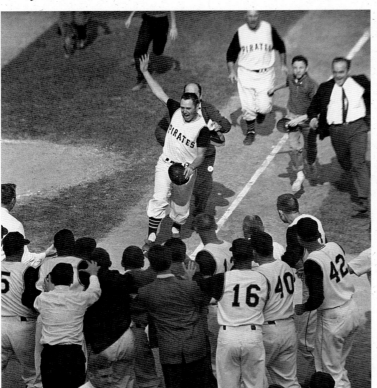

rapped a single, and then the Yanks' Tony Kubek misplayed a possible double-play grounder at short, and the ball hit him in the throat. Another single by Dick Groat, and then a successful bunt by Bob Skinner kept things rolling. Pirate star Roberto Clemente chopped a ball to the right side of the diamond, then simply outhustled Yank pitcher Jim Coates to the bag, driving a second run in. Pirate catcher Hal Smith capped off the rally with a three-run homer. The Pirates went into the ninth with a completely amazing 9-7 lead.

But the Yankees weren't through. With two on and one out, Mickey Mantle lined a single to right field, bringing the Yanks back within one and leaving runners at first and third. Yogi Berra swatted a two-hop bouncer right to first baseman Rocky Nelson at the bag. All "the Rock" had to do was step on first and toss to second for an easy tag on Mantle, and the Series would be over. (By touching first base, Nelson had removed the force play at second.) But Mantle, a man with highly developed baseball instincts, knew that too, and in an instant had the poise *not* to run toward second, but to go backward instead, to first. Nelson raised his hand to make the throw but saw what Mickey was doing and, startled, tried to dive and tag the runner on the ankles. Too late. The runner scored from third, and, incredibly, the game was tied.

There has never been a more clutch heads-up play in baseball history.

But that was all moot a few minutes later (3:36 P.M.—every Pirate fan knows that number like his or her own zip code) when Bill Mazeroski homered on the second pitch from Ralph Terry. The totally remarkable Pirates had beaten the nearly invincible Yankees in a highly improbable World Series capped off by a near-mystical Game 7. It's said Mickey Mantle cried in the clubhouse. Five days later the Yankees held a press conference to announce that Casey Stengel had "retired."

No manager was ever subject to as much second-guessing as Casey was for his decisions in the 1960 World Series, especially his choice of pitchers. But in retrospect, the truth seems to be that the ever-opportunistic Pirates *made* Stengel's decisions suspect by the way they responded to them. They took advantage of every edge they could get to turn everything their way. At the press conference, the Yankees said they wanted to change the team's direction, to go with youth (they also got rid of general manager George Weiss at that time). Casey's reaction: "I'll never make the mistake of being 70 again." In some ways, it was the beginning of the end for the Yankee dynasty that had reigned since Ruth.

CASEY'S METS

They were the lovable losers of New York baseball. The Mets were born in 1962, lost 120 games in their inaugural season, and were no-hit by Sandy Koufax. Yet fans loved this hapless ballclub managed by the grandfatherly Casey Stengel. On the eve of the Mets' home opener, the city hosted a ticker tape parade celebrating the return of NL baseball to New York. The new National League team in town inherited the fans of the Brooklyn Dodgers and New York Giants, who had defected to the West Coast in 1958. No matter how poorly the Mets played, former Dodger and Giant fans would never, ever switch their allegiance to the Yankees.

Stengel, who directed the Yankees to ten AL pennants, managed the Mets from 1962 to mid-'65, when a broken hip forced him to retire. Despite his winning ways in the Bronx, the Mets were 175-404 during his tenure.

"I thought he was great," said Al Jackson, who pitched under Stengel from 1962 through '65. "To me, I learned a great deal from the man because he had a lot to give. He was very smart and a great baseball man."

The franchise attempted to build a team with faces familiar to New York baseball fans. Stengel had worn the uniform of the Giants, Dodgers, and Yankees. Other Brooklyn alumni signed by the Mets in the early years included Roger

Casey Stengel points to Roger Craig's "lucky" number 13.

Craig, Don Zimmer, Joe Pignatano, Gil Hodges, and Duke Snider. Even Yankee legend Yogi Berra played four games for the '65 Mets and signed on as a coach. Unfortunately, the formula hardly equated to wins for the team.

If one player epitomized the misery of these Mets, it was "Marvelous" Marv Throneberry. In one game against the Cubs, the lovable clown slugged what appeared to be a triple. However, he was called out on appeal for failing to touch second base. When Stengel came out to argue the call, the umpire pointed out that Throneberry had also missed first base! On Stengel's birthday during the '62 season, he joked to his notoriously clumsy first baseman that they would give him a piece of cake—if they didn't think he would drop it.

Even while the team struggled to win, fans flocked to the Polo Grounds in record numbers to watch. One of the early attractions was the opportunity to watch the Giants and Dodgers return to the city of their origin. Almost 50,000 fans attended "Willie Mays Night," and 55,704 came to see the Mets play the Dodgers. The latter was the largest attendance figure in the NL for 1962. In the first four seasons of their existence, the Mets outdrew the Yankees—even though the Bronx Bombers won pennants in '62, '63, and '64. When the Mets moved to Shea Stadium in 1964, more than 2.5 million fans walked through the turnstiles.

In 1961, President John F. Kennedy nearly caught a ball during the first game ever played by the expansion Washington Senators. A Red Sox fan, Kennedy loved the sport so much that he appointed a staffer (whom he jokingly called the "undersecretary of baseball") to keep records for him.

EXPANSION

Baseball's half-century of geographical stability had been knocked inside-out in the 1950s, when nearly one team in three packed up and took its show somewhere else. But when the '50s ended, there were still only 16 teams. If baseball was going to reach new markets, it would have to do it with new teams. In typical fashion, the moguls of the game didn't initially grasp this concept. It took someone to punch them up-to-date. And that person was none other than Branch Rickey, the genius who had engaged in shoving matches with the big boys for 40 years.

The New York City folks who had grown up on the Dodgers, the Giants, and their fellow NL combatants weren't likely to turn tail and become Yankee fans. It didn't take long for New York to get officially upset that they were without National League baseball. The mayor appointed a committee to bring it back. One of its members was an ambitious young attorney named William Shea. Shea was that rare creature among politically connected types; he knew when he didn't have all the answers. So he hired the 77-year-old, semiretired (but still voluble) Mr. Rickey to consult with the committee. Rickey was as cocksure and cantankerous as he had been when he had gone toe-to-toe with such heavyweights as Landis, MacPhail, and Durocher.

Shea took the logical first step, which was to try to persuade another NL team to move to New York. But no one was swinging at his pitch. So he asked NL President Warren Giles if his league would consider expanding—adding another team— so it could have a New York presence. The history books say Giles's response was "Who needs New York?" It wasn't the right thing to say.

So Shea and Rickey cooked up the idea to start a new baseball league that would be direct competition to the current baseball structure. They would call their group the Continental League, and it would include franchises in Houston, Denver, Toronto, Dallas, Atlanta, Buffalo, Minneapolis-St. Paul, and, of course, New York.

The new league plan absolutely scared the stuffing out of the big-league owners. They had been nervous to start with; several times in the '50s Congress had held hearings on whether or not baseball deserved their beloved antitrust exemption, and congressional action seemed likely again. There hadn't been a challenge to their fiefdoms since the Federal League flickered out in 1915, but the owners knew their history well enough to understand that if Rickey went through with his plan, it was going to cost them a lot of money. Players would want bigger salaries to stay where they were, and there would be a loss of revenue as the new league chopped off pieces of the comfortable broadcasting pie the owners enjoyed so much.

The expansion Los Angeles Angels, owned by entertainer Gene Autry, debuted in the American League in 1961. Southpaw Bo Belinsky, wild on the mound and off the field, nevertheless posted a 3.56 ERA in 1962, helping the Angels to a stunning 86-76 record.

Worst of all, there would be lawsuits. And countersuits. And counter-countersuits. The owners could easily foresee that a lot of the money that belonged in their pockets was soon going to be the property of players and lawyers. They hemmed and hawed, they stalled and sued, but, with no leg to stand on, ultimately they caved.

For the 1961 season, the American League expanded into the lucrative southern California market with the Los Angeles Angels. They also let Calvin Griffith move his ever-woeful Washington Senators to Minneapolis-St. Paul and,

in an effort to keep the D.C. politicos at bay, replaced Griffith's men with an expansion franchise. The new franchise kept the Washington Senators moniker, even though it had no connection to the team that had been there since the beginning of the century.

In their first expansion (in 1961), the AL replaced a Washington team that had been a miserable failure for decades. In try number two ('69), the AL replaced the Kansas City team Charlie Finley had recently yanked to Oakland and also put a team in Seattle. But that team folded after one season, moving to Milwaukee as the Brewers for 1970. The "new" Washington Senators packed up and left for Texas in 1972, and ultimately the Milwaukee team joined the National League.

For whatever reason, the AL never really took advantage of expansion the way the NL did. The American League, instead of breaking new ground, kept trying to heal old wounds.

Major League Baseball, which had started the 1950s with 16 teams in 10 cities, would wrap the '60s with 24 teams in 22 towns.

The Washington Senators morphed into the Minnesota Twins prior to the 1961 season. Despite the frigid weather in Minneapolis, Harmon Killebrew (right) blasted 46 home runs and Bob Allison (left) had 29 dingers that year.

MANTLE AND MARIS

Babe Ruth's record of 60 home runs in 1927 was a huge achievement that captured the imagination of baseball fans for all time. Nearly every season one could find a sports article asking "Is this the year the Babe gets passed?" or, even more commonly, "Can Rocky (or Hank or Ralph or Willie or Duke or Ernie) beat the Babe?" But as the 1961 season dawned, only two players had ever actually come close: Jimmie Foxx in 1932 and Hank Greenberg in 1938 each slugged 58. Greenberg reached 58 with five games left but couldn't muster up any more.

In 1961 not one, but *two* men—Mickey Mantle and Roger Maris—were in full rush to bust the Babe's record. Better yet,

they were teammates, and best of all, they were Yankees. But personally they couldn't have been more different. Mantle, of course, was the golden boy of New York (and of all baseball, for that matter)—that amazing combination of speed, power, aw-shucks good looks, and high-living good times. He had been groomed to succeed Joe DiMaggio as both the Yanks' center fielder and as their superstar in the Ruth/Gehrig/DiMaggio mode. He had already won the Triple Crown (hitting 52 homers while doing it) in 1956.

Playing next to Mickey in the Yank outfield was Roger Maris, who was shy where Mantle was outgoing, intense where Mick was flamboyant, and frankly, much more of a defensive specialist than a power hitter when the Yanks acquired him from Kansas City in early 1960 after just three years in the majors. But Roger found his power stroke that year, and it wasn't the short porch at Yankee Stadium that made the difference; he hit just one-third of his homers there. He slugged 39 homers and took Most Valuable Player honors in 1960. When Mickey knocked 40 out of the park that year, the New York press quickly dubbed them "The M&M Boys."

With the league's expansion to ten teams in 1961, offense was up everywhere. And Roger and Mickey put on a wonderful show. By July 25 they were neck and neck; Maris with 40 long balls (ahead of Ruth's pace), and Mantle not far behind at 38.

The Mantle–Maris relationship was one of opposites attracting. Mantle (left) was as excessive as he was charismatic, Maris (right) as temperate as he was insular. Nevertheless, the two were friends, roommates, and fiercely protective of each other.

However, by late August a series of injuries knocked Mantle off the pace. He ended his season with 54 homers while Roger went on to the promised land.

Maris had rapped his 50th on August 22; his 59th came in Game 155 on September 20. In the last game of the season he belted number 61 in front of a mere 23,000 fans in Yankee Stadium. Reaching the legend of Ruth required a performance of heroic proportions. Maris hit 15 homers in June, including a stretch of six consecutive games with at least one homer and four in one doubleheader. Thirty of his long balls came at Yankee Stadium—tying a Lou Gehrig record. And how much did he fatten up on expansion pitchers? He slugged 13 homers against the Angels and Senators, but that was as many as he hit against the White Sox. Four other Yanks hit more than 20 home runs, setting the all-time record, and the team's 240-homer season stood as the best for a long time.

There was controversy, too. Mantle was the fans' choice to break the Babe's record, by far. Maris, not used to the attention, got ripped in the press for being surly and bitter, when all he probably wanted was to be left alone. Later in life he said his

Boston's Tracy Stallard buried two pitches in the dirt before offering one to Roger Maris that he could drive—which he did (here) for his record-breaking 61st home run, on October 1, 1961.

As a minor-leaguer, Roger Maras (accent on the second syllable) changed his moniker to Maris to dodge catcalls of fans who found convenient ways to heckle his real name. That sort of sensitivity, combined with media myopia and pro-Babe Ruth sentiment, devastated him emotionally during his season-long home run chase.

career in baseball would have been a lot more fun if he hadn't hit 61 homers in one season.

Even worse, the commissioner of baseball ruled that it didn't count. Sort of. Commissioner Ford Frick, a longtime pal (and business partner) of Babe Ruth, made the announcement in July that for 61 homers to be recognized as breaking Ruth's record, it had to be done in 154 games, even though the season was now eight games longer. Otherwise it would be noted in the official record book with "a distinctive mark." He never said "asterisk." Major League Baseball eventually tired of that nonsense and removed the "distinctive mark" in 1991. Unfortunately, Maris had died of cancer six years earlier.

BASEBALL REACTS

"Distinctive mark" or not, the bosses of baseball seemed threatened by the effect expansion was having on offensive stats. (The addition of two new teams meant there were 20 pitchers in the league who weren't good enough to have been there the year before.) In addition to the Mantle–Maris chase of Ruth, other players had career years of their own the first season they faced watered-down expansion pitching. In the American League there was another factor: The ballpark where the Los Angeles Angels played was notorious for being homer friendly—if not actually a launching pad. (When producers set out to find a site to film the TV show *Home Run Derby*, that's where they went.) The first-year Los Angeles Angels wound up with five 20-plus homer hitters themselves.

"Stormin'" Norman Cash of the Tigers reaped the hugest benefits. Cash was in just his second big-league season in 1961. In his first year he batted a reasonable, though hardly spectacu-

BASEBALL CARDS

They were distributed with tobacco in the early part of the 20th century, and by the 1950s they were packaged with bubble gum to appeal to younger baseball fans. During that time the baseball card became as much a part of baseball culture as a ballpark frank or a Sunday doubleheader. The small cardboard photos of the players, complete with statistics on the back, became the obsession of young fans everywhere.

The major companies that produced cards were Bowman, Topps, and Goudey. Topps, which would become the company most synonymous with baseball cards, put out their first set in 1951. They also established the standard 2½"×3"-size card.

In the '50s and '60s, kids collected cards and saved

Children compare baseball card collections.

them for fun and out of loyalty to their favorite teams. The cards possessed great sentimental value, and, for young fans, it was a hobby not unlike collecting stamps or comic books. Kids would swap cards to attain their favorite players or "flip" them in attempt to acquire additional cards. Many kids stuck cards in their bicycle frames to make a fluttering noise against the spokes when they rode to the nearest ballfield. Collectors often stored their cards in shoeboxes for years—until Mom or Dad cleaned out the attic and tossed them into the garbage.

Over the years, the pastime of collecting baseball cards evolved into big business, with the rarest and most treasured cards commanding exorbitant prices. The cards of such Golden Age players as Willie Mays and Mickey Mantle—at least those that survived in decent condition—are valued in the thousands. And in 2000 a Honus Wagner card sold on eBay for $1.27 million!

lar, .286 and hit 18 home runs. But in 1961 he was unstoppable, walloping the ball at a .361 clip, slugging 41 homers, and tacking on 132 RBI. He took the batting title handily, although he was nowhere near a Triple Crown title. His own teammate, Rocky Colavito, bombed 45 long balls and drove home 140 runs. Later in his career, Cash 'fessed up: He admitting doctoring his bat by replacing some of the wood with cork so that it would be as hard as a 36-ounce bat but weigh only 34 ounces, so it would be easier to swing faster. Either Cash went back to the regular bat or the corked bat stopped working, but Norm Cash never hit above .283 during the final 13 years of his big-league career.

Two-time NL batting champion Tommy Davis had a banner year in 1962. Even while he was driving in truckloads of runs, however, his relaxed attitude toward the game still compelled some critics to view him as "lazy."

Norm Cash, who hit .264 over 16 other seasons, was one of the more unlikely batting champs in history. The Tigers first baseman later admitted that, while swatting .361 in 1961, he used a corked bat.

Over in the National League, the expansion era batting noise came from Tommy Davis, outfielder for the Dodgers. When expansion hit the National League (in 1962), Davis, like Cash and Jim Gentile, had minimal big-league experience. But that year he batted .346, and his 230 hits were the most in the NL in 32 seasons. The real marvel was his 153 RBI, the most in baseball since 1949 and the most in the National League in 25 years. In the rest of his career, which included a second batting title, Davis never drove in more than 89 runs.

The lords who ran the game were worried. The number that seemed to unsettle Commissioner Frick the most was that unseemly total of 3,001 home runs. (No one pointed out that if the extra games due to expansion were

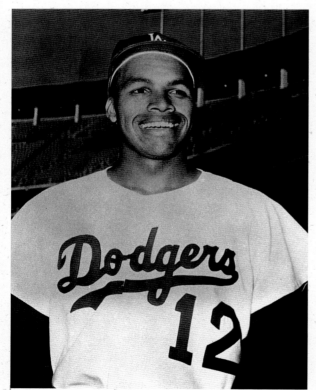

Commissioner Ford Frick waved his hat, and the lords of baseball followed his command. The rule changes they imposed in the early '60s swiftly and decisively shifted the balance of power back to the pitchers.

factored in, that's about how many long balls big-league batters had hit in 1959.) The big guns seemed to be worried that just about everybody would start breaking Babe Ruth's record and hitting .360 every year, and the game would be forever sullied. (What they were really thinking is that guys with big offensive stats want bigger paychecks.) The Baseball Rules Committee, although technically under the owners' control, harkened to Frick's loud hints and took it upon themselves to fix the situation. They increased the size of the strike zone to include the batters' shoulders and the bottom of their knees. It was their stated intention to "bring back" the strike zone to what it had been in 1950—but by including the batters' knees, they effectively made it what it had been in 1887. Frick also encouraged them to re-legalize the "damp delivery," the spitball, but they didn't go for that one.

And that settled that. Bill James explained what happened in his *Historical Baseball Abstract*: "Home run output in 1963 dropped by 10 percent, and total runs dropped by 12 percent. . . . Batting averages dropped by 12 points. The second dead-ball era had begun."

MAURY REINTRODUCES SPEED

There was never a less likely revolutionary than Maury Wills. Although he wasn't short, he wasn't muscular, either, weighing in at about 170 pounds. There was apparently nothing special

This, the 100th stolen base of Maury Wills's 1962 season, was quite a momentous milestone, as no post–WWII player had swiped more than 56. Wills finished with 104 that season—eight more than Ty Cobb's previous record.

about his skills, either. He wasn't much of a fielder and was weak at the plate as well. His team, the Dodgers, loaned him to the Tigers. The Tigers sent him back. Even the baseball card company, Topps, *on the advice of Dodger management*, refused to offer him a card contract.

But the history of the game is full of tales of young players with minimal talent who became much better through a combination of hard work and intelligence. Wills moved all the way from below-average to competent to All-Star. On a tip from his manager at Spokane, Wills turned himself into a switch-hitter and earned a spot with the big club, even though he was already almost 27 years old. He was slumping in early 1960 when the Dodgers hired Pete Reiser to be his personal coach, working with Maury on batting, baserunning, and motivation for two hours before every game. Wills led all National League shortstops with 40 errors that year; he also stole 50 bases, highest in the National League since Max Carey had swiped 51 in 1923. Under Reiser's guidance, he studied pitchers until he knew their motions on the mound better than they did themselves.

Wills made baseball sit up and take notice in 1962—the year he helped change the game as surely as Babe Ruth's bat had, as surely as Bob Gibson's arm would. That year he stole 104 bases, eight more than Ty Cobb had when he set the record in 1915. (Of course,

Luis Aparicio was already using the stolen base as an offensive weapon over in the American League, and had been for several years. But Luis was leading the junior circuit with 50 or so— not 100.) Since this was the year after the Maris "asterisk" achievement, Wills made a point of successfully breaking Cobb's record in the same number of games Cobb had needed to set it. (He had broken the modern National League record of 81 two weeks earlier.) In some ways Wills's record was a little cleaner than Cobb's; he was caught stealing only 13 times all season, Cobb had been nailed 38 times. Wills finished the season with 100 steals, then pilfered four more in the three playoff games. (The Dodgers and Giants had tied for first again, and all playoff stats were included in season totals.) That number was more than any *team* in either league had stolen in any of the first seven years of the 1950s (in other words, pre–Luis Aparicio). Wills also led the league in another speed measurement— triples—and had 130 runs and 208 hits. For his achievement he was named Most Valuable Player, beating out Willie Mays.

The opposition tried everything to stop Wills, including watering down the basepaths. Wills complained, even calling Giant manager Al Dark "The Swamp Fox" for what he made sure his grounds crew did to the area where Wills had to get his start. And of course some traditionalists snorted and scoffed when Wills swiped a base or two when a game was all but over.

What was significant about the record wasn't merely the number; it was the effect it had on the game. The reasoning was perfect: With pitchers dominating, waiting for the home run was a less effective way of constructing an offense. The Dodgers of 1962 had approximately the same batting and slug-

One out of every 7.6 National League stolen bases in 1962 was credited to Maury Wills. Although the other facets of his game were unexceptional, his 104 swipes were so unique and revolutionary that he was voted the league's Most Valuable Player.

ging averages as they had in 1961, and they actually walked fewer times. But they scored 107 more runs and won 13 more games. Wills went on to lead his league in steals for six consecutive seasons, which was tough considering the beating his body took—diving back to first on pickoff attempts and sliding hard into second and third. (He said that by the end of the 1962 season, his legs were so bandaged he "looked like a mummy.") He also tied the NL record for most years leading in singles, with four. It wasn't long until every winning team seemed to have a Wills-like guy; soon thereafter nearly every team did.

Maury's 104 steals led all baseball in 1962—by 72! But by 1964 there were four men with more than 40 steals. In 1965 Maury stole 94, and two new kids, Lou Brock and Bert Campaneris, were next, with 63 and 51 swipes. As artificial turf (with its ability to speed up baserunning) became more prevalent, basestealing became more and more important. In 1975 Davey Lopes had 38 consecutive successful stolen bases. Vince Coleman stole more than 100 bases three years in a row (1985–87). Wills's record fell to Brock (118) and then to Rickey Henderson (130). The Kansas City Royals, the expansion team born in 1969 that finished second in its third year of existence and made it to the postseason in its eighth year, was consciously built on speed—basestealing and baserunning and defense—because of the quickness of the turf in its new ballpark.

Lou Brock was among the first players to truly change games—and the game itself—with his speed. Traded by the Cubs to St. Louis for Ernie Broglio (in a true "steal"), Brock stole 43 bases that year to spark the Cardinals to the World Series. He's shown here in the '67 Series.

INCREDIBLE HULKS

It was the dawn of a new age. Rocket scientists shot men into space, families found themselves glued to the first color television sets, and a new generation of prodigious power hitters proved that size matters.

Within a span of four short years (1959–63), pitchers realized their worst nightmare: the advent of brawny, oversize batters who looked like club-swinging Paul Bunyans. Willie McCovey (6′4″, 210) and Frank Howard (6′7″, 255) were successive National League Rookies of the Year, while Boog Powell (6′4″, 240) and Willie Stargell (6′3″, 225) proved equally imposing specimens for a '60s version of Murderer's Row. They frightened pitchers merely by approaching the plate. Sometimes they even scared their own teammates. Maury Wills, Howard's fleet teammate in Los Angeles, once broke from third base as the ball left the pitcher's hand. Howard missed the sign and took a full swing. Fortunately, Wills arrived home after Howard's mighty rip.

"He's the strongest man I've ever seen in baseball," said Hall of Famer Ted Williams, who won Manager of the Year honors with the 1969 Senators after Howard hit a career-best 48 home runs. In 1968, Howard hit 10 homers in 20 at-bats over a six-game span, and he led the majors with 172 homers while winning two home run crowns (1967 and '70).

Stargell surfaced in 1963, three years after Howard was named NL Rookie of the Year. The cavernous dimensions of Forbes Field, Pittsburgh's home park, hardly fazed the left-handed hitter: Willie walloped seven balls over the right-field roof. He later hit four into the upper deck of Three Rivers Stadium and became the only man to hit two balls out of Dodger Stadium in L.A.

"I've never seen a batter who hit the ball any harder," said former manager Harry Walker of Stargell, who also hit a 535-foot shot at Montreal's Olympic Stadium. "For sheer crash of bat meeting ball, Stargell is simply the best."

Frank Howard (left) and Willie McCovey (right)

Though Powell, who also hit left-handed, never won a homer crown, he provided plenty of power for the O's. He racked up three 3-homer games in four years, won a slugging title, and finished his career with four 30-homer campaigns.

"Every time he swings I cringe," said Birdie Tebbetts, a catcher-turned-manager, of Powell. "Every time he fouls one off, I shudder."

Willie McCovey inspired even more fear in opponents. The ball he lined at the Yankees' Bobby Richardson for the final out of the 1962 World Series might have been the hardest he ever hit. An inch or two either way and the Giants, who had runners at second and third in a 1-0 game, would have been world champions. The first person to hit two homers in an inning twice, McCovey led the NL in home runs and slugging three times each. But he might not have done that if not for a batting tip from Ted Williams. After Ted told the struggling youngster to switch to a lighter bat, the big first baseman prospered. He finished his career with 521 homers, the same number as Williams.

Casey Stengel, manager of the original 1962 New York Mets, once asked starting pitcher Roger Craig, "Where would you like us to defense McCovey, upper deck or lower deck?"

Harmon Killebrew was even better, finishing with 573. And he hit them a long way. The first man to clear the left-field roof at Tiger Stadium, he also hit a 530-foot homer that smashed a seat in Minnesota's Metropolitan Stadium. According to Donald Honig in *The Power Hitters*, "If ever anyone wielded a blunt instrument at home plate, it was Harmon Killebrew. There was nothing subtle about the Idaho strongboy; it was always his intention to mash a pitched ball as hard and as far as he could."

The Killer won his first home run crown in 1959, his first year as a regular, and kept on hitting no matter where he played in the field (third, first, or left field). From 1961 through '64, he took three of his six home run titles, averaging 47 homers each year. Though the 5′11″, 210-pound Killebrew lacked the height of the other new sluggers, he compensated in stature; no other right-hander hit more home runs in the AL.

"IF WILLIE HAD ONLY HIT IT TWO FEET HIGHER . . ."

The Dodgers of 1962 were riding high thanks to Wills's speed and the (finally) matured arm of Sandy Koufax. But Koufax developed a circulatory problem in his pitching hand, and the team, now playing in their brand-new stadium, began to stumble. Meanwhile their old nemesis, the Giants, were making their move. The Giants had a starting staff that outdid the Dodgers—at least this year. Giants ace Jack Sanford won 16 consecutive games on his way to a 24-7 season. The other righty in the rotation was 24-year-old Juan Marichal, and two Billys—O'Dell and Pierce—provided portside efficiency.

The Dodgers lost 10 of their last 13 games, including their final four, while the Giants' 2-1 victory on the final day of the season—on a Willie Mays home run—gave them 16 wins in September. The teams ended the season tied for first place. For just the fourth time in National League history, a dead heat in the pennant race forced a postseason playoff—and the Dodgers were participants all four times. All the talk in 1962 was about a "replay" of the stunning 1951 playoff series that made Ralph Branca and Bobby Thomson household names.

In 1962, in what turned out to be Willie "Stretch" McCovey's first and last World Series, he turned in a tremendous offensive performance. Here, Yankee Bobby Richardson beats out the throw to first in Game 5 of the Series. Days later, in Game 7, Richardson beat him again when he snagged McCovey's ninth-inning screaming line drive that would have won the Series for the Giants.

The Dodger malaise from the end of the season continued through Game 1 (they were shut out, 8-0) and most of Game 2, but they managed to squeeze out a rally for a win. They took the lead early in Game 3, but the Giants roared back with four runs in the top of the eighth to win 6-4 and move on to meet the Yankees in the fall classic.

Both teams in the 1962 World Series were offensive powerhouses. Both had led their respective leagues in runs, hits, RBI, batting average, and slugging percentage. The Giants had also topped the league in homers, with 204. The Yank total of 199 was just ten less than the AL leader. The Giants trotted three future Hall of Famers up to the plate: Willie Mays, Willie McCovey, and Orlando Cepeda. Just a bit behind them in hitting skills were Harvey Kuenn and Felipe Alou, with Felipe's brother Matty waiting on deck.

The Yanks were that old familiar swaggering bunch: Mantle, Maris, and Moose Skowron were on long-ball duty; second baseman Bobby Richardson, MVP of the 1960 Series (even though the Yankees had lost) hit better than .300; and when shortstop Tony Kubek went to the military, rookie Tom Tresh took his place and won the Rookie of the Year Award. Sharing time as regulars under their flexible system were reliables Yogi Berra, Dale Long, Hector Lopez, and Johnny Blanchard.

Despite all the firepower, this was a pitching-dominated World Series. Every game but one featured a complete game by one hurler or another. Game 1 was Whitey Ford's show; his boys won 6-2. Jack Sanford returned the favor in Game 2, pitching a three-hit shutout while Willie McCovey took Ralph Terry downtown in the seventh inning with a monster shot that left fans agape. In Game 3, neither team scored until the seventh inning, when Maris knocked in two runs and scored a third, giving Bill Stafford a complete-game victory.

In Game 4 Giants second baseman Chuck Hiller, who had homered only three times all year, swatted a grand slam to bust open a 2-2 game. It was the first Series slam ever by a National Leaguer. The Giants won 7-3. Ralph Terry netted his second win of the Series in Game 5; the Giants' Billy Pierce spun a three-hitter in Game 6 to even the Series at three games apiece.

Tom Tresh, 1962 AL Rookie of the Year, played shortstop primarily, but his stab of Willie Mays's seventh-inning liner into the left-field corner safeguarded the Yankees' World Series Game 7 win. Tresh, who later named his only son Mickey, led the Yanks with a .321 Series average.

Game 7 turned out to be a masterpiece. Ralph Terry, who had given up the Series-winning home run to Bill Mazeroski in 1960, faced Jack Sanford. Between the two, they let only one man reach base through the first four innings. Two singles and a walk loaded the bases for the Yankees with none out in the fifth, so even though Tony Kubek grounded into a double play, one run scored. The Giants didn't put a man on base until the last of the sixth, when Sanford himself slapped a single. In the seventh inning Tresh, playing left field, made a fine running catch of a Willie Mays one-out line drive. Then

Willie McCovey tripled over Mantle's head in center but was stranded at third.

You could taste the tension in the top of the eighth when the Yankees loaded the bases with none out. But Roger Maris hit it hard to Chuck Hiller, who threw out the Yank trying to score, then Ellie Howard grounded into a double play. The score remained 1-0.

Ralph Terry struck out to end the Yankee ninth, but he probably had other things on his mind. In the last of the inning, Matty Alou beat out a bunt. Terry righted himself and fanned both Matty's brother Felipe and Chuck Hiller. With two out, Mays ripped a double to right. Only a spectacular grab and throw by Roger Maris froze Matty at third.

Young Giants second sacker Chuck Hiller (#26) hit only three long balls during the regular season, but his 1962 World Series grand slam was the first ever by a National Leaguer. It provided the final margin in San Francisco's 7-3 win in Game 4.

Up came McCovey. He didn't have to equal his monumental home run off Terry in Game 2 or his triple two innings earlier. Just a single would win the World Series for the Giants. The count was 1-and-1 when McCovey swung, smashing a bullet right at Bobby Richardson, who caught it to end the game. (It has been inaccurately reported that the ball almost got past Richardson and that he had to make a super catch. That's not true. The only question was whether Richardson could catch the screaming ball and still remain upright.) And so the Yanks won the game, and the Series, in a game without an RBI by either team.

When he retired Willie McCovey for the final out of the 1962 World Series, Ralph Terry had to be thinking about that home run he'd surrendered to Bill Mazeroski in '60. But the Yankees' 23-game winner tossed leather to sky when Mac's scorching liner was caught, preserving his 1-0 shutout.

SANDY

Another change that helped contain batting averages and polish ERAs was the new stadiums being built at this time. With old franchises moving and new ones being born, ten new sites opened for major-league play in the 1960s. The men responsible for the stadium designs seemed to have one thing in common: They much preferred pitching over hitting. Nearly all the new parks were slanted toward the hurler's advantage. And no one reaped the benefits of this slant more than the Dodgers, once they moved out of the bizarre Coliseum and into the lovely pitcher's heaven, Dodger Stadium at Chavez Ravine.

Sandy Koufax could always throw hard—his problem was getting it over the plate. Signed as a bonus baby, he spent the first three years of his career doing mop-up duty in Ebbets Field and averaging close to a walk every two innings. When he got to the West Coast, things began to shift for him. He worked hard to improve, and occasionally he'd strike out a pile of batters in a game. By 1960 he held opposing batters to the lowest average of anyone in the National League, but his frustration of only reaching a record of 8-13 almost drove him from the game. (Hundreds of batters wish he had gone back to selling light fixtures then and there.) In early 1961, Koufax got some special technical advice from catcher Norm Sherry and pitching coach Joe Becker. He made the adjustments, then continued to experiment himself, until he found the perfect combination of form and fire. In 1962 the Dodgers moved into

Koufax opened the 1963 World Series by striking out a record 15 batters. Here, he rejoices in his Game 4 victory as the Dodgers completed the first postseason sweep of the Yankees in 41 years.

A physician once described Sandy Koufax's arthritic elbow as resembling that of a 90-year-old man. Following the 1966 season, at age 30, the great lefty shocked the game by becoming the only player ever to retire the year after winning a Cy Young Award.

their beautiful new ballpark, and Koufax began his move toward the Hall of Fame.

For the next five seasons he was as dominating as any pitcher ever had been or ever would be. During that period Koufax won 111 games and lost just 34. He won the ERA title in each of those years and had the lowest opponent batting average from 1962 to '66. He pitched four no-hitters, and three times he struck out more than 300 men. At the time, only three pitchers had ever fanned 300: Rube Waddell and Walter Johnson did it twice and Bob Feller once. Along the way Koufax set a single-season record of 382 Ks that wasn't broken until Nolan Ryan came along. He won three pitching "Triple Crowns" (leading the league in wins, ERA, and strikeouts). In 1963 he tossed 11 shutouts, the most by any major-league pitcher in one season in 47 years.

That year's Dodger team was the perfect opposite of the sluggers who dominated when they had "Brooklyn" on their uniforms. The Dodgers led the league in just one offensive category: stolen bases. Only two L.A. hitters—Maury Wills and Tommy Davis—batted better than .300. Five other teams in the league outscored the Dodgers.

But they had a terrific defensive infield, with Ron Fairly at first, aging but efficient Jim Gilliam at second, Wills at short, and Ken McMullen at third. The two speedy outfielders (Tommy and Willie Davis) made up for the slow one (Frank Howard). And their pitching was remarkable.

Koufax was simply out of this world, but he wasn't alone. Don Drysdale, the big sidearmer with the sneer and the knockdown pitch, notched 19 victories with his 2.63 ERA. Ron Perranoski won 16 games out of the bullpen and saved 21 more. Johnny Podres, who just *looked* old (he was only 30), won 14 games himself. They won the pennant by six games and headed to the World Series for another faceoff with the Yankees—the eighth time the two teams had done battle in the World Series, but the first one involving cross-continental air travel.

Sandy set the tone for the whole Series in the first game, setting down the first five Yankees on strikeouts. He struck out ten more by the time the game ended, setting a new record for Ks in a Series game. The Dodgers, helped by the presence of former Yankee Moose Skowron, scored five runs off Whitey Ford. In Game 2 the Yankees didn't score until the bottom of the ninth and lost to Podres and Perranoski 4-1. Drysdale stepped up in Game 3, tossing a three-hit shutout. The Dodgers got only four hits themselves, but the one run the Dodgers pushed across in the first was enough. Koufax returned to throw a six-hitter in Game 4, with the only Yank run scoring on a Mantle homer. A crucial error by Joe Pepitone, who lost sight of a Clete Boyer throw in the white shirts behind

Don Drysdale (left) and Jim Bouton (right) were the opposing starters in Game 3 of the 1963 World Series. The first Series game ever played at Dodger Stadium was a classic: A first-inning RBI single by L.A.'s Tommy Davis held up, as Drysdale completed a three-hitter to beat the Yankees 1-0.

third base, set up the run that got the Dodgers the win. They had swept the Yankees in the World Series, something that hadn't happened in the past 24 Yankee Series appearances. But this was not the Murderer's Row of ancient times. In the 1961, '62, and '63 Series, Mickey Mantle's batting figures were .167, .120, and .133; Maris's, .105, .174, and .000. This was a team headed downhill.

In 1964 Koufax and Drysdale both performed well again, but the rest of the staff failed miserably. At season's end five teams were within five games of first; the Dodgers weren't one of them. A solid season from young Claude Osteen helped right the ship for the 1965 season, and the Dodgers returned to the Series. This time their opponents were the Minnesota Twins, a crop of young sluggers who had been bombing the ball for years but never winning anything. Manager Sam Mele began to emphasize "little ball"—steals, hit-and-runs—in lieu of big bombs. They were led on offense by their shortstop (and league MVP) Zoilo Versalles and buttressed by excellent hitters such as Tony Oliva (winning his second batting title in his second full year in the bigs) and sluggers Bob Allison and Harmon Killebrew. Killebrew missed nearly 50 games with injuries, and the team home run total slipped 71 from the year before. To compensate, pitching coach Johnny Sain whipped his staff, including Mudcat Grant, Jim Kaat, and Jim Perry, into shape, and the Twins won the flag by seven games.

Tony Oliva went from playing barefoot in the streets of Pinar Del Rio, Cuba, to winning three American League batting titles. Political unrest precluded him from returning to the island to see his family throughout the first 13 years of his pro career.

Zoilo Versalles, shortstop for the pennant-winning Twins, was the AL's Most Valuable Player in 1965. Although "Zorro" led the loop in total bases, doubles, triples, and runs—and won a Gold Glove—he hit only .217 over the next (and last) five seasons of his career.

In Game 1, Don Drysdale was rattled around for seven runs in less than three innings, while Mudcat responded by tossing a ten-hit victory. Koufax sat the game out because it fell on the Jewish holy day of Yom Kippur. When he returned the next day, he was outpitched by Kaat, who allowed just one run on seven hits in a complete-game 5-1 win. Minnesota was up two games to none, and while the Dodgers were down, they were not out of it. According to baseball writer Roger Angell, "After I had visited the clubhouse and heard Sandy Koufax's precise, unapologetic and totally unruffled analysis of the game, I came away with the curious impression that the Twins . . . were only slightly behind in the Series." Writer George Vecsey seemed to agree; his column was headlined, "All Twins Have Is a Fat Lead."

Back home, Claude Osteen put the Dodgers back on track, winning a five-hit shutout. No one should have been surprised. While pitching for the expansion Washington Senators, Osteen had gone 5-0 against the men from Minneapolis. Drysdale tied the Series at two with another five-hitter in Game 4, then Koufax tossed a four-hitter to win Game 5. With Grant going against Osteen in Game 6, it looked as though the Dodgers were about to dominate again.

In 1965, Sandy Koufax (left) and Don Drysdale (right) accounted for 49 of the Dodgers' 97 wins, including (here, postgame) a pennant-clincher by Koufax over the Braves on October 2. The next season, the pair's dual holdout led to their becoming the game's highest-paid pitchers.

But Game 6 was the Mudcat Grant Show. The Twins hurler, known for his second career as a jazz/pop organist/singer, sang a tune with his arm as well as his bat that the Dodgers couldn't dig. He pitched a complete game, allowed only one run, and swatted a three-run homer himself. The Series was up to the decisive seventh game.

Dodgers manager Walter Alston sent Koufax to the mound, even though Sandy had only two days rest. Koufax didn't seem to mind. His curveball was nonexistent, but his hard stuff was plenty nasty. Sandy spun a three-hitter and fanned ten, and a "Sweet" Lou Johnson home run that clanged off the foul pole in the fourth inning was the only run the Dodgers needed. The Dodgers were champions again. In two World Series, Koufax had pitched five games, completed four of them, tossed 42 innings, and struck out 52 opponents. His ERA was an astonishing 0.86. The Yankees and Twins had gotten a healthy (and scary) dose of what National League batters had to deal with on a regular basis.

In the 1965 fall classic, colorful pitcher Mudcat Grant beat the Dodgers twice, and (here) helped himself when he uncorked a three-run homer in Game 6.

Philadelphia skipper Gene Mauch was despondent as he watched his team drop its eighth straight game, on September 28, 1964. By the time the streak reached ten, the Phillies had blown a 5½-game lead with 11 to play.

PHILS FALTER,
CARDS CAPITALIZE

In the early part of the decade, the Philadelphia Phillies seemed to be a club on the way up. Late in 1960, they had hired a 34-year-old manager who had proved his ability to manage at Triple-A. Even though he suffered through a major-league-record 23-game losing streak in 1961, manager Gene Mauch knew what he wanted. He and general manager John Quinn began to build. They acquired budding talent from other teams: Tony Gonzalez and Johnny Callison to play the outfield, Ruben Amaro for short, Tony Taylor for second, and Cookie Rojas as a

utility player. They picked up veteran sticks such as Gonzalez, Frank Thomas, and Wes Covington. On the mound they had homegrown southpaw Chris Short. Promising youngster Dick (then called Richie) Allen was ready to move up to the big club. The Phils advanced to fourth place in 1963.

In the off-season, Mauch told Quinn he needed a solid number one starter. Quinn found Jim Bunning in Detroit. But the Tigers wanted Don Demeter, starting Phils third baseman, in the swap. Mauch convinced Quinn that he could make the talented, if egocentric, Allen into a third baseman. The pieces fell into place, and the Phillies were atop the NL by the end of June. On Father's Day, Bunning fired a perfect game at the woeful Mets. Allen was on his way to Rookie of the Year honors. The word "genius" was appearing next to Mauch's name more and more frequently.

On September 20, the Phils were coasting. They were 30 games above .500, 6½ games up with 12 to play. They were wondering who they'd face in the World Series. But the next day they lost a 1-0 game to the Reds when Chico Ruiz stole home, and something turned. They lost nine more in a row, with Bunning taking three of the losses and Short two. The Cards and Reds flew by them, winning eight and nine in a row, respectively. The Phils still had a chance on the last day, but, when they won, all they succeeded in doing was knocking the Reds out of the race, as the Cards won and clinched. What caused the Phils to flop? For one thing, reliable slugger Frank Thomas hurt his thumb. Worse, though, was that young manager Mauch panicked and began using his two pitching aces on just two days rest each. It didn't work out.

The Cardinals' season turned on two events. One was the acquisition of Lou Brock from the Cubs for pitcher Ernie Broglio on June 15, just before the trading deadline. Broglio

Jim Bunning was the first pitcher of the modern era to win 100 games in each league. His most significant win came with the Phillies in 1964, when he authored the first perfect game of the 20th century for the National League.

had been a reliable, if unspectacular, starter, winner of 21 games just four seasons before and 18 in 1963. He "gave you innings," as the cliché goes. St. Louis first baseman Bill White said, "None of us liked the deal. . . . Lou had a lot of talent, but he didn't know anything about baseball." But manager Johnny Keane gave Brock the green light to be what he could be, and Brock responded in a big way. He not only batted .348 for the rest of that season and stole 33 bases in a Cardinal uniform, but by the time he finished his 19-year career he had set the career record for stolen bases (later broken by

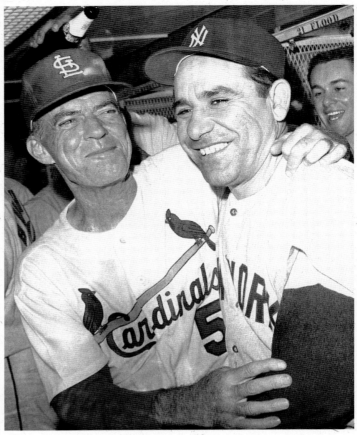

Less than 24 hours after this photo was shot at the conclusion of the 1964 World Series, the pennant-winning managers—Johnny Keane (left) and Yogi Berra (right)—were unemployed. Keane resigned from St. Louis, and Berra was fired by the Yankees, who replaced him with Keane four days later.

Rickey Henderson). Broglio, on the other hand, would win just seven games in the next three years and be gone from baseball after 1966.

The second turning point was a midseason blowup between shortstop Dick Groat and manager Johnny Keane. It took a clubhouse meeting to clear the air. With that, the ballclub kicked it up a notch. They started to win, and they chased down the foundering Phils the last week of the season. Even though the team was winning, owner Auggie Busch was disappointed with general manager Bing Devine and fired him on August 17. He was also fed up with Keane, whom he planned to axe after the season.

On the field, the Cards were as solid a team as any NL aggregation that had recently appeared in the Series. Most of their infield had started that season's All-Star Game. Ken Boyer at third and Bill White at first supplied superb defense and timely power hitting. Groat, though he lacked the physical skills of many others, was a guy who used intelligence and hard work to reach the top of his field. The Cards outfield featured Curt Flood along with Brock and late-season pickup Mike Shannon—all first-rate fielders, and Flood posted a .311 average, too. With a well-armed pitching staff—Ray Sadecki, Bob Gibson, and Curt Simmons won 20, 19, and 18 games, respectively—the Cards were ready. Having survived a scorcher of a pennant race, they were steeled for pressure.

Almost no one remembers that the American League had a pennant race that year, too. The Yankees had been in third place as late as mid-August, but an 11-game winning streak begun on September 16 propelled them to the top. The White Sox kicked off a nine-game streak a week later, but it wasn't enough. The race ended with the Bronxmen a game ahead of Chicago and two up on Baltimore. But things were different in New York: Yogi Berra was the Yankee manager, not the catcher. Jim Bouton was elbowing Whitey Ford for the number-one starter spot. Mickey Mantle was on his last legs; Roger Maris had driven in just 71 runs. Instead of dominating their opponents as they had in the past, these Yanks had been pushed to extra innings 26 times. The message was loud and clear: These weren't your parents' Yankees.

Roger Angell said this of the 1964 World Series: "I cannot remember two Series opponents that were more closely matched in strength, weaknesses and combative optimism." The Cards were quoted saying how much they were in awe of playing in Yankee Stadium, but because the two frequently met in Florida spring training exhibition games they were hardly in awe of the team. This Series marked the second time in history the Yanks had appeared in five consecutive World Series—a record not likely to be broken anytime soon.

Cardinals catcher Tim McCarver would find more fame as a broadcaster than a player, but his finest moment in uniform was this three-run homer in the tenth to defeat the Yankees in Game 5 of the 1964 World Series. His .478 average paced St. Louis to a seven-game title.

Whitey Ford started Game 1 (to the average young fan of the time, this seemed as immutable a fact as sunshine in Los Angeles), but this year's model Ford had a sore arm and wasn't his old self, and the Cards pocketed the game. The Yanks turned it around in Games 2 and 3, both times leaping on 38-year-old knuckleball reliever Barney Schultz for victories. The Cards returned with the help of a Ken Boyer grand slam to take Game 4, and a three-run homer by Card catcher Tim McCarver was the difference in Game 5. Joe Pepitone swatted a Yank grand slam to win Game 6.

Game 7 pitted Gibson against Mel Stottlemyre for the

third time in the Series. Gibson dominated early, and the Cards put together back-to-back three-run innings in the fourth and fifth. The Yanks clambered back but couldn't complete the job. The Cards had beaten the Yankees, and the men of the Bronx had lost consecutive World Series for the first time since 1921–22. After the season the Yankees fired Berra as manager and hired Johnny Keane in his place. It was that kind of year.

THE DYNASTY TAKES A TUMBLE

The New York Yankees' run of success was unprecedented in any sport. From 1926 through 1964—39 years!—they had a winning record every single season. They appeared in 29 World Series (going back to 1921) and won 20 of them. They twice played in five consecutive Series, and one of those times won all five. They also had a run of four consecutive world championships. But by 1965 the Yankee era was definitely over. They were able to finish above .500 only once in the next five years. In 1966 they actually finished tenth, as low as you could go in the American League, 26½ games out of first. (*The Yankee Encyclopedia*, pinstriped to the core, proudly points out this is the best record of any tenth-place finisher in AL history.)

Yogi Berra was the first to admit he was aesthetically challenged, but, on October 4, 1964, he was sitting pretty with an AL pennant in his first season as Yankees manager. He was axed after a World Series loss but returned to skipper the Bombers again 20 years later.

The cracks in the Yankee edifice had started appearing several years before. The dismissal of Stengel and Weiss after the '60 Series loss left a hole in the team's baseball savvy that was never filled. The '61 team rode the bats of Mantle and Maris and the pitching of Ford and not much else to win in an expansion year. The older players were aging fast, and the younger players didn't strike terror into the heart of any opposing players. Tresh, Bouton, and Pepitone were hardly Keller, Reynolds, and Gehrig. The '62, '63, and '64 Series proved this Yankee team was far from invincible.

The 1964 season marked the downslide for several other reasons. That year, manager Berra was losing control of the team; at one point he boarded the team bus after an upsetting loss and heard utility infielder Phil Linz playing his harmonica. Yogi swatted the instrument out of Linz's hands, and the two shouted at each other. The whole incident was stupid and ugly. That kind of stuff happened to bush league teams; it was definitely *not* in the Yankee mode. In addition, that year the Yankees became the first big-league club owned not by a rich individual or a handful of wealthy sports fans, but instead by a corporation. Worse yet, the corporation was CBS, a television network. Pundits from around the country wailed at the predicament this would create for the national pastime. (As always they turned out to be somewhat right and somewhat wrong, but for all the wrong reasons.) One flagrant blunder made by the new bosses was the dumping of Mel Allen, longtime and much beloved broadcaster, whose upbeat delivery perfectly matched the glory of the team on the field.

In 1965 the amateur draft was instituted. This was an obvious move to counter the wealth of the Yankees and the Dodgers and improve competitive balance. Before the draft, those two teams, with more money, could hire more scouts and sign more players than the poorer teams could. The mystique of the glorious histories of these two teams had an effect as well. If you were a talented high school ballplayer, would you rather become a Yankee or a Tiger? A Dodger or a Cub? The two rich teams saw the draft as a direct slap in their faces, and they were absolutely right. (It wasn't until the era of free agency that the Yankees would return to prominence, once again able to spend money other teams just didn't have.)

The New York fans didn't hang around for tradition's sake. In 1964, even though they lost 109 games and the Yanks won the pennant, the New York Mets outdrew those legendary Bronx Bombers. The "Amazin's" would continue to win the battle for the New York fan's heart (and ticket money) for the next 11 years.

Roger Maris was traded in December 1966; after winning only a pair of games in '66 and '67 alike, Whitey Ford hung up his spikes. Mantle ended his brilliant, though pained, career after the next season. If you add up his homers (536), his walks (1,733), and his strikeouts (1,710), you could claim that Mickey

Mickey Mantle's popularity stretched far and wide, even as his career waned. These youngsters reach out for a touch of greatness before the start of a 1965 Yankees–Senators exhibition game in San Juan.

Mantle played around eight seasons without ever putting the ball in play. The glory of the Yankees was history.

It's possible that the real reason for the Yankees' plunge from dominance to mediocrity and worse was their failure to sign young African-American and Latin talent. They were among the last teams to integrate. And when the Yanks did enlist a young African American or Latino, they tended not to select the best. While the Braves were signing Rico Carty and the Pirates Willie Stargell, the Yanks picked up Roy White and Hector Lopez. Of course, the American League lagged behind the senior circuit in that regard in general. In 54 NL offensive races from 1961 through 1978, whites won only four batting titles, one slugging title, and five home run crowns. When Elston Howard won the 1963 AL MVP Award, he was the first black man to win in his league; the NL already had honored a non-white 11 times. Regardless, the Yankees' inability or unwillingness to take advantage of the burgeoning market of non-white talent was a huge mistake.

Elston Howard was the first African American to play for the Yankees and, in 1963, the first to be awarded the American League MVP Award (here presented by league president Joe Cronin). The announcement provoked its share of hate mail and racist commentary.

THE LATIN INCURSION

Prior to Jackie Robinson in 1947, Major League Baseball's doors were closed to dark-skinned Latin Americans as well as African Americans. However, the majors did feature several light-complected Latinos. Cuban-born Esteban (Steve) Bellan played big-league ball in the 19th century; fellow Cuban Armando Marsans appeared in 100 games or more four times in the 1910s. Most of these players were Cuban; most were middle

Ozzie Virgil began to play baseball with U.S. Marines in the 1950s and eventually became the first Dominican to reach the majors. The sport enjoyed explosive popularity in the Dominican Republic, which went on to become an extraordinary source of talent. Here, Dominican kids practice with American G.I.s in 1965.

infielders. A few appeared during the war years, then disappeared soon thereafter. One exception was Hi Bithorn, a Puerto Rican pitcher who won 333 games for the Cubs and one for the White Sox in the mid-'40s (18 in 1943).

By the '50s, the quality of Latino players as well as the quantity was increasing. Sandy Amoros patrolled left field for the Dodgers, and Bobby Avila won a batting title for the Indians. Slick fielder Chico Carrasquel spent several years as the regular White Sox shortstop before being replaced by Luis Aparicio, who helped bring the stolen base out of the mothballs and remake it an important part of the game. Both were born in Venezuela.

The second wave of players impacted by baseball's opening its doors to African Americans came in the form of dark-skinned players from Latin America. The first dark-skinned Latino ballplayer really made a stir. The lovable Minnie Minoso was a fine player who played with such a sunny disposition and childlike enthusiasm that he was instantly a fan favorite. He hit better than .300 eight times in a 17-year career and showed power and baserunning skills as well. He led the league in triples and steals three times each. Bill Veeck "unretired" Minnie for two games in 1976 so he could be a four-decade player. Then Veeck did it again in 1980, making Minnie the first five-decade player. Minnie even played one game in an independent minor league in 1993, making him a six-decade pro baseballer. (The team was owned by Veeck's son Mike.)

First baseman Minnie Minoso was, in 1949, the first dark-skinned Latino to reach the bigs. He was 28 when he debuted but also played briefly—at the behest of master promoter Bill Veeck—at ages 53 and 57, making him (along with only Nick Altrock) a five-decade player.

The three Alou brothers made their major-league debuts for the Giants between 1958 and 1963. Felipe, the oldest, was the first Dominican to become a major-league regular. He was a strong and smart hitter with plenty of pop in his bat. He later earned respect around the game as an excellent manager, even under adverse conditions—namely, managing the Montreal Expos. Brother Mateo (Matty) learned the art of poking singles from Pirate manager Harry Walker and became a batting champ in 1966. Jesus never played regularly but acquired a reputation as a high-quality pinch hitter.

Luis Tiant seemed to be born old. He came to the majors at age 23, but he already looked like he'd been around the track more than once. Tiant's quality pitching stats (229 career wins, six 15-plus win seasons, two World Series) fail to give an accurate picture. Tiant's pitching motion ran counter to "the rules" that every pitching coach tries to teach. He came overhand,

As the last of the American Negro Leagues disbanded in 1960, Major League Baseball diversified rapidly. Sixty percent of the '66 Pirates' non-pitchers at-bats were by players of color, including (left to right) Matty Alou, Manny Mota, Roberto Clemente, and Willie Stargell.

sidearm, three quarters, with high, low, and no leg kicks. He could pause in mid-motion, cast his eyes skyward, and then deliver a devastating slider over the corner. He could be herky-jerky or smooth as silk. He had a repertoire of deliveries like the guy at the piano bar has a repertoire of songs. The hitters, more often than not, were left humming to themselves. And after the game, the photos often showed "El Tiante" smoking a victory cigar that looked to be a foot long.

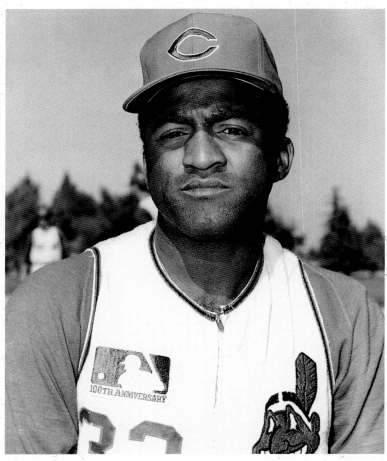

Latino players such as Luis Tiant not only bolstered baseball's talent base but demonstrated a colorful exuberance for the game that helped fuel the sport's popularity to extraordinary levels in the 1960s. "Looie" led the AL in ERA twice, including '68, when he held batters to a then-record 5.3 hits per nine innings.

In 1964 two Latino players exploded onto the big-league scene, each possessing the kind of hitting skills seldom seen in rookies. Dominican Rico Carty was with the Braves; Tony Oliva (whose real name was Pedro, but he had used his brother Tony's passport to get out of Cuba) was with the Twins. Carty hit an amazing .330 his first season and would have been second in National League batting average if he had come to the plate four more times (enough to quality for the title). To this day there are people who feel he should have won the Rookie of the Year Award instead of Richie Allen. Carty's career was checkered with bad luck. He sat out an entire season with tuberculosis; one year his shoulder was separated seven times. But when he was healthy, he was a strong slugger who combined a fine average and decent power. In 1970 he batted .366. But as the final indication of his bad luck, he finished his career with a .299 average—just two hits short of the coveted .300 mark.

Tony Oliva was plagued by bad knees throughout his career. His roommate, Rod Carew, remembered hearing Oliva frequently moan and cry at night from the pain and wander through the hotel trying to find ice to pack on his knees to ease the suffering. Like Carty, Oliva showed up with a bang—a .323 average his first year, enough to win the AL batting crown. Then he won it again his second year, making him the first player to top the league his first two seasons. He would top the .300 mark five more times before his knees forced him out of the game. In the dead-ball '60s only one other American League hitter had a 200-hit season (New York's Bobby Richardson).

The nickname Orlando Cepeda brought with him to the big leagues from Puerto Rico was "The Baby Bull," not because Orlando was small but because his father, one of the greatest players in Puerto Rican baseball history, had been called "The Bull." Orlando was a Giant who never played in New York, so, unlike Willie Mays, the San Franciscans took him immediately to their hearts: He was "theirs." Homering off Don Drysdale in his first game didn't hurt, either. Cepeda rocketed to the Rookie of the Year Award in 1958, with 25 homers, 38 doubles, and 96 RBI. In 1961 he was awesome, knocking 46 balls out of the park and driving home 142. The next season he belted 35 homers and knocked home 114 as his team went to the World Series, only to lose in seven games to the Yankees. Then Cepeda injured a knee lifting weights; he was afraid to admit it, so he struggled through the 1964 season, putting up good numbers despite the pain. But fans and manager Al Dark suspected the big slugger of just being lazy. Cepeda finally opted for surgery, but he was still in the doghouse when he returned from rehab. He was dealt to the Cardinals in '66, where he compiled another All-Star season and helped them to the World Series.

It has been reported that one key member of the Giants organization in the early '60s was overheard making derogatory comments about Latinos. Orlando Cepeda (shown) responded by hitting 379 home runs—the most by a Puerto Rican until Juan Gonzalez passed him in 2001.

The greatest Latino pitcher of the decade was Juan Marichal, a man who defined pitching consistency and quality for more than ten years, but unfortunately also pitched during the career peaks of Koufax and Bob Gibson, so he never won a Cy Young Award. Marichal was a joy to watch on the mound—unless you were 60 feet, six inches away with a bat in your hand. He used no windup, but his leg kick often had him nearly scraping the ball on the ground behind him as he began to throw. He had a baffling assortment of deliveries, and he threw them all with pinpoint control. He averaged fewer than two walks per game for his entire career. Marichal won six games his first year, 13 his second, and 18 his third. He then began a run of seven sensational seasons during which he led the league in wins, complete games (including 16 consecutive in 1968), shutouts, and innings pitched twice each. He averaged 21 victories a season and five shutouts during that time. For the decade of the '60s, Marichal won 191 games, more than anyone else in baseball— 27 more than Gibson. In fact, Marichal won more games than Gibson every one of those years.

In June 1963 Marichal became the first Giant pitcher since Carl Hubbell to toss a no-hitter. Then, just two weeks later, he banged up against Warren Spahn in what may have been the greatest pitchers' duel of all time. Both Spahn and Juan threw 16 innings in that game; neither one allowed a run until Willie Mays homered for a 1-0 Giant win. Perhaps the clearest evidence of Juan Marichal's greatness was his performance in All-Star Games. He appeared in eight games against the best the American League had to offer, threw 18 innings, had a 2-0 record, and allowed only one earned run.

Few non-Anglos achieved celebrity in 1966 America, but Juan Marichal was a pioneer. Only weeks before he graced this Time *magazine cover, the "Dominican Dandy"—who had grown up under dictatorship—bought a full-page ad in his nation's largest newspaper, urging citizens to vote in their presidential election.*

¡Arriba!

Words can hint at the greatness of Roberto Clemente on the baseball field, but they fail miserably when trying to describe his greatness as a man. Several times eager filmmakers have tried to tell his story, but they have always given up. What he did, the way he lived, his devotion to his family, his country, and his fellow people, and the stunningly selfless way he died are all so far beyond what any of us even dream of that the only credible response is stupefaction. Baseball has had all kinds of heroes, but Clemente's heroism runs deeper and truer than anyone else's.

As a player, Clemente was the opposite of the easygoing Minnie Minoso. Clemente brought a fierce intensity to everything he did. He was driven to excellence, and his most superlative performances always followed some perceived slight, as he rose past the insult to succeed even more dramatically. The way he stood at the plate, the way he swung the bat, ran, and threw seemed to push his body past every conceivable limit. His swings didn't just come from the heels; they came from the purposeful place of exceeding fire within him.

By the time Clemente was 14 years old he was a playing against Negro Leaguers and major-leaguers in his home of Puerto Rico. As a teen he played in the same outfield with Willie Mays in a winter league. Even then he belonged. Signed by the Dodgers, Clemente was confused

Embittered by his eighth-place finish in the MVP vote, Roberto Clemente never wore his 1960 world championship ring. Instead, he donned the one he earned as MVP of the '61 All-Star Game, where his teammates included Willie Mays (center) and Hank Aaron (right).

Pirates fans embraced the stylish, stately Roberto Clemente (here as the defending NL batting champ at the start of the '62 season). "The Great One" became the second ballplayer (Jackie Robinson was first) to appear on a U.S. postage stamp.

when he was immediately assigned to Triple-A Montreal and was treated a little strangely. He would have a great game and then be benched for several games, or he would be pinch-hit for in the first inning with two men on base. The team hadn't told him they were trying to hide him from other teams' scouts, who could draft him away from the Dodgers for just $4,000. So discouraged was Clemente, he almost quit baseball.

But the Pirates saw through the Dodgers' ruse and snatched him up. He was an immediate sensation in the outfield; in his first two seasons as the Buc right fielder he gunned down 18 and 20 unaware base-runners trying to advance. By the time his career ended he had led the league in assists five times. Clemente had his first great year in 1960, as did the whole Pirate team. His stellar play—both defensive and offensive—and his unmatched hustle on a simple bouncer to first base in the eighth inning of the final game of the World Series helped the Bucs take the lead.

Roberto Clemente finished lower than third in the batting race only four times during the '60s. This hit was special: No. 2,000 of his career, in Pittsburgh on September 2, 1966. He would get exactly 1,000 more before his career was tragically cut short.

The next season Clemente chose to use a heavier bat, figuring it would reduce his tendency to overswing on bad pitches. He then won his first batting title with a .351 mark. This was the second year of a string of twelve .300-plus seasons. Like Carty and Oliva, Clemente suffered from a host of physical problems, from backaches to bone chips in his throwing elbow. But even though Clemente complained about his ailments to anyone who would listen, the pains didn't keep him out of the lineup. He appeared in more than 143 games eight seasons in a row (and four times played in more than 150).

Today, with other sports seemingly attracting African-American youth more than baseball, players of Latino origin and descent are becoming the rich new legacy of Jackie Robinson, as baseball welcomes incredible talent regardless of national origin or skin color.

BASEBALL GOES SOUTH

The only reason Boston Braves owner Lou Perini was able to move his team to Milwaukee in 1953 was because the American League had blocked the attempt of St. Louis Browns owner Bill Veeck to move there. Perini, whose position in Boston was miserable, realized Veeck had been on to something, and he packed up his team and slid into amazing riches in Milwaukee. By 1962, however, Perini was looking to retire from baseball ownership, and he sold the team to an association of several investors, headed by Braves GM John McHale. But the investor group consisted of six former minority stock-holders in the Chicago White Sox. They weren't Milwaukeeans; they didn't live there, and didn't want to. The absentee owners had no idea how deeply the town loved their Braves. Bottom-line oriented, the moguls noticed that attendance for the team was no longer breaking records and began a search for a new town.

Atlanta-Fulton County Stadium housed Major League Baseball's first southern team, beginning in 1966. After the novelty wore off, the Braves drew fewer than one million fans in 12 of 19 seasons from 1972 through 1990. Three times in the mid-'70s, fewer than 1,000 showed up for a game.

The obvious place was Atlanta, the large, progressive southern city where Major League Baseball had no presence at all. Minor-league ball had been a big hit throughout many parts of the South for decades, and Atlanta was no exception. However, Charlie O. Finley, owner of the Kansas City Athletics, also liked the smell of Atlanta. He proposed to move his ensemble there, but the AL owners stiffed him just the way they had stiffed Veeck—and apparently for the same reason: They just didn't like the guy. So the American League missed out on not one but two fine cities as new moneymaking venues for their teams.

Construction began on Atlanta–Fulton County Stadium in 1964. Baseball officals announced that a major-league team was coming their way; they just couldn't say which one yet, which didn't please anyone. Bad feelings were running high everywhere. Milwaukee fans were miffed that they were being mentioned as an ex-baseball city. The National League didn't like the secretive way the Braves were proceeding. So, fearful of legal action that would cost everybody a lot of dough (the team still had a year left on its lease), the National League prevented the owners group from moving for the 1965 season, forcing them to stay in Milwaukee for a "lame duck" year that only intensified the animosity. The owners thought they had the answer: They offered the city half a million dollars to break the lease. However, this only made them (and Major League Baseball) look even grubbier. That year a car sales representative named Bud Selig started a personal campaign to return big-league ball to Milwaukee.

This move was quite different than the move from Boston, where the Braves had been second-class citizens at best. For the town that had taken the Braves into their hearts, "The shift out of Milwaukee was one of the ugliest affairs in baseball history," according to Morris Eckhouse. It was carpetbaggery at its worst, matched only by Charles O. Finley's slip-sliding of his A's from Kansas City to Oakland two years later.

DOME ON THE RANGE

When it opened in 1966, it was called "the Eighth Wonder of the World."

Even though it was built in a state where almost everything is oversize, the Houston Astrodome was overwhelming from the start. Just the idea of a covered ballpark was a novelty. The dome not only had to be air-conditioned to protect occupants from the searing Texas heat, but it had to be high enough to allow for balls hit high into the air. It stood 18 stories high, had room for 30,000 cars, and generated $30,000 air-conditioning bills each month. The first ballpark with theater seating, the Astrodome had an initial capacity of 42,217 (later expanded to 54,816). Fans were entertained by indoor fireworks, a scoreboard "home run spectacular" featuring a snorting bull, and a grounds crew dressed in spacesuits.

Things didn't always work as planned. The 4,500 plastic skylights caused a glare that resulted in fielders "losing the ball" in the roof. After conditions deteriorated to a point where outfielders wore batting helmets for day games, the team painted the skylights and reduced the day lighting by 25 to 40 percent. The subsequent lack of sunlight killed the original grass surface, which was replaced a year later by the artificial AstroTurf (a low-maintenance synthetic that created fast "AstroTurf hits" and high-bounding outfield balls, though infielders appreciated the true hops). The hard surface created a new problem of turf injuries: shinsplints, sore knees, and other wear and tear.

Other problems also surfaced: Ed Kranepool of the New York Mets once complained that the Astrodome air-conditioning was blowing out when the Astros batted but blowing in when the visitors batted. Mike Schmidt was deprived of a tape-measure homer when his long blast to center field struck a loudspeaker during a game in 1974. Under prevailing ground rules, the Philadelphia slugger had to settle for a single (though it was arguably the longest single in baseball history!).

Two years later, on June 15, 1976, the only rained-in game in baseball history occurred when torrential rains flooded the city with ten inches of water. The Astros and visiting Pittsburgh Pirates got to the rainproof Astrodome, but the umpires, fans, and most stadium personnel could not.

The Astrodome, in service from 1965 to '99, was the first of several domed ballparks, some of them with retractable roofs. Another, originally named Enron Field, replaced the Astrodome in 2000.

Houston Astrodome

In 1966 the Boston–Milwaukee Braves added Atlanta to their resume. They drew 1.5 million fans to their bright new ballpark, which was about three times as many as had come to see the team in the rancorous lame duck year, although just 600,000 more than they had drawn in 1964. The new park was homer-friendly, so it was quickly dubbed "The Launching Pad," which helped draw fans. So in terms of the bottom line, the move ranked as a success, but it was nothing like the shift from Boston to Milwaukee, which set attendance records. The Braves attendance for 1966 was only sixth best in the National League. The Braves moguls had gotten what they wanted, but baseball got a huge black eye in the process.

When the Braves moved from Milwaukee to Atlanta in 1966, Mobile, Alabama's Hank Aaron became baseball's first superstar from a southern team. Though his years in the Peachtree state were fraught with racial enmity, he spoke stridently with words of justice and a bat of magic.

A POWERHOUSE BUILT ON PITCHING

The second team to move in the 1950s, the St. Louis Browns, could hardly have done any worse when they shifted to Baltimore and became the Orioles. The miserable Browns had broken the *half*-million mark in attendance just four times in 30 years. But the new Baltimore ownership quickly realized that they had to become more than the town's newest novelty act. To succeed, they had to construct a winning team. So they began to build... slowly, but wisely. With Paul Richards as their first general manager (he was the field manager too), succeeded by Lee MacPhail (although the dead opposite of his dad, Larry, in personality, he had a keen baseball mind), they put together a pitching staff of young fireballing hurlers lacking in experience, control, and knowledge but able to learn how to pitch at the big-league level. Then they picked up the other pieces where they could. They landed Hoyt Wilhelm on waivers in 1958. Hoyt, who hadn't made it to the majors until he was 28, won the National League ERA crown as a Giant his rookie season. In his first year in Baltimore, he took the AL crown.

Wilhelm was a rarity: a knuckleball pitcher who had always been a knuckleball pitcher. But Wilhelm's knuckler

Brooks Robinson (leaping) and pitcher Dave McNally (who just completed a 1-0 Game 4 shutout of the Dodgers) were key operatives in Baltimore's 1966 sweep—the franchise's first World Series win.

was in a league of its own. More than a few catchers set records for passed balls trying to snag Hoyt's best pitch: that bizarre, dancing, mind-of-its-own delivery that surprised the pitcher throwing it as often as the batter trying to hit it. But manager Richards had an idea; he devised a super-huge glove for the catchers to use when on the receiving end of Wilhelm's floaters. As big as 50 inches in circumference (about 17 inches across), the glove was ruled illegal a few years later when new regulations set a limit on the size of the mitts, but it sure worked wonders for Hoyt.

Hoyt Wilhelm's knuckleball—a pitch typically thrown with the fingertips, not the knuckles—made him the first relief specialist elected to the Hall of Fame. In 1960, Orioles manager Paul Richards developed an oversize mitt so his catchers could snare it.

The O's were built one piece at a time. In 1955 they brought up an 18-year-old kid who would take a few years to develop into a big-league hitter, but who was born a sensational star with the glove—Brooks Robinson. Robinson became not just the

team's star, but its soul as well. His stolid, dependable work ethic matched up perfectly with the blue-collar town's fans. By 1960 he ranked third in the voting for league MVP. That year he began a string of 16 consecutive Gold Gloves. It didn't take long for him to earn the nickname of "The Human Vacuum Cleaner." When he retired he took nearly every fielding record for third basemen with him. The O's stationed big bomber Boog Powell in the outfield in 1962 and the next year traded for Luis Aparicio, at 29 years old still a fine fielder, as their shortstop. Baltimore began to knock on the door of the American League leadership, but the Yankees weren't letting anyone in.

Shown here in the midst of a four-hitter that bested Sandy Koufax in Game 2 of the 1966 World Series, Jim Palmer was one of four Orioles to combine for 33 straight innings of goose eggs to climax a sweep of the Dodgers.

The first "Kiddie Corp" pitching staff was growing a little long in the tooth by 1965, but a second wave was coming. Baltimore's starting rotation that year featured "old timers" (26-year-olds) Steve Barber and Milt Pappas, along with 22-year-old Dave McNally and 20-year-old Wally Bunker. The real prize was a rawboned 19-year-old, Jim Palmer. Management had such faith in his potential that they pulled the trigger on a blockbuster trade after the 1965 season, dealing one of their aces, Pappas, to Cincinnati for the supremely talented (but 30-year-old) Frank Robinson. When Reds President Bill DeWitt was asked how he could deal his star, he answered, "He's an *old* 30." It was

Frank Robinson, Moe Drabowsky, and Brooks Robinson (left to right) were heroes of the 1966 Series opener. The "Robbies" pounded back-to-back home runs, while Drabowsky tied a record by fanning six straight Dodgers as part of his 6⅔ innings of shutout relief.

one of those quotes that goes down in baseball lore and is still remembered today.

All Frank Robinson did in 1966 was win the Triple Crown. With him as offensive centerpiece, the Orioles topped the AL in runs scored, batting, and slugging. On the defensive side, no team had fewer errors. They won the pennant by nine games. However, they were set to face the Dodgers of Koufax and Drysdale in the World Series, so no one really gave them much of a chance.

They proceeded to shock the world. In one of the best team pitching performances in World Series history, the unsung O's toppled the Dodgers, who had won the Series in 1963 and 1965. In Game 1, neither Oriole starter McNally nor Drysdale could pitch out of the third inning, but Baltimore reliever Moe Drabowsky (known as much for the high-quality hot feet he gave in the bullpen as anything else) allowed the Los Angelenos just one hit over the final six-plus innings, and the O's took a 5-2 victory. Amazingly, the run the Dodgers pushed across in the third inning would be their last tally of the Series. Palmer tossed a four-hit shutout at the Dodgers in Game 2, and even though only one of the four runs Koufax allowed was earned (Willie Davis was playing an adventurous center field), it was

plenty. Orioles 6-0. (Roger Angell pointed out that the Orioles had six runs, while the Dodgers had six errors.) Sadly, though, it was the last game Koufax would ever pitch; his chronic arm problems forced him from the mound forever.

Game 3 matched Claude Osteen, star of the '65 Series, against Bunker. Wally allowed six hits but no runs; Claude gave up just three Oriole safeties, but one of them was a 430-foot smash into the bleachers by Paul Blair. With it, the Orioles took a three games to none lead in the Series. McNally and Drysdale locked up again for Game 4, with much different results from the first contest. Both men allowed just four hits. But McNally permitted just singles, while one of the hits off Drysdale was a Frank Robinson home run. It was the first time ever that an American League team not named the Yankees had swept a World Series.

AN UNBELIEVABLE SEASON

The Boston Red Sox players of the 1960s loved playing for owner Tom Yawkey. He treated them well, paying them what they deserved or better. But even more enjoyably, there was no real pressure on them to win. Yawkey's mild-mannered style of avoiding conflict and confrontation had resulted in a "country club" atmosphere. No one forced them to work; they could relax, play the game, and relish their paychecks. The closest they had gotten to a pennant since Ted Williams had left was a sixth-place finish. But in 1967 they brought in a new manager. In his first big-league assignment, Dick Williams laid down the law immediately. He removed the responsibility of "team captain" from star Carl Yastrzemski's shoulders. Yaz was

In high school, Carl Yastrzemski once hit safely in 26 consecutive plate appearances. He finished his pro career as the only American League player to accrue both 3,000 hits and 400 home runs, a feat only Cal Ripken, Jr., has accomplished since.

miffed—until he realized that Williams was making it clear Yaz's job was to hit; Williams would take care of the rest. Williams quickly installed rookies Mike Andrews at second and Reggie Smith in the outfield. He tightened up the pitching staff. Jim Lonborg, who had relaxed through a comfortable career with a lifetime 19-27 mark, picked up on Williams's intensity as well. All in all the 1967 personnel weren't that different from the bunch who had lost 90 games the season before. The difference could be found in Williams's drive for perfection. The Red Sox were quickly transformed into a team with a knack for executing the basics flawlessly, which is one mark of a winner, if not the only one.

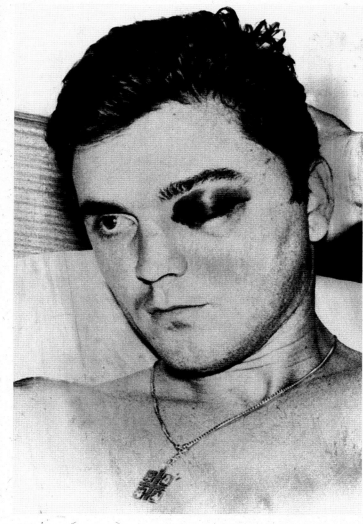

Tony Conigliaro hit 56 home runs before his 21st birthday. (Mel Ott, with 61, is the only player ever to have beat that pace.) Unfortunately, the promising career of the Boston outfielder was derailed by beaning in 1967. Effectively blind in his left eye, Conigliaro made two comebacks but could not sustain them.

The Sox didn't start out beating the world. At the All-Star break they were just two games over .500, six games back, in fifth place. But right after the midsummer classic they gelled, taking ten straight. Lonborg was pitching better than he ever had, and Yaz was superb.

By August 18 the Sox were just 3½ games back. But they suffered a terrible blow that day when their young superstar-to-be, Tony Conigliaro, took a bone-crushing fastball in the face. Although he was just 22, he had already slugged 104 big-league homers. He came back valiantly years later, but he was never what he could have been. The Sox shrugged off the near-tragedy, Yaz picked up the slack, and the team kept charging.

However, they had a raft of competition. The White Sox, Twins, and Tigers were not far away. On August 22, the four teams were separated by just a single game. In fact, at no time after August 6 was there a wider gap between first and fourth than 3½ games. It was simply the hottest pennant race anyone had ever seen.

Lonborg was dominating the league, and the Red Sox were getting solid pitching performances from Jose Santiago, Gary

Bell, and John Wyatt. But Yaz was the story. If he wasn't carrying the team on his back, he was at least pushing the cart. Time after time he delivered the crucial hit or made the game-saving catch. During the last two weeks of the season he batted .523 with five homers and 16 RBI. No player had ever responded to such a challenge in such a fashion. While many players (indeed, many *people*) buckle under pressure and perform worse in tough situations, for half a season in 1967 Carl Yastrzemski relished that pressure like it was a Fenway Frank with the works.

Going into the season's final week, the four

teams were only 1½ games apart. Chicago flopped first, getting plowed under by the Senators. As the final weekend started, the Tigers' schedule featured two doubleheaders against the Angels while the Red Sox were hosting the Twins. To win it all, Boston had to sweep the last two games and hope the Tigers lost at least one of their four. In those final two must-win games, Yaz was all over the place. He drove home six runs (including three on one homer) and made a great throw to slam the door shut on a late-inning Twin rally in the final game. Meanwhile, the Angels took one game each in their two doubleheaders with the Tigers to give the Sox the title free and clear.

Their opponent in the '67 World Series was the reconstituted Cardinals. In 1966 the St. Louis team moved from the cramped, hot, ancient quarters of Sportsman's Park into the brand-new, ultramodern, air-conditioned locker room of Busch Stadium. They dealt Dick Groat and Ken Boyer and obtained Orlando Cepeda and Roger Maris. Maris, always a fine right fielder, forced Mike Shannon to move to third base, and Mike took to the switch. The addition of power and defense was

The 1967 Red Sox were the first team of the century to win a pennant after finishing in ninth place the previous year. The Fenway faithful— more than a few of whom would wait in line for as long as it took to get World Series tickets— hoped in vain for their first world title in 49 years.

exactly what the club needed. Cepeda, who had been accused of malingering in San Francisco, was welcomed to the boisterous Card clubhouse with open arms. He gave as good as he got, was rechristened "Cha Cha" for the loud dance music he played in the clubhouse, and proceeded to win the MVP Award. Catcher Tim McCarver finished second in the voting, Lou Brock was seventh, and Julian Javier was ninth. The Cards took the NL flag by 10½ games. In July, Card ace Bob Gibson had his leg broken by a drive off the bat of Roberto Clemente. It seemed likely that Gibby would be out for the season, but he returned down the stretch and made three starts in the World Series.

The Red Sox wished he hadn't. He threw a six-hitter at them in Game 1, with the only run he allowed coming on a solo homer by his mound opponent, Jose Santiago. Lonborg started Game 2 and returned the favor with a one-hit shutout—the first World Series one-hitter in 20 years. Yaz knocked in four of his team's five runs.

In the 1967 World Series, Carl Yastrzemski—here stroking one of his three home runs—swatted .400. But because his teammates hit just .193, the long title drought persisted for the Red Sox. (The pitcher is Dick Hughes, the only man ever to cough up three homers in one World Series inning.)

In Game 3, Card hurler Nelson Briles won a complete game, 5-2. Gibson was impressive again in Game 4, tossing a shutout, and the Cards had the Sox down three games to one. In Game 5, fans from both sides were chewing their fingernails. The Red Sox took a 1-0 lead into the top of the ninth, and then former Yank Ellie Howard popped a bases-loaded single to drive in two runs for the Sox, shutting the door on the men from St. Louis.

The Red Sox cranked three homers (but all solo shots) in the fourth inning of Game 6 against Card starter Dick Hughes. A two-run homer by Lou Brock tied the game at four heading into the last of the seventh, when the Bostonians exploded for four runs. Cards manager Red Schoendienst yanked everybody out of his bullpen that he could, using a total of eight pitchers in the game, to no avail. The Series was tied.

The question for Game 7 was whether Dick Williams would start his ace, Lonborg, against Gibson on just two days rest. Williams did, and his plan failed. Lonborg allowed home runs to Gibson and Javier, seven runs in all in his six innings of work, while Gibson was once again masterful, throwing a three-hitter. The final score was 7-2. With this performance, Gibson became only the third pitcher in the previous 47 years to win three games in one World Series. The Red Sox "Impossible Dream" season missed the final icing on the cake.

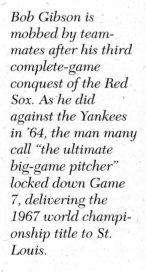

Bob Gibson is mobbed by team-mates after his third complete-game conquest of the Red Sox. As he did against the Yankees in '64, the man many call "the ultimate big-game pitcher" locked down Game 7, delivering the 1967 world championship title to St. Louis.

Facing an American League that scuffled to a meager composite batting average of .230 in 1968, Denny McLain became baseball's only 30-game winner from 1935 to the present. He was famous, flamboyant—and ultimately fallible, incarcerated multiple times later in life for offenses ranging from cocaine dealing to embezzlement.

THE YEAR OF THE PITCHER

The misguided effort to make sure expansion didn't lead to batters breaking Ruth's home run record every year reached its full, miserable culmination in 1968. It has gone down in history as "The Year of the Pitcher," but Roger Angell suggests a better moniker would be "The Year of the Infield Pop-up." The trend, which had begun in the late '50s, was goosed by baseball establishment's overreaction to the brief flicker of extra offense in the expansion years: They increased the size of the strike zone. As newer, more pitcher-friendly ballparks were built, offensive totals shrunk more. Pitchers who were already strong and smart took advantage, becoming even stronger and smarter.

But 1968 was by far the most embarrassing for anyone who called himself a big-league hitter. The leagues' *combined* batting average that year was .237, or a little less than the '62 Mets batted as a team when they tried to nail down the crown as the worst team of all time. One of every five games was a shutout. The home run total that had irritated Commissioner Frick in 1961 took a tumble too; by '68 it was down by 735. Fewer runs were scored per game than in any season since 1908, when one baseball per game was all Christy Mathewson needed to win 37 games, and Big Ed Walsh 40. Only five National League batters managed to hit .300 or better in '68; and if Carl Yastrzemski

hadn't had a hot bat on the last day of the season, the AL would have had none. (In fact, Yaz was the only ALer with more than 100 at-bats who hit .300.) The historically mighty New York Yankees batted just .214 as a team. Seven big-league pitchers had an ERA below 2.00; 14 more were under 2.50. Compared to any other season since the arrival of Ruth, 1968's totals always come out worse.

Two exceptions stand out: Matty Alou, whose simplicity-defined batting style ("Keep your head down and poke it to the opposite field") worked even when pitchers ruled the earth, batted .342, .338, .332, and .331 from 1966 to '69; and Frank Howard, who was so big his strike zone was already twice as huge as anyone else's. In 1968, when the rest of the major-leaguers were flailing and fanning, the big guy hit 44 homers.

Ford Frick was replaced as commissioner in 1965, but one has to wonder if he looked fondly at the style of baseball he had helped create, because, as said before, fans respond to offense. It was abundantly clear: The 1968 style of baseball was boring fans to tears. One almost gets the feeling that the several super World Series of the decade were about the only reason for fans to maintain any interest. At least one historian claims that because the game was so dull, fans fell away and, instead of paying attention to baseball, started organizing protest movements and marching against this or that. True or not, many people even today will

No one told Frank Howard that 1968 was "The Year of the Pitcher." That year, the hulkish "Hondo" set a still-standing record of ten home runs in a six-game span and began a three-year streak of at least 40 round-trippers and 100 RBI.

WILD MAN BLUES

Steve Dalkowski spent nine years in the minors trying to harness a fearsome fastball that was less predictable than a wild stallion. He never succeeded.

A 5'10", 170-pound southpaw, Dalkowski struggled through the

Steve Dalkowski

minors, mostly in the Baltimore Orioles organization, as managers and pitching coaches tore their hair out trying to teach him control.

Two 1957 games were shining examples of their frustration:

• On August 17, Dalkowski was pitching for Kingsport of the Appalachian League when he walked 21 batters and made *six* wild pitches in a 9-7 loss to Wytheville.

• On August 31, the lefty picked up a win, beating Bluefield 7-5, but had 18 walks to go with his 24 strikeouts.

"Hearing him warm up on the sidelines was like hearing a gun go off," said Dalton Jones, a major-leaguer who faced Dalkowski while still in the minors. "I kept thinking, 'If this guy ever hits me, he'll kill me.' I batted against Nolan Ryan

and Sudden Sam McDowell but Dalkowski was noticeably faster."

The bespectacled pitcher once threw six straight wild pitches and hit the man in the on-deck circle. One of his fastballs shattered an umpire's mask, while another ripped the earlobe off a batter.

Just how fast he pitched is subject to conjecture, since the wild lefty played before the era of radar guns, but he easily exceeded 100 miles per hour. He fanned 1,396 men in 995 innings but walked almost as many (1,354). As a result, the Connecticut native finished only 46-80 with a 5.59 earned run average.

Wild off the field as well as on, Dalkowski was 26 and beset by arm problems when he pitched his last game in 1965, having never reached the majors.

tell you the world began to fall apart in the late 1960s; any correlation between dull baseball and social upheaval may be left to the mind of the reader.

RECORD BREAKERS

When good pitchers are given the advantage of high mounds, big ballparks, and an expanded strike zone, they will set records. The list of league leaders for pitching stats in the 1968 season of course includes such proven pros as Juan Marichal and Don Drysdale (who set the consecutive-scoreless-inning record at 58⅔), Luis Tiant, and Dave McNally. A host of newcomers first made their mark that year, too, including Jerry Koosman, Steve Blass, and Tom Seaver. And there are some unexpected names, now mostly forgotten, as well: Bobby Bolin, Stan Bahnsen, and Bob Veale. In September, Gaylord Perry and Ray Washburn pitched no-hitters on consecutive days in Candlestick Park.

By 1968, Denny McLain had already made a name for himself, though not always on the positive side of the ledger. He was a pitching star who loved the limelight. He played the organ in a Las Vegas lounge act and would appear on TV at the

drop of an *Applause* sign. In 1966 McLain won 20 games for the Tigers, and he would have done the same in 1967 if a mysterious toe injury hadn't cost him his last six starts. Fans gave him the razz for that (the Tigers had been eked out of the pennant by the Red Sox) when the '68 season started, but he won them over with one of the most dominating seasons in pitching history. He started the season by winning 18 of his first 20 decisions and ended it with 31 victories, baseball's first 30-game winner since Dizzy Dean won 30 in 1934, and the ninth highest total in the 20th century. His earned run average was 1.96, almost two runs a game better than it had been in '67. The flamboyant McLain went from bum to beloved in Detroit. He won the Most Valuable Player Award that year and was the unanimous choice for Cy Young honors.

Dizzy Dean, base-ball's last 30-game winner (1934), congratulates Denny McLain on his 30th following the Tiger right-hander's defeat of Oakland on September 14, 1968.

Over in the National League, Bob Gibson had a pretty fair year himself. He won 22 games while losing only 9. He had 28 complete games and 13 shutouts and fanned 268 batters. He held opponents to a .184 batting average and a .233 on-base percentage. His ERA of 1.12 was the third lowest in 20th-century NL history, behind only superb seasons by Dutch Leonard and Mordecai Brown, more than 50 years before. It was simply one of the greatest seasons by a pitcher ever. But the truth is, it is probably even greater than most people realize. Throughout the season, Gibson was plagued by poor run support from his Card mates. He lost five of his first eight decisions that year; in those five losses his team scored a total of four runs. Gibson saw the need to take charge, and he proceeded to pitch five consecutive shutouts. From early June through early August, Gibson pitched 99 innings, allowing *only two earned runs*. But his teammates still weren't hitting for him. He was on the losing end of the Perry no-hitter, 1-0. As Peter M. Gordon pointed out in the *Baseball Research Journal*, Gibson allowed four runs in a game only once. He was never removed from a game in the middle of an inning—in other words, he was never knocked from the box. Gordon calculated that if the Cards had scored just four runs every time Gibson pitched, his record would have been 31-2. If they had scored just three runs each time (not that awesome an offense, even in "The Year of the Pitcher"), his record would have been 27-5.

Naturally, the baseball world was watching with interest when the World Series began with Gibson's Cards going against McLain's Tigers. And, as often happens, the pundits missed the whole thing, and the guy they *didn't* expect became the star.

Bob Gibson went 22-9 with a 1.12 ERA en route to the 1968 NL MVP and Cy Young awards. Gibson, who amassed 13 shutouts that season, allowed only two runs over a 99-inning stretch.

MR. TIGER

During a 22-year career spent entirely with the Detroit Tigers, Al Kaline proved himself a remarkable model of consistency. Though he never had a 30-homer season, he hit a career total of 399. He also posted a lifetime average of .297.

The 6'2", 185-pound right-hander led the American League once each in hits, doubles, batting, and slugging. His second season may have been his best: In 1955 he led the league with a .340 average and 200 hits, both career peaks. Only 20 at the time, Kaline became the youngest batting champion in baseball history. Bedeviled by injuries, he topped 150 games played in only two more seasons and led the league in only two more categories, slugging .530 in '59 and lacing 41 doubles in 1961.

Al Kaline

Kaline's shining hour came in 1968, when Detroit topped Baltimore by 12 games to take the American League pennant. Limited to 102 games that season by a broken arm suffered when he was hit by a pitch in May, Kaline squeezed into the Tiger lineup in time to help them win the World Series. Manager Mayo Smith, desperate to add more offense against a St. Louis pitching staff led by Bob Gibson, made a bold move late in the season, moving Mickey Stanley from center field to shortstop and switching Jim Northrup from right to center to make room for Kaline to return to his regular spot in right. All three played well defensively, but Kaline's bat was the key: He hit .379, homered twice, and led both teams with eight runs batted in. The Tigers won in seven games.

A Baltimore high school star who went straight to the majors after accepting a $30,000 bonus, Kaline never quite lived up to his initial image as Detroit's answer to Mickey Mantle. But his 11 Gold Gloves, 15 All-Star selections, and 3,007 lifetime hits helped him win election to the Hall of Fame on his first try in 1980.

Patrons paid 71 cents per Bob Gibson strikeout in Game 1 of the '68 Series. In 2002—based on the minimum ticket price of $250.00—it would have cost 14 dollars and 71 cents per K to see a 17-whiff game.

Detroit manager Mayo Smith knew that offense would be critical in a Series with such potent pitching, so he made a bold move. He brought longtime batting star Al Kaline back to a regular spot in the lineup, in right field, even though an injury had limited him to just 74 games there all season. To keep the best bats handy, Smith moved Mickey Stanley from center field to shortstop, replacing Ray Oyler, who had hit .135 during the season and would have been blown out of the box by Gibson, and made right fielder Jim Northrup his center fielder.

In Game 1, McLain allowed three runs in the Cardinal fourth, and that was all Gibson needed, as he let the Tigers hit safely only five times while striking them out 17 times, breaking Sandy Koufax's World Series record by two. Detroit's big lefty

Mickey Lolich, who sported the body of a beer-league soft-baller, defeated Nellie Briles in Game 2 to even the Series.

The Cards unwrapped their power bats in Game 3, as both McCarver and Cepeda slugged three-run homers. Game 4 featured Gibby against McLain again, and the outcome was the same. Lou Brock led off with a home run, and Gibson once again tossed a five-hitter. Final score: Cards 10, Tigers 1.

Many Detroit fans were still grumbling about the over-jazzy version of "The Star-Spangled Banner" sung by Jose Feliciano before Game 5 when Orlando Cepeda hit a first-inning two-run homer that gave the Cards a 3-0 lead over Lolich. But big Mickey hung tough for the rest of the game, and the Tigers responded with two runs in the fourth and three in the seventh for a 5-3 victory. In Game 6, McLain faced Ray Washburn, not Gibson, and he pitched a complete game, allowing only one run. A Jim Northrup grand slam helped the Tigers score ten times in the third inning to tie a Series record.

Game 7 pitted Gibson against Lolich, both architects of a pair of complete-game victories in the Series. Lolich was tough; Gibson seemed tougher. Through two outs in the seventh inning, he had allowed just one hit, an infield roller by Mickey Stanley. But two singles and a misplayed fly ball in center gave the Tigers three runs. A ninth-inning solo homer by Mike Shannon was all the offense the Cards could manage. The Tigers had won the Series, not on the much-heralded pitching of Denny McLain, but on the sturdy arm of Mickey Lolich, who went 3-0.

The '68 Series was the sixth of the decade to go seven games. Two of the others were four-game sweeps, but almost as breathtaking for their sudden surprise.

The lords of baseball decided it was time to rethink the pitchers' advantages.

In 1968, Mickey Lolich was the "other" Tigers ace, but he was the singular star of the World Series. Lolich and Bill Freehan celebrate after he beat Bob Gibson in Game 7—his third win. The stocky southpaw was born right-handed but switched as a toddler after a motorcycle fell on his shoulder.

A MAN ON THE MOON AND MORE

Ask a baseball historian to list the half-dozen most important seasons in baseball history, and it's not likely that 1969 will be in the top ten (unless the historian is a big Mets fan). But in its own quiet way, 1969 shook the game to its roots.

For one thing, there was a second round of expansion. And this time it was thought through a lot better than it had been at the time of the knee-jerk reaction to Branch Rickey and Bill Shea's Continental League challenge. The National League moved into Canada, with a team in Montreal, and farther into southern California, placing a team in San Diego. The AL wasn't quite as savvy, putting a team in Kansas City to replace the A's, who had split for Oakland, and one in Seattle, which wouldn't last two years there. But K.C. and Seattle (although in different incarnations) remain in the bigs today and are doing fine. By expanding to 12 teams in each league, baseball was forced for the first time to split into two divisions for each (the prospect of having 12th place teams was just too terrifying).

EXPANSION AND DIVISIONAL PLAY

From 1962 to '68, both the American and National League had ten teams, thanks to expansion that added two teams to each circuit shortly after the decade began. League winners went directly to the World Series matchup. However, ten-team leagues meant that postseason hopes ended quickly for the majority of teams.

With the addition of four new teams in 1969, the leagues decided to adopt a 12-team format but split each league in half, creating divisions loosely based upon geography. A best-of-five "League Championship Series" was created to determine pennant winners as well as to raise additional revenue.

This second wave of baseball expansion brought big-league baseball to Montreal and San Diego (National League), and Seattle, which won a short-lived franchise called the Pilots (it moved to Milwaukee a year later). The other expansion franchise was awarded to Kansas City, which had lost the Athletics to Oakland in 1968.

Baseball purists complained that the LCS lessened the chances of the team with the best record over the 162-game regular schedule to reach the World Series. A team with a hot hitter or pitcher might be more likely to win, they said, while a sudden slump or critical injury could deprive a deserving team of a trip to the fall classic. That very first year, in fact, the red-hot "Miracle" New York Mets roared down the September stretch in the original NL East

Frank Robinson scrambles safely back to third in a game against the expansion Seattle Pilots.

and upset the Atlanta Braves, sweeping them in the 1969 NLCS, while the Baltimore Orioles beat the Minnesota Twins in the American League.

Atlanta had been placed in the West only to accommodate the Mets, who had refused to agree to divisional play unless the league-champion St. Louis Cardinals shared their division. So St. Louis and its natural rival, the Chicago Cubs, wound up in the East, while Atlanta and Cincinnati were placed in the West. Twenty-five years later, when baseball went to a three-division format, the Braves finally found their rightful spot in the NL East.

So now, for the first time, a team had to win two rounds of postseason play to land the ultimate championship.

The second big change for the '69 season was adjusting the embarrassing imbalance between hitting and pitching that had all but ruined the game in the '60s. The first thing the rulemakers did was shrink that immense strike zone: Now it went only as high as the armpits and as low as the top of the knees—about a six-inch decrease for most batters. But most dramatically, the maximum legal height of the pitching mound was lowered from 15 inches to 10—a 33 percent drop. In truth, it may have been an even steeper falloff. Bill James maintains that prior to 1969 there was no true enforcement mechanism to make sure teams weren't stacking their mounds even higher than 15 inches. He points to the significant difference between home and road ERAs for Cleveland and Los Angeles as possible proof. So the leagues began to check the mounds carefully. Adjusting the height of the mound was the first rule change that directly affected the playing field's dimensions in the 20th century.

Along with all that, as if the pitchers needed *more* help, the occasional liquid artist moundsman had been getting away with throwing the spitball. So the rule was clarified to forbid the pitcher from putting his hand to his mouth while he stood on the mound. Of course these changes had an impact: With the dilution of pitching due to expansion as an added factor, the American League batting average climbed 16 points, the National League seven. The fans liked it, too: Attendance rose by 2,700 per game, or more than four million overall. In another attempt to boost the offense, the rules committee authorized several minor leagues to experiment with having another player bat for the pitcher every time he came up.

The last year of the decade was notable for another reason, too: It was the year the first baseball strike almost happened. The owners had been strong-armed by new Players Association director Marvin Miller into signing the first "Basic Agreement" in 1968, which included, among other things, a

Shrewd labor leader Marvin Miller was a thorn in the side of baseball owners. He led the players in a revolution that eventually changed the face of baseball forever.

raise in the minimum salary and increased meal money. It also established a procedure for arbitration of grievances (which would have an earthquakelike effect in just a few years) and included a provision that seemed harmless at the time but has come to mean huge headaches for big-league owners: No rules changes could be implemented without the players' approval. The owners, having had a year to really read the thing, tried to back off several of their commitments when the agreement's one-year term was up, and the players threatened to strike. Commissioner Bowie Kuhn was able to placate the more rambunctious owners, then essentially gave the players everything they wanted. One book written about the labor movement in baseball is titled *The End of the Game As We Knew It* (which is a quote from longtime baseball guy Paul Richards), and it couldn't be more correct.

The 1969 season provided plenty of unexpected on-field excitement, too. In the National League, the Chicago Cubs had hired Leo Durocher as their manager following the 1965 season. In his first year there, the eternally irascible Leo finished tenth (or about what his predecessors, the "College of Coaches"

When Leo Durocher took the helm for the eighth-place Chicago Cubs, he promised things would be different the next year. They were: In 1966 the Cubs slid to the NL basement, finishing in tenth place. But it wasn't long before the Cubbies began to improve.

IN THE BLEACHERS

Many historians believe the "Golden Age of Baseball" was an era when games were played on lazy summer afternoons, with enthusiastic spectators screaming support from the bleachers.

Fans considered themselves lucky to get a "live" opportunity to watch players in woolen flannels perform for minuscule salaries and it didn't cost them much: often a dollar or less for the cheapest seat in the house. (And that left enough change for a beer and a hot dog!)

Bleacher seats were a staple in old ballparks, especially those belonging to the original 16 teams, before baseball's first expansion. Though the ballpark-building boom of 1966–76 created circular, symmetrical bowls that swallowed up the stand-alone bleachers of the past, a few of the old parks survived with their bleachers intact.

The expansion New York Mets spent their first two seasons in the old Polo Grounds. Bleacher fans there, who adopted the Mets as lovable losers, showed off so many supportive signs from the bleacher seats that the team created a "Banner Day" promotion on which the fan with the most creative banner received a prize. That promotion helped compensate for a 120-loss season in 1962 and titanic home runs into the center-field bleachers *on successive nights* by Lou Brock and Hank Aaron, when Joe Adcock had been the only major-leaguer who had ever reached that distant target before.

When the Cubs found themselves surprise contenders in 1969, Wrigley Field fans suddenly awoke from the lethargy of rooting for perennial losers. Wearing bright yellow hard hats usually found on construction workers, the self-proclaimed "bleacher bums" became so rambunctious that the team had to erect a chicken-wire fence for fan safety. One of the bleacher bums' customs, later adopted by fans in other fields, was their refusal to keep home run balls hit by opponents.

"I would have hated being an opposing player in Wrigley Field at that time," said Randy Hundley, a catcher with the '69 Cubs. "They didn't hold anything back. If they knew something personal about a guy, they'd let it rip. They used to get on Willie Davis about his ex-wife. He was ready to go into the stands to fight them."

Beer consumption often contributed to the rowdy behavior of bleacher denizens. In Washington's final big-league game in 1971, souvenir-hungry fans stormed the field while the game was still being played, and with their team leading, no less. The umpires were forced to call the game, and it went into the record books as a forfeit to the visiting Yankees. Three years later, Cleveland's Nickel Beer Night promotion produced a riot that resulted in another forfeit against the home club. And Bill Veeck's Disco Demolition Night between games of a 1979 doubleheader at Comiskey Park fomented a forfeit against the White Sox.

Realizing that exuberance was preferable to inebriation, many teams eliminated roving beer vendors in the bleachers, forcing fans to leave their seats for refills, and stopped all sales of alcohol after the seventh inning. A few even banned beer in the bleachers—something present-day Wrigley fans can't even fathom.

Joyful fans root for their team from the bleachers.

had done), but he pushed, pulled, snarled, and shoved his minions into third place the next two seasons. The Cubs, who hadn't drawn a million fans to Wrigley Field since 1952, slid past that in 1968. Baseball was hot in the Windy City, and it was the Cubs, not the White Sox, who were attracting the attention.

Durocher's Cubs shot out of the gate in '69 with an 11-1 record. By August 14 they had a nine-game lead on the second-place Cardinals. In third, just one game behind St. Louis, were the Mets. The "Amazin's" had been a ninth-place club just the year before, but their team 2.72 ERA was a hairsbreadth from being the second best in the league. It was a good omen. Under manager Gil Hodges's stern leadership, they suddenly grew up. They didn't score much, but they pitched superbly. Had no one told them of the new rules? They were still pitching (and batting) like it was 1968. Hodges did his Casey Stengel impression; he moved players in and out. He used five outfielders and a pair of second and third basemen. Tom Seaver, on his way to 25 wins, rang up victories in his last ten starts.

On May 21 the Mets had an 18-18 record (which was the best they had ever been so far into the season). Then they tore off an 11-game win streak. By the middle of June they had

TOM TERRIFIC

Yes, one man can turn a team around.

It happened for the New York Mets when Tom Seaver reached the big leagues in 1967. That year, on a club that lost 101 games, he went 16-13 and earned NL Rookie of the Year honors. His golden arm and spirited leadership transformed baseball's laughingstocks into the 1969 world champions.

Although he would later pitch for the Reds, White Sox, and Red Sox, Seaver logged 198 of his 311 wins as a Met. The New York media dubbed him "Tom Terrific" and "The Franchise." In the Mets' magical '69 season, Seaver went 25-7 with a 2.21 ERA. He led New York back to the Series again in 1973 while posting a 19-10 mark and a 2.08 ERA.

Seaver generated his pitching power from his muscular thighs and thorough follow-through. In fact, his right knee would sometimes tap the mound after he unleashed a searing fastball. As a result, he struck out 200 or more batters for nine consecutive seasons and an ML-record ten overall (since broken). On April 22, 1970, he fanned 10 straight batters (another big-league record) and 19 overall. Seaver won the Cy Young Award in 1969, '73, and '75.

When Seaver retired in 1986, he had amassed 3,640 strikeouts while posting an ERA of 2.86. In Hall of Fame balloting in 1992, 98.84 percent of the voters selected him for enshrinement—the highest percentage of any player in history.

Tom Seaver

It seemed the 1969 Mets were as much about voodoo as victory. During the Cubs–Mets game on September 9, a black cat skittered between Glenn Beckert and the Cubs dugout. The Cubs lost the game and, the next night, lost the NL East lead to the "Miracle Mets."

moved up into second place with a 30-26 mark. And when they acquired veteran first baseman Donn Clendenon, they knew the magic was on their side. In his first 16 games in a Mets uniform, he drove in the lead or winning run in every game. And while the Mets stayed hot, the Cubbies fell apart, going 8-17 in September. The Mets took 22 of their last 27. They *were* amazing. One day Steve Carlton struck out 19 Mets to set the single-game strikeout record, and the Mets *still* won the game. On September 10, the Cubs lost the seventh of eight in a row, and the Mets zipped past them. New York City was in a tizzy. The Yankees dynasty was just a memory; the Mets were a hustling bunch of nobodies with a superior pitching staff.

When all the dust had settled, the Cubs were eight games back. In his book *Nice Guys Finish Last*, Durocher points out that the Mets were pitching out of their heads all year. He mentions that the Mets' *fifth* starter, Jim McAndrew, at one point put together consecutive wins with 1-0, 2-1, 6-0, and 3-0 scores. Some say Durocher overmanaged, that his team was just tired out. Leo says otherwise, pointing out that a late-season, late-night bed check (and with a day game scheduled the next day) indicated 13 Cubs were out on the town. They may have been tired, but not from playing ball.

Another surprise took place over in Baltimore. The team that had swept the Dodgers in the 1966 Series had taken a stumble. In mid-1968 team ownership replaced Hank Bauer with new manager Earl Weaver. The feisty, unprintable philosopher was making himself very clear when it came to the style and personality of his team. With "pitching, defense, and three-run homers" at its core, he led his team to 109 victories, the third-highest total in American League history. The O's won their half of the American League by 19 games, and, like the Mets, swept their opponents in the first League Championship Series.

Earl Weaver is considered one of the greatest managers of all time. A visionary strategist and incendiary competitor, he disdained "small-ball" strategies, not even instituting a sign for the hit-and-run play. In 17 seasons, he skippered Baltimore to six division crowns, four pennants, and the 1970 World Series title.

Of course the ga-ga New York fans were dishing out the hyperbole, calling the season "The Miracle at Flushing Meadows" (that's where Shea Stadium is located), but although the Mets were unexpected, they were no joke. Their team ERA was second in the league; 28 times they shut out their opposition, tops in the NL. They believed in manager Hodges's ability to make the right move at the right time, and they hustled from the opening pitch until the final out. Too, the NL East was by far the weaker division; the Mets didn't have to outplay the Braves of Aaron and Mathews and the Giants of Mays and McCovey. They just had to outlast Durocher's over-partied Cubs and the sagging Pirates and Cards.

Earlier that summer, the United States Space Agency successfully landed astronauts Neil Armstrong and Buzz Aldrin on the moon, which gave Mets fans a pretty obvious joke. Shortly thereafter, a music festival in upstate New York attracted several hundred thousand young people and came to be known as Woodstock. Protests against the U.S. involvement in Vietnam were at a fever pitch. It was a pretty heady summer.

So no one knew what to expect when World Series time came around. The Mets had been 100-1 longshots to win it before the season started, but that was before they dominated the NL East. The Orioles looked very strong; in fact, they were just beginning. This would be their first of three consecutive World Series appearances, and the first of five division titles in the next six years.

Oriole hurler Mike Cuellar was too much for the Mets in Game 1, and Don Buford led off with a homer against Tom Seaver. In Game 2, lefties McNally and Koosman locked up in a classic mound duel. The Mets had a 1-0 lead on a Clendenon homer when the O's came to bat in the seventh, still hitless. But a single by Paul Blair, a stolen base, and another one-base knock by Brooks Robinson tied it up. However, on the list of

Karl Ehrhardt—aka "The Sign Man"— was an integral part of the Mets experience at Shea Stadium in 1969. In the team's "bad old days," Ehrhardt's critical commentaries sometimes were confiscated, but in this special season, they were a thumb to the nose at Yankee Stadium's no-banner rule.

"Least Likely World Series Heroes" is the Mets' Al Weis. The shortstop who batted .215 for the season rapped a two-out single in the top of the ninth that gave his Mets the lead. They won 2-1.

Game 3 belonged to Tommie Agee, the Mets center fielder who had been American League Rookie of the Year in 1966 but had sputtered since. He led off the game

with a homer off Jim Palmer, then made two spectacular catches to save about five runs. Met hurlers Gary Gentry and Nolan Ryan benefited from his stylish play. The Mets won 5-0 and, amazingly, were up on the O's two games to one.

Game 4 was crucial, and it was a classic. The only score until the ninth inning was a Donn Clendenon solo homer for the Mets. With their backs against the wall, the Orioles responded. Two singles put Frank Robinson at third and Boog Powell at first after one out. Brooks Robinson lashed a line drive into right center that Ron Swoboda (never known for his defense) snatched off the grass with a sensational diving catch.

This Tommie Agee first-inning homer ignited the Mets to a 5-0 triumph in Game 3 of the 1969 World Series. He preserved his handiwork with two sensational catches in center: a wall-banger with two men on in the fourth, and a dive with the bases juiced in the seventh.

Donn Clendenon, the 1969 World Series MVP, is low-fived after his two-run homer in the final contest. His blow immediately followed the controversial award of first base to Cleon Jones, in which Mets manager Gil Hodges produced a shoe polish-scuffed baseball as evidence his batter had been hit by a pitch.

Frank tagged and rushed home to score and tie the game, but Boog had to stay at first. When the next batter also swatted a deep fly to right, Swoboda chased that one down, too. The Mets won the game in the tenth when a throw to first on a bunt play caromed off the runner and the man on second hustled in to score.

You could almost see it coming in Game 5. The Mets took it and the Series,

5-3, on homers by Clendenon and Al Weis (just his third of the year) and two clutch errors by the O's. It was true that men walked on the moon in 1969, but if you said that was more impossible than what the Mets accomplished that year in any saloon in New York City, you'd be in for an argument.

The decade had begun with baseball fat and sassy. But new pressures affected how it was played and where. Major-league owners responded clumsily, and the game suffered, but with further changes things seemed to be coming to order. No one knew that the biggest change was still on the horizon.

BASEBALL ENCYCLOPEDIA BRINGS STATS TO THE MASSES

It was the year man first walked on the moon, so it only seems fitting that baseball statistics also took a great leap forward during 1969. Macmillan Publishing's release of *The Baseball Encyclopedia* in '69 offered the first definitive source for lifetime and season-by-season statistics for every player in MLB annals, along with league standings, batting and pitching leaders, and team stats covering each year since the NL's 1876 formation. In addition to serving as a great means of ending barroom debates, the seven-pound tome affectionately dubbed "Big Mac" would, as hardball historian Bill James put it, "facilitate and thus encourage baseball mania."

The two men most responsible for the *Encyclopedia's* contents were Lee Allen and John Tattersall. Allen, historian for the Baseball Hall of Fame in Cooperstown, had spent the previous 30 years combing newspaper accounts and talking with old ballplayers and their descendants to verify everything from birth and death dates to nicknames. Tattersall, a shipping executive, was an expert in 19th-century baseball who had spent four decades amassing scrapbooks, publications, and box scores from

the game's earliest days. When these two men combined their talents, the result was a must-read for everybody from big-league beat writers to everyday fans.

Like any good research book, Big Mac (which in 1996 released its tenth edition) was updated and improved upon many times. Editors used a computer database to make sure every batting, pitching, and fielding record added up, and as a result of double-checking through

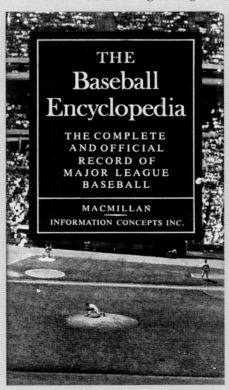

Macmillan's Baseball Encyclopedia

the years, several numbers—including the lifetime batting averages of a few Hall of Famers—were changed. Other nuggets included stats and biographical information for the long-neglected Negro Leagues and the All-American Girls Professional Baseball League, the latter of which was made famous by the movie *A League of Their Own*. Even data for Eddie Gaedel, the 3'7" pinch hitter St. Louis Browns owner Bill Veeck sent to the plate in one 1951 game, made the book: one game played, one walk.

The release of many copycat record books did little to tarnish the *Encyclopedia's* image, but the release of *Total Baseball* and the Internet explosion (24-hour availability of stats online) have sadly pushed it back onto many fans' bookshelves to gather dust. Even though it's much easier today to just type in Mark Fidrych's name than to flip through nearly 3,000 pages to find out he had 24 complete games as a rookie, the importance of Big Mac should not be forgotten. It helped bring forgotten players to life, gave the game its most accurate and permanent historical record, and helped stats (and fantasy leagues) grow in popularity.

1970s

DYNASTIES AND DOLLARS

Lowering the pitching mound and adding four more teams opened up the game in the early '70s. The era of the one-dimensional slugger was gone. Teams discovered that the more weapons they had, the better their chances to win. Call it "The Baltimore Theory of Balance," if you will, but by putting that philosophy to use, several organizations constructed impressive teams that were capable of more than just one sweet season. By the time 1979 rolled around, seven different teams had appeared in the postseason at least three times. It was the decade of the dynasty. Three years into the decade, baseball (or half of it) instituted the game's strangest rule change. Three years later, players who signed a big-league contract were no longer bound to one team for life. It was a revolution of grand style.

Pete Rose lunges into third base in Game 7 of the 1975 World Series. "Charlie Hustle," who popularized the headfirst slide, was emblematic of the power of sheer will to overachieve.

THE DYNASTIES ARE BORN

There are essentially two reasons why several teams became consistent winners for the decade of the 1970s. The first is that, with a 25 percent increase in just eight years in the number of teams, there were still some (expansion) clubs around who hadn't yet been able to solidify into competitive organizations. Which is another way of saying the big guys could still beat up on them. Second, the victory by the Mets over the Orioles in the '69 World Series looked to everyone like a fluke, which it was. The Orioles were built to be balanced, the Mets were not. It was actually a symbolic (although not factual) win by Baltimore. With hitters' batting averages coming back to normal places, and with speed and power still important factors, there were more different ways to win a game than anyone had mounted in a long time. Sure, a team with a couple of slow-footed bombers and a solid pitching rotation could win once in a while, but a team that wanted to win more often needed more tools in its bag. A wider variety of capabilities decreases the likelihood of slumps. So a team that was truly balanced—starting pitching, relieving, speed, defense, power, and on-base percentage—could become a consistent winner, even a dynasty. After free agency entered the picture, filling the hole in the lineup that made the difference could be a matter of simply opening the checkbook.

Jim Palmer (left), age 25, and Tom Seaver (right), age 24, were all the rage as the starting pitchers of the 1970 All-Star Game. They tossed three shutout innings apiece in what turned out to be a 12-inning classic that ended on Pete Rose's famed run-scoring wipeout of catcher Ray Fosse.

THE O'S SET THE TONE

When the Orioles hired Earl Weaver as their manager in mid-1968, he was hardly the new kid on the block. Weaver had been managing in their farm system for ten years. He had been instrumental (along with Paul Richards) in developing "The Oriole Way," a specific set of rules and guidelines that applied to every player and coach in the entire organization, from rawest recruit to World Series star. Thomas Boswell's fine essay, "Why Baltimore Wins More Games than Anyone Else," describes the system in detail. It's true that before "The Oriole Way" teams had developed personalities and styles of play, usually based on the approach of their top guy—Rickey, MacPhail, Yawkey—but never before had the philosophy been spelled out so clearly and consistently, so that everyone could get on board. It was genius. And it worked.

Before the 1969 season Baltimore acquired enigmatic pitcher Mike Cuellar and center fielder/leadoff hitter Don Buford. They gave the shortstop job to youngster Mark Belanger. It was just what the doctor ordered. The O's won 109 games in

LOOKALIKE BALLPARKS

Build it and they will come. That theory, expressed so vividly in the film *Field of Dreams*, also applied to the wave of new ballparks that sprang up during the '70s. These brand-new stadiums carried with them the air of novelty. Curious fans, hoping their teams would play better in new environs, came out for a look, causing significant spikes in attendance.

The symmetrical new parks, designed to replace decrepit fields plagued by inner-city locations, had better lighting, more seating, and a cleanliness that almost made them seem sterile. The fact that many of the parks were remarkably similar added to the aseptic feel. It appeared that each had been carved from the same cookie cutter. By comparison, only two of the 16 ballparks in use during the first half of the 20th century were symmetrical. The other 14 had individual angles and quirks that were often quite peculiar. But that was their charm.

Busch Memorial Stadium, opened in 1966, and San Diego Stadium, opened in 1969 (later renamed Jack Murphy Stadium and Qualcomm Park), both held 50,000. This was the same capacity as both Cincinnati's Riverfront Stadium, which had replaced the ancient Crosley Field bandbox, and Pittsburgh's Three Rivers Stadium, successor to Forbes Field. Riverfront and Three Rivers, whose names caused as much confusion as their similar designs, both opened in 1970.

A year later, the Phillies moved from Connie Mack Stadium (formerly Shibe Park) to a cookie-cutter model slightly larger than its cross-state rival. Veterans Stadium, also called The Vet, held 56,371 at its opening but squeezed in several crowds of 62,000 for big games.

Three other fields also opened during the decade: Royals Stadium, the first park with its own waterfall, in 1973, and both the Seattle King-dome and Montreal's Olympic Stadium four years later. The Canadian ballpark became the home of the Expos after the 1976 Olympics. Though Royals Stadium was the only new ballpark with charming features, it—like the other new parks—used artificial turf, which was cheaper to maintain than grass.

The advent of cookie-cutter architecture for ballparks reversed the early-century trend, leaving only six asymmetrical fields by the time baseball had expanded to 26 teams. The plethora of lookalike parks did not sit well with fans and media.

As Stanley Cohen wrote in *The Man in the Crowd*, "I had become accustomed to an entirely new generation of ballparks, round as doughnuts, merry nursery rooms, and as artificial and undistinguished as the suburbs in which they nestled. They look, all of them, like gigantic tiered wedding cakes with their centers sucked out."

Busch Memorial Stadium

1969 before dropping the Series to the overachieving Mets. The club was a textbook of balance. In a league that batted .246, eight of their nine regulars batted .280 or better. They led the league in on-base percentage and were second in team batting average. On defense, they made fewer errors than any other team in the league. Their pitchers led the AL in shutouts, in fewest walks allowed, and ERA. Then they got better.

Three Oriole pitchers won 20 or more games in 1970, and each pitched around 300 innings. The offense led the league in runs scored this time around. Five regulars (and one part-timer) swatted 17 homers or more. Boog Powell had 35, Frank Robinson 25. They almost led in fielding percentage again, missing by just a single point. They won one fewer game (108) than they had in '69 and took the AL East by 15 games. Once again, they swept the Twins in the LCS.

This time their opponent in the World Series was the Cincinnati Reds. First-year manager Sparky Anderson had not yet constructed his team in the Baltimore Balance mode. This club was a bunch of sluggers: Johnny Bench slugged 45 homers and Tony Perez knocked 40. Perez's 129 RBI total was second to Bench's 148, which had been topped by only one NLer in 33 years. Every outfielder belted at least 15 homers; even "light" hitter Pete Rose swatted 15. The World Series promised to be a bombs-away adventure.

In April 1970, Brooks Robinson put a tag on his luggage that read "1970 World Champions." Six months later he was both prophet and World Series MVP. His offensive contributions—such as this Game 4 long ball—were second-ary to his succession of jaw-dropping plays at third base.

Lee May's homer spurred the Reds to a Game 4 win over the Orioles—their lone victory of the 1970 World Series. The big first baseman—a future Oriole and, later, a highly regarded batting coach—drove in eight runs in the five games.

Instead, it turned on sensational glovework by Brooks Robinson. In Game 1 (the first World Series game played on artificial turf—they were in the Reds' brand-new Riverfront Stadium), the Reds jumped to a 3-0 lead against Jim Palmer, but the Orioles tied it up thanks to homers by Boog and Ellie Hendricks. Lee May opened the sixth for the Reds by slamming a ball over third base that should have been a double. Somehow Brooks grabbed it deep behind the bag, well into foul territory, and let loose a marvelous throw to nail the runner. This was just the first lesson in the 1970 Brooks Robinson Fielding Clinic. The Reds' jaws were still on the ground when Brooks homered in the seventh to give his team the lead they would keep.

In Game 2 the Reds took a 4-0 lead after three innings, but the Orioles banged one home in the fourth and another five in the fifth to win 6-5. Brooks made three more spectacular saves in Game 3, preventing at least two doubles, then popped a couple doubles himself. Pitcher Dave McNally settled everything down with a grand slam, and the O's enjoyed the final tally of 9-3.

Brooks was 4-for-4 in Game 4, but the Reds won 6-5 on a three-run homer by Lee May in the eighth inning. As he had in Game 2, Mike Cuellar started out poorly for Baltimore in Game 5, but the O's scored two runs each in the first, second, and third innings, and the Reds couldn't push across another run. The

Screwball artist Mike Cuellar was a complete-game victor, and Series MVP Brooks Robinson (#5) was protecting third base in the 1970 Series clincher. Cuellar, 24-8 that season, was a four-time All-Star and the ultimate "thinking-man's pitcher."

O's had a 9-3 lead, and the Series was theirs. But not until "Brooksie" capped it off with some sensational glovework at the hot sack. His diving catch of a Bench liner to third in the ninth effectively stopped the Reds cold. The "Big Red Machine" would need some tinkering if it was going to run with Baltimore.

The Baltimore men led the league in runs scored again in 1971. And the pitching may have been even better than the previous two years. All four Baltimore starters won 20 games or more that year, the first time that had been accomplished since 1920. McNally won 21; Pat Dobson, Jim Palmer, and Cuellar each rang up 20. They won their division by a dozen games and swept the LCS, this time over the Oakland A's.

Jim Palmer was establishing himself as one of the greatest pitchers of all time. He won 20 games eight times in the '70s; only two other AL pitchers have equaled a string like that. When he missed the 20-win circle it was because of injuries, not poor performance. Despite his lanky appearance, his style was classically smooth, and he was capable of laying down a bunt, slapping a single, or making a great defensive play when it meant the difference between winning and losing. He was the first AL hurler to win three Cy Young awards, and, if you ask him, he'd probably tell you he should have won more. He was the youngest pitcher ever to throw a World Series shutout and the only pitcher to have Series wins in three decades.

People who believe that in a short series the better pitching staff will win would have expected the 1971 World Series to be another mismatch. The oddsmakers concurred, making the Orioles 9-5 favorites over the Pirates as the Series started. The O's pitching was already famous; the Pirates' top hurler was the eccentric Dock Ellis. The Bucs had plenty of punch in their

Jim Palmer's prosperous career included three Cy Young awards and the singular achievement of World Series pitching victories in three decades. In 1970 (here), five of his 20 wins were shutouts.

lineup, leading the league in runs, hits, triples, homers, and slugging average. Their left fielder, Willie Stargell, belted 48 homers in '71, 20 more than any Oriole. And when the Bucs lost on the wet field of Baltimore in Games 1 and 2, their terrible play was almost an embarrassment to the sport.

But no one noticed that the Pirates had a secret weapon in right field: No. 21, the brilliant Roberto Clemente. Before the Series, Oriole Frank Robinson had popped off that he was going to show Clemente how right field should be played. Well, it was Clemente who gave the lesson—to Frank, and to the world.

Clemente simply captured the Series and made it his own. He had two hits in both the first and second games. In the fifth inning of Game 2, the Orioles were already up 4-0 when Frank Robinson slammed a ball to deep right with two men on base. Second-sack runner Merv Rettenmund tagged and went to third. He was safe, but Clemente's throw missed him by inches. The looks on the Baltimore faces were visible to all; they'd never come across anything like this before. For the rest of the Series, they didn't stray far from their bases.

In Game 3, Clemente drove in the first Pirate run, and then, with the Pirates leading 2-1 in the bottom of the seventh, he led off with a bouncer back to the pitcher, Mike Cuellar. Cuellar figured it was routine and prepared a lollipop toss to first, but Clemente was tearing down the line at full, manic speed. Cuellar tossed the ball wild, Clemente was safe, and in a

Pirates manager Danny Murtaugh presided over the first World Series game ever to be played under the lights, on October 13, 1971, in Pittsburgh. Murtaugh, a self-effacing storyteller, skippered the Bucs in four separate stints and won two world titles.

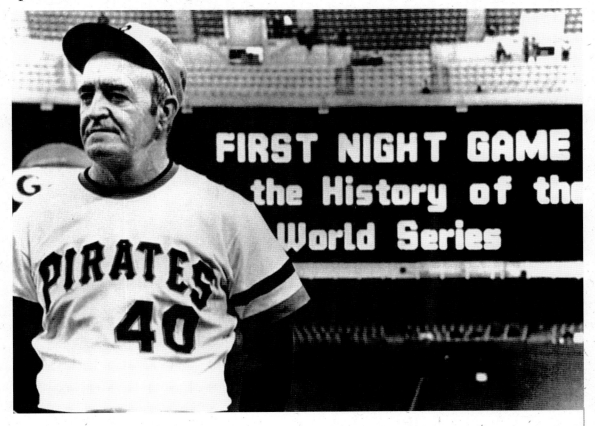

minute Bob Robertson belted a three-run homer that extended the Bucs' lead to 5-1.

Clemente was also superb in the Game 4 Pirate victory, swatting three singles. (That game marked the first night World Series game—61 million people watched.) He drove in a run in Game 5 as the Pirates took the Series lead. Clemente had a triple and a homer in Game 6 and made a sensational throw to keep the winning run from scoring for Baltimore in the ninth, although the Orioles did win in ten. In the final showdown, Clemente homered for the Pirates' first run in Game 7, in a pitcher's duel in which Steve Blass outpitched Cuellar 2-1. The Pirates had won the Series.

Clemente batted .414 for the Series, and by hitting safely in all seven games (which he had also done in 1960) he set the record for the longest consecutive World Series hitting streak by a National Leaguer. But it was almost his final taste of glory. The next year, Clemente rapped his 3,000th hit late in the season, and then the Pirates lost the NLCS to Cincinnati on a ninth-inning wild pitch. The superstar Puerto Rican had always been

Roberto Clemente was 37 years old when his hitting (including this homer that spurred Pittsburgh to a Game 7 win), coltish baserunning, and dazzling defense earned him 1971 World Series MVP kudos. As he had done in 1960, he hit safely in all seven Series games.

active in community service, particularly in his dream of building a sports complex in Puerto Rico for the island's youth. So when a devastating earthquake struck Nicaragua in December 1972, it surprised no one when Clemente went to work. With the same tireless passion that marked his on-field play, he solicited donations of food and money, packed boxes, and badgered airlines for the best deals on renting planes to deliver the supplies. When he heard that some of the supplies were being "liberated" by thieves and sold for profit, Clemente took matters into his own hands. On New Year's Eve, he boarded a plane he had rented with his own money. The cargo plane, overloaded with supplies, crashed into the ocean shortly after takeoff.

The word "tragic" is tossed around nowadays as a slightly more serious-sounding synonym for "sad" or "unfortunate." But Clemente's death was a tragedy in its truest sense. A man acted boldly in a cause he knew was just, but the consequences turned out to be much graver than anyone could have known. Major League Baseball waived the rule in which a player had to be five years gone from the game in order to be eligible for the Hall of Fame, and Clemente was the first Latino player enshrined there. At his inauguration ceremony, Commissioner Bowie Kuhn said, "He had about him a touch of royalty."

The 1971 Orioles were the only flag-winners ever with four 20-game winners on staff, but it was unheralded Pirates righty Steve Blass (#28) who dominated the World Series. After throwing a three-hitter in Game 3, he came back with a four-hitter in Game 7 (pictured).

PITCHING WONDERS

While the Baltimore Orioles and the Oakland A's climbed to world titles with strong pitching arms in the early 1970s, other noteworthy hurlers emerged on non–pennant-winning teams. Three of these pitchers in particular—Steve Carlton, Nolan Ryan, and Mark Fidrych—left an indelible mark on the game.

The Lefty Was All Right

A master on the mound and somewhat of a mystery off of it, Steve Carlton ranks among the greatest left-handed pitchers of all time. "Lefty" broke into the major leagues with the St. Louis Cardinals in 1965 and emerged as a true force in 1969 when he developed the devastating slider that became his signature pitch. He threw it nearly as hard as his fastball, and the pitch broke down and in against right-

handed batters. Despite his success, acrimony marked his relationships with management and the media. After a second contract holdout, the Cardinals traded Carlton to Philadelphia in 1972.

In his first season with the Phillies, Carlton became the fifth pitcher in history to win 20 games for a last-place team, notching an incredible 27 of the Phillies' 59 victories. He also tossed 8 shutouts and 30 complete games and fanned 310 batters to earn the Cy Young Award.

In 1975, Carlton was reunited with catcher Tim McCarver and found new life in his arm due to an intense conditioning program, which included swirling his arm in a vat of uncooked rice as well as practicing a variety of martial arts and the art of meditation. He went 23-10 with a 2.64 ERA in 1977 to

notch his second Cy Young Award. It was also the season that Carlton stopped talking to the media.

Carlton pitched for 24 seasons, winning 329 games—second to Warren Spahn among southpaws—and his 4,136 career strikeouts rank second only to Nolan Ryan. Carlton, a first-ballot Hall of Famer, compiled six 20-win seasons and was the first pitcher to win four Cy Young awards.

The Ryan Express

Mets fans are still steaming about the Nolan Ryan trade.

The hard-throwing right-hander was only 24 when the team packaged him with Leroy Stanton, Don Rose, and Francisco Estrada in order to acquire Jim Fregosi, hard-hitting shortstop of the California Angels, after the 1971 season. Fregosi, only 29 at the time, fizzled into oblivion within two years, while Stanton became a dependable outfield regular. Ryan's response was even better.

That first year, he became the Angel ace with 19 wins, 329 strikeouts, and a 2.28 earned run average. During his eight-year stay with the team, he won seven strikeout crowns, threw four no-hitters, and posted a pair of 20-win seasons. Two of the no-hitters came in the same season, 1973. He also fanned a record 383 batters in 1973.

To most batters, Ryan's 100-mph fastball was a blur. Only umpires got a good enough look to determine whether it was a ball or a strike. Too often, they decided the pitch missed its mark: Ryan issued more walks than any pitcher in baseball history. But just the

Steve Carlton

Nolan Ryan

thought of his uncanny velocity was enough to intimidate opposing hitters.

"Nolan Ryan is the only guy who could put fear in me," Reggie Jackson admitted. "Not because he could get me out but because he could kill me. You just hoped to mix in a walk so you could have a good night and go 0-for-3."

Dubbed "the Ryan Express" (after the '70s war film *Von Ryan's Express*), the pitcher tied Sandy Koufax when he notched his fourth no-hitter in 1975. Though he averaged more than four walks per game during his tenure with the Angels, Ryan also recorded more than a strikeout per inning, threw 40 shutouts, and racked up 156 complete games. The Houston Astros were glad to give the native of Alvin, Texas, a four-year, $4.5 million deal in November 1979. Nine years later, he signed with the Texas Rangers.

Ryan's likable, easy persona made him one of the game's most popular figures throughout his playing days. When an elbow injury forced him to call it quits in 1993, Ryan retired with major-league records for no-hitters (7), years played (27), and strikeouts (5,714). No pitcher has come within 1,577 whiffs of his monumental record.

The Bird Is the Word

Mark Fidrych exploded onto the baseball scene in 1976 as a charismatic rookie with the Detroit Tigers. Although he began the season in the bullpen, he made his way into the rotation five weeks later and never looked back. Fidrych, 21, started the All-Star Game, finished 19-9, and led the AL with a 2.34 ERA and 24 complete games.

Nicknamed "The Bird" because he resembled Big Bird from *Sesame Street*, Fidrych was truly one of a kind. He talked to the baseball between pitches, crouched to manicure the pitching mound with his hands, and returned any ball "with a hit in it" to the umpire. Detroiters, who hadn't had a sports team to cheer about in years, packed Tiger Stadium to see this joyous character. While the Tigers made a fortune off The Bird's gate appeal, Fidrych earned less than $17,000 in '76—including the dimes he fished for in pay phone coin returns.

But success was short-lived for Fidrych. A knee injury in spring training 1977 forced him to alter his delivery, and he was never the same again. In 1977 he started just 11 games and went 6-4 with a 2.89 ERA. He was also plagued by shoulder injuries, and by 1980 he was out of baseball, his major-league career having lasted just five seasons.

Mark Fidrych

THE SWINGING A'S

While the Orioles couldn't translate their everyday excellence into more than a single World Series championship, the Oakland Athletics won five straight division titles from 1971 to '75, appeared in three World Series in a row, and won all of them. That moves them into the slender trivia category titled "Only Us and the Yankees."

The Oakland team was the dead opposite of the corporate discipline the Orioles proffered. The A's were a bunch of strong personalities, some downright wacky. But you couldn't really blame them for it. Heading up their organization was one of the wackiest owners of all time (and one of the most disliked): Mr. Charles O. Finley. Finley was a forward-thinker; he is on record as proposing night games during the World Series as well as the designated hitter. (He also liked the notions of designated runners and orange baseballs!) Finley was known for his unique ability to both sum up the situation perfectly and completely miss the point. And although Finley wasn't lacking for money, he didn't feel his ballplayers should get much of it.

Like Bill Veeck, he ran unique promotions to encourage fan support. But there was something else in Finley's character that inspired the wrath of those around him. He bought a mule,

Unconventional A's owner Charlie Finley was a powerful, penurious—and polarizing—force during the '70s. On Opening Days, he forced his players to ride onto the field on mules such as "Charlie O," the team mascot.

made it team mascot, and named it after himself, which was fine. But then he went to team announcer Harry Caray, whose trademark "Holy cow!" had been bellowing from his lips for nearly 30 years, and asked him to change it to "Holy mule!" Improving the look of the team's uniforms was okay, but Finley wound up

Vida Blue was among the most "colorful" players of the 1970s. He won the AL MVP and Cy Young awards in '71, when he went 24-8 with a 1.82 ERA. Rebellious and brassy, he haggled over salary and threatened to play pro football.

dressing his men in green and gold combinations that turned the stomach, not the head. As a result of this behavior, and plenty more like it, Finley was simply a person it was impossible to be lukewarm toward.

The fans of the area never really perked to Finley or his team. Even during the team's five-year swing of dominance as one of the best teams in the league, in the game, and perhaps even of all time, the A's eked past the million mark in attendance just twice.

The A's weren't a team in any sense of shared effort except one. Even among their distinct set of personalities, which led to well-publicized clubhouse fistfights as well as lesser squabbles, the team was fiercely united in a single sentiment: how much they disliked Finley. By all estimates, this was a superior team. Managed by the forceful Dick Williams, they won 101 games in 1971. Rookie Vida Blue was a pitching marvel; he won 24 games and lost just 8. Just 21 years old, the lefty had already thrown a no-hitter the season before. In '71 he fanned 301 men, making him only the third AL pitcher since Bob Feller to reach 300. His ERA was a remarkable 1.82. He won both the Cy Young and Most Valuable Player awards. Catfish Hunter and Blue Moon Odom (both of whom had been given their nicknames by Finley) played vital roles on the pitching staff, and

Rollie Fingers was rapidly establishing himself as one of the game's great relievers (as well as sporter of one of the most remarkable mustaches).

The A's starting outfield averaged just below 25 years of age: Reggie Jackson, who had clubbed 47 homers two years earlier; Joe Rudi; and Rick Monday. Dave Duncan was becoming a stalwart receiver, and proven commodities Bert Campaneris (speed and defense) and Sal Bando (power and defense) handled the left side of the infield. The Orioles outplayed them in the 1971 LCS, but Finley's A's were making their move.

In 1972 the Athletics won eight fewer games, and Blue's holdout turned the season sour for him, but the A's were growing up. A deal of Monday for Cub lefty Ken Holtzman made up for Blue's decline; the A's led the AL in homers,

As per this announcement on Candlestick Park's scoreboard in 1972, major-league players called the first strike in the game's history on April 1. This one lasted less than two weeks, but during the next 30 years seven more work stoppages would occur.

and Campaneris stole more bases than anyone else in the league. Their appearance in the LCS against the Tigers was a harbinger of things to come. They won the first game 3-2 with a two-run comeback in the bottom of the 11th. After Odom shut out Detroit in Game 2, Joe Coleman returned the favor in Game 3. Game 4 was another nail-biter, with Oakland slipping out to a two-run lead in the top of the tenth only to have the Tigers chase home three in the last half to pull out the victory. Odom started Game 5, and once again it was a one-run decision, as Vida Blue finished up a 2-1 win for Oakland.

In the World Series that year the two teams couldn't have looked more unalike. The scruffy, mustachioed, multihued A's took on the clean-cut, classic-uniform-style Cincinnati Reds. The Reds were beginning to lay claim to the "dynasty" title themselves; this was their second Series appearance in three years. When it was over, the Athletics had won four games to the Reds' three, with six of the seven games decided by just one run. Part-time catcher/first baseman Gene Tenace drove in 9 of the 16 runs his Oakland team scored.

In 1973 the A's finished the season with 94 wins, then

In baseball's grand tradition of improbable World Series heroes, it was Gene Tenace's turn for the Reggie Jackson–less (hamstring) A's in 1972. This swing produced the first of his two home runs in Game 1. Tenace finished with four clouts and nine of the team's 16 RBI.

scraped and clawed their way to a five-game LCS win over the Orioles. Catfish, who along with Blue and Holtzman had each won 20 games in the regular season, took two of the victories, but the highlight was an 11-inning double-sided pitching masterpiece in Game 3. Both Holtzman and Mike Cuellar had allowed only three hits and one run as the A's came to bat in the last of the 11th, but leadoff hitter Bert Campaneris swatted Cuellar's second pitch over the fence for a 2-1 A's victory.

The National League champions were the New York Mets, who had managed to win the Eastern Division with an embarrassing 82-79 record, as the Pirates, Cards, and Expos all coughed up furballs the last two weeks of the season. Then the Mets, surprising as ever, toppled the powerful Reds in an LCS marked by fistfights and fan rowdiness. The World Series was no less amazing.

Oakland took Game 1, with Ken Holtzman more or less outpitching Jon Matlack. Holtzman allowed one run, Matlack two, but both of Oakland's runs were unearned. The American League had instituted the designated hitter in 1973, but it wasn't to be used in the Series, which was fine with Oakland, as Holtzman doubled and scored his team's first run.

Game 2 was wild and woolly. The Mets took a 6-4 lead into the last of the ninth, but with two outs and a man on second, a walk and singles by Reggie and Gene Tenace tied it up. Joe Rudi threw out a runner at home in the 10th. In the top of the 12th,

This exchange with umpire Augie Donatelli in the 1973 World Series would be the last spat of Willie Mays's career. The great center fielder delivered his farewell hit—an RBI single in Game 2 that would prove decisive for the Mets—and then retired at age 42.

Willie Mays (finishing out his career back in New York) singled in the go-ahead run. Consecutive errors by Oakland second baseman Mike Andrews pushed the Met lead to four. It was the longest game in World Series history to that point, running 13 minutes over four hours. After the loss, Finley forced Andrews to sign a paper saying he was injured so that he could try to replace him before the next game. No one fell for Finley's ploy.

The dugout intrigue surrounding Finley's boys never let up. Before Game 3, manager Williams told his players he could no longer put up with Finley and would quit after the Series. The Mets leaped to a 2-0 first-inning lead, but the A's scored one each in the sixth, eighth, and eleventh to win 3-2. New York took the next two games, 6-1 and 2-0, with Rusty Staub the offensive hero in Game 4 and Jerry Koosman joining with team cheerleader Tug McGraw to shut out Oakland in Game 5.

For Game 6, two of the best righty pitchers of the generation faced each other: Catfish versus Tom "Terrific" Seaver, in the must-win game for Oakland. Reggie Jackson had three hits and drove home two runs in the 3-1 A's victory. After six games, the A's had yet to hit a homer. No AL team had been zeroed on the homer board in a Series since 1918. Someone must have mentioned that to the A's before Game 7, as Jackson and Campaneris both hit two-run blasts in the third inning, and Oakland won its second consecutive Series, with a 5-2 effort.

For the second year in a row Rollie Fingers had appeared in six of his team's World Series games. He would appear in three more World Series before he retired and would leave the game with 341 saves, more than anyone else up until then. A subpar starter, he had found that relieving suited his mentality and his stuff to a tee. In Game 2 of the 1972 Series, Johnny Bench came to bat against Fingers in the eighth inning with the score tied at two, one out, and Reds runners on first and third. The count was two and two when Bobby Tolan stole second on ball three. There were now men on second and third. Manager Williams purposefully strode to the mound and ceremoniously called for the intentional walk. Fingers and catcher Tenace went through the motions, and when Bench relaxed, Tenace snuck back behind the plate. Fingers threw a strike, and the befuddled Bench could only watch as he was called out. It was one of those plays that makes the breath catch in your throat.

The A's had a new manager for 1974, the less-than-tactful Alvin Dark. But they didn't seem to mind—they took their

Rollie Fingers got a well-deserved celebratory champagne dousing after saving the clincher in the 1972 World Series against Cincinnati. Six of the seven games—one won and two saved by the future Hall of Fame reliever—were decided by one run.

Reggie Jackson (right) tallied nine hits and six RBI to earn the MVP crown of Oakland's 1973 World Series nail-biter over the Mets. An argument also could have been made for shortstop Bert Campaneris (left), who chipped in with nine hits, six runs, and three steals.

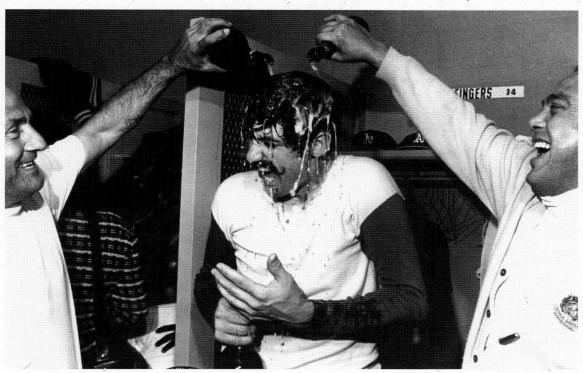

division by five games and won three of four to beat the Orioles once again in the LCS. This was the year of the first all-California World Series, as the Dodgers had bumped off the Pirates in the NLCS.

The A's had a fight in the clubhouse before Game 1 (nothing new there), then beat the L.A. team 3-2. The Dodgers took Game 2 but then handed the A's Game 3 with catcher Joe Ferguson's errors in consecutive innings helping Oakland to three runs.

Oakland also won Game 4 behind the pitching of Holtzman and Fingers. In Game 5 they had a 3-2 lead in the top of the eighth when a Dodger singled to lead off the inning but tried to reach third when the center fielder bobbled the ball. He was out by a mile, and L.A.'s chances were done. The *San Francisco Chronicle* called it "one of the biggest bonehead plays in World Series history.... The adventurous, strategy-defying [runner] was on his way to a paragraph in the same history book that features the names of Fred Merkle, Mickey Owen and Lou Brock." The runner's name? Bill Buckner. Yes, the same Bill Buckner who would make an even more egregious error for Boston in the 1986 World Series.

In 1975 the A's repeated as Western Division champs for the fifth consecutive season, but the powerful Red Sox swept them in the LCS, and their championship reign was over. Soon free agency would appear, and the Athletic stars would eagerly abandon ship to play for someone—anyone—other than the despised Charlie Finley. The team wouldn't appear in a World Series again for 14 years.

MOVE OVER BABE, HERE COMES HENRY

While several teams were succeeding consistently enough to be considered dynasties, the '70s also featured at least one sensational example of individual success. It

After watching the great Jackie Robinson play an exhibition game in Mobile, Alabama, a 12-year-old Hank Aaron was inspired to pursue baseball. At 40, Aaron himself became a lightning rod for race relations as his pursuit of Babe Ruth's home run record stirred America's cauldron of bigotry.

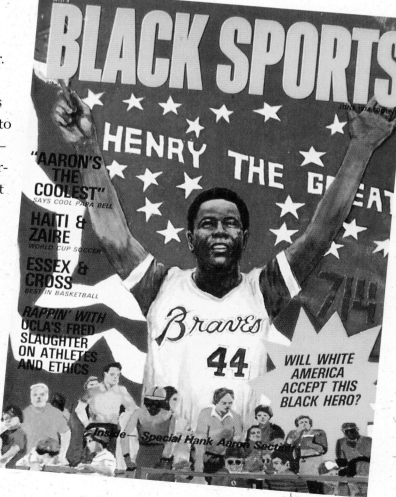

came in surprising fashion at the hands of a man who embodied the essence of perseverance even in the face of steep odds.

Henry (Hank) Aaron's professional career began in the Negro Leagues, where he played for the Indianapo-lis Clowns. He joined the Milwaukee Braves in 1954, getting his chance when Bobby Thomson broke a leg. (This was not unlike what happened to Willie Mays, who got his chance when Thomson moved from cen-ter field to third base.) Along with fellow sluggers Eddie Mathews and Joe Adcock (and superb pitchers such as Warren Spahn), Aaron

helped the Braves to first-place finishes in 1957 and '58 and a tie for the top rung in '59. They won the world championship the first of those years. The National League at that time had three amazing right fielders playing every day: Aaron, Clemente, and Frank Robinson. Fans of the era had the same furious debates as fans had often had earlier in the decade about Mantle, Mays, and Snider. Robinson had terrific power—and a huge chip on his shoulder that often exploded into fisticuffs. Clemente was haughty and proud, the vastly superior fielder of the three but far behind the other two in slugging ability. Aaron was simply excellent, and quietly so, every single year.

A glance at the lifetime stats of great players quickly shows the seasons in which they fell below what was expected: when they failed to deliver, when they drove in 80 runs instead of 100, when they played only 90 games instead of 150. Aaron's stats, however, were consistently at the highest level. He slugged 20 home runs or more 20 seasons in a row. (Ruth did it only 16 times.) He scored 100 runs in 13 consecutive seasons. And he tallied more than 100 RBI over and over again. So even though Aaron wasn't making headlines like Clemente or Robin-son or a dozen other flashier players, he was proving his great-ness with long-term excellence.

After drawing a walk in the second inning on April 8, 1974, Henry Aaron scored his NL-record-breaking 2,063rd run. But that was just an appetizer. His next time up, he sent an Al Downing slider over Fulton County Stadium's left-field fence for his 715th home run, breaking Babe Ruth's career record.

Aaron himself outlined the reason for the shape of his career. "Patience. It's something you pick up pretty naturally when you grow up black in Alabama. When you wait all your life for respect and equality and a seat in the front of the bus, it's nothing to wait a little longer for the slider inside."

Henry Aaron holds aloft the ball he hit for his record-setting 715th home run. Other than in 1971, when he hit 47, Aaron never hit more than 45 in any season. However, he blasted at least 20 a major-league-record 20 times.

At age 35, Aaron was considering retirement in the spring of 1969 when historian Lee Allen sat him down for a chat. Allen pointed out that Henry was only a few home runs behind Mel Ott for the all-time National League record, and that Aaron stood a good chance to reach the 3,000-hit plateau as well as set the all-time record for at-bats. Aaron perked up. He realized he could quickly change the nature of his relatively silent career, and then he could use his reputation to make a difference in the situation of blacks in sports and throughout American life, as he put it in the title of his autobiography, *I Had a Hammer*. Of course, Allen never mentioned Ruth's record of 714 lifetime homers. That record was untouchable, or so everyone at the time agreed.

So Henry kicked things up a notch, increasing his home run total from 29 in 1968 to 44 in '69. Then he hit 38, then 47 (the most he ever knocked in one season—and he was 37 years old!), followed by 34. All of a sudden he had passed those other milestones, including Stan Musial's lifetime total bases mark, and he was just 41 homers behind the all-but-impossible 714. He began a sensational finishing kick with one of the greatest seasons anyone has ever had. In 1973, at age 39, Aaron slugged 40 homers—one in every 9.8 at-bats, or, in other words, McGwire/Ruth territory. He began the 1974 season just one behind the Babe.

But the hate mail had been coming for a while. When Roger Maris chased Ruth's single-season record in '61, he was scorned and slandered for not being as great (or as likable) as Babe Ruth or Mickey Mantle. Hank Aaron carried an additional burden: He was black. The racist invective was disgusting; the death threats would have terrified other men. When people heard about the hate mail, supporters began to write, too, and Aaron received a plaque from the United States post office for getting more mail than any nonpolitician that year—930,000 pieces.

Hate mail or not, Aaron was on a mission. He tied Ruth in his first plate appearance of the season. Two games later, against Los Angeles, he walked in his first at-bat, then came around to score a run that broke Mays's lifetime NL record. No one noticed. The next time he came to the plate, he used his marvelous, magical wrists to loft an Al Downing pitch over the left-field fence in Atlanta. As he circled the bases, announcer Milo Hamilton shouted, "There's a new home run champion of all time, and it's Henry Aaron!" With day-in, day-out consistent excellence over 20 years, Henry Aaron had pushed aside the unbreakable record. Aaron finished his career with 755 homers, a mark for the next guy to shoot for.

THE WILD CARD HITTER

One of the offshoots of the pain and suffering from "The Year of the Pitcher" was experimentation with having another player bat in the pitcher's spot without affecting the hurler's ability to stay in the game. It was first called "The Wild Card Hitter," then "Designated Pinch Hitter," before "Designated Hitter" or "DH" was approved for use by the Ameri-

THE FIRST BLACK MANAGER

Twenty-eight years after Jackie Robinson smashed baseball's color barrier, another Robinson became MLB's first black manager. Frank Robinson opened the 1975 season as the skipper of the Cleveland Indians. He was quoted as saying that he wished Jackie was alive to see it.

At 39, Robinson was still an active player when he was hired to manage the Cleveland Indians. Baseball's first player/manager since Solly Hemus played 24 games for the 1959 Cardinals, Robinson relished his role. He even homered in his first at-bat for Cleveland, helping the Indians beat the Yankees 5-3 on April 7.

A combative player who became an outspoken manager, Robinson broke new ground when the Indians appointed him. But years later, he said it wasn't enough.

During his Hall of Fame induction speech, Robinson referred to the "systematic exclusion" of blacks from positions of authority in baseball, and said he wished he had spoken out on the topic at the time.

The first man to win Most Valuable Player honors in both leagues, Robinson finished his playing career in 1976 with 586 home runs, trailing only Hank Aaron, Babe Ruth, and Willie Mays.

Frank Robinson

He didn't enjoy the same success in his first managerial stint—mainly because his team didn't have the horses.

Under Robinson, Cleveland went 79-80 in '75, finishing fourth in the AL East, and then went 81-78 in '76. Though the team remained in fourth place, it posted its third winning season since 1959. A year later, however, the situation deteriorated rapidly. The Indians were plodding along at 26-31 when Robinson became the first black manager to be fired. He later managed the Giants, Orioles, and Expos, winning the Manager of the Year Award with Baltimore in 1989.

can League before the 1973 season. The AL was trying to catch up to the senior circuit in attendance. Since expansion, the AL had been within 1.5 million of the other loop in only one season. The reasons were simple, and they didn't really have a lot to do with levels of offense. In fact, in the ten years since both leagues first expanded, the American League had out-homered the NL every year but two. The NL wasn't outscoring them by a lot, either. In those ten seasons the AL outscored the NL three times, and five other times the difference was fewer than 300 runs (or less than one-third of a run per game). The American League's problem wasn't a lack of offense; the National League was simply playing a more interesting brand of ball. Part of the reason for that was that the NL was the first to embrace African Americans, a giant swell of talent. The AL was an early leader in recruiting Latin Americans, but the status of Clemente, who was more than a baseball star—he was a true international hero—encouraged young Latinos to gravitate toward the NL. The American League had expanded less wisely than the NL, too.

Interestingly, the idea of taking the bats out of the pitchers' hands was first suggested by National League President John Heydler in 1928, but it failed to go through when the AL rejected the idea. That didn't deter the owners of American League teams 45 years later. In 1973, for no good reason whatsoever, the American League voted in the DH. The results were

He jokingly called himself a "designated Hebrew," but it was for being the first designated hitter (on April 6, 1973) that the Yankees' Ron Blomberg earned his own display in Cooperstown. He drew a bases-loaded walk in his first at-bat as DH.

not what they had hoped for; even though it picked up their offenses a bit (and increased the number of complete games by 20 percent), they still didn't match the National League in attendance until the next expansion year, 1977.

Most baseball purists believe the designated hitter rule severely damaged the game. Players who were not even good enough defensively to flop around first base or left field could become genuine stars (and command star salaries). Similarly, players whose careers should have been long over got a chance to extend them, in quest of (now dubious) statistical records or, at the least, more secure retirement accounts. Who really wanted to see their favorite heroes end their career with a whimper? Even worse, strategy was diminished, because managers never had to face that ultimate of strategic decisions: Which is more important at this instant of this game—offense or defense?

In addition, the gap between the leagues grew wider, not closer. Managers who only knew American League baseball were befuddled by the complexity of options the other league offered. (Today it's high praise to call an AL manager a "National League–style manager.") Worst of all, the DH created the inexplicable situation that baseball, of all sports, is the only one where the two halves of the top professional echelon play by two different sets of rules—indeed, with two different numbers of players.

On April 6, 1973, Ron Blomberg of the New York Yankees stepped to the plate as the AL's first designated hitter. He quipped, "I've been the DH all my life—designated Hebrew." Playing as DH, Al Kaline reached the 3,000-hit level, which he might not have achieved otherwise. Players who had once been stars but whose physical problems had all but ended their careers got second chances—Tony Oliva, Orlando Cepeda, Frank Robinson. Players who had never been comfortable in the field got to hang around, too—Carlos May and Hal McRae.

Hall of Famer Orlando Cepeda bounced around with four teams in the final three years of his career. After limping through the 1971 and '72 seasons, Cepeda was able to survive as a designated hitter in '73, driving in 86 runs for the Red Sox.

THE MACHINE THAT RAN ON PRIDE

The Cincinnati Reds appeared in the World Series in 1961 and in 1970 and lost both times, once to the fearsome Yankees, once to the methodical Orioles. After finishing fourth in the NL West in 1971 when star catcher Johnny Bench slumped, the Reds picked up second baseman Joe Morgan and pitcher Jack Billingham in a big trade with Houston. Morgan became the "generator of the Big Red Machine," consistently excellent, providing speed and power, leadership and guts, defense and batting. For his part, Billingham provided consistent quality innings. Bench snapped back with 40 homers and 125 RBI in

CLOSE, BUT FEW CIGARS

Baseball historians remember the '70s as the decade of the "Big Red Machine," Charlie Finley's final Oakland dynasty, and the Yankee resurrection in which the Bronx Bombers returned to the World Series for the first time in 12 years. Only avid students of the game, however, remember the other challengers of the time: teams that won multiple divisional titles before falling under the postseason playoff system introduced in 1969.

Though the Pittsburgh Pirates powered their way to world championships both times they reached the World Series, against the Baltimore Orioles in both 1971 and 1979, they lost the National League Championship Series three times in between.

Willie Stargell anchored both Pirate pennants, with help from Roberto Clemente in '71 and successor Dave Parker in '79. Pittsburgh prevailed against persistent NL East challengers, outlasting the Cardinals during Joe Torre's MVP season in 1971 and the Expos, led by Andre Dawson and Gary Carter, eight years later. But the Bucs proved no match for Sparky

Anderson's Reds, who beat them in the playoffs twice, or the Dodgers during Mike Marshall's heyday.

Pennsylvania's other club, the Philadelphia Phillies, also proved potent during the period. The Phils flattened opponents en route to three straight NL East crowns from 1976 to '78 but fell flat against the Big Red Machine in '76 and a lethal dose of Dodger blue the next two years. Even the combination of Mike Schmidt, who strung together three straight home run crowns (1974–76), and Steve Carlton, with Cy Young awards in 1972 and '77, wasn't enough.

The Kansas City Royals had the same problem: three divisional titles

but no trips to the World Series. Unfortunately for the Royals, their emergence as an AL West powerhouse coincided with the Yankee comeback. Even with the league's best win total (102 in '77), Kaycee couldn't escape the shadow of the pinstripes. The '77 Royals had more wins, more saves, a better earned run average, and more stolen bases than the Yankees but lost a best-of-five AL Championship Series in the last inning of the last game, when New York scored three runs for a 5-3 victory. New York denied George Brett's team three years in a row, 1976–78, though Brett already had the first of three batting titles (each earned in a different decade) under his belt.

Only the dawn of a new decade gave the also-rans of the '70s their own day in the sun: The 1980 World Series pitted the Philadelphia Phillies, winners of their first flag in 30 years and just their second since 1915, against the Kansas City Royals, a 1969 expansion team getting its first taste of the fall classic. The Phils prevailed, winning their only world championship.

The 1976 Phillies: (left to right) Steve Carlton, Tim McCarver, and Tommy Hutton

'72, and the Reds finished 10½ games in front of Houston and Los Angeles. Manager Sparky Anderson had his team cooking.

But their opponent in the 1972 LCS was the Pirates. Pittsburgh had Steve Blass heading up a tough pitching staff and a lineup blessed with a crop of .300 hitters, including third baseman Richie Hebner and outfielders Al Oliver, Gene Clines, Vic Davalillo, and the inestimable Roberto Clemente. First baseman Willie Stargell rapped 33 homers and garnered 112 RBI to go along with his .293 average, while catcher Manny Sanguillen batted a solid .298. The Bucs led the National League in hits, doubles, and triples.

The result was one of the most thrilling best-of-five League Championship Series ever played. The Pirates landed a 5-1 win in Game 1. The Reds jumped out to a 4-0 lead before the Bucs batted in the first inning of Game 2, and it was all they needed. In Game 3 the Reds once again hopped in front, but the Pirates pulled themselves back with solo runs in the fifth, seventh, and eighth to nail down a 3-2 victory. The Bucs could have taken the title the next day, but sneaky Cincy lefty Ross Grimsley slammed the door on the big Buc bats with a two-hitter, while his teammates scored seven times.

Game 5 featured the teams' two best pitchers, the Pirates' Blass and the Reds' Don Gullett. The Pirates had knocked Gullett around in Game 1, and in the final game they had him out of the box, down three runs to one, in the fourth inning. But the Reds bullpen tightened the screws and stiffed the Buc batters. The last of the ninth began with Pittsburgh up 3-2 and the dominant Pirates closer, Dave Giusti, on the

Joe Morgan's first-inning homer off Steve Blass (shown) would account for the Reds' only tally in their loss in Game 1 of the 1972 NLCS, but they eventually vanquished the Pirates in five. It took a two-run rally in the bottom of the ninth in the finale to do it.

hill. But Johnny Bench got hold of a high outside pitch and muscled it over the right-center wall. Tie game. Two singles followed, and a fly ball advanced the lead runner to third. Pirates pitcher Bob Moose induced the second out on a harmless pop-up, then threw a breaking pitch that bounced in front of the plate and wickedly away from catcher Sanguillen. The winning run raced home for Cincinnati in an ending that was positively stunning for everyone.

In that year's World Series, the Reds played the mighty A's mighty close, losing in seven games. The Reds took their third divisional title in four years in 1973, but the Mets won the LCS in a nasty performance in which Pete Rose punched out Bud Harrelson and then nearly got beheaded by trash when he went out to play left field the next inning. It was not one of the game's finer moments. In 1974 the Dodger pitching was too much for anyone but the A's.

The "Big Red Machine" returned to championship levels for its two most glorious seasons—1975 and '76. This was a powerhouse team, with Bench, Morgan, and Rose all performing at Hall of Fame levels and Tony Perez operating as an RBI machine. Some have maligned the pitching staff, but their lack of high individual win totals was more a function of how manager Anderson distributed the starting duties (widely) and used his bullpen (frequently) than of any inherent weakness. Every year a Red or two showed up in the top five in one or another pitching stat.

Tony Perez, Johnny Bench, Joe Morgan, and Pete Rose (left to right) fueled the Big Red Machine, baseball's dominant team of the decade. From 1970 to '79, Cincinnati won nearly 60 percent of its games, captured six division titles (plus three second-place finishes), and took a pair of world titles.

Pete Rose was, simply stated, one of the great hitters of the era. He began as a pure singles hitter, but then added some home run power to his swing, averaging 13 homers over the seven seasons from 1965 through '71. Later in his career he dropped the long ball in favor of doubles and won five doubles titles. Even though he extended his career simply to push past Ty Cobb's lifetime hit mark, it is a fact that when he was in prime form, he had the bat to make things happen. And no matter where he was placed defensively, he did a solid job. When he retired, he had led the league in hits seven times and batting average three times.

The Reds, winners of 108 games during the 1975 regular season, finished the year 20 games ahead of the second-place Dodgers. They had to get past the mighty Pirates again to reach the World Series, a job that took them just three games.

Then they turned their attention to the Red Sox of Boston, the never-quite-good-enough team some writers claim had been cursed forever because they had committed the unpardonable sin of selling Babe Ruth in 1919. The last time the Red Sox had been to the Series (1967), they lost in seven games. They could have won the pennant in 1949, but they dropped the final two games of the season to the Yankees. In 1946 they won the pennant but lost the World Series—again in seven games.

This World Series went seven games, too, and it was such a tangled knot of comebacks, slipups, turnarounds, and heroics that many now list it as the greatest World Series of all time. Roger Angell summed it up perfectly: "In six of the seven games, the winning team came from behind. In one game, it came from behind twice. In five games the winning margin was one run. There were two extra inning games, and two games were decided in the ninth inning. Overall, the games were retied or saw the lead change hands 13 times." It was just plain breathtaking baseball.

The Red Sox won the first game 6-0 behind Luis Tiant's dazzling display of pitching contortions, and that was as dull as this Series got. The Reds were down 2-1 heading into the ninth inning of Game 2. Johnny Bench led off with a double into the right-field corner. He moved to third with one out, but George Foster's fly

44 STRAIGHT

It began with a harmless single against the Chicago Cubs at Cincinnati's Riverfront Stadium on June 14, 1978. Within a month, however, Cincinnati's Pete Rose had tongues wagging. Could "Charlie Hustle" best Joe DiMaggio's 56-game hitting streak of 1941?

Rose raced past Tommy Holmes, whose 1945 streak of 37 straight had stood as the modern National League standard for 33 years, and set his sights on Wee Willie Keeler, whose 44-game streak in 1897 occurred when the Baltimore Orioles were a National League club. He caught Keeler on July 31 with a sixth-inning single off a fastball from Braves knuckleball specialist Phil Niekro.

"It's a long way from 44 to 56," Rose told reporters. A pair of unlikely Atlanta pitchers, rookie southpaw Larry McWilliams and veteran reliever Gene Garber, would prove just how long the very next night.

The 6'5" McWilliams walked Rose in the first, then used his reach to spear a waist-high liner that seemed headed for center field. He

Pete Rose

later retired the rampaging Red on a grounder to short. Against Garber, Rose lined into a double play in the seventh and fanned in the ninth. "He was batting like it was the final inning of the seventh game of the World Series," Garber said later. "We were leading 16-4 and he was trying to bunt." Rose, on the other hand, felt that Garber had nibbled at the corners without ever giving him anything to hit.

"I suppose it's a load off my shoulders," Rose said, "but I would have liked to get a hit tonight and again tomorrow so I could go back home with the streak intact. But they won't boo me when I get back to Cincinnati."

to left was too short to score him. Speedy Dave Concepcion hustled out an infield single to score Bench and came home on Ken Griffey's double to tie the Series.

They also won Game 3, although in even more spectacular fashion. Red Sox Dwight Evans slapped a two-run homer to tie the game at five in the top of the ninth. In the last of the tenth, the Reds got a man on, and pinch hitter Ed Armbrister was sent up to bunt him over. Armbrister bunted, all right, but then he stopped dead in front of catcher Carlton Fisk, who was charging out from behind the plate to grab the ball. The two got tangled; Fisk pushed Armbrister aside and threw to second to force the lead man, but his arm bumped the runner and his throw went wild. The baserunner wound up at third, and nothing the Sox said or did could persuade ump Larry Barnett that Armbrister had interfered with the play. The storm raged in the press for days. (It still hasn't died. Go into any sports saloon in Boston today and say "Armbrister" or "Barnett.") Someone pointed out that since a rotation system was in place for selecting which umpires called the World Series, not one of the umps on the field that night had ever worked a Series before. So even though Barnett's call seemed incorrect, none of the other umps would stand up and make the sensible call. Two batters after Armbrister, Joe Morgan belted a long single and the Reds were ahead, two games to one.

Tony Perez homered twice, including this three-run, sixth-inning shot, in Game 5 of the 1975 World Series. Years later, manager Sparky Anderson would acknowledge that the good-humored but intense "Doggie" was indeed the leader of the star-saturated Big Red Machine.

"El Tiante" returned for Game 4, and although he was only a shadow of his Game 1 self, he still threw a complete-game victory. This time it took him 163 pitches, nine hits, four walks, and four runs. The Red Sox scored first in Game 5, but Tony Perez shook off a Series-long slump to hit two homers, driving in four of his team's runs in a 6-2 win.

Rain delayed Game 6 for three days. As it turned out, fans needed the time to catch their breath. Tiant started for the third time for Boston, and they jumped to a 3-0 lead on rookie sensation Fred Lynn's homer in the first. With two on in the fifth, Lynn nearly decapitated himself leaping into the wall trying to catch a Griffey triple. Griffey knocked home two and scored the tying run a minute later. When the Reds scored two in the seventh and one in the eighth for a 6-3 lead, it looked as though the Sox's chances were evaporating. The clubhouse attendants had the Reds' champagne on ice and ready to pour.

There were two on and two out in the bottom of the eighth when non-slugger (though he had hit a pinch-hit homer in Game 3) Bernie Carbo clubbed another pinch-hit homer to knot the game once more. The stomping and screaming in Fenway Park reached into millions of homes around the country. The score was knotted at six apiece. With Red Sox on first and third with no outs in the bottom of the ninth, Fisk was intentionally walked to load the bases. George Foster, who was not known for his glovework, snagged a fly ball near the foul line and threw a strike home to nail an overeager Boston baserunner and extend the game into the tenth. In the 11th, Joe Morgan cracked a line drive toward the right-field stands, but Dwight Evans came from nowhere

to make a leaping grab; he recovered in time to rocket the ball back to first, completing a double play on the runner who had taken off from first. Millions of people watching the game on TV were afraid to move for fear they might miss something.

The whole world has seen the film of Carlton Fisk frantically waving, trying to blow his potential home run ball fair with the force of his arms in the last of the 12th. As the ball flew over the fence, baseball gave the sports fans of America a sudden jolt of heroism to join the innings of excellence and the moments of surprise. This was as good as it got. Elation rocked through Red Sox Land.

Carlton Fisk cajoles, coaxes, and wills his 12th-inning drive into fair territory. Almost unbelievably, the blast whammed off the foul pole, giving Boston a victory in Game 6 of the '75 World Series.

Manager Sparky Anderson (left) and Johnny Bench (right) were bubbly after winning the 1975 World Series. Anderson managed the controls of 17 consecutive winning teams in Cincinnati and Detroit from 1972 through '88. Bench, by consensus, is the most complete catcher of all time.

The joy in Boston lasted just one day. The next night, Joe Morgan's two-out bloop single knocked home the run that won the Series for Cincinnati, and the city of Boston watched its dream float out of reach.

But few people realize today what this Series meant for baseball. At this time many of the people who made their living discussing such things agreed that "baseball was dead." Football was the game everyone loved; no one cared about baseball. But this Series, particularly the "hand me the heart medicine" excitement of Game 6, led to a resurgence of interest in the national pastime. A *Sports Illustrated* cover the following spring showed a ballpark loaded with roaring fans and the headline "Baseball Is Back."

The next season the Reds took their division handily once more and again swept their opponent (this time Philadelphia) in the LCS. Their competition in the World Series in 1976 featured a set of new faces as the New York Yankees returned to the fall classic for the first time in a dozen years. The Reds were still mighty tough, and, frankly, the Yankees were still a few bricks shy of a load. It took the barest minimum: After just four games, the Reds donned the championship robes once again.

The Reds finished out the '70s as the winningest team of all. They averaged 95 victories per year and drew 21 million fans to their home park that decade. With their clean-shaven faces, close-cropped hair, and black baseball shoes, they weren't just the antithesis of Finley's A's; their looks set them apart from most young men of their age at that time. They were something quite different, and they had the pride to let that be clearly known. Six times in that decade a Red was named Most Valuable Player (Morgan and Bench two times apiece, Rose and Foster once each). The team just consistently demonstrated stability and superior play even under intense pressure and especially in clutch situations.

But during an interview in the clubhouse after the '76 Series victory, Cincinnati GM Bob Howsam said of his guys, "This isn't just a great team. It's the last great team built the right way." He was talking about the most radical change in the game since the 19th century, which would make its appearance that year.

Joe Morgan's Game 1 homer set the Big Red Machine on the road to a World Series sweep of the Yankees in 1976. The repeat National League MVP that year, "Little Joe" also had starred in the '75 fall classic, knocking home the winning runs in Games 3 and 7.

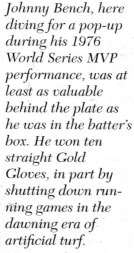

Johnny Bench, here diving for a pop-up during his 1976 World Series MVP performance, was at least as valuable behind the plate as he was in the batter's box. He won ten straight Gold Gloves, in part by shutting down running games in the dawning era of artificial turf.

THE FIRST FREE AGENTS

Thanks to the mercy of a Supreme Court that had ruled many years ago that baseball was not a business—or at least not one subject to antitrust legislation—most of the major changes impacting the game had come from inside. The owners, their assistants, and the people they hired, such as architects to build new stadiums, had made their own decisions, many of which were ill advised or even downright stupid. They were a function of management stupidity, however, not any dictate from above. The single exception was baseball's reaction to Branch Rickey's threats to begin a new league, and we saw how that turned out.

That was true until baseball found itself forced to let its players become "free agents," that is, sign with whichever team they chose. No longer could a team sign a player once and keep him as its property forever, regardless of his wishes. It started with Cardinals outfielder Curt Flood, who said no to a trade to the Phils after the 1969 season. In a famous letter to Commissioner Bowie Kuhn, which echoed John Montgomery Ward's 1887 article "Is the Base-Ball Player a Chattel?" (which led to the founding and brief existence of the Players' League), Flood made this point: "I do not feel that I am a piece of property to be bought and sold irrespective of my wishes. I believe that any system which produces that result violates my basic rights as a citizen . . ." Of course, the issue of being bought and sold meant something much deeper to Flood, an African American, than it had to John Ward.

In two years of litigation, Cardinals outfielder Curt Flood (right, with attorney Allan H. Zerman) argued that it was unconstitutional to force him to play for the Phillies, to whom he had been traded. Baseball's "reserve clause" was (narrowly) upheld, but the action paved the legal way for free agency.

Fans were aghast. Flood had turned down a $90,000-a-year contract. What could he be thinking? Flood sued Major League Baseball; ultimately the Supreme Court ruled that Flood's suit had no merit because the exception from antitrust status still held. The principled action ruined Flood's career. In some ways he was the anti–Jackie Robinson; Flood stood up for his rights and got slammed, not praised.

But Marvin Miller, baseball's labor leader, saw a chance to change things. The key lay in the language of the standard player's contract, the section that had come to be known as the "reserve clause." Simply stated, this clause held that if a player could not agree to con-

tract terms with his team, the team could "reserve" the player for its roster by renewing his contract for one year. Since the dawn of time, the owners had taken this to mean that they could keep renewing a contract one year at a time, again and again, for "one year."

The first challenge to the reserve clause came from Catfish Hunter of the Oakland A's, who had signed a contract with Charlie Finley that required Finley to make payments to a deferred compensation fund. But the ever-frugal Finley hadn't bothered. The first basic agreement, which the owners had unwillingly signed in 1968, set out the criteria for deciding such a grievance. The grievance board consisted of three people: one union rep, one management rep, and an impartial arbitrator—in this case, a man named Peter Seitz. Of course the deciding vote came down to Seitz, who decided that the contract was null and void because Finley had breached it. Thus, Catfish could sign with whomever he wanted; he was a "free agent." When Yankees owner George Steinbrenner made him the biggest offer, Catfish became a Yank.

Even though the Hunter situation was a special case, Miller liked the result. Next, two players, Dave McNally and

Post–Golden Age ballplayers owe their healthy bankbooks to Marvin Miller, a brilliant but reasoned economist who liberated them from the absolute rule of owners by galvanizing the union. As director of the Players Association, he orchestrated the first strike in 1972, setting in motion an enduring pattern of favorable legal decisions.

*The Yankees reaped
the benefits of Cat-
fish Hunter's last of
five consecutive
20-win seasons after
signing him away
(for millions of
dollars) from the A's
in the winter of '74.*

Andy Messersmith, played without contracts for a year and then
filed grievances claiming the contracts couldn't be renewed
again. The grievance board heard the case of the two pitchers,
and Seitz again cast the deciding vote. He ruled that contracts
could not be renewed in perpetuity, meaning the reserve clause
was dead. Baseball owners went berserk. Having brought the
bad news, the messenger was immediately slain (the owners
fired Seitz unanimously), as if that would make any difference.

But now both sides faced an ugly predicament. The owners were faced with the possible chaos of every player being
free to jump anywhere he liked. And, although they never said
it out loud amidst all their self-serving pontificating about "freedom," the labor leaders realized that if every player became a
free agent they would be left with a huge mess to sort out. In a
free market, each player's worth would be determined by how
much he was needed. That might actually keep salaries down
for all but the best players. Wouldn't it be better if only a few
players could become free agents each year? Then, if there
were only two shortstops available, they would each be worth a
lot more than if there were 24 from which to choose. Though it
took some time and caused some pain, the owners and players
worked out a deal permitting free agency after a certain number of seasons in the bigs.

And this was the action Cincy GM Howsam had made
reference to. From that time on, thick wallets would always

make the difference, or so the owners howled. No longer could a relatively poor team compete with canny scouting and smart management. The much-hated Charlie Finley saw all his good players leap into free agency in what seemed like minutes. He left baseball for good. "Baseball in Chaos" read the cover of *Sports Illustrated*.

Did the sudden spending change things? There were as many free-agent busts as there were bargains. Worst of all were the pitching signings. Messersmith, who had won 19 games the season before, moved from Los Angeles to Atlanta, and he won a total of just 18 more games in the majors. McNally went 3-6 with the Expos before retiring. Wayne Garland, a 20-game-winner as an Oriole, got injured as an Indian and won just 28 more games before hanging it up. Out in California, Angels owner Gene Autry spread around some of his royalty checks from the song "Rudolph the Red-Nosed Reindeer" by hiring free agents Don Baylor, Bobby Grich, and Joe Rudi. Two of them got hurt, and although the Angels would eventually contend, they weren't champion material and wouldn't be for a long time.

The fact is, even though a lot of money was thrown around in the first few years of free agency, it didn't seem to make a whole lot of difference . . . except in one place. New York City.

MONEY TALKS

With the advent of free agency in 1970, owners engaged in wild bidding wars that made many players millionaires. Reggie Jackson joined the Yankees in 1977 with a five-year deal worth $2.9 million. Not quite two years later, Dave Parker became the first man to average a million a year when the Pirates gave him a five-year, $5 million pact.

With greed and avarice fueling their thinking, teams lavished small fortunes on the likes of Bill Campbell, Wayne Garland, and Mike Torrez. In 1978, slugger Larry Hisle's annual salary skyrocketed from less than $50,000 to $525,000 a year as his six-year pact with Milwaukee made him a millionaire. Garland, a 25-year-old pitcher coming off a 20-7 season in 1976, got a ten-year Cleveland contract that called for $2.3 million. His annual take was almost $200,000 more than the Orioles paid him the year before. A colossal bust, Garland lost 19 in his first Indian season and went 2-3 in 1978 before needing rotator cuff surgery.

At least Pete Rose was worth it: At age 37, the future all-time hit king, who had been paid $375,000 by the 1979 Reds, inked a four-year Philadelphia contract that would pay him $3.225 million. "With the money I'm making," he said after signing, "I should be playing two positions."

Reggie Jackson

Thanks to free agency, runaway salaries became the norm: From 1978 through '81, teams agreed to 43 contracts that paid recipients seven figures per season. Even though a quarter-century has passed since the advent of free agency, owners still haven't figured out how to stop the salary spiral.

HIT MACHINES

From 1976 through '78, George Brett's Royals and Mike Schmidt's Phillies played in October—yet they never met in the World Series, each the victim of three straight League Championship Series heartaches. Nevertheless, sluggers Brett and Schmidt—along with an effective, consistent line-drive basher in Minnesota named Rod Carew—ranked among the best bashers of the 1970s.

A Royal Slugger

George Brett was one of the most consistent hitters of the '70s. He hit for average and power and was almost single-handedly responsible for bringing credibility to the Kansas City Royals—at the time a lowly expansion team.

George Brett

Brett debuted for the Royals in 1973 and spent his entire 21-year major-league career with the club. He emerged as a star during the 1976 season when he, teammate Hal McRae, and Minnesota All-Star Rod Carew were vying for the AL batting title. The race was still up for grabs when the Royals met the Twins in the final game of the season. Brett, McRae, and Carew each had two hits going into the ninth inning. In thrilling fashion, Brett secured his first batting title (of three) with an inside-the-park homer in the ninth.

Brett came the closest of any hitter to batting .400 in a season since Ted Williams accomplished the feat in 1941. In 1980, Brett finished up the season at .390, falling short of the coveted .400 mark but taking home the AL MVP Award.

During Brett's tenure in Kansas City, the team won five division titles, including three in a row beginning in 1976. The third baseman was the cornerstone of the Royals' success. He was a clutch performer in the postseason, with a .340 lifetime average in the ALCS and a .373 average in World Series action.

Throughout his career, Brett hit over .300 11 times, had 90 or more RBI five times, and even managed to lead the AL in triples three times. He was the first player to win a batting title in three different decades, taking home the crown in 1976, 1980, and 1990. Brett ended his Hall of Fame career with 3,154 hits, 317 home runs, and a .305 lifetime average.

Mighty Mike

Only Babe Ruth won more home run titles than Mike Schmidt. The Philadelphia third baseman, who batted only .196 in his first full season, led the National League eight times, three of them in consecutive seasons (1974–76). Along the way, he won three Most Valuable Player awards and led his team to five NL East divisional crowns and, the crowning glory, the 1980 world championship (the Phillies' first world title in 97 years), for which he took home the Series MVP title.

A notorious streak hitter who learned to cut down on his once-alarming strikeout totals, Schmidt remains the only man in baseball history to twice hit four consecutive home runs. He is baseball's all-time home run king (with 548) among non-outfielders.

"Someone was always trying to get me to change my stance to cut down on strikeouts," said Schmidt, who spent his entire 18-year career with the Phils. "But I believed in myself. I was a power hitter."

The 6'2", 203-pound right-handed hitter led the league in slugging percentage five times, home runs eight times, and runs

Mike Schmidt

batted in four times. He also produced some tape-measure shots. In 1974, he smashed a Claude Osteen fastball into an Astrodome speaker suspended 329 feet from home plate and 117 feet above the field. Due to league rules, the smooth-fielding infielder was forced to settle for a single.

When he retired, Schmidt's career home run total ranked seventh in baseball history. His power plus his defensive expertise (ten Gold Gloves) convinced Hall of Fame electors to make Mike Schmidt the 26th player chosen during his first year of eligibility.

The Bat Magician

A slashing hitter who uncoiled out of a crouched stance, Rod Carew batted over .300 for 15 consecutive seasons and was one of the game's most consistent hitters. White Sox infielder Alan Bannister once said about Carew, "He's the only guy I know who can go 4-for-3."

Born on a train in the Panama Canal Zone, Carew moved to the United States when he was 16. He was discovered by a pro scout on the sandlots of New York and signed to a deal with the Minnesota Twins. After six years in the minors, he came up as a second baseman with the Twins in 1967 and was named American League Rookie of the Year when he hit .292 that season. He established his bat wizardry early, winning a batting title in '69. Minnesota won the AL West in '69 and '70; Carew and Co. ran into the Baltimore buzzsaw both years.

A contact hitter who was capable of spraying line drives to all fields, Carew lacked power but made up for it with other talents. He was a master bunter: In 1972, he had 15 bunt-hits but not a single home run. (That year, he became the only man ever to win the batting title without a single home run.)

In 1977 Carew was moved to first base and responded with the most productive season of his career. He made a valiant run at the .400 mark last topped by Ted Williams, though Rod fell short, finally finishing with a .388 average. He also clubbed 14 home runs, scored 128, drove in 100, and was a runaway choice for league MVP.

He was also an excellent base-stealer, swiping more than 20 bags in seven of his 19 big-league seasons. In 1969 alone, he stole home seven times.

Although he won six batting titles in the 1970s—including four straight from 1972 to '75—he was traded to the California Angels in 1979. He would finish out his career with the Angels, making two postseason appearances. He was elected to every All-Star Team from 1967 to 1984.

In his final season, Carew hit .280 and became the 16th player in baseball history to reach 3,000 hits. He was voted into the Hall of Fame in 1991, his first year of eligibility.

Rod Carew

THE RETURN OF THE YANKEES

The Yankees, who had fallen off the radar screen shortly after they were sold to CBS for around $13 million in 1964, proved to be no bargain for the entertainment conglomerate. Nine years later they were sold again, to a group of investors including a Cleveland shipbuilder named George Steinbrenner. The sale price was an astonishingly low $10 million.

With longtime trade maker Gabe Paul as the general manager, and before the free agency ruling, the Yanks began making smart deals. Before long they had acquired speedy Mickey Rivers, solid starter Ed Figueroa, third base fielder-with-power Graig Nettles, model-of-infield-consistency Willie Randolph, and relief ace Sparky Lyle. Catcher Thurman Munson, a multisport standout at Kent State, dropped out of school to join the Yanks and immediately established himself as a winner. When Charlie Finley's tight pockets made Catfish Hunter a free agent in 1974, the Yanks snapped him up. He won 23 games in his first year in the Bronx, leading the league for the second year in a row.

Graig Nettles was a defensive difference-maker as third baseman for the 1978 Yankees. The six-time All-Star was especially luminous in Game 3 of the World Series, making several dazzling plays in a win over the Dodgers.

The Yanks were now a strong team headed by a strong manager, Billy Martin. After less than half a season at the Yankee helm in 1975, he took his team to the pennant in '76, topping Weaver's O's by 10½ games.

The Boys from the Bronx met the upstart Kansas City Royals in the LCS. The Royals had only been invented in 1969, but their manager, Whitey Herzog, had constructed a team around speed (they played on an artificial surface), and their hitting instructor, guru Charlie Lau, worked miracles with their young bat talent. The teams alternated wins in their first four games. Coming into the final game, both teams had scored an

Although the Reds would obliterate the Yanks in the 1976 World Series, Yankee fans enjoyed a moment of bliss when Chris Chambliss belted a game-winning homer in the ninth inning of the deciding game of the AL Championship Series against Kansas City.

identical number of runs. The two teams traded the lead for several innings, but the Yankee 6-3 advantage looked like it would hold—until K.C. third baseman George Brett powered a three-run homer in the eighth to tie it up. In the last of the ninth, first up for the Yanks was Chris Chambliss, another savvy Yank pickup. He knocked one over the right-field fence, and the Yanks were back on top for the first time in a dozen years. The crowd at Yankee Stadium, overcome with joy, became a mob. They tore onto the field. By the time Chambliss reached second, he had to tag it with his hand as a fan ran off with it. Third base was long gone; he just sort of stepped where he figured it must have been. Even after he returned to the dugout, his teammates had to take him back out to make absolutely sure he stepped where home plate once was. The delirious Yankee fans almost tore down "The House that Ruth Built," causing about $100,000 worth of damage.

But the Reds rolled over the Yankees in a World Series dubbed "the dullest in history" by *The Sporting News*. So Steinbrenner decided to invest a few more dollars in his team. He grabbed the biggest free agent out there, former Oakland A's slugger Reggie Jackson. The brash Jackson relished the New York spotlight but infuriated his teammates. He and Billy Martin were bound to clash. In the middle of a sticky pennant race, Martin unceremoniously yanked Jackson from his outfield position in the middle of an inning for what he deemed lazy play.

*The irrepressible egos
of Yankees manager
Billy Martin (left)
and superstar Reggie
Jackson (right)—
chummy prior to a
1977 World Series
game in L.A.—
alternately clashed
and melded. Martin
stood up to Jackson's
narcissistic petulance,
but owner George
Steinbrenner sided
with his star and
forced Martin to
resign in '78.*

Reggie challenged his manager in the dugout; the two nearly came to blows, and the "Game of the Week" cameras caught it all. The Yanks needed all the power they could muster that season. Injuries held Catfish to just nine wins; no Yankee pitcher won more than 16. But Nettles and Reggie each hit more than 30 homers, Munson joined them in amassing 100-plus RBI, and the Yanks wriggled through a tight pennant race with Boston and Baltimore to take the division. A key move was Martin's August 10 shift of Jackson into the cleanup slot; Reggie (naturally) felt he belonged there, and he hit 13 homers from then on.

The Royals were back for a second dose of Yankee magic in the ALCS. Once again the teams swapped victories for the first four games. This time Game 5 reached the ninth inning with K.C. holding onto a 3-2 lead. But the Yanks stormed back: a single, a walk, a single, and a sacrifice fly gave them the lead. A Brett error helped them tack on an insurance run. The Yanks had battled the Royals in another close Series and come away with another victory. In no time they had a new nickname: "The Best Team Money Could Buy."

The '77 World Series pitted the Yanks against the Dodgers in an echo of the many great Series these two franchises had played. The Dodgers had a rookie manager, Tommy Lasorda, but they had a veteran team. Every regular was at least 28 years old; three were past 30. Their pitching staff, which led the NL in ERA, was headed by Tommy John (in his second year after his famous arm surgery) and Rick Rhoden. The core of the Dodger unit was their infield, from first to third: Steve Garvey, Davey Lopes, Bill Russell, and Ron Cey— the longest lasting infield unit ever. And they had

power, too: Garvey and Cey were joined by outfielders Dusty Baker and Reggie Smith in hitting at least 30 home runs. This was the first time a team had that many players at that level in one season.

Game 1 was dead even after nine, then ten, then eleven innings, but Paul Blair (who had entered the game in the ninth as a defensive replacement for Reggie Jackson), singled home the Yankee

Played during a steady downpour in Philadelphia, Game 4 of the 1977 NLCS was the clincher for the Dodgers. Lefty Tommy John (foreground) befuddled the Phillies in a 4-1 win, while Steve Garvey (rear) contributed with a .308 batting average.

winner in the 12th. Burt Hooton stifled the Yank bats in Game 2, but Mike Torrez returned the favor in Game 3. Ron Guidry, on his way to becoming one of the great Yankee lefties of all time, was nearly flawless in Game 4, but Don Sutton pitched a complete game for the Dodgers in Game 5 while the Dodgers pounded on free agent and former Red Don Gullett. The Yanks led three games to two.

While baseball seasons take months to wind their way home, World Series memories seem to exist in glorious moments: Maz's and Fisk's homers, Owen's passed ball, Slaughter's "Mad Dash." But in Yankee Stadium on the night of October 18, 1977, Reggie Jackson provided a trifecta of moments that hasn't been equaled since, earning himself the honorific "Mr. October." What he did in this game was beyond belief.

In the eighth inning of Game 5, Reggie had clouted a long home run. In Game 6, "the other Reggie" (Smith) homered for Los Angeles to give them a 3-2 lead in the third. But in the Yankee half of the fourth, Munson singled and Jackson took Burt Hooton's first pitch downtown. The Yanks had a 4-3 lead. Jackson came to bat again in the fifth with a Yank on first and two down. He sent the first pitch he saw from Elias Sosa even farther back in the right-field stands. Consecutive homers for Reggie on consecutive pitches; Yanks up 7-3. Meanwhile, Mike Torrez was pitching high-efficiency baseball for the New Yorkers.

Jackson batted again in the eighth, this time against Charlie Hough. Hough's first offering was his famous knuckle curve, but the ball didn't seem to knuck or curve, and it didn't stay around for long. Reggie absolutely creamed it. That made three homers on three swings. Jackson became only the second player to hit three homers in one Series game (Ruth was the other). He set Series records with five homers, four in consecutive games, ten runs scored, and 25 total bases.

The '77 Yank season had been wild and woolly. But compared to what happened in '78, it was almost a yawner. The season began all–Red Sox. Boston had added pitchers Mike Torrez and Dennis Eckersley to its starting rotation, and the two combined for 36 wins. The acquisition of Jerry Remy at second base and the maturation of third baseman Butch Hobson solidified the infield. The outfield was superlative: future Hall of Famer Carl Yastrzemski in left, former AL MVP Fred Lynn in center, and reliable gloveman/clutch power hitter Dwight Evans in right. Catcher Carlton Fisk was second on the team in RBI. DH Jim Rice (who shared time in left with Yaz) was the big bomber (46 homers), and some folks were saying he was the best hitter in the game.

The men from Boston roared out to their best start in 32 years. By July 19 they were 34 games over .500, and people were wondering if they would shatter the Indians' 1954 AL

Reggie's three home runs in Game 6 to nail down the Yankees' 1977 World Series win came on consecutive pitches (left to right) in the fourth, fifth, and eighth innings. Mr. October's career rate of one home run for every 2.7 World Series games was exactly the same as Babe Ruth's.

After waiting 15 years for a world crown, the Yankees were back in '77. Controversial owner George Steinbrenner (left) was enamored with Billy Martin (right) following the AL title-winning game, but between 1975 and '88, "The Boss" would hire and fire the feisty manager five times.

record for wins in a season. Even when the Sox lost nine of their next ten, they were still way out in front.

Meanwhile, things weren't going well in the Bronx. Manager Martin and superstar Jackson had more run-ins, and Martin yapped off about the respective character of his boss and his star. It cost him his job (although Steinbrenner relented a few weeks later and promised Billy his job back in the future). On July 19, just before Martin was booted, the Yankees were in fourth place.

It's almost a given that a team struggling under a tyrannical manager will play better under a mellower one. That's what happened when Bob Lemon's quiet style replaced the edginess of Martin. The fact that the New York newspapers went on strike meant there were fewer rumors flying around the clubhouse, and that helped calm things, too. The team's individual personalities were free to be, well . . . free. They were living up to the nickname "The Bronx Zoo." Graig Nettles said, "When I was a little boy, I wanted to be a baseball player and join the circus. With the Yankees, I've accomplished both." Jackson strutted and bragged; Munson glowered and snarled. Mickey Rivers spoke a language all his own. Perhaps the quietest member of the team was "The Gator," Ron Guidry, who was having a Koufax-like year (25-3, 1.74 ERA) even when others flopped or stumbled. And to make sure nothing got out of hand, reliever Goose Gossage seemed mostly unhittable. The Yanks began to charge.

The Sox hung in. A late August push had them seven games in front of the blistering Yanks at the end of the month. On September 7, the Sox had a four-game lead when New York came to Fenway for a four-game Series. The Yanks had won 30 of their 44 games under Lemon. Meanwhile, a series of injuries to key players (Yaz and Evans among them) was taking its toll on the Sox, who were barely over .500 for their previous 49 games.

What happened in those four games has gone down in history as "The Boston Massacre." The Yanks scored quickly and often, winning the first game 15-3. The Red Sox made seven errors in the second game to hand the New Yorkers a 13-2 victory. The third game was a battle of the aces: Guidry against Eckersley, but erratic defense cost the Sox again and Guidry wound up on the front end of a 7-0 win. The Yankees belted 18 hits to win the fourth game 7-4. The total score for the four games was Yanks 42, Sox 9. Even more important, the pennant race was all tied up.

The Yankees continued their winning ways, and the Sox continued their stumble. The men from New York moved out to a 3½-game lead in mid-September. But the Red Sox turned it around, winning their last eight games and 12 of their last 14 to force a playoff for the division title. Both teams had won 99 games and lost 63.

All that was left of this gasping, groaning season was a one-game playoff in Fenway Park to determine the champ. It was only the second playoff in American League history, and the Red Sox had been there for both. Torrez started against Guidry.

The world seemed right for the Red Sox fans as longtime Sox hero Yaz started the scoring with a solo homer in the second and Rice knocked in another in the sixth. The Yanks hit consecutive singles in the seventh, and Bucky Dent came to bat. Dent batted ninth in the Yank lineup for a reason: He was a .243 hitter with little power. In his almost-six-year career, he had hit a total of 22 home runs. But the "Green Monster" of Fenway changes many things. Dent popped an 0-2 pitch from Torrez up and over the wall, and the Yanks were up 3-2. The shaken Torrez walked the next hitter, then Munson cracked a double that added a fourth run. Jackson homered the next inning, and the Yankees had a 5-2 lead.

But this classic wasn't over yet. The Red Sox hadn't given up all year, and they weren't about to start now. In the bottom of the eighth, Remy doubled, then Yaz, Fisk, and Lynn tagged singles to bring two runs home. With the score 5-4, fastball-machine Goose Gossage replaced Guidry in the eighth.

In one of the sharpest U-turns in major-league history, ping-hitting Yankee Bucky Dent tagged Boston's Mike Torrez for a game-winning homer in a 1978 AL East playoff game. The Red Sox blew a 14-game lead in a collapse "highlighted" by a late four-game sweep in which New York outscored them 42 to 9.

With one out, Rick Burleson walked. Remy hit a fly to right that Yankee fielder Lou Piniella lost in the bright late afternoon sun. But he kept his cool and stood stock-still. Burleson had to play it safe, and when the ball bounced right in front of Piniella, Boston only had men at first and second. Rice's long fly moved Burleson to third, but if he had been there on Remy's hit he would have scored the tying run. Up now with two out was Carl Yastrzemski. No one in Red Sox history had ever been such a clutch player; the memory of his stunning performance both offensively and defensively in the 1967 "Impossible Dream" season was still fresh in the minds of the Boston faithful. He had fought through the hellacious pressure of the season with back and shoulder miseries, made even worse by pulled ligaments in his right wrist. (Only the latter finally took him out of the lineup.) Everyone knew Gossage was going to be throwing fastballs. His first one was out of the zone. Yaz popped the next one foul near third, where Graig Nettles

If K.C.'s Willie Wilson (right) represented an irresistible force, New York's Thurman Munson (left) was an immovable object. Munson, here in the 1978 ALCS, was a barricade of a catcher, a clutch and combative warrior.

squeezed it, and the Yankees had done it to the Red Sox again, although never more painfully.

The Yanks banged up against the Royals in the '78 LCS and won again (even though George Brett did his Mr. October impersonation, hitting three homers in Game 3). They went on to face the Dodgers in the World Series . . . again. This Dodger team was sitting on a brand-new record: They had just become the first major-league club to draw more than three million fans to their park in one year.

The Yankees seemed a bit out of gas as the Series began. All four of the pitchers they sent to the mound in Game 1 got scored upon, and the Dodgers had an 11-5 win. In Game 2 Ron Cey singled in one run and homered in three more to give the Dodgers a 4-3 edge going into the ninth inning. Yanks stood on first and second with one out when rookie flamethrower Bob Welch entered the game to face Thurman Munson. The intense catcher swatted a liner to right, but right at Reggie Smith. Two down. Next up was Jackson. It was a classic battle: young pitcher bringing heat, well-established fastball hitter trying to connect. Jackson fouled off several fastballs; Welch missed with three. The count was full when Welch fired a screamer high and over the plate. Reggie swung with everything he had and missed it. The Dodgers led the Series two games to none.

In the course of that taut contest Yank third sacker Nettles had made three first-rate plays. After Game 3 he was all anyone could talk about. Nettles made four great stops, two with the bases loaded. He might have saved five runs and turned the Series around. The Yanks won 5-1.

Game 4 was delayed 40 minutes by rain in the third inning, and soon after it resumed Reggie Smith walloped a three-run homer off Guidry to give the Dodgers a three-zip lead. But in the last of the sixth, the Yankees had scored one run and had

Munson on second and Jackson on first when Lou Piniella tapped a perfect double-play ball to shortstop Russell. He stepped on second, forcing Jackson, then threw to first for the inning-ending play, but Jackson artfully stuck out his rear end and the ball ricocheted into short right field. Munson scored, and Piniella was safe at first. The Dodgers screamed, but the Yanks had life. Munson doubled in the tying run in the eighth, and Piniella knocked home the winner in the tenth. The Series was tied at two games.

New York unloaded the sticks in Game 5, winning 12-2 with keystone combination Bucky Dent and Denny Doyle surprisingly going 6-for-9 and

He was liberally listed at 160 pounds, but from 1977 through '85, no American League lefty had more wins, shutouts, strikeouts, complete games, or a lower ERA than Ron Guidry. In '78, "Louisiana Lightning" won his lone World Series start (here) and the Cy Young Award.

Throughout his decade as a Dodger and seven seasons with the A's, Bob Welch won 211 games. As a 21-year-old rookie in 1978, he wedged his way into World Series lore with a nerve-racking, nine-pitch, ninth-inning strike-out of Reggie Jackson with Game 2 on the line.

scoring four runs. They went back to Los Angeles for Game 6, but it didn't matter much. Jackson knocked a two-run homer in the seventh that capped the Yank scoring, Doyle–Dent went 6-for-8, and Hunter and Gossage combined for a 7-2 win.

The brash, bold, and occasionally out-of-control Yankees were back atop the baseball world, where Babe Ruth had first put them nearly 50 years before. And they had done it against the old challengers, the Dodgers.

There had been many changes since the Babe came to town. In 1961 his single-season home run record was surpassed ("distinctive mark" or no) by Roger Maris. It had stood for 34 years. In 1974 his lifetime homer record of 714 was toppled by Henry Aaron after 38 seasons. In 1962 Ty Cobb's single-season stolen-base record of 96—a record that had lasted 47 years—was broken by Maury Wills; and 15 years later Cobb's lifetime steals record that had stood for 49 years was also outdone, by Lou Brock. Baseball had relished its Golden Age. But new stars, new heroes, were coming along to challenge the greats of all time. In 1978 Mark McGwire was 15 years old; Barry Bonds was 14.

The pugnacious, partying 1978 Yankees were immortalized as the "Bronx Zoo" in reliever Sparky Lyle's tell-all book. However, there was much love between Series MVP Bucky Dent (left) and Rich "Goose" Gossage (center) after they defeated the Dodgers in the 1978 World Series.

Epilogue

A State of Flux

As the 1970s drew to a close, baseball seemed to be on the upswing. The start of the decade had witnessed a decline in fan interest, with professional football poised to eclipse baseball in popularity. But the spectacular 1975 Red Sox–Reds World Series and the reemergence of the Yankees as a powerhouse club—one capable of roaring back from a 14-game deficit in a thrilling '78 AL East race—had reeled the crowds back in. Legendary performers the likes of Willie Mays and Henry Aaron were passing from the spotlight, but charismatic young stars such as Reggie Jackson and George Brett were smoothly taking the stage.

Those watching from the stands weren't the only ones smiling. A 1976 U.S. Court of Appeals ruling had abolished the reserve clause and, with it, a century of total control by major-league owners. Players with six years of tenure could now become "free agents" when their contracts expired and sell themselves to the highest bidder. Many did just that, and the average player salary doubled in the first year after the ruling. Already owner of the single-season strikeout record, pitcher Nolan Ryan set another mark following the 1979

Nolan Ryan (shown here after his 300th career victory) was perhaps baseball's most beloved figure from the mid-'70s into the early '90s. His seven no-hitters and 5,714 whiffs seem to be marks that will stand indefinitely.

season when he signed a three-year contract with the Houston Astros worth *$1 million per year*.

Freedom and prosperity, however, were not enough to stop the rift between players and owners. In 1981, insistence by the latter group that teams be compensated with a veteran player for each one lost in the annual reentry draft was cited as the main cause of a player strike that began on June 11 and lasted 50 days. One-third of the year's games were wiped out, and an extra round of "split-season" playoffs lacked the normal postseason intensity. Attendance, which had risen each year from 1976 to '80, dropped off down the stretch.

Fans were forgiving, and in 1982 they returned in record numbers. This was the trend for the remainder of the decade, as labor strife continued amidst several exciting pennant races, the emergence of spectacular young players, and historic feats by veteran performers. Pete Rose passed the immortal Ty Cobb in 1985 en route to establishing a new all-time hit record of 4,256, and Nolan Ryan outdid former strikeout champ Walter Johnson by taking his lifetime total past the once unfathomable 5,000 mark. Cobb's tenure atop the career stolen-base charts also ended at the feet of leadoff hitter extraordinaire Rickey Henderson, and Reggie Jackson and Mike Schmidt each blasted his 500th home run.

Pete Rose acknowledged the crowd on September 11, 1985, after he broke Ty Cobb's record with his 4,192nd career hit. Throughout his career, "Charlie Hustle" was one of baseball's most popular players ever. His banishment from the game for alleged gambling remains a contentious issue.

These accomplishments and the rise of splendid young talents such as Roger Clemens, Tony Gwynn, and Cal Ripken, Jr., in the 1980s were enough to at least temporarily overshadow the off-field troubles. Rumors of an extensive drug problem among major-leaguers were substantiated by the 1983 conviction of three Kansas City Royals players for cocaine use and testimony during two 1985 Pittsburgh trials that identified 17 players as drug users. Each was suspended and ordered to donate up to 10 percent of his salary to drug-fighting charities. Since the average player salary had risen from $51,000 in 1976 to nearly $450,000 in 1988, this wasn't much of a hardship.

Signs that the next decade would prove challenging surfaced during 1989. In August, Commissioner Bart Giamatti banned hit king Pete Rose from the game for life when evidence indicated that "Charlie Hustle" had bet extensively on baseball, including, some speculated, games in which his own Reds team took part. One week after making this excruciating decision, the hugely popular Giamatti died of a heart attack. And in October, minutes before an Oakland A's–San Francisco Giants World Series game, an earthquake rocked the Bay Area, killing 63 people and forcing a ten-day postponement of the Series.

The 1990s started on similarly shaky ground. Players refused to agree to an ownership proposal for a new five-year Basic Agreement that included revenue sharing and strict salary caps, then were literally shut out of spring training by a 32-day owner lockout. Eventually the full season was salvaged and a revenue-sharing task force established, but the experience triggered bad feelings all around. Executive Director Donald Fehr of the Major League Baseball Player's Association vowed never to accept a salary cap, even though many fans saw it as the only way small-market teams such as Milwaukee and Pittsburgh could compete in the big-money era.

Failure by the two sides to reconcile had drastic results.

By overcoming all manner of adversity and probability to play in a record 2,632 consecutive games, Cal Ripken, Jr., became more than simply a baseball player. His work ethic, humility, and understated style turned him into a cultural icon.

On August 12, 1994, a player's strike began that lasted 234 days—not ending until the following April. The World Series was canceled for the first time since 1904, and players and teams who had been enjoying a successful year were denied the chance to see it to fruition. Fans had trouble feeling sorry for athletes now averaging well over $1 million annually, and eventually their apathy turned to anger. After a U.S. District judge issued an injunction restoring baseball's old work rules despite the lack of a collective bargaining agreement, attendance plummeted in many big-league cities during the '95 season.

Cal Ripken, Jr.'s toppling of Lou Gehrig's "unbreakable" record of 2,130 consecutive games played that September is

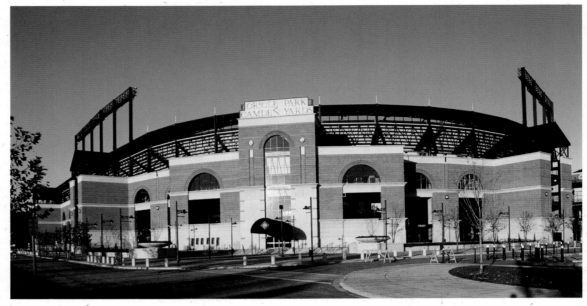

The great Mark McGwire–Sammy Sosa long-ball race of 1998 was more than just a pursuit of numbers. With its spirit of competitive camaraderie, it captured imaginations nationwide. McGwire (left) got the record, with 70 home runs to Sammy's (right) 66, but the big winner was the game itself.

Baltimore's Oriole Park at Camden Yards, which opened in 1992, stands as an appropriate symbol for baseball today: fan-friendly and state-of-the-art, but also drenched in nostalgia.

often credited with "saving" baseball in the wake of its longest-ever work stoppage, but it was much more than one individual that got the sport through its darkest period since the Black Sox scandal. A split from four to six MLB divisions, the addition of a third playoff round, and "wild card" postseason spots were all moves opposed by traditionalists, but even they couldn't deny the excitement generated by having additional teams in the playoff hunt. Eleven new ballparks were built during the 1990s (more than in any other decade), including many with a nostalgic look and feel that fans embraced. Although attendance through 2002 had still not quite reached its record pre–'94 strike levels, for the most part it was gradually improving.

The action taking place in these new locales was more explosive than ever, as balls cleared walls at a dizzying pace. Whereas just one player had reached 50 home runs in a season between 1966 and '89 (George Foster in 1977), seven players made the mark during the '90s—including one pair of very special sluggers. In 1998, Mark McGwire (70 homers) and Sammy Sosa (66) captivated the sports world when both toppled Roger Maris's record of 61 round-trippers in a season. The amazement was short-lived; by 2001 Barry Bonds had raised the bar yet again, to 73 homers. Some speculated that watered-down pitching resulting from the addition of four new expansion teams (Colorado, Florida, Arizona, and Tampa Bay) had caused this power surge, while others believed steroid use was behind it. Whatever the reason, crowds loved the show, and those who preferred great pitching instead of slugging could always turn to the exploits of Red Sox flamethrower Pedro Martinez or Diamondback teammates Randy Johnson and Curt Schilling—perhaps the best one–two hurling punch since Koufax and Drysdale.

There certainly are still reasons to worry about the state of the game nearly a quarter-century after Bucky Dent's Yankees closed out the Golden Age in style. The 2002 World Series drew the lowest seven-game TV ratings in history, continuing a drop of 50 percent in just 11 years. These and other playoff games ended well past midnight, all but assuring that the next generation of potential fans would miss them. Another strike was narrowly averted in August 2002, and even with a new agreement that included revenue sharing, many skeptics believe the big-market teams will always have an unfair edge—especially the Yankees, who won four World Series from 1996 through 2001. Then, of course, there are those yearly salaries—up to an average of $2.38 million.

Yet as long as folks can still sit back on a summer night and enjoy the beauty of a hard-breaking fastball, a diving stab in the hole, or a game-winning shot over the wall, there is hope for America's pastime. As baseball's wisest and most experienced observers have noted, the game will survive and prosper because it is greater than any one moment. Its beauty lies in its timelessness.

Much as they had during other hefty chunks of baseball's Golden Age, the New York Yankees established another dynasty by the end of the 20th century. Their celebration of a World Series title here in 2000 was their third in a row and their fourth in five years.

Index

A

Aaron, Hank, 43, 84, 92, 98, 147, 161, 165, 166, *166*, 167, 169, *169*, 170, 186, 228, *228*, 232, *232*, 251, 276, *276*, 277, *277*, 278, *278*, 279, 306, 307
Adcock, Joe, 162, 166, 170, 186, 251, 277
Agee, Tommie, 256, *256*
Agganis, Harry, 165, *165*
Albert, Steve, 158, 159
Alexander, Grover Cleveland, 40, *40*, 41, 55, 75, *75*, 76, 137, 156
Allen, Lee, 257, 278
Allen, Mel, 92, 93, 158, *158*, 159, 221
Allen, Richie, 217, 225
Allison, Bob, 198, *198*, 214
Alou, Felipe, 209, 210, 224
Alou, Jesus, 224
Alou, Matty, 209, 210, 224, *224*, 242
Alston, Walter, 154, 216
Altrock, Nick, 223
Amaro, Ruben, 216
Amoros, Sandy, 155, *155*, 223
Anderson, Sparky, 262, 282, 286, 288, *288*
Andrews, Mike, 237, 274
Angell, Roger, 215, 219, 236, 241, 285
Antonelli, Johnny, 156
Aparicio, Luis, 184, *184*, 185, 188, 223, 234
Appling, Luke, 96
Arft, Hank, 176
Arlin, Harold, 78, 92
Armbrister, Ed, 286
Armstrong, Louis, 86
Ashburn, Richie, 137, *137*, 139
Atlanta Braves, 230–232
Auker, Eldon, 59

Autry, Gene, 197, 293
Avila, Bobby, 157, *157*, 223

B

Bagby, Jim, 35, 95
Bahnsen, Stan, 243
Baker, Dusty, 299
Baker, Frank, 17, 51
Ballplayers, The (Kavanagh), 53
Baltimore Orioles, 232–236, 260–267, 282
Bander, Chief, 51
Bando, Sal, 272
Banks, Ernie, 84, 87, 128, 177, *177*, 178, *178*
Bannister, Alan, 295
Barber, Red, 80, 92, *92*, 113, 158, 159
Barber, Steve, 234
Barnett, Larry, 286
Barnstorming, 22, 23, 24, 46, 80, 84, 85
Barrow, Ed, 16, *16*, 33, 69
Baseball cards, 201
Baseball Encyclopedia, The, 257, *257*
Baseball Research Journal (Gordon), 245
Basestealing, 203–206
Bauer, Hank, 134, *134*, 170, 254
Bauman, Joe, 180, *180*
Baylor, Don, 293
Bearden, Gene, 126
Beazley, Johnny, 105
Becker, Joe, 211
Beckert, Glenn, 253, *253*
Behrman, Hank, 121
Belanger, Mark, 261
Belinsky, Bo, 197, *197*
Bell, Bill, 180
Bell, Cool Papa, 84, 86, *86*, 87
Bell, Gary, 237–238
Bell, Gus, 162

Bellan, Steve, 222
Bench, Johnny, 84, 262, 264, 275, 282, 284, *284*, 285, 288, *288*, 289, *289*
Bentley, Jack, 17
Berg, Moe, 71, *71*
Berra, Yogi, 123, *123*, 133, *133*, 134, *134*, 135, *135*, 138, *138*, 154, *154*, 155, 157, 159, 170, 194, 209, 218, *218*, 219, 220, *220*
Bevens, Bill, 124, 125
Bickford, Vern, 126, 127
Big Sticks: The Batting Revolution of the Twenties (Curran), 28
Bilko, Steve, 180
Billingham, Jack, 282
Binks, Bingo, 112, 127
Bishop, Max, 17
Bithorn, Hi, 223
Black, Joe, 151
Black Sox scandal, 16, 19, 20, 21, 22
Blair, Paul, 236, 255, 299
Blanchard, Johnny, 209
Blass, Steve, 243, 266, 267, *267*, 283
Blomberg, Ron, 280, *280*, 281
Blue, Vida, 271, *271*, 273
Boley, Joe, 17
Bolin, Bobby, 243
Bonds, Barry, 306, 311
Borowy, Hank, 112
Boston Red Sox, 16, 46, 70–71, 236–240
Bottomley, Jim, 30, *30*, 32, 56
Boudreau, Lou, 96, 116, 126, 127, *127*, 150, 173
Bouton, Jim, 213, *213*, 219
Boyer, Clete, 213
Boyer, Ken, 218, 219, 238
Bramham, William, 76
Branca, Ralph, 125, 139, 141, *141*, 142, 143, 148, 208
Breadon, Sam, 73, 79

Bressler, Rube, 25
Brett, George, 282, 294, *294*, 297, 298, 304, 307
Brewer, Chet, 82
Brickhouse, Jack, 158
Briles, Nelson, 240, 247
Brock, Lou, 206, *206*, 217, 218, 239, 240, 247, 251, 306
Broeg, Bob, 28
Broglio, Ernie, 206, 217, 218
Brooklyn Dodgers, 101, 102, 118, 123, 124, 125, 139–143
Brown, Joe L., 192
Brown, Mordecai, 244
Brown, Warren, 112
Bruton, Bill, 166
Buck, Jack, 92
Buckner, Bill, 276
Buford, Don, 255, 261
Buhl, Bob, 163, 167, 170
Bunker, Wally, 234, 236
Bunning, Jim, 217, *217*
Burdette, Lew, 167, 168, 169, *169*, 170, 171, 186
Burleson, Rick, 303
Busch, Auggie, 218
Bush, Donie, 32
Bush, Guy, 66
Bush, Joe, 33

C

Cadore, Leon, 24, 26, *26*
Callison, Johnny, 216
Calloway, Cab, 86
Campanella, Roy, 84, 139, 150, 154, *154*, 165, 184, *184*, 186
Campaneris, Bert, 206, 272, 273, 274, 275, *275*
Campbell, Bill, 293
Cannon, Jimmy, 157
Cantillon, Joe, 31
Caray, Chip, 159
Caray, Harry, 158, 159, 270
Caray, Skip, 159
Carbo, Bernie, 287
Carew, Rod, 225, 294, 295, *295*
Carey, Max, 204
Carlton, Steve, 137, 253, 268, *268*, 282, *282*

Carrasquel, Chico, 223
Carter, Gary, 282
Cartwright, Alexander Joy, 76, *76*
Carty, Rico, 222, 225, 229
Case, George, 107, *107*
Casey, Hugh, 101, 123, *123*
Cash, Norman, 201, 202, *202*
Catcher Was a Spy, The (Dawidoff), 71
Cepeda, Orlando, 209, 226, *226*, 238, 239, 247, 281, *281*
Cey, Ron, 298, 299, 304
Chambliss, Chris, 297, *297*
Champion, Aaron, 7
Chandler, Happy, 115, 121
Chapman, Ben, 121
Chapman, Ray, 14, 16, 19, 20, *20*, 33, 165
Charleston, Oscar, 83, *83*, 84, 86
Chase, Hal, 13
Chicago Cubs, 31, 41, 42, 177–178
Cicotte, Eddie, 13, 21, *21*
Cimoli, Gino, 193
Cincinnati Reds, 272–276, 282–289
Clabaugh, Moose, 180
Clark, Stephen, 75
Clemens, Roger, 308
Clemente, Roberto, 167, 178, 194, 224, *224*, 227, 228, *228*, 229, *229*, 239, 265, 266, *266*, 267, 277, 282, 283
Clendenon, Donn, 253, 255, 256, *256*, 257
Cleveland Indians, 156–157
Clines, Gene, 283
Coates, Jim, 194
Cobb, Ty, 11, 21, 25, *25*, 27, 29, 76, 92, 96, 166, 204, 205, 284, 306, 308
Cochrane, Mickey, 51, *51*, 52, 53, *53*, 59, 84, 165
Colavito, Rocky, 161, 162, 202
Colbert, Nate, 98
Coleman, Jerry, 136
Coleman, Joe, 272
Collins, Eddie, 13, 51, 75, *75*
Collins, Jimmy, 10
Collins, Joe, 153
Combs, Earle, 33, *33*, 34, 35, *35*

Comiskey, Charles, 13
Complete History of the Negro Leagues, A (Brewer), 82
Concepcion, Dave, 286
Conigliaro, Tony, 237, *237*
Connolly, Tommy, 20
Continental League, 197
Coolidge, Calvin, 18, *18*
Coombs, Jack, 51
Cooper, Mort, 105
Corwin, Al, 141
Coveleski, Stan, 31
Covington, Wes, 217
Cox, Billy, 105, 139, 151
Craig, Roger, 195, *195*, 207
Cramer, Doc, 59
Crandall, Del, 166
Crane, Sam, 113
Cronin, Joe, 62, 70, *70*, 96, 222, *222*
Crosley, Powel, 80
Crues, Bob, 180
Crutchfield, Jimmie, 86
Cuellar, Mike, 255, 261, 263, *263*, 264, 265, 266, 273
Culberson, Leon, 117
Curran, William, 28
Cuyler, Kiki, 32, 39

D

Dalkowski, Steve, 243, *243*
Dandridge, Ray, 84
Daniel, Dan, 91
Dark, Alvin, 142, 205, 226, 275
Davalillo, Vic, 283
Davis, Curt, 100, 101
Davis, Tommy, 202, *202*, 212, 213
Davis, Willie, 212, 235, 251
Dawidoff, Nicholas, 71
Dawson, Andre, 282
Day, Leon, 84
Dean, Daffy, 54, *54*, 57
Dean, Dizzy, 54, *54*, 57, *57*, 59, 81, *81*, 85, 86, 244, *244*
Delahanty, Ed, 9
Demeter, Don, 186, 217
Dent, Bucky, 302, 303, *303*, 305, 306, *306*, 311
Designated hitters, 279–281
Detroit Tigers, 58–60

Devine, Bing, 218
DeWitt, Bill, 234
Dickey, Bill, 62, 63, *63*, 68, 84, 101, 135
Dihigo, Martin, 84, 86, 87
DiMaggio, Dom, 93, *93*, 117
DiMaggio, Joe, 33, 63, *63*, 66, *66*, 68, 70, 91, *91*, 92, 93, *93*, 94, *94*, 95, *95*, 97, 99, 101, 106, *106*, 124, 125, 130, 131, 134, *134*, 144, 146, 163, 166, 199, 285
DiMaggio, Vince, 93, *93*
Dixon, Rap, 83, *83*
Dobson, Pat, 264
Doby, Larry, 84, 122, *122*, 173
Doerr, Bobby, 70, 116
Dolan, Cozy, 21
Donatelli, Augie, 274, *274*
Donovan, Dick, 185
Doubleday, Abner, 6, 74, 76
Douthit, Taylor, 56, 57
Downing, Al, 279
Doyle, Denny, 305, 306
Drabowsky, Moe, 235, *235*
Dressen, Chuck, 140, 142, 143, 150, 152, 153, 154
Dropo, Walt, 162
Drug use, 308
Drysdale, Don, 213, *213*, 214, 215, *215*, 226, 235, 236, 243, 311
Dugan, Joe, 17–18, 33
Duncan, Dave, 272
Dunn, Jack, 17, *17*, 52, 53
Durocher, Leo, 49, 57, 100, 101, 113, 120, 121, 127, 139, 140–141, 143, 145, 152, 157, 159, 180, 250, *250*, 253
Dykes, Jimmy, 42, 177

E

Eagen, Ben, 17
Earnshaw, George, 17, 41, 52, 57, 62
Easter, Luke, 162
Easterling, Howard, 87
Eckersley, Dennis, 300, 302
Eckhouse, Morris, 231
Ehmke, Howard, 41, 42

Ellis, Dock, 264
End of the Game As We Knew It, The, 250
English, Woody, 64
Ennis, Del, 139
Era, The, 1947–1957: When the Yankees, the Dodgers, and the Giants Ruled the World (Kahn), 123, 144
Erskine, Carl, 139, 142, 151, 152, 183, *183*
Essegian, Chuck, 187
Estrada, Francisco, 268
Evans, Dwight, 286, 287, 300

F

Face, Elroy, 178, *178*
Farley, James, 76
Farm system, 53–58
Fear Strikes Out (1957), 168
Federal League, 12, 13, 197
Fehr, Donald, 309
Feller, Bob, 81, 85, 105, 106, 115, 116, *116*, 156, *156*, 163, 164, *164*, 212, 271
Ferguson, Joe, 276
Fidrych, Mark, 269, *269*
Field of Dreams (film), 261
Fields, Wilmer, 83, 84
Figueroa, Ed, 296
Fingers, Rollie, 272, 275, *275*, 276
Finley, Charles, 125, 198, 230, 231, 270, *270*, 271, 272, 274, 276, 282, 291, 293, 296
Fisher, Jack, 190–191
Fisk, Carlton, 136, 286, 287, *287*, 299, 300, 302
Fitzsimmons, Freddie, 62
Flood, Curt, 159, 218, 290, *290*, 291
Ford, Whitey, 133, 136, 169, 193, *193*, 209, 213, 219, 220, 221
Fosse, Ray, 260
Foster, George, 285, 287, 289, 310
Foster, Rube, 84, 86
Foster, Willie, 84
Fox, Nellie, 185, *185*
Foxx, Jimmie, 51, 52, *52*, 62, 70, *70*, 71, 97, *97*, 198

Frazee, Harry, 16, 17
Free agency, 290–293, 307
Freehan, Bill, 247, *247*
Fregosi, Jim, 268
Frick, Ford, 75, 76, 121, 201, 202, 203, *203*, 241, 242
Friend, Bob, 163, 178
Frisch, Frankie, 32, *32*, 56, 57, *57*, 59, 74
Furillo, Carl, 151, 152, 186

G

Gaedel, Eddie, 174, *174*, 175, 257
Gallagher, Mark, 134
Garagiola, Joe, 134–135, 164
Garber, Gene, 285
Garcia, Mike, 156, *156*
Gardella, Danny, 115
Garland, Wayne, 293
Garvey, Steve, 298, 299, *299*
Gedeon, Elmer, 106
Gehrig, Lou, 33, 34, 41, 46, *47*, 51, 55, 59, 62, 64, 67, *67*, 68, *68*, 69, *69*, 70, 91, 94, 130, 146, 153, 165, 200, 309
Gehringer, Charlie, 58, *58*, 59
Gentile, Jim, 202
Gentry, Gary, 256
Giamatti, Bart, 308, 309
Gibson, Bob, 218, 219, 220, 227, 239, 240, *240*, 244, 245, *245*, 246, 247
Gibson, Josh, 83, *83*, 84, *84*, 86, 87
Giles, Warren, 196
Gillespie, Earl, 159
Gilliam, Jim, 186, 212
Gionfriddo, Al, 121, 124, *124*
Giusti, Dave, 283
Glenn, John, 136
Glickman, Marty, 158
Gomez, Lefty, 52, 62, 66, *66*, 70
Gonzalez, Juan, 226
Gonzalez, Tony, 216, 217
Gordon, Joe, 101, 105
Goslin, Goose, 31, 58, *58*, 59
Gossage, Goose, 301, 302, 303, 306, *306*
Gowdy, Curt, 190

Gowdy, Hank, 39
Graney, Jack, 158
Grant, Mudcat, 214, 215, 216, *216*
Gray, Pete, 108, 110, *110*
Greenberg, Hank, 58, *58*, 59, *59*, 98, 102, 103, 104, *104*, 105, 106, 111, 112, *112*, 115, 161, 198
Greenlee, Gus, 87
Grich, Bobby, 293
Griffey, Ken, 286, 287
Griffith, Calvin, 197
Griffith, Clark, 110
Grimm, Charlie, 112
Grimsley, Ross, 283
Groat, Dick, 194, 218, 238
Grove, Lefty, 17, 41, 51, *51*, 52, 53, 57, 62, 70, 71, 74, *74*
Guettler, Ken, 180
Guidry, Ron, 299, 301, 302, 305, *305*
Gullett, Don, 283, 299
Gwynn, Tony, 308

H

Haas, Mule, 52
Hack, Stan, 91
Haddix, Harvey, 186, *186*
Haefner, Mickey, 117
Hafey, Chick, 30, *30*, 32, 56
Haines, Jesse, 40
Hallahan, Bill, 74
Hamilton, Billy, 9
Hamilton, Milo, 279
Hamner, Granny, 138, *138*
Harrelson, Bud, 284
Harridge, Will, 75, 76, 175
Harris, Bucky, 31, 32, *32*, 39, 124
Hartnett, Gabby, 63, 64, *64*
Hartung, Clint, 142
Harwell, Ernie, 92, 159
Hauser, Joe, 180
Hayes, Frankie, 97
Hazle, Bob, 168, 169
Hearn, Jim, 140
Hebner, Richie, 283
Heilman, Harry, 26, 27, 28, *28*, 29, 30
Henderson, Rickey, 206, 218, 308

Hendricks, Ellie, 263
Henrich, Tommy, 101
Herman, Billy, 79, *79*, 100
Hershberger, Willard, 90, *90*
Herzog, Whitey, 136, 296
Heydler, John, 71
Higbe, Kirby, 100, 101
Hildebrand, George, 36
Hill, Carmen, 32
Hiller, Chuck, 209, 210, *210*
Hisle, Larry, 293
Historical Baseball Abstract (James), 114, 160, 203
Hoak, Don, 186
Hobson, Butch, 300
Hodges, Gil, 142, 162, 186, 195, 252, 254, 256
Hodges, Russ, 143, 159, *159*
Holmes, Tommy, 166, 285
Holtzman, Ken, 272, 273, 276
Home Run Derby (television), 201
Hooper, Bob, 156, *156*
Hooton, Burt, 299
Hoover, Herbert, 57
Hope, Bob, 173
Hornsby, Rogers, 26, 28, 29, *29*, 32, 40, 50
Hoskins, Dave, 156, *156*
Hough, Charlie, 300
Houtteman, Art, 156, *156*
Howard, Elston, 84, 210, 222, *222*, 240
Howard, Frank, 207, *207*, 212, 242, *242*
Howsam, Bob, 289, 292
Hoyt, Waite, 17, 33
Hubbell, Carl, 61, 62, *62*, 74, *74*, 227
Huggins, Miller, 38, 69, 130
Hughes, Dick, 239, *239*, 240
Hulbert, William, 8
Hundley, Randy, 251
Hunter, Catfish, 271, 273, 274, 291, 292, *292*, 298, 306
Hustler's Handbook, The (Veeck), 174
Huston, Tillinghast, 33
Hutton, Tommy, 282, *282*

I

I Had a Hammer (Aaron), 278
"I Play Baseball for Money, Not Fun" (Kahn), 147
Irvin, Monte, 84, 122, 140, *140*, 141, 142

J

Jackson, Al, 195
Jackson, Joe, 13, *13*, 21, *21*, 27
Jackson, Reggie, 41, 269, 272, 273, 274, 275, *275*, 293, *293*, 297, 298, *298*, 299, 300, *300*, 301, 304, 305, 306, 307, 308
Jakucki, Sigmund, 111, *111*
James, Bill, 108, 114, 160, 203, 257
Jansen, Larry, 140
Javier, Julian, 239, 240
John, Tommy, 298, 299, *299*
Johnson, Ban, 10, 20
Johnson, Judy, 83, *83*, 84, 87
Johnson, Lou, 216
Johnson, Randy, 311
Johnson, Walter, 11, 30, 31, *31*, 39, 75, *75*, 76, 116, 188, 212, 308
Jones, Cleon, 256
Jones, Dalton, 243
Jones, Sam, 33, 177
Jones, Sheldon, 140
Jones, Willie, 139
Judge Landis: Twenty-Five Years of Baseball (Spink), 55

K

Kaat, Jim, 214
Kahn, Roger, 93, 123, 144, 147, 180
Kaline, Al, 246, *246*, 281
Kansas City Royals, 282
Kavanagh, Jack, 53
Keane, Johnny, 218, *218*, 220
Keeler, Willie, 9, *9*, 76, 95, 285
Kell, George, 127, 131
Keller, Charlie, 63, *63*, 101
Kelly, George, 36
Keltner, Ken, 95
Kennedy, Frosty, 180
Kennedy, John F., 196, *196*
Killebrew, Harmon, 161, *161*, 198, *198*, 207, 214

Kiner, Ralph, 117, *117*, 159, 162, 178

Klein, Chuck, 48, *48*, 68, 73

Klem, Bill, 113

Kluszewski, Ted, 185, 187

Koenig, Mark, 34, 64

Konstanty, Jim, 137, 139, *139*

Koosman, Jerry, 243, 255, 274

Korean War, 136

Koslo, Dave, 140

Koufax, Sandy, 92, 159, 165, 188, *189*, 195, 208, 211, *211*, 212, *212*, 213, 214, 215, *215*, 216, 235, 236, 246, 269, 311

Kranepool, Ed, 231

Kubek, Tony, 194, *194*, 209

Kucks, Johnny, 155

Kuenn, Harvey, 161, 209

Kuhn, Bowie, 250, 267, 290

Kuzava, Bob, 146, 153, *153*

L

Labine, Clem, 141, 151

Lajoie, Nap, 27, 75, *75*, 76

Landis, Jim, 185

Landis, Kenesaw Mountain, 14, 16, 19, *19*, 20, 21, 22, 23, 24, 36, 38, 54, 55, 60, 71, 73, 75, 76, 79, *79*, 81, 100, 103, 104, 111, 116, 173, 180

Lane, Frank, 161, 162

Lanier, Max, 115

Larsen, Don, 135, *135*, 155, *155*

Lary, Frank, 164

Lasorda, Tommy, 298

Lau, Charlie, 296

Lavagetto, Cookie, 113, 124

Lazzeri, Tony, 34, 40, 55, 66, *66*, 180

League of Their Own, A (film), 257

Lemon, Bob, 156, *156*, 163, 164, *164*, 301, 302

Leonard, Buck, 84, 86, *86*, 87

Leonard, Dutch, 244

Leonard, John, 101, 152

Lieb, Fred, 34, 39

Life and Times of Hank Greenberg, The (Kempner), 59

Lindstrom, Fred, 39

Linz, Phil, 220

Lisenbee, Hod, 108

Littlefield, Dick, 182

Lloyd, John Henry, 84

Lockman, Whitey, 142

Loes, Billy, 151

Logan, Johnny, 166

Lolich, Mickey, 247, *247*

Lollar, Sherm, 176, 185, 187, *187*

Lonborg, Jim, 237, 239, 240

Long, Dale, 209

Lopat, Ed, 132, *132*

Lopes, Davey, 206, 298

Lopez, Al, 156, *156*, 185

Lopez, Hector, 209, 222

Los Angeles Dodgers, 179–182

Louis, Joe, 86

Low and Outside (Mead), 56

Lown, Turk, 185

Lyle, Sparky, 296, 306

Lynn, Fred, 287, 300, 302

M

Mack, Connie, 12, 33, 34, 41, 42, 50, 51, *51*, 53, 58, 75, *75*, 97, 101, 148

MacPhail, Larry, 78, 80, 99, 100, 105, 113, 152, 179, 232, 261

MacPhail, Lee, 232

Maglie, Sal, 115, 140, 142

Maisel, Fritz, 17

Man in the Crowd, The (Cohen), 261

Mantilla, Felix, 186

Mantle, Mickey, 128, *129*, 134, 144, *144*, 145, *145*, 146, *146*, 147, 149, 165, 169, *169*, 194, 195, 198, 199, *199*, 200, 201, 209, 210, 214, 219, 220, 221, *221*, 222, 277

Marberry, Firpo, 31

Marichal, Juan, 208, 226, 227, *227*, 243

Marion, Marty, 99, 150

Maris, Roger, 92, 198, 199, *199*, 200, *200*, 201, 205, 209, 210, 219, 220, 221, 238, 278, 306, 311

Marsans, Armando, 222

Marshall, Mike, 282

Martin, Billy, 153, 154, *154*, 296, 297, 298, *298*, 301, *301*

Martin, Pepper, 56, *56*, 57, 144

Martinez, Pedro, 311

Mathews, Eddie, 166, *166*, 170, 186, 277

Mathewson, Christy, 11, *11*, 73, 76, 188, 241

Matlack, Jon, 273

Mauch, Gene, 216, *216*, 217

May, Carlos, 281

May, Lee, 263, *263*

Mays, Carl, 17, 20, 33, 36, *36*

Mays, Willie, 84, 98, 128, 136, 140, *140*, 141, 144, 145, *145*, 146, 149, 156, 157, *157*, 162, *162*, 165, 167, 195, 208, 209, 227, 228, *228*, 274, *274*, 277, 279, 307

Mazeroski, Bill, 193, 194, *194*, 195, 209, 210, 299

McAndrew, Jim, 253

McCarthy, Joe, 50, 66, *66*, 69, 109, 130, 132

McCarver, Tim, 219, *219*, 239, 247, 268, 282, *282*

McCovey, Willie, 207, *207*, 208, *208*, 209, 210

McDevitt, Danny, 186

McDougald, Gil, 165

McDowell, Sam, 243

McGraw, John, 9, 31, 32, 33, 36, 38, 60, 61, 131

McGraw, Tug, 274

McGwire, Mark, 92, 278, 306, 310, *310*

McHale, John, 230

McInnis, Stuffy, 51

McKechnie, Bill, 90

McLain, Denny, 241, *241*, 243, 244, *244*, 247

McMullen, Ken, 212

McNally, Dave, 233, *233*, 234, 236, 243, 255, 263, 264, 291, 293

McNeely, Earl, 39

McQuinn, George, 111

McRae, Hal, 281

McWilliams, Larry, 285

Meadows, Lee, 32

Medwick, Joe, 55, *55*, 57, 59, 60, *60*, 100

Mele, Sam, 214

Messersmith, Andy, 292, 293

Meusel, Bob, 23, 34, 35, *35*, 40

Meyer, Russ, 128

Microsoft Complete Baseball, 53, 115, 140

Mid-Week Pictorial, 27

Miljus, Johnny, 41

Miller, Bing, 52

Miller, Marvin, 249, *249*, 291, *291*

Milosevich, Mollie, 127

Milwaukee Braves, 165–171, 230–232

Minoso, Minnie, 223, *223*, 228

Mitchell, Dale, 135

Mize, Johnny, 99, *99*, 152

Monday, Rick, 272

Monroe, Marilyn, 93

Moon, Wally, 186, 187, *187*

Moore, James, 82, 84, 85, 87

Moose, Bob, 284

Morgan, Joe, 282, 283, *283*, 284, *284*, 286, 287, 288, 289, *289*

Moses, Robert, 182, 183

Mossi, Don, 156, *156*

Mota, Manny, 224, *224*

Mranville, Rabbit, 144

Mueller, Don, 142

Mulcahy, Hugh, 102

Munson, Thurman, 296, 298, 299, 301, 302, 304, *304*, 305

Murtaugh, Danny, 265, *265*

Musial, Stan, 86, 97, *97*, 98, *98*, 99, 105, 147, 162, 163, *163*, 278

N

Narleski, Ray, 156, *156*

National Association of Base Ball Players, 7, 8

National League of Professional Base Ball Clubs, 8

Neal, Charley, 187

Necciai, Ron, 180

Negro Leagues, 82–87

Nelson, Lindsay, 184

Nelson, Rocky, 194

Nettles, Graig, 296, *296*, 298, 301, 303

Newcombe, Don, 84, 122, 136, 139, 142, 151, *151*, 163

Newhouser, Hal, 111, *111*, 156, *156*

New York Giants, 31, 32, 33, 36, 38, 39, 60–62, 139–143, 182–184

New York Yankees, 16, 17, 32, 33, 35, 36, 38, 40, 41, 43, 62–67, 101, 102, 123, 124, 125, 130–135, 220–222, 296–306

Nice Guys Finish Last (Durocher), 253

Nichols, Kid, 9

Niekro, Phil, 285

Night games, 46, 49, 64, 77–78, 99, 104, 115, 270

Northrup, Jim, 246, 247

Nuxhall, Joe, 108

O

Oakland Athletics, 270–276, 282

O'Dell, Billy, 208

Odom, Blue Moon, 271

Oeschger, Joe, 24, *24*, 26

O'Farrell, Bob, 40

Ogden, Jack, 17

Oliva, Tony, 214, *214*, 225, 229, 281

Oliver, Al, 283

O'Malley, Walter, 143, 176, 179, 180, 181, *181*, 182, 183

O'Neil, Buck, 87

O'Neill, Harry, 106

Ormsby, Bob, 116

Osteen, Claude, 214, 215, 236, 295

Ott, Mel, 60, 61, *61*, 237, 278

Owen, Marv, 59

Owen, Mickey, 100, 101, *101*, 115, 299

Owens, Jesse, 107

Oyler, Ray, 246

P

Pafko, Andy, 139, 143, 151, *151*, 152

Page, Joe, 125

Pagliaroni, Jim, 191

Paige, Satchel, 81, *81*, 83, *83*, 84, 85, 87, 125, *125*, 126, 173, *173*

Palmer, Jim, 234, *234*, 256, 260, *260*, 264, *264*

Pappas, Milt, 234

Parker, Dave, 282, 293

Pasquel, Jorge, 115, *115*

Passeau, Claude, 112

Patterson, Red, 131

Paul, Gabe, 296

Peckinpaugh, Roger, 39, *39*

Pennock, Herb, 17

Pepitone, Joe, 213, 219

Perez, Tony, 262, 284, *284*, 286, *286*

Perini, Lou, 175

Perranoski, Ron, 213

Perry, Gaylord, 243

Perry, Jim, 214

Pesky, Johnny, 116

Philadelphia Athletics, 41, 42, 50–53

Philadelphia Phillies, 137–138, 139, 216–220, 282

Pierce, Billy, 185, 208, 209

Piercy, Bill, 23

Piersall, Jimmy, 168, *168*

Pignatano, Joe, 195

Pinelli, Babe, 135

Piniella, Lou, 303, 305

Pipgras, George, 63, 70

Pipp, Wally, 34

Pittsburgh Pirates, 31, 32, 39, 41, 177–178, 282

Plank, Eddie, 51

Platooning, 133

Podres, Johnny, 151, 155, 213

Post, Wally, 162

Powell, Boog, 207, 234, 256, 262

Power Hitters, The (Honig), 207

Prince, Bob, 159

Puckett, Kirby, 177

Q

Quinn, John, 216, 217

R

Radio, 46, 78–80, 92, 99, 123

Randolph, Willie, 296

Raschi, Vic, 132

Rawlings, Johnny, 36

Reagan, Ronald, 78, *78*, 156, *156*

Reese, Pee Wee, 96, 121, 139, 150, *150*, 151, 152, 181, *181*, 184, *184*

Reiser, Pete, 100, *100*, 113, 124, 204

Remy, Jerry, 300, 303

Rettenmund, Merv, 265

Reynolds, Allie, 132, 133, 152

Rhoden, Rick, 298

Rhodes, Dusty, 157

Rice, Jim, 300, 303

Richards, Paul, 232, 260

Richardson, Bobby, 208, *208*, 209, 210, 226

Rickey, Branch, 30, 46, 53, 54, 55, *55*, 73, 90, 99, 100, 106, 110, 118, 119, *119*, 120, 121, 123, 159, 164, 177, 178, 180, 181, 188, 192, 196, 197, 248, 261, 290

Rigney, Bill, 182, *182*

Riley, James, 82, 84, 85, 86

Ripken, Cal Jr., 67, 308, 309, *309*

Rivers, Mickey, 296, 301

Rizzuto, Phil, 88, *89*, 96, 130, *130*, 134, *134*, 150, 152, 158, 159, *159*

Roberts, Robin, 137, 138, 139, 163, *163*

Robinson, Brooks, 151, 152, 233, *233*, 235, *235*, 255, 256, 262, *262*, 263, *263*, 264

Robinson, Frank, 167, 234, 235, *235*, 236, 248, *248*, 256, 262, 265, 277, 279, *279*, 281

Robinson, Jackie, 59, 82, 83, 84, 85, 86, 87, 118, *118*, 119, *119*, 120, *120*, 121, *121*, 122, 123, 127, 139, 141, 150, 151, *151*, 153, 154, *154*, 167, 180, 182, 186, 222, 228, 279

Robinson, Wilbert, 35

Rodriguez, Alex, 177

Roe, Preacher, 98, 151

Rogan, Bullet, 84

Rogell, Billy, 59

Rojas, Cookie, 216

Roosevelt, Franklin Delano, 72, *72*, 77, 103, 104, 107

Root, Charlie, 64

Rose, Don, 268

Rose, Pete, 92, 258, *259*, 260, 262, 284, *284*, 285, *285*, 289, 293, 308, *308*, 309

Roseboro, John, 186, 187, *187*

Rowswell, Rosey, 159

Rudi, Joe, 272, 273, 293

Ruel, Muddy, 39

Ruffing, Red, 17, 62, 68, 70

Ruiz, Chico, 217

Ruppert, Jacob, 16, *16*, 33, 65, 69

Rush, Bob, 163, 186

Russell, Bill, 298

Ruth, George Herman "Babe," 11, *11*, 14, *15*, 16, *16*, 17, 18, 22, 23, 24, 25, 26, 27, *27*, 28, 33, 34, 35, *35*, 38, 41, *41*, 43, 44, *44*, 45, *45*, 46, 51, 52, 55, 62, 64, 65, *65*, 66, 67, 68, *68*, 69, 71, 75, *75*, 76, 80, *80*, 96, 130, 133, 146, 149, 153, 157, 167, 198, 200, 201, 203, 242, 278, 279, 285, 300

Ryan, Nolan, 92, 116, 212, 243, 256, 268, 269, *269*, 307, *307*, 308

S

Sadecki, Ray, 218

Sain, Johnny, 126, *126*, 167, *167*, 168, 214

St. Louis Cardinals, 32, 38, 40, 41, 53–58, 99, 216–220

Sanford, Jack, 208, 209

San Francisco Giants, 162

Sanguillen, Manny, 283, 284

Santiago, Jose, 237, 239

Saucier, Frank, 175

Sauer, Hank, 162, *162*

Schang, Wally, 33

Schilling, Curt, 311

Schmidt, Mike, 231, 282, 294, 295, *295*, 308

Schoendienst, Red, 168, 169, *169*, 240

Schultz, Barney, 219

Schumacher, Hal, 62

Score, Herb, 165

Scott, Jim, 21, *21*

Scully, Vin, 92, 158, 159

Seaver, Tom, 243, 252, *252*, 260, *260*, 274

Seitz, Peter, 291, 292

Selkirk, George, 63, *63*

Seminick, Andy, 139, *139*

Shannon, Mike, 218, 238, 247

Shaw, Bob, 185

Shawkey, Bob, 17, 33

Shea, William, 196, 197, 248

Shepard, Bert, 108, *108*

Sherry, Larry, 186, 187, *187*

Sherry, Norm, 211

Short, Chris, 217

Shotton, Burt, 150

Simmons, Al, 42, 51, 52, 62, 73

Simmons, Curt, 137, 218

Sisler, Dick, 137, 139

Sisler, George, 28, *28*, 30, 75, *75*, 76, 94, 137

Skinner, Bob, 194

Skowron, Bill, 170, 171, *171*, 209, 213

Slaughter, Enos, 99, 117, *117*, 299

Smalley, Roy Sr., 177

Smith, Al, 95, 149, 185

Smith, Elmer, 35, 43, *43*

Smith, Hal, 194

Smith, Hilton, 84

Smith, Mayo, 246

Smith, Red, 95

Smith, Reggie, 237, 299, 304, 305

Snider, Duke, 144, 147, *147*, 149, 152, 153, 186, 195, 277

Sockalexis, Louis, 35

Sosa, Elias, 299

Sosa, Sammy, 310, *310*

Southworth, Billy, 126

Spahn, Warren, 106, 126, *126*, 127, 133, 145, 167, 168, 169, 227, 268, 277

Spalding, Albert, 6, *6*, 8, 80, 124

Speaker, Tris, 21, 75, *75*, 122

Spink, J. G. Taylor, 20, 55

Sporting News, The, 20, 74, 79, 98, 180, 190, 297

Sports Illustrated, 288, 293

Stafford, Bill, 209

Staley, Gerry, 185

Stallard, Tracy, 200

Stanky, Eddie, 139–140, 143
Stanley, Mickey, 246
Stanton, Leroy, 268
Stargell, Willie, 207, 222, 224, *224*, 265, 282
Staub, Rusty, 274
Stearnes, Turkey, 84, 86, 87
Steinbrenner, George, 291, 296, 297, 298, 301, *301*
Stengel, Casey, 31, 38, 127, 128, 130, *130*, 131, *131*, 133, *133*, 136, *136*, 146, 151, 153, 169–170, 190, 192, *192*, 195, *195*, 207, 220, 252
Stephens, Vern, 115, 127, 131, 150
Stirnweiss, Snuffy, 107, *107*, 108
Stoneham, Horace, 176, 182, 183
Stottlemyre, Mel, 219
Strikes, players', 272, 308, 309
Stuart, Dick, 162, 180
Suehsdorf, A. D., 34, 119
Sukeforth, Clyde, 143
Sunday baseball, 73
Suttles, Mule, 86
Sutton, Don, 299
Swoboda, Ron, 256

T
Tattersall, John, 257
Taylor, Harry, 124
Taylor, Tony, 216
Taylor, Zack, 175
Tebbetts, Birdie, 207
Ted Williams: A Portrait in Words and Pictures (Stout), 191
Teenagers, Graybeards, and 4-Fs, 107–108
Television, 80, 158–159, 179
Tenace, Gene, 273, *273*
Terry, Bill, 29, 48, *48*, 49, 58, 60, 69
Terry, Ralph, 195, 209, 210, *210*
Thomas, Frank, 162, 217
Thompson, Hank, 140, *140*
Thomson, Bobby, 141, 142, *142*, 143, *143*, 145, 152, 159, 162, 208, 277
Throneberry, Marv, 195
Tiant, Luis, 86, 224, 225, *225*, 243, 285, 286, 287

Tolan, Bobby, 275
Torre, Frank, 166, 170
Torre, Joe, 282
Torrez, Mike, 293, 299, 300, 302, 303, *303*
Total Baseball (Pietrusza), 77, 257
Travis, Cecil, 96, 105
Traynor, Pie, 32, 61
Tresh, Tom, 209, *209*
Trucks, Virgil, 164
Turley, Bob, 163, 171

U
Updike, John, 192

V
Vander Meer, Johnny, 49, *49*
Vaughan, Arky, 96
Veach, Bobby, 29
Veale, Bob, 243
Vecsey, George, 215
Veeck, Bill, 113, 122, 125, 126, 172, *172*, 173, *173*, 174, 176, *176*, 185, 223, 230, 251, 257, 270
Veeck, Mike, 223
Versalles, Zoilo, 214, *214*
Virdon, Bill, 157, 194
Virgil, Ozzie, 223, *223*
Voiselle, Bill, 126, 127

W
Waddell, Rube, 116, 212
Wagner, Honus, 11, 12, *12*, 75, *75*, 76
Walberg, Rube, 70
Walker, Fleetwood, 82
Walker, Harry, 117, 207, 224
Walsh, Christy, 44
Walsh, Ed, 21, *21*, 42, 149, 241
Wambsganss, Bill, 35–36, 43, *43*
Waner, Paul, 32
Ward, Arch, 73
Ward, John Montgomery, 290
Washburn, Ray, 243, 247
Washington Senators, 30, 31, 39
Weaver, Buck, 21
Weaver, Earl, 254, *254*, 260, 296
Weis, Al, 256
Weiss, George, 158, 195, 220

Welch, Bob, 304, 305, *305*
Wells, Willie, 84, 86
Wertz, Vic, 156, 162
White, Bill, 218
White, Jo-Jo, 59
White, Roy, 222
"Why Baltimore Wins More Games than Anyone Else" (Boswell), 260
Wilhelm, Hoyt, 178, 233, *233*
Williams, Dick, 236, 240, 271, 274, 275
Williams, Smokey Joe, 84
Williams, Ted, 70, 71, 91, *91*, 92, 95, 96, *96*, 97, *97*, 98, 99, 103, *103*, 105, 106, 116, 117, 127, *127*, 131, 136, *136*, 144, 163, 166, 188, 190, *190*, 191, *191*, 207, 236, 237, 294, 295
Wills, Maury, 188, 203, 204, *204*, 205, *205*, 207, 208, 212, 306
Wilson, Hack, 26, 42, 50, *50*
Wilson, Jud, 83, *83*
Wilson, Willie, 304, *304*
Winning Team, The (1952), 156
Wood, Joe, 21
World War II, 102–109
Wright, George, 8, *8*
Wright, Glenn, 32
Wright, Harry, 8, *8*
Wrigley, Philip, 79, 109
Wyatt, John, 238
Wyatt, Whitlow, 101, 113
Wynn, Early, 156, *156*, 163–164, 185

Y
Yankee Encyclopedia, The, 220
Yastrzemski, Carl, 236, *236*, 237, 239, *239*, 241, 242, 300, 302, 303
Yawkey, Tom, 70, 190, 236, 261
Young, Cy, 10, *10*, 31, 75, *75*
Young, Ross, 36, *36*
Yount, Robin, 98
Yvars, Sal, 141

Z
Zimmer, Don, 181, *181*, 186, 195

Acknowledgments:

Publications International, Ltd., has made every effort to locate the owners of all copyrighted material to obtain permission to use the selections that appear in this book. Any errors or omissions are unintentional; corrections, if necessary, will be made in future editions.

Page 69: "Luckiest Man" speech delivered by Lou Gehrig on July 4, 1939. Reprinted by permission of the Estate of Eleanor Gehrig by CMG Worldwide, Inc., www.LouGehrig.com, ™/© 2003.

Page 101: Quote by Mickey Owen from "Dodgers Stress Luck of Rivals...," © October 6, 1941 by *The New York Times*. Reprinted by permission of The New York Times Co.

Page 132: Quote by Dave Egan of *The Boston Record*. Reprinted by permission of *The Boston Herald*.

Page 276: Quote about Bill Buckner. Reprinted by permission of the *San Francisco Chronicle* conveyed through Copyright Clearance Center, Inc.

All Yogi Berra quotes contained within this text are reprinted by permission of LTD Enterprises, Inc., Little Falls, NJ.

Picture Credits:

Front cover: **The Brearley Collection, Boston, MA.**

Back cover: © **Bettmann/Corbis** (bottom); **Transcendental Graphics** (top).

AP Wide World Photos: 5, 29 (bottom), 52, 55, 56, 60, 61, 66 (bottom), 69, 70, 75, 81, 90, 91, 92, 95, 96, 97 (bottom), 100, 101, 104, 107, 108, 110, 111 (top), 115, 117 (bottom), 126, 129, 133, 136, 138, 139, 141, 144, 149 (bottom), 150, 151, 153, 154 (top), 155 (top), 156 (bottom), 162, 163 (top), 167, 168, 170, 171, 180, 181 (bottom), 182, 184, 186, 187, 189, 190, 191, 193, 194 (top), 200 (top), 204, 209, 210 (bottom), 211, 213, 215, 219, 221, 225, 229, 239, 240, 243, 245, 255, 256, 259, 261, 263 (bottom), 266, 267, 269, 272, 273, 275, 277, 278, 279, 287, 289 (bottom), 291, 297, 300, 303, 304, 305 (bottom), 306, 310 (bottom); **John Biever/Sports Illustrated:** 307; © **Corbis:** 18, 23, 78, 135, 147 (top), 154 (bottom), 161, 182, 223 (top); Lucien Aigner: 82, 85, 87; Paul Almasy: 231; Bettmann: 13, 16, 17 (top), 22, 25, 33, 35 (top), 38, 42, 45, 47, 57, 58, 63, 66 (top), 72, 74, 79, 89, 93, 94, 97 (top), 102, 103, 105, 109, 113, 114, 118, 119, 120, 121, 131, 134, 137 (bottom), 140, 145 (bottom), 146, 155 (bottom), 156 (top), 157 (bottom), 158, 159, 160, 164, 165, 166, 169, 172, 173, 175, 176, 178 (top), 179, 181 (top), 185, 192, 194 (bottom), 195, 196, 197, 198, 201, 203, 205, 206, 207, 208, 212, 216, 218, 220, 223 (bottom), 224, 228, 233 (bottom), 234, 235, 238, 241, 244, 246 (top), 248, 249, 250, 251, 253, 260, 262, 264, 271, 274, 281, 282, 283, 286, 289 (top), 290, 292, 293, 298, 299, 301; Bettmann/UPI: 137 (top); Lance Nelson: 310 (top); Reuters NewMedia: 309, 311; Charles E. Rotkin: 230; © Schenectady Museum; Hall of Electrical History Foundation: 77; Joseph Sohm/ChromoSohm Inc.: Contents; Underwood & Underwood: 21 (bottom), 30, 39, 43; UPI: 124, 265; **Getty Images/Time Life Pictures:** 227; **Dick Johnson:** 257; **National Baseball Library & Archive, Cooperstown, NY:** 6, 9, 10 (bottom), 12, 14, 17 (bottom), 19, 20, 21 (top), 24, 26, 31, 32, 34, 35 (bottom), 36, 37, 48, 49, 51, 53, 54, 67, 71, 76, 83, 84, 86, 98, 106, 112, 122, 123, 125, 127, 130, 132, 142, 143, 145 (top), 148, 149 (top), 152, 157 (top), 163 (bottom), 174, 177, 178 (bottom), 187, 202 (bottom), 210 (top), 214 (top), 217, 222, 226, 233 (top), 237, 242, 247, 252, 254, 270, 280, 288, 296, 305 (top); AP Wide World Photos: 263 (top); **PhotoFile:** 10 (top), 28, 29 (top), 40, 50, 59, 64, 111 (bottom), 202 (top); ©1984 The Sporting News: 11 (top); T.V. Sports Mailbag: 116, 117 (top), 147 (bottom), 199, 214 (bottom), 232, 236, 268, 284, 285, 295, 308; **Transcendental Graphics:** 7, 11 (bottom), 41, 44, 65, 68, 80, 294; © 1974 Black Sports magazine: 276; M. Brown: 227; Kenneth A. Felden: 99, 246 (bottom); Horace Marchant: 27; B. Sloate: 8.